D1053444

THE PHARAOH'S TREASURE

PAPYRUS

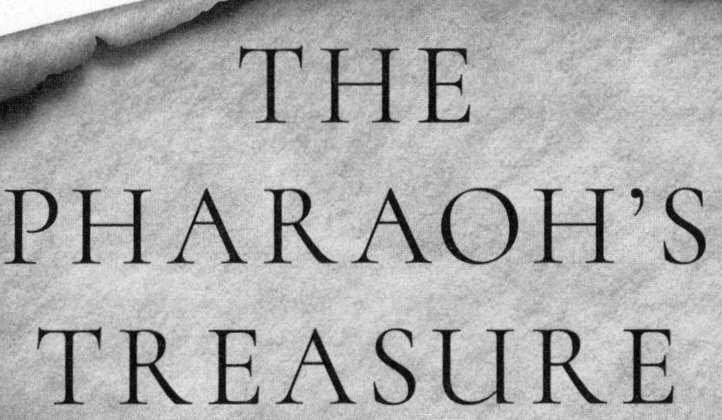

THE PHARAOH'S TREASURE

The Origin of Paper and the Rise of Western Civilization

JOHN GAUDET

PEGASUS BOOKS
NEW YORK LONDON

THE PHARAOH'S TREASURE

Pegasus Books Ltd.
148 W. 37th Street, 13th Floor
New York, NY 10018

First Pegasus Books cloth edition October 2018

Interior design by Maria Fernandez

Frontispiece: *Clio, Goddess muse of history, consulting an ancient papyrus scroll (based on a wall painting in Herculaneum, 1755).*

Library of Congress Cataloging-in-Publication Data is available.

ISBN: 978-1-68177-853-2

10 9 8 7 6 5 4 3 2 1

Printed in the United States of America
Distributed by W. W. Norton & Company

To all those who had faith in me; and to those who didn't,
but will have, once they've read this book.

CONTENTS

	Author's Note	xiii
	Prologue	xvii
PART I	***Guardian of Immortality***	1
ONE	*The Inspector Puts Pen to Paper and Makes History*	3
TWO	*Prisse, like Moses, Carries Home Stone Tablets and Paper Scrolls*	24
THREE	*The Undertaker's Special and the World's First Bestseller*	32
FOUR	*The Book of the Dead, Guardian of Immortality*	45
FIVE	*Papyrus Paper, Your Ticket to Paradise*	54
SIX	*The Sands of the Nile Give Up their Treasures*	69
SEVEN	*The Affair of the Oranges*	74
EIGHT	*The Floodgates Open*	83
PART II	***Egypt, Papermaker to the World***	91
NINE	*The Birth of Memphis and Paper*	93
TEN	*A Gift from the Gods*	107
ELEVEN	*The Monopoly*	112

TWELVE *Growing and Managing Papyrus for Paper* 120
THIRTEEN *The Emperor and the Lewd Papermaker* 127
FOURTEEN *Taking on the World—and Leaving a Legacy* 136

PART III *The Enemy of Oblivion* 151
FIFTEEN *Early Libraries, Paper, and the Writing Business* 153
SIXTEEN *A Library to End All Libraries and the Sweet Smell of History* 167
SEVENTEEN *The Romans and the Book Trade* 177
EIGHTEEN *Roman Libraries* 186
NINETEEN *Those Precious, Tender-hearted Scrolls* 200
TWENTY *Saving the Day* 210
TWENTY-ONE *Media One Makes Its Mark in the World* 216
TWENTY-TWO *The Last Bastion, the Church of Rome* 230
TWENTY-THREE *Constantinople and the Long Goodbye* 238
TWENTY-FOUR *End of the Road and the Battle of the Talas River* 254
TWENTY-FIVE *The Mystery of the Disappearing Plant* 264
TWENTY-SIX *The Pharaoh's Own Conquers the Vatican* 274
TWENTY-SEVEN *The Road Back* 285
EPILOGUE *The Road Ahead* 293
Acknowledgments 307
Supplementary Illustration Credits 311
Appendix 313
References 317
Endnotes 327
Index 345

MAPS

Map 1: Egypt during the Old Kingdom and the Tura Caves. *p. 5*

Map 2: Egypt in Roman times, showing papermaking centers. *p. 98*

Map 3: The Great Swamp in the Fayum Region. *p. 121*

Map 4: The Roman Empire in the 1st century. *p. 128*

Map 5: Sixteenth century map of Alexandria. *p. 173*

Map 6: The world in the time of Cassiodorus. *p. 211*

Map 7: The world of Islam 750 A.D. *p. 255*

Map A: Vegetation map of the Sahara. *Image insert, p. 3*

Map B: Location of the ancient Nile and Memphis. *Image insert, p. 6 (top)*

Map C: Papyrus paper distribution. *Image insert, p. 6 (bottom)*

Map D: Location of important papyrus finds in Egypt. *Image insert, p. 7*

"Then was paper discovered, and therewith was eloquence made possible. Paper, so smooth and so continuous, the snowy entrails of (papyrus stems); paper which can be spread out to such a vast extent, and yet be folded up into such a little space . . ."

—Cassiodorus, 527 A.D.
(Letters of Cassiodorus, Book XI Letter 38)

"Some historians speculate that paper was the key element in global cultural advancement. According to this theory, Chinese culture was less developed than the West in ancient times because bamboo, while abundant, was a clumsier writing material than papyrus."

—Case Paper Company, Harrison, NY
(www.casepaper.com/company/paper-history)

"Consider the book. It has extraordinary staying power. Ever since the invention of the codex in the third or fourth century A.D., it has proven to be a marvelous machine—great for packaging information, convenient to thumb through, comfortable to curl up with, superb for storage, and remarkably resistant to damage. It does not need to be upgraded or downloaded, accessed or booted, plugged into circuits or extracted from webs. Its design makes it a delight to the eye. Its shape makes it a pleasure to hold in the hand. And its handiness has made it the basic tool of learning for thousands of years, even before the library of Alexandria was founded early in the fourth century B.C."

—Robert Darnton, "The New Age of the Book."
(*New York Review of Books*, 1999.)

Author's Note

When is paper not paper? Many modern dictionaries and writers reserve the term "paper" for modern paper made from wood or rag pulp. Since paper made from papyrus was made with thin strips rather than from pulp it is often placed in the category of "writing materials," and falls outside the modern classification for paper, even though the Victorians called it "natural paper."[1]

It wasn't always like that. In the early days, Roman historians such as Pliny the elder, simply used the Latin word, *papyrum* to signify "the paper plant, or paper made from it." Before him the Greeks took *papyros* to mean "any plant of the paper plant genus." There was never any question in their minds that "paper" meant anything but sheets or rolls of paper made from the stems of the papyrus plant. The question does remain: where then did the Greek word *papyros* come from? Several authors believe it derives from the Egyptian "*pa-per-aa*" (or *p'p'r*), literally "that of the pharaoh" or "Pharaoh's own" in reference to the crown's monopoly on papyrus production. After this came a natural progression when the modern word "paper" evolved from the Latin word *papyrus*, which arrived in English by way of *papire* (Norman French and Middle English 1150–1500 A.D.)

People were still using "paper" in the generic sense in the seventeenth century, at a time when paper was handmade from pulp. The earliest pulp paper was not even called "paper" by the Europeans, to whom it was first known as "cloth parchment," since from the thirteenth century it was made mainly from linen rags.[2] Thus, papermaking machines were yet to be introduced when Father Imberdis—a Jesuit priest who described the manufacture of rag paper in his hometown in France in 1693—used the Latin term "*papyrus*" for the pulp paper of his time.[3]

We get a whiff of the confusion that would follow when in 1943, the dean of American papermaking, Dard Hunter, tried to explain why the word "paper" appeared in a 1635 translation of Pliny's famous text on making papyrus paper in ancient Egypt.[4] Hunter cautioned the reader to understand that it was all a mistake, although the English was a verbatim translation of the Latin text. Someone, presumably the translator, had translated the Latin "papyrus" as "paper." Other than noting that papyrus was not "true paper," Hunter goes no further in his commentary, and we are left in confusion. Is the lightweight writing material made from papyrus to be considered paper, or is it not?

It seems to me that people today have it backwards; paper was in fact born in ancient Egypt and remained paper forever after, much like the terms "wood" or "lumber" apply to the hard, fibrous material that forms the main body of a tree. No one challenges the concept regardless of the tree species used, or whether it has been chipped (then molded into reconstituted wood), or shaved into thin sheets (then glued and laminated into plywood), or just sawn into rough boards, it still falls under the generic category of "wood" and we look for it in a lumberyard.

Perhaps a great deal of the misunderstanding comes from the fact that many people do not realize that a sheet of papyrus paper doesn't differ much from a sheet of heavyweight, handcrafted bond paper of today. In ancient times it was close to the modern sheet in size, though it differed in color. It was not dead white; it looked more like something the Crane paper company would call "kid finish," a yellow-tinged heavy paper considered by many to be the height of sophistication. The fibers in papyrus paper sometimes bother a fine steel pen unless the sheet has been given a smooth finish by rubbing or polishing, but a modern ballpoint pen or a quill pen runs easily across its surface. In other words, for all intents and purposes it is paper.

Another mistaken impression is that papyrus paper is fragile; when in reality, it is an especially durable writing surface. Papyrus books and documents from ancient and medieval times had a usable life of hundreds of years. Worse yet, perhaps, was the notion created not long ago in the best-selling novel *The Da Vinci Code* that papyrus paper is so delicate that it will dissolve in vinegar. In the novel, a vial of vinegar is said to exist inside a secret document holder called a "cryptex." Anyone who uses a wrong code or forces the cryptex open causes the vial to shatter, releasing the vinegar. Sophie, the heroine, says that if this happens, the papyrus paper will be reduced to mush, "a glob of meaningless pulp." This is nonsense. Papyrus paper can be dipped, soaked, and pummeled in vinegar with little or no effect, but the slander stuck, and papyrus paper is now diminished in the eyes of the public. It appeared to over 200 million readers to be a fragile cousin of modern tissue paper, even though the fact, not fiction, is that if the famous Nag Hammadi codices from the third and fourth century had been written on modern wood or rag pulp paper instead of papyrus paper, the texts would have disintegrated into dust long ago.

The problem centers around the practice of reserving the term "paper" for only modern rag paper, which I believe does a disservice to a medium that served human civilization so well for thousands of years and deserves its own special spot in the pantheon of intellectual history, alongside the invention of the personal computer and the Gutenberg press. I think of modern paper made of wood or rag pulp or from animal skin as all simply modifications of the original, which was the lightweight sheet known to the Egyptians as "*p'p'r.*"

When I refer to "paper" in this book I refer to paper in the wide sense. Wherever possible, I will specify the basic material from which the paper was made.

Prologue

Paper was born in Egypt toward the end of the Stone Age and was put to work almost immediately. Paper made from papyrus soon became a necessity for the thousands of scribes, priests, and accountants who made a living from the obsessive recording of temple goods and property, and the agricultural accounting that was part of ordinary life in ancient Egypt. Four thousand years later, after an interesting and varied history, papyrus paper was replaced by modern paper made from rag and wood pulp. The story told in this book is an account of what happened during those early days when papyrus paper was the most common medium used throughout the world.

The making of this kind of paper, and the books and documents that came from it, represents one of the most astonishing and exciting stories in the history of the world. It is a tale of human endeavor that spans a period from the late Neolithic almost to the time of Gutenberg; a period that covers more than three-quarters of recorded history, yet it has never been told in its entirety until now.

Why not? It seems writers and historians over time have been enamored with the story of parchment and vellum used in place of papyrus in Europe from 300 A.D. to 1450 A.D. And they have also been much taken by the story of rag paper and its discovery by the Chinese. Developed further by the Arabs in 750 A.D. Chinese rag paper evolved into the handmade paper of the Europeans, the sort of paper used by Gutenberg in 1450 and that started the modern age of books and printing. Lost in the shuffle are the early paper products used from the end of the Stone Age until 1450 A.D. What sort of paper did people use for business records, letters, and books during all that time, and why haven't people written about this?

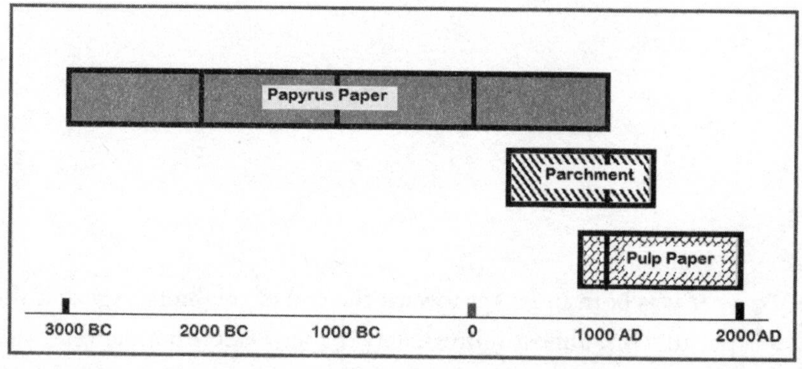

Comparison—different forms of paper through history.

To begin with, there are no examples of ancient paper before 5,100 years ago. From then until the Middle Kingdom of Egypt, we have thousands of fragments and some small rolls that represent the first records, which include accounts of building materials used for the pyramids in 2566 B.C. After this, one fragile roll of papyrus dated to 1800 B.C. stands out; it contains the first surviving literary effort, the lectures and notes of two viziers of ancient Egypt.

The era of funerary scrolls began around 1550 B.C.; thousands of scrolls and pages of papyrus have been found preserved in tombs dating from that period. These books of the dead, which first appeared in 1700 B.C.,[1] were used to guide the deceased in the afterworld. Produced up until the time of Christ, they dominated the world of ancient paper until the literary efforts of the Greeks and later Romans finally provided enough documents and fragments on which historians could begin to feed. Parchment and pulp paper appeared in later years, but the paucity of material and lack of early documents that remained intact meant that the story has been difficult to write about. It was also easy to pass over, so it was lost in the shuffle. It was as if history had dealt out the cards, but had neglected to include several aces in the deck. This present book is intended to restore the balance and to identify the earliest paper as a key element of global cultural advancement.

I have divided this vast history into three parts, in order to capture the rise, apex, and decline of papyrus paper:

1. *Guardian of Immortality:* ancient Egyptian paper and books, their discovery and significance

2. *Egypt, Papermaker to the World*: the earliest form of paper, how it was manufactured, how it came to rule the world

3. *The Enemy of Oblivion*: the ancient Romans' love affair with papyrus paper, book scrolls, and libraries, early Christian books, parchment, Chinese paper, the rise of rag paper and the printed book.

❧

A second source of inspiration for this book was an illuminating essay by Robert Darnton—historian, writer, Princeton emeritus professor, and former director of the Harvard University Library. The essay first appeared in the journal *Daedalus* in 1982 and again in *The Kiss of Lamourette* in 1990, a book I bought because of the chapter on publishing, "A Survival Strategy for Academic Authors." This last offered some of the best, most practical advice I'd ever gotten about how to get a book published on the ecology, life cycle, and history of the papyrus plant. He especially advocated the two t's, tactics and titles, which must appear innovative even when the subject is quite ordinary. A good example was the book *On the Rocks: A Geology of Great Britain*.

Well, once my book was published,[2] I moved on to the idea of taking on the task referred to above, how to identify the earliest paper and books as key elements of global cultural advancement. I was encouraged again by my reading of Professor Darnton, this time from his essay in chapter seven, which was about how a field of knowledge could take on a distinct identity. Titled "What is the History of Books?" it put forward Darnton's argument that the history of books was its own, new, and vital discipline even then in the 1980's. This idea resonated with me as I set out a few years ago to write this present book.

Darnton made much of the purpose of those in pursuit of this new discipline, which would help them understand how exposure to the printed word affected the thought and behavior of mankind, before and after the invention of movable type. In essence, the goal of any such endeavor should be to understand the book as a force in history. In my case, I felt that the study of the earliest books—those made of the first "*p'p'r*" paper of the ancients, which came from plants growing in the swamps of Egypt and was preserved for us by the hot, dry sands of the Nile—were as of yet underrepresented.

Is the study of the history of books worth it? After all, some might argue that books and paper, which are the objects of my story, are on their way out. Well, not quite. Darnton and many others (including, as he points out, Bill Gates) prefer printed paper to computer screens for extensive reading. In short, Darnton assures us, the old-fashioned codex printed on folded and gathered sheets of paper is not about to disappear into cyberspace.

Darnton warned anyone who might set out along the path that led to the understanding of the book as a force in history, that they would have to cross a no-man's land located at the intersection of a half-dozen fields of study. The ancillary disciplines to be considered included the histories of libraries, publishing, paper, ink, writing, and reading. One question that arose immediately from my perspective is that I often think of books and paper as Media One.[3] This set aside paper, as I see it, as an invention that lent itself to the long-term needs of modern man. It also distanced paper from the many antique media used in earlier times that were less than global or of limited use because they were so cumbersome.

What then was Media Two? The answer to me was clear; Media Two was the second media invention that was of great service to modern man:

the telegraph. More accurately, the long-distance transmission of text messages *without* the physical exchange of Media One or any other object bearing the message. Thus, as Wikipedia tells us, semaphore (a system of flag waving) is a method of telegraphy, whereas pigeon post is not.

The first big break in Media Two came in the nineteenth century with the invention of electrical telegraphy, then wireless radio, all of which were followed by a second big break with the arrival of natural language interfaces. This happened in the Internet Age and allowed for the evolution of technologies such as electronic mail and instant messaging; these are all still part of this second phase of information transmission, divorced as it is from the physical exchange that paper represents. Paper was the first innovation that allowed for the true expansion of the human intellect and its creative, expressive, and even moral possibilities. No wonder it is still considered a key element in global cultural advancement.

THE PHARAOH'S TREASURE

PART ONE

Guardian of Immortality

ONE

The Inspector Puts Pen to Paper and Makes History

Our story begins in the last year of the reign of Pharaoh Khufu (2589–2562 B.C.) His Great Pyramid was almost complete and it was no coincidence that his life would end perhaps at the moment the last stone was put in place. It was well within his power to do whatever he wanted, after all; he was a god on earth, was he not? In the last year of his existence and in his haste to have all in readiness for his death, he may have driven the people of his realm to work harder than usual. As king and overseer of the known world, he would probably never brook riots or insurrections; in any event he had no need to worry in that regard, since he had several very efficient management techniques that served him well. And, god or no god, good management has a way of winning out.

Great Pyramid of Cheops during the inundation (Wikipedia).

Though labeled a tyrant by Greek historians, Khufu reminds us more of a velvet glove than an iron fist. Firstly, his call to workers to report each year to build his pyramid would always be obeyed. And why not? The supply of meat, beer, food, and living conditions—including medical care—at Giza were all of an unusually high level and quality for that age.[1] Consequently, there was no need for slave labor. Khufu's people came voluntarily by the thousands to work willingly on his monumental constructions in order to insure their own afterlife.[2]

The work also coincided with the inundation, a period when farm work was at a minimum anyway, so why sit around waiting for the floodwater in the fields to lower enough for planting, when beefsteaks and beer could be had at Giza? It also happened that in that same season, building blocks for his pyramid arrived in quantity daily at the pyramid river port. High water on the Nile worked well for the heavy wooden barges used to transport these enormous stones. Everything functioned in favor of the king, as it had done for Egyptian royals for hundreds of years.

In addition to working conditions and the timely arrival of supplies, Khufu's management style and choice of staff were faultless. Proof of this lies in what he left behind, the Great Pyramid, engineered to within 0.05 degrees of accuracy along a north-south axis. A magnificent creation to his memory, this tombstone was composed of 2.3 million massive blocks and completed within twenty years.[3] It is the only one of the Seven Wonders of the Ancient World that remains.

We are concerned here with one of Khufu's managers, an inspector named Merer, a functionary brought into the news in 2013 by Professor Pierre Tallet of the Université Paris-Sorbonne. Merer, until then an unknown leader of a royal team of expeditors, became famous when he was discovered to be the author of the oldest surviving writing on paper in the history of the world.[4]

He had been appointed by Khufu to oversee the acquisition and transportation of stone for the Great Pyramid. The stone Merer delivered was a special white limestone from the Tura caves not far from Cairo. Polished with fine sand, this limestone served as the outer covering of the pyramid and turned the outside into a blinding white surface that must have been spectacular when the sun hit it during the height of the day. No wonder people in those days as well as today thought that this pyramid might have come from heaven or outer space—no ordinary man was capable of such things. Of course, they had not counted on people such as Khufu or Merer.

The limestone from Tura was the finest and whitest of all the Egyptian quarries, so it was used for facing the richest tombs, pyramids, sarcophagi, and temples. It was found deep underground and the caves that the quarries left behind were adapted by British forces during World War II to store ammunition, aircraft bombs, and other explosives.

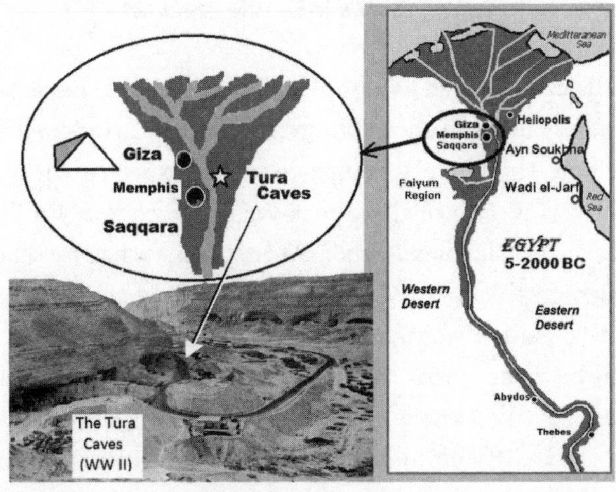

MAP 1: *Egypt during the Old Kingdom and the Tura Caves.*

Tallet found Merer's diary during an expedition in 2013 to Wadi el-Jarf, an ancient Red Sea port (Map 1) used by the Egyptians thousands of years ago.[5] Tallet was leading a joint Egyptian–French archaeological team with Gregory Marouard from the Oriental Institute of Chicago. The site of the ancient port is in a remote part of the Egyptian desert about 140 miles east of Giza. It consists of a 492 foot-long stone jetty, a navigational marker of heaped stones, a large storage building, and a series of thirty galleries carved into limestone outcrops farther inland from the sea.

Modern sheet of papyrus paper, left; Ancient papyrus paper 1075–945 B.C., right (after Wikipedia & Brooklyn Museum).

These galleries provided living space, as well as workshops, boat storage space, and warehousing in ancient times; after being abandoned for so many years these were the last places anyone would expect to find an antique diary. But it was in two of these rock-cut galleries that Professor Tallet found an unusual cache of old paper. At first glance, he saw that they were written in hieroglyphics as well as hieratic, the cursive script that the ancient Egyptians used for everyday communication. When Tallet was asked how he felt when he came across these hundreds of pieces of ancient papyrus paper, he replied, "You know, when you are working full tilt every day on a site like that it's difficult to realize the full significance of such a find."

Tallet also told *Discovery News*, "Although we will not learn anything new about the construction of the Khufu monument, this diary provides for the first time a look into what was going on behind the scene." After examining hundreds of fragments, along with some larger pieces, sheets, and even scrolls, Professor Tallet concluded that the paperwork was the production of Inspector Merer and his team, an efficient group of workmen, scribes, craftsmen, sailors, and stevedores. What was such a group doing in Wadi el-Jarf? Tallet concluded that Merer and his team had been sent there by royal command to collect and transport copper back to Giza.[6] At that time, copper rivaled gold in terms of utility and value as a trade item. Khufu lusted after the output of local copper foundries. Why? Because copper was used in forming the tools his pyramid builders needed. Indeed, according to some, Khufu may have amassed the largest concentration of copper anywhere in the world in order to have the tools needed to build his gigantic marvel.[7] The production of thousands of copper tools required in turn a large amount of wood needed to produce the hot fires necessary for working the metal. In fact the construction of the pyramids at Giza must have used so much wood that deforestation of the Giza region was inevitable, especially because acacia trees—the preferred fuel—were not easily replaced because of the arid conditions that developed in this region.

The metal came from several sources, including the Sinai region that lies just across the Red Sea, opposite the ancient ports of Ayn Sukhna and Wadi el-Jarf. At Ayn Sukhna, Professor Tallet had uncovered the remains of ovens for smelting copper before he discovered Merer's journals.[8]

Khufu was also known to have sent several expeditions to Lebanon to trade copper tools and weapons for precious Lebanese cedar; the wood was essential for building the stately funerary boats that he sequestered in large pits on the southern side of his Great Pyramid.[9]

It is evident that Merer and his team were important links in the trade and development of Egypt. And this royal team had to be supplied and fed while on the road. Now, thanks to Tallet, we have detailed daily and monthly accounts kept by the team of the foodstuffs they received and consumed. Local officials had to provide for them since they were on assignment from Pharaoh. The names of those contributing to the maintenance of this team were also entered on the sheets, perhaps serving as an official receipt to let Pharaoh know exactly how the various provinces were carrying out their obligations. There is an entry for every item that had to be delivered to the team. On the papyrus account sheet, alongside the accounting of food and supplies, Merer and his clerks drew three boxes: one to indicate the amount anticipated, then an entry of what was actually delivered, and finally what was still pending. The most complete of these sheets was the delivery record of different types of cereals, or the "account of bread."[10]

A second set of documents discovered by Professor Tallet consists of time sheets, grids with horizontal lines subdivided into thirty boxes with columns to record the daily activities of the team over the course of a month. This mostly concerns their progress fetching limestone slabs at Tura and delivering them to Giza. The team scribes entered tasks and project goals on lists separated by horizontal lines. At every stage of the operation, a notation of progress or date of completion would be added to track overall progress. Forward progress was definitely needed to satisfy the boss, who in this case was a pharaoh with a reputation for quick and harsh reactions.

Sound familiar? Michael Grubbs of Zapier thought it was. He cites Merer's bread account and time sheets as the first ever spreadsheet.[11] Apparently, four and a half thousand years ago man was just as bad at mentally processing information as today. In modern times we repackaged data tables—more commonly known today as spreadsheets—to organize arrays of information as accurate, easy-to-use data sets that our brains can't otherwise recall. But the invention of the first "spreadsheet," as it were, was not thanks to Microsoft Excel, but to papyrus.

> Spreadsheets help us sort and label in a way that makes sense, so we can reference it and perform calculations later. The practice actually dates back thousands of years, to the papyrus spreadsheets in the diary of Merer, an Egyptian Old Kingdom official involved in the construction of the Great Pyramid of Khufu. Back then, paper was one of your only options for cataloguing huge amounts of data. Now, we've got computers to do the work for us. (Michael Grubbs, "Google Spreadsheets 101: Beginner's Guide.")

Lastly we come to the third set of papers found at the site, the journal or diary, which consists of the best-preserved sheets in the cache. They contain detailed accounts of various missions carried out by the Merer team, mainly their work before their arrival at the port of Wadi el-Jarf. The team organized the loading, transport, and delivery of stone from Tura, and thus Merer made daily entries of the times of arrival, overnight stays, and the duration of each phase of the operation.

The Tura quarry is located twelve and half miles south of Giza. From the diary it is clear that the trip required two days to reach Giza sailing with the current. Once unloaded, the barge would be rowed or sailed back upriver and returned to Tura in one day. Recall that unlike the majority of the world's rivers, the Nile flows north. Sailing on the Nile is at most times an easy task for a light boat; little effort is involved either way. The prevailing wind is from the north, thus boats can sail upstream and then drift down with the river current on their return journey; or in Merer's case, just the opposite. This is easy to remember when you think of the hieroglyph for the expression "travel up the river or south," which is a small drawing of a papyriform boat with sail set. The same glyph with sail furled is used to mean, "travel down the river or north."

One complicating feature of river travel in ancient times was that the course of the Nile shifted, so that the route from Tura to Giza most certainly would not be as direct as it is today. It has been suggested that Khufu and those before him constructed waterways and canals that connected the pyramid-building area to harbors, reservoirs, and basins that would ease the passage of stone barges to the site.[12]

As noted by Tallet, the diary makes for straightforward reading.

"Day 24: heaping up of stone with the crew, personnel from the palace, and the noble Ankhaef [a vizier, half-brother of Khufu]."

"Day 26: ship laden with stones; spends the night beside the Lake of Khufu."

"Day 27: departure, bound for the Horizon of Khufu [aka the Great Pyramid] to deliver the stones."

"Day 28: departure, headed for Tura Caves."

"Day 29: day spent with the crew to pick up other stones at Tura . . ." and so on.[13]

Tallet speculated that Merer's team carried the paperwork and diary with them to the port during their last copper run, then left it all behind when they heard Pharaoh had died. With Khufu dead, their work came to an end. By then, the pyramid was perhaps complete and there was no longer any reason to stay in Wadi el-Jarf, which being an arid, very hot isolated station was hardly a place to linger.[14]

❧

Tallet was interviewed in 2015 by Alexander Stille, an author and professor at Columbia's School of Journalism. Stille thought the professor found the comments of the press and popular media both amusing and mildly annoying. And who could blame him for being annoyed? Ealier Tallet had made the case for Merer's diary being, ". . . to this day the oldest registered papyrus ever unearthed in Egypt,"[15] a fact that seems to have been pushed aside by Madison Avenue-type spinmeisters in the popular media. In their view, ancient Egypt means only the "three M's": monuments, massive pyramids, and mummies. As far as they are concerned the real keys to development, the mundane items of ordinary life that made Egypt great and are studied by the professor, can go begging. Things like pottery kilns, copper smelters, simple water-lifting devices, homemade ploughs and farm animals like oxen for agricultural production, all must wait. The building of monuments and pyramids are more buzzworthy.

It is true that the pyramids provided a national economic stimulus and a focus for mobilization of resources, but economists tell us that the real basis for Egypt's greatness came from agriculture and the management of agricultural production. The Egyptians remeasured and reassigned land after every inundation based on past assignments, they assessed expected crops, they collected part of the produce as taxes, and then stored and redistributed it to those on the state's payroll. Regional storage facilities with hundreds of storehouses provided produce in case there was a shortfall. All of this was recorded and tracked using spreadsheets, and so the country soon became a nation dependent on lightweight paper to process and manage data sets.

Paper thus became one of the many basic things that made Egypt the wonder of its time. Spreadsheets of the type used by Merer became invaluable to the Egyptian way of life. It was also the medium used to record the immediate thoughts or sayings of the priests, pronouncements of the kings, and the substance of history in the ancient world. As such, it was far more important than Khufu or his pyramid. In essence it was the pharaoh's greatest treasure.

Professor Tallet has spent twenty years working on the edges of Egypt's ancient culture, a culture that leveraged what Stille calls, "a massive shipping, mining, and farming economy" needed to propel their civilization forward. Part of this process involved the small miracle performed by Merer every day of his adult lifetime, using paper to free up the minds of his team members for bigger and better things. Lightweight paper made from plants helped carry out the business of the moment and, most importantly, helped process and use data sets to move the agenda of Pharaoh forward. All of this pointed again toward the importance of paper.

Paper wasn't their only means. Other media, such as tablets made of lead, copper, wax, and clay; pieces of shell or pottery; tree bark; leather; cloth; slips of bamboo; and palm leaves were all used to a greater or lesser extent. Papyrus paper was, however, the first medium in the modern sense. It weighed almost nothing, and yet allowed the writing that had until then been restricted to the walls of tombs or sides of monuments or lids of coffins or the impressed surface of clay and paintings on pottery to lift off and take wing. This was the first stage in the ultimate journey that brought us all to what is known today as "the cloud."

In earlier times, clay tablets were also a means of passing text around. Evolved from tokens used around 4000 B.C. to record basic information about crops and taxes, clay tablets allowed for the development of Sumerian cuneiform 'wedge writing,' a script that began around 2500 B.C. The fragility and weight of clay tablets were liabilities that were not shared by paper or parchment. Properly baked clay is fairly permanent, but sun-dried clay is not. New Testament scholar Robert Waltz tells us that a number of cuneiform tablets from Mesopotamia, while initially perfectly legible, are now decaying because they were displayed in museums that did not maintain proper humidity. This quality would preclude their spread after the Bronze Age to areas other than arid regions. These tablets did serve well in the royal archives of Mesopotamia. Distinguished librarian and scholar Frederick Kilgour noted that 95 percent of the half million tablets surviving today were made for record keeping. But there were complaints from ancient readers that the writing used was almost unintelligible to scribes other than the Sumerians. And as a social medium, clay tablets had another disadvantage: their weight. Waltz estimated that a complete New Testament would require about 650 tablets and would be too heavy for an ordinary person to carry, plus you'd need a way to keep the tablets in order.

Luckily for the written word, papyrus paper arrived in about 3000 B.C. just in time to help kick-start Western civilization and literature as we know it. From then on, as cuneiform clay tablets faded into the background, the world could breathe easier as words became as transmittable and as easy to spread as the scrolls they were written on.

The Egyptians made papyrus paper from thin slices of the white inner stem of the papyrus plant, which were pressed together, and then dried to make millions of sheets. From the end of the Neolithic period in 3000 B.C. the Egyptians, and later the Greeks, Romans, and Arabs, would swear by it.

What a godsend. And the early Christians likewise were relieved when they looked around for something to record their early letters and scriptures on and found papyrus paper in sheets, rolls, and the folded pages of notebooks that formed the earliest books, called "codices." Lucky for them, and again for us, the plant the Egyptians used was among the fastest growing, most productive plants on earth. Under the hot sun and cloudless skies of old Egypt, it prospered in the ancient swamps, which were millions of acres in size.

The First Piece of Paper Ever

Tallet's discovery revealed the first piece of paper with writing on it, but we know paper existed even prior to that time. The person who discovered this did so by dint of hard work. With great difficulty, he had cleared tombs of viziers, sacred bulls embalmed and encased in a giant sarcophagi, and Nubian kings, and he had seen it all in the process. He had even been present and lent a helping hand when Howard Carter cleared out the tomb of King Tut in 1923. Solid, reliable, pipe-smoking Walter Emery was there in Saqqara because he had earned the right. On a Penguin book cover, his smiling face looks out from eyes framed by horn-rimmed glasses. Dark haired and ruddy cheeked, in the photograph he looked exactly like what he had been in early life: a marine engineer. But the place where he stood that day late in March 1936 was very far from any ocean or sea; it was an arid, dusty necropolis, a place used in ancient times by the inhabitants of Memphis, the capital that lay south of present-day Cairo.

As a young Egyptologist, Emery had shown himself capable of managing large and important excavations, and because he was a trained draftsman and analyst of structures, he was the right man to excavate these tombs. And his wife Molly helped immensely by taking charge of the camp logistics. The famous archaeologist Flinders Petrie had himself wanted to "do" Saqqara, but had been turned down. In the early days when Petrie had longed for the area, it had been set aside as a preserve for government archaeologists. Many years later the chief inspector of antiquities at Saqqara died and Emery was put in charge.

His first excavation season began in the autumn of 1935, once the hot summer had passed. His first move was to look long and hard at the solid, massive mastaba called "Tomb 3035," a mound that dominated the area. His engineer's eye told him that, of all the places in the necropolis, this was the right place to start.

It was rumored that it was the burial place of Hemaka (ca. 3100 B.C.[16]), an important man who had been chancellor and royal seal-bearer and second in power only to Pharaoh Den in the First Dynasty. This tomb was considered a masterpiece of architecture, and throughout history had attracted many visitors who had picked the place clean. Was there anything of importance left? Luck, intuition, and hard work paid off when, after a year's work, Emery discovered forty-five storage rooms, or magazines.

Then came the hard part, the backbreaking work; carefully clearing each of the forty-five rooms. Starting in magazine A, his crew had proceeded through the alphabet to Z, where he stood this day. Clearance meant 400 men digging, sifting, sweeping, brushing, and even dusting under close supervision. All the previous twenty-five rooms had been cleared, but to date only a handful were found to contain anything of value. In some of the rooms he had discovered ancient oil and wine jugs. Over the last few weeks in magazines W, X, and Y his crew had turned up more and more artifacts. Today in magazine Z they had uncovered a large number of objects, among them an inlaid gaming disc showing hunting dogs in pursuit of a gazelle. Numerous other gaming discs were recovered in Z, along with arrows, tools, flint scrapers, flint knives, and pot seals made of clay. It was in this room he had found the name of Hemaka on two ivory labels and the handle of a sickle.

More than satisfied with his find, he photographed the site. These last three objects had dated the site and given him the confidence he needed to begin drawing a detailed plan for publication. It also meant that he could name and date Tomb 3035 as definitely belonging to Hemaka.

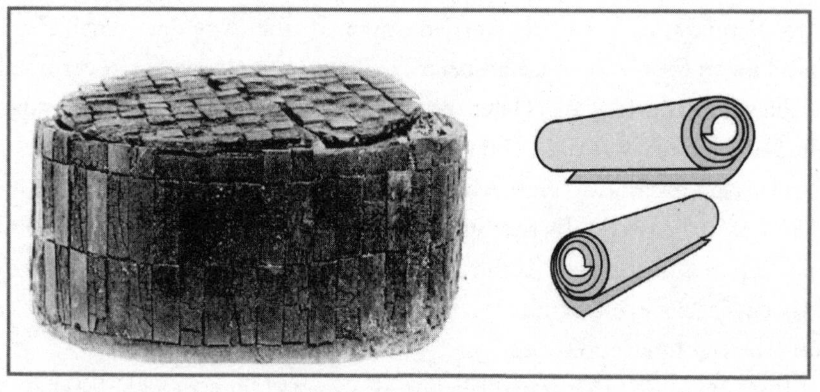

Inlaid wooden box found in Hemaka's tomb (after Emery, 1938) and two blank papyrus scrolls.

Suddenly one of the workmen motioned him over. There, under a layer of sand and debris, was a small, circular, inlaid wooden box. Carefully hefting the box, he waited as the men gathered round. Here was a container that had sat for over 5,100 years. They were certain that inside would be gold trinkets, semi-precious stones, or some exquisite relict of those early days when history was just beginning. They held their breaths as Emery gently pried opened the lid.

Inside were two rolls of papyrus paper, the sole contents of the box. Imagine their disappointment as they then learned that the rolls were blank. The crew went back to work and Emery turned his attention to other things.

In King Tut's tomb Carter had his solid gold coffins; in the great Tomb of Hemaka Emery had his drawings, and the largest single collection of early dynastic objects ever discovered, including a cache of 500 arrows. He was satisfied.

The instant he opened the box had been an important moment in the history of the world. Then and now, despite thousands of rolls of papyrus paper recovered from Egypt; thousands of copies of the *Book of the Dead*; despite two thousand charred rolls found in a villa in Italy; despite the hundreds of thousands of fragments, sheets, and rolls dug up at Oxyrhynchus and other rubbish sites; and the ancient diary and spreadsheets of Merer; no one has yet turned up an older example of paper, let alone two intact rolls. He had by chance uncovered the most ancient paper ever found.

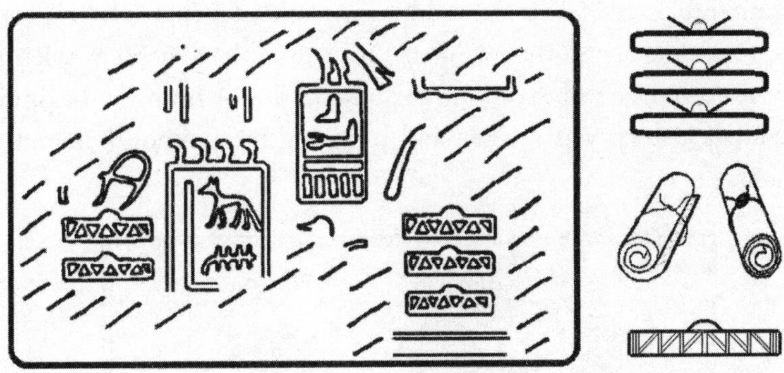

Papyrus roll hieroglyphs on clay seal King Qa'a (from Emery, 1954). Right, various drawings of book rolls and their glyphs.

The most intriguing part of his discovery was that the rolls were blank. What did that mean? During the First Dynasty (3100–2890 B.C.) simple outlines on seal impressions in the time of King Qa'a, the last ruler in this period, showed scrolls sealed with a daub of Nile mud. The drawing of such a sealed scroll served as a hieroglyph for "book" or "writing."[17] This showed that papyrus paper was already in existence with the arrival of the first kings of Egypt. By then Egyptians had developed hieroglyphics, as well as hieratic, an elegant cursive script.

Looking back on all this, Cambridge University Egyptologist Toby Wilkinson concluded that the uninscribed rolls of papyrus paper discovered by Emery were not only proof that papyrus paper existed 5,000 years ago, but also that Egyptian writing already existed in the First Dynasty (a span of eight kings from Narmer to Qa'a from 3150–2750 B.C.)[18] Wilkinson based his conclusion on the fact that hieratic script was tied to papyrus paper, which lent itself to this speedier form of writing.

The Pharaohs' Treasure

It is interesting and important to note from the beginning that ancient Egyptians were quite aware of the true value of the papyrus plant, and that, as it happened, Egypt was the only one among the many early hydraulic civilizations blessed by this plant. This is a fact that seems to have escaped modern historians, and there is precious little in the general or scientific literature to indicate how or why this plant, almost from the beginning of recorded history, was revered and treasured by common folk and the pharaohs.

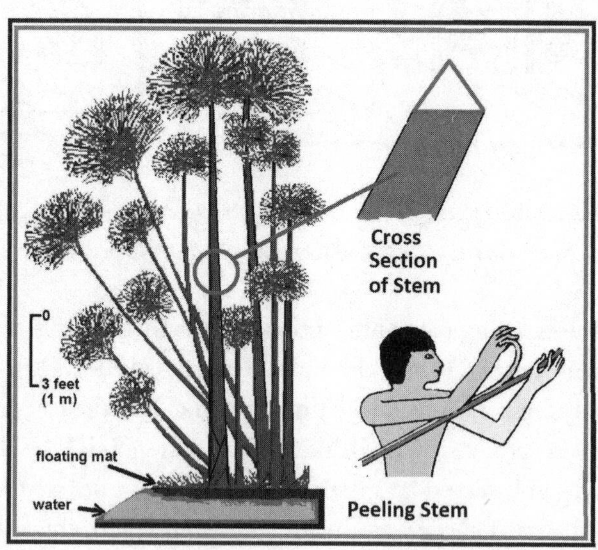

Papyrus plants growing at the edge of a papyrus swamp on the River Nile.

What made the plant so unusual was the flexibility of its stem. At maturity, most other reeds are too stiff to be worked into a great number of handicrafts or to be made into paper or rope. Once papyrus stems are cut they can be dried and used like any other of the reeds common to the hydraulic empires of Mesopotamia, the Indus valley, Somalia (Shebelle-Juba), Sri Lanka, China, pre-Columbian Mexico, and Lake Titicaca (Bolivia-Peru) to build boats, fences, and houses. Beyond that, the most common reeds are of limited use. It happens that the grass reed or *bardi* (Phragmites), *totora* sedge (Schoenoplectus) and the bulrush or *khanna* (Typha), are all hollow or too rigid at maturity, and therefore not useful for making paper or rope, as was done for thousands of years with the more flexible papyrus.

Given its flexibility, how then was papyrus able to grow up to an average of fifteen feet under normal conditions? The papyrus plant grows a light, tough green skin around a wide triangular core of pith, an ingenious invention of nature that packaged a pith useful for paper making while the outer green skin can be easily peeled away. That in itself provides an excellent source of material for weaving and handicrafts of all sorts. The pith and skin made papyrus an outstanding resource and, because of its size, unique even among plants of its own kind.

Because of its versatility, productivity, and adaptability, papyrus played an important role in the life of Egyptians and thus appeared in the earliest hieroglyphs. The word for the papyrus stem was "*djet*" or, as a water plant, "*tjufy*," or the more general term for marsh plants, "*mehyt*."[19] A sign for a papyrus plant was used in writing the word "*wadj*," which meant fresh, flourishing, or green—as in the "Great Green" or Mediterranean Sea. After it had been made into paper rolls it was called *djema*, which meant "clean" or "open," in reference to the fresh writing surface.[20] A long-stemmed papyrus plant folded twice symbolized an offering or gift, a clump of papyrus (phonogram *ha*) represented the Nile delta or Lower Egypt, stems lined up on a base were used in the expression for the inundation season.

When the papyrus stem was joined with a cobra (the symbol for Wadjet, patroness of the Nile delta), it represented the adjective green (phonogram *wadj*); whereas stems tied into a bundle then bent into a loop (an early form of life jacket or cattle float) meant "protection."

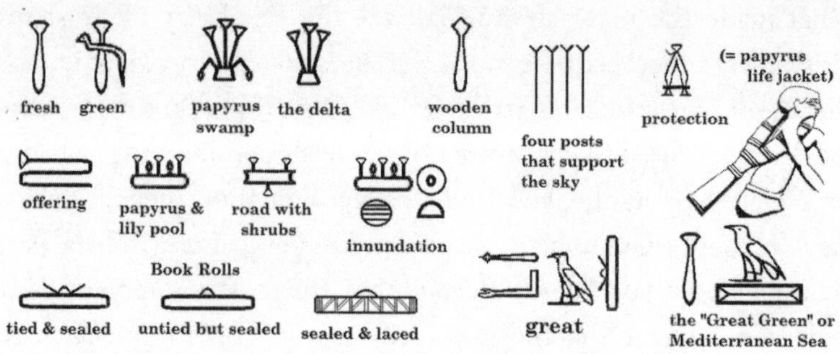

Various hieroglyphs featuring papyrus or papyrus paper.

Simple ouline drawings of the plant stem became part of the symbol for a street (perhaps "road with shrubs" was an indication that early Egyptian roads were built along the top of dikes with papyrus plants on both sides or bordering roads that ran between and through papyrus swamps); or the symbol of the four pillars that support the sky, which are the four corners of the earth; or the symbol of the outline of a wooden column modeled after the common stone papyriform columns used in temples throughout Egypt.

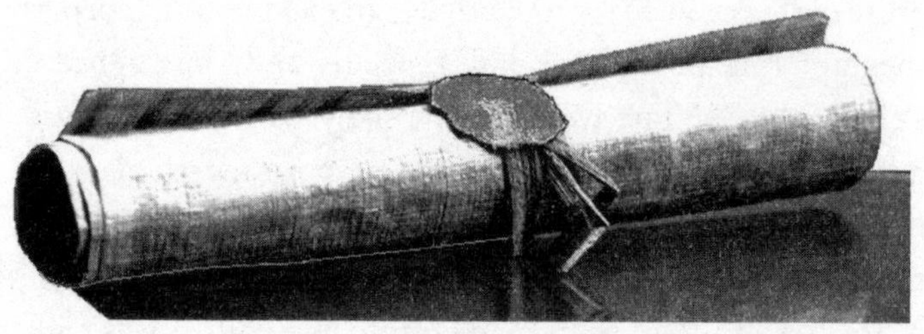

Replica roll sealed with clay (Wikipedia & Papyrus Mus. Siracusa, photo by G. Dall' Orta).

As to the paper, a roll of papyrus paper shown tied with a string and sealed with a daub of clay (or without the string but still sealed) is an ideogram for "roll of papyrus," with its own phonetic value ("*m(dj)3t*"). This comes from the fact that hieroglyphic writing is phonetic with certain symbols standing for certain sounds, unlike the English alphabet where some letters have many sounds or can be silent. Thus when an ancient

Egyptian said "*m(dj)3t*" he knew anyone listening would understand that he had just called for another roll of paper.

Combined with other signs, the papyrus roll appears in the expression for "great." What we are missing, however, is the path that led the Greeks to the word *papyros*. Several authors believe it is an obvious derivative of the ancient Egyptian "*pa-per-aa*" (or *p'p'r*) literally "that of the pharaoh" or "Pharaoh's own," in reference to the crown monopoly on papyrus production.

All of the ways that images of papyrus were included in Egyptian writing were indications of how they recognized the importance of the plant. It was almost as if they could foretell that paper that was already being produced from it, would in the coming years be a significant factor in the development of the world. In more immediate terms, it turned out to be an important foreign exchange earner for Pharaoh. It was the export and sale of millions of sheets and rolls of paper, and millions of feet and coils of papyrus rope over thousands of years that made papyrus a treasure—a jewel not shared by any of the other early global river-based cultures. The income from papyrus was a steady, significant flow into the Pharaoh's coffers. This flow went on regardless of the rise and fall of grain stocks, which were subject to droughts. And the income from the products of Egyptian papyrus swamps could always be counted on. As we will see, it was an unusual set of circumstances that interrupted the export flow of paper.

❧

From 30 B.C. to 640 A.D., Egyptian rule gave way as the Romans took control of the country and the management of the paper industry, which went on to supply the whole of the Roman Empire with scrolls and sheets. One Roman statesman, Cassiodorus, openly admitted that he did not know how the civilized Western world would have got on without it,[21] since by his day it was used for books, records of business, correspondence, orders of the day for the Roman army, even the first newspaper, the *Acta Diurna*—the newspaper that was originally carved on stone—was then written on papyrus paper and became then a lot easier to carry around.

All of this seems to pale in light of the new electronic world of pads, pods, PCs, phones, and tablets. But for all the innovation and technological miracles, the physical proof of evolution of the human mind still centers on the scrolls and books made of papyrus paper, which are counted among the earliest historical documents.

The importance of papyrus' role was recently reinforced when a scrap of papyrus paper surfaced in 2012 and made headline news. It was announced by Karen King, professor at Harvard Divinity School, that she had obtained a fragment from a private collector who wanted to remain anonymous. It contained the words, "Jesus said to them, 'My wife . . . '" King obtained the papyrus two years before that. At first blush, she said, it appeared genuine. "Christian tradition has long held that Jesus was not married, even though no reliable historical evidence exists to support that claim." King later wondered whether this fragment should lead us to re-think whether Jesus was married, rather than to re-think how Christianity understood sexuality and marriage in a very positive way, and to recapture the beauty of human intimate relations.

This event proved that papyrus paper is still a force to be reckoned with. It also reminded me of the day I found an old piece of notepaper. In my case I'm sure the press were not interested, especially as I found it in a pair of trousers slated for the Goodwill people. It was a note to myself and I recalled just how important that message was at the time. There it was, preserved in its entirety, a reminder to pick up an antique pearl necklace. My wife still treasures the anniversary gift that it engendered, and an archaeologist going through a Goodwill midden years from now would probably have found it hard to contain his excitement at such a find.

The conservation of records at such a personal level pales in comparison to what we face in the future on a global scale. At a conference on this topic in the nineties, one speaker described ". . . the threat to all our magnetic records posed by a high altitude [over thirty kilometers] nuclear explosion, which would generate gamma radiation and erase all magnetic records within a wide area . . ." In the discussion period, someone asked who would be alive then to save our heritage. The speaker said that the atmosphere protects us, only the electromagnetic radiation gets through, and had he understood the question correctly? The person replied, 'Yes—You're promoting the use of paper.'"[22]

If that technician is correct, then it really is important to write things down. And today, the lawyers and accountants would agree. They would further caution you that once something is written down you should sign it, scan it, and send a copy to them, "and make sure you mail me the original." Presumably on paper.

Once done, such a record is as good as carved in stone, but much more portable—a point that Moses would come to appreciate when he was commanded to appear in 1200 B.C. at God's bidding atop Mount Sinai. Here, according to Hebrew tradition, the text of the Ten Commandments was written with the finger of God on two original stone tablets, as well as on subsequent replacements. After this, Moses was faced with task two: recording the Torah, virtually a history of the world as well as a code of ethics and behavior for his followers. Since the Torah also recounts the creation of the world and the origin of the people of Israel, their descent into Egypt, and the drafting of the Torah on Mount Sinai, it is in part or whole a significant undertaking, composed of many pages. If Moses had turned to a chisel and hammer, it may never have happened. Instead, he must have reached for a scroll of papyrus paper. Why? Because Mount Sinai was and still is located in the Sinai Peninsula near the city of Saint Catherine in Egypt, a nation in which, at that time, papyrus paper was the medium of choice. And a pen? We know that at a later date, among the Gnostic documents there is reference to God as having a pen of gold. Whether Moses was so equipped, we don't know, or whether God loaned him His pen we are ignorant, but according to the story when he came down the mountain carrying two tablets in his arms he must have had a copy of the Torah written out on a paper scroll sequestered someplace in the folds of his robe. At this point the Bible tells us that Moses was ready to direct his people onto the path of righteousness and he never looked back. Again the same message comes through: if it's important, write it down.

As we will see in the next chapter, Prisse d'Avennes, a Frenchman in Victorian times coming out of Egypt and, like Moses, carrying stone tablets and scrolls, items that were destined to be part of the foundations of recorded history, must have, again like Moses, reflected on the choice of medium. If papyrus paper was, after all, the dominant medium of its age, then, as Marshall McLuhan (the famous philosopher and professor of communication technology) would argue, such media shaped the way we perceive and understand our surrounding world. And this is exactly what happened, as papyrus paper went on to affect the Western world for almost four thousand years.

One school of media scholars, led by Donald Shaw at the University of North Carolina, has recently drawn attention to what they refer to as the "emerging Papyrus Society," a society in whch there is a more personalized mix of personal messages, as in ancient times when messages were the ones more easily transportable by papyrus paper. This need of modern man for a personal, portable means of communication, is the result of a long period of evolution that started with the move away from messages painted and carved on rock faces. Once the move was made to the new medium—mobile, flexible, portable paper—it never stopped. This was a pivotal moment in world history; we had been set free. In essence, papyrus paper was the midwife at the birth of civilization and had literally cut the cord. It freed man from his dependency on writing on unwieldy surfaces. It allowed man to carry his messages and records with him as he moved around, an innovation the like of which was not seen again until the introduction of wireless technology in the twentieth century. And, once set in motion, this new media assisted in the advent of the first newspaper. In later days, newspapers, news magazines, radio, news channels, and TV programs directed the news to listeners and viewers in a vertical fashion—top-down to the entire community. These major media are fighting a losing battle with the new horizontal media: social networking, blogs, web sites, cable TV, satellite radio, etc.

> All this will come as a surprise to modern Internet users who may assume that today's social-media environment is unprecedented. But many of the ways in which we share, consume, and manipulate information, even in the Internet era, build upon habits and conventions that date back centuries. Today's social-media users are the unwitting heirs of a rich tradition with surprisingly deep historical roots . . . social media does not merely connect us to each other today—it also links us to the past. (Tom Standage, "Writing on the Wall: Social Media—The First 2,000 Years.")

Since attention spans are limited, people today mix and match media to a greater degree, which led Shaw to consider another dimension to the meaning of his modern day Papyrus Society. It seems that papyrus paper required two layers of papyrus pith in its manufacture: one laid horizontally and one laid vertically. To Shaw, this matrix is a physical metaphor for the challenging modern media mix of vertical power and horizontal spread. (It also can be seen, as pointed out by Shaw and his colleagues, as a balancing between the power of vertical, institutional society, represented by magnificently rising pyramids, and the ease and convenience of social media to convey information, such as papyrus paper once allowed.)

One goal of this book will be to provide a history of paper and books during the early days of antiquity. Another goal will be to present an overview of how papyrus lent itself to the task of producing these books and how, in doing so, it helped revolutionize the world.

TWO

Prisse, like Moses, Carries Home Stone Tablets and Paper Scrolls

Once Prisse d'Avennes had packed his treasures into twenty-seven large cases, he needed to carry his trophies downstream to Cairo. In the spring of that same year, 1844, on the other side of the world, the first electrical telegram was sent by Samuel Morse from Washington, DC, to a railroad depot, asking the question of questions, "What hath God wrought?" Prisse was certain the Egyptians would ask the same question once he had gone, but in reference to him: "What hath d'Avennes done?"

He had little time to ponder how such things as the invention of Morse would change his world, which was still a paper world. His small crew had been working every night for almost a year, secretly cutting over sixty sculptured panels from the Amun temple in Karnak near the port town of Luxor, formerly Thebes (Map 1). Having done this without a permit (*firman*) or diplomatic immunity, he stopped work in 1844 when he found out that the local governor of the Quena region had been tipped off about what he and his team had been doing.[1] The minute his tent had been placed under government watch, Prisse decided it was too risky to stay; it really was time to get out while he could. By noon the next day he had rented and loaded a large *felucca* boat. That night, as the moon rose over the river Nile, he made his escape.

Falucca on the Nile with crew in the 1840's (Wikipedia).

As they pushed off from the pier, the captain of the felucca took the tiller and several of his crew rowed while Prisse and his workmen lay down on the deck for a well-deserved rest. The river current and the rowers carried them steadily away from shore and out into the main stream.

Prisse d'Avennes was perhaps the most skillful treasure hunter to ever come to Egypt. Strangest of all was the fact that he hadn't intended it that way. When he first arrived in 1826 at the age of nineteen, he carried with him a diploma in drafting and engineering from a respected French school and a pedigree—he came from the French branch of a family descended from the English noble family of Price of Aven. His parents and grandparents were prominent administrators and lawyers and he was intent on assisting the viceroy, Mohammed Ali Pasha, and his son, Ibrahim Pasha, with engineering and water development projects. In the process, and over the course of many years, he acquired a proficiency in Arabic, Turkish, Greek, Coptic, Amharic, Latin, English, Italian, and Spanish. He also taught topography and fortifications in Egyptian military academies, traveled widely in the East and, after taking the name Edris-Effendi, embraced Islam.

Though contentious by nature and in the habit of alienating his colleagues, he succored the sick and poor and remained a model of deportment. He was never thought of as a man who would steal, and he disparaged those who did. He is famously quoted as saying, ". . . learned society has now descended like an invasion of barbarians to carry off what little remains of its [Egypt's] admirable monuments . . ." If anyone could claim the moral high ground, it was this man.

Émile Prisse d'Avennes 1807–1879, French archaeologist, architect. (Wikipedia).

What happened? What changed his character so? Why on that night in 1844 was he lying down on a felucca with a band of rogue workmen, a group no better than a gang of thieves, in an escapade that was entirely against local law? He knew he had committed a crime, one of serious proportions, but he had been driven to it by his bosses, the Pashas. They made it known throughout Europe that they would trade antiquities, including obelisks, ancient tombs, and any and all pharaonic treasures for cotton gins, steam engines, mechanical looms, metal works, and sugar mills. They encouraged the leveling and recycling of all ancient monuments in their haste to rebuild Egypt as a modern country. When Prisse learned that they planned to demolish the Temple of Amun in Luxor, he acted. He became a man who would steal for a cause, not for gain.

Prisse's men removing the stone panels in Karnak, 1843 (Wikipedia).

Through superhuman exertions and with virtually no resources, save a few men and fewer tools, and working mainly under cover of darkness, Prisse removed the carved stone blocks from the temple walls that included the figures, cartouches, hieroglyphic signs, and details of all known Egyptian kings. Known as the Karnak King List, this incomparable record included the details of over five-dozen royal predecessors, ranked in dynastic order. The writer Mary Norton tells us that he also succeeded in extracting several tablets (stelae)—one with domestic scenes dating from 4000 B.C.,[2]—and a papyrus scroll that turned out to be as important as all his other loot. Discovered in Thebes, Prisse bought that scroll from one of the *fellahîn* whom he employed when he was excavating at the necropolis there. It has since been dated to 1800 B.C. and refers back to the nobility of Khufu's time. Known as the Prisse Papyrus, it is said to be the oldest literary work on paper in the world.

When he neared Cairo, he tied up his felucca in Boulac, the nearby Nile river port, and left his foreman in charge of the boat and its cargo. He sought out the French vice-consul and implored him to place his precious cargo under diplomatic protection, but the official refused. Undeterred, Prisse returned to his boat. Along the way he met the famous archaeologist and scholar, Richard Lepsius, leader of a Prussian team that had just started assembling an expedition that would travel up the Nile. Sanctioned by the Pasha, Lepsius would later come away with his own impressive collection, including a dynamited column from the ill-fated tomb of Seti I, and sections of tiled wall from Pharaoh Djoser's Step Pyramid at Saqqara. All of these were official presents from Mohammed Ali Pasha in thanks for a dinner service presented to him by Lepsius in the name of the Prussian king. Prisse invited Lepsius back to his boat and entertained him that night with coffee while the famous man sat on one of the cases, not knowing what was in it.

In May 1844, a full year after he had first sunk his chisel into the monumental walls of the Temple of Amun, Prisse sailed downriver to Afteh. If he had waited another twenty-five years, perhaps it would have been easier to get away, since by 1869 the Suez Canal would be in place. Instead, Prisse had to transit the Mahmoudieh Canal, which connected the Nile to the sea at Alexandria and delivered fresh drinking water and food to that city. The canal had been dug by the Pasha, Prisse's old boss, at a loss of 15,000 men. Prisse had his felucca towed in tandem with a barge and steam tug up the canal to the port of Alexandria where he unloaded his crates and boarded the French steamboat *Le Cerbère* that called at Malta and Gibraltar en route to Marseille.[3]

So, after many years of dedicated work in Egypt, he left for France and glory. On arrival, he presented the stone tablets that comprised the Karnak King List to the Louvre and was awarded the Legion d'Honneur in 1845. What then was the outcome of Prisse's efforts? His King List had simply joined a host of others.

There have been many other king lists discovered since his time, including the Palermo Stone carved on an olivine-basalt slab and broken into pieces and acquired by F. Guidano in 1859 (it is kept in Palermo); the Giza King List painted on gypsum and cedar wood, taken in 1904 by George Reisner from a mastaba at Giza (it now rests in the Museum of Fine

Arts in Boston); the South Saqqara Stone carved on a black basalt slab that was discovered in Saqqara in 1932 by Gustave Jéquier; the Abydos King List of Seti I carved on limestone that is still in place on the wall of the Mortuary Temple of Seti at Abydos in Egypt; the Abydos King List of Ramses II carved on limestone, dug up in Abydos by William Bankes in 1818 (now in the British Museum); and the Saqqara King List carved on limestone and found in 1861 in Saqqara (now in the Egyptian Museum, Cairo).

Surprisingly, the most reliable kings list in history for the chronology of the period prior to the reign of Ramesses II (1200 B.C.) wasn't even cut in stone, but written out on papyrus paper. It is called the Turin King List. Inscribed with red and black ink, it was acquired by the famous collector, Drovetti in 1820 at Luxor. Even though it is damaged, it includes all the early kings of Egypt up through at least the Nineteenth Dynasty. Kept in the Museo Egizio in Turin, it is yet another excellent example of the advantage of copying out messages from stone to paper. In this case, a papyrus scroll has trumped many of the previous carved or painted monumental artifacts.

The second remarkable thing is that, with the exception of the two Saqqara lists and the Abydos Seti list, all of the above were discovered by Victorian and Edwardian collectors and are now kept outside of Egypt. Should they be repatriated, especially if they were illegally exported? These are questions that have been argued for years, but there is less talk today of repatriation to Egypt since the Arab Spring revolutions of 2011. After the fire-bombing of the Egyptian Scientific Institute near Tahrir Square in Cairo in December 2011, volunteers spent days trying to salvage what was left of the 200,000 historic books, priceless journals, and extraordinary writings kept in the institute. This presents a conundrum, should people acquire by any means (including illegal transactions) in order to "rescue history?" or should they demand the return of hundreds of thousands of objects from around the world? Any massive repatriation would overwhelm the curators and resources of the museums in Egypt, making the situation worse.

Perhaps the solution lies in what seems like a general philosophy offered by Salima Ikram, the well-known archaeologist and professor of Egyptology at the American University in Cairo. After advising that, without question, certain items should be returned to Egypt, she pointed out that many items on display overseas "are the best ambassadors that Egypt has."[4] She wondered what would happen if everything went back to Egypt. A mass repatriation would leave a vacuum in the world. "How will anyone know about Egypt? How will anyone be excited?" The impasse has not been resolved despite the impending opening of the long-planned Grand Egyptian Museum at Giza, which could harken a return of the many Egyptian antiquities in museums around the world, should the organizations that currently have these artifacts prove willing to return them. As a consequence, for now, many of these kings lists will probably remain where they are.

❧

The diary and spreadsheets of Merer are the tip of an iceberg when it comes to pinpointing when the use of paper first exploded into the mainstream. We have some idea of how extensive paper use had become in ancient days when a host of ancient fragments and scrolls were uncovered by nineteenth century collectors and archaeologists. Included among these nineteenth century discoveries is an assortment of business papers relating to the cults of an ancient royal family, the Abusir Papyri from the Old Kingdom (about 2686–2181 B.C.), and a scattered array of literary papyri including the Westcar Papyri (1800–1650 B.C.) that contains five stories about miracles performed by priests and magicians (these tales were told at the royal court of Pharaoh Khufu by his sons).

When the Prisse Papyrus was handed over to the Bibliothèque Nationale in Paris in 1845, it was divided and glazed and has been on exhibit for 170 years. Spread out flat, it measured about twenty feet, seven inches, with an average height of about 6 inches. It contains eighteen pages of bold, black and red hieratic script that is said to be the earliest literary use of papyrus paper. The papyrus relates "The Maxims of Ptahhotep," itself a copy of a work written by the Grand Vizier Ptahhotep, during the reign of Djedkare Isesi (2475–2455 B.C.). The maxims are directed to Ptahhotep's son. The scroll also contains lessons and advice from another vizier, Kagemni, who served during the earlier reign of Pharaoh Sneferu (2600 B.C.), father of Khufu.

Leila Avrin, author of *Scribes, Script, and Books*, believed that "The Maxims of Ptahhotep" began an age of classical literature in Egypt that blossomed during the Middle Kingdom, a new wave of middle-class ancient literature that sprang up as writers became aware of social evils and the use of the short story as a genre. Among ancient Egyptian texts, which fall in this class and surfaced over the years, we find *The Eloquent Peasant*, *The Dispute Between a Man and his Ba*, and *The Story of Sinuhe*. There is also *Teaching of King Merikare*, a literary composition taken from three fragmentary papyri produced in 1540–1300 B.C.

Along with these is the classic papyrus containing *The Tale of the Shipwrecked Sailor*, a story told of an ancient voyage to a king's mines (2000–1650 B.C.). Considered to be the oldest fantasy text ever written, it involves a hero who sets out on a sea journey, encounters a storm, lands on an enchanted island, and battles a monster that turns out to be the prototype for the greatest imaginary monster of all time—the dragon.

Mathematical and medical papyri dating back to 2400–1300 B.C. were also recovered by collectors and archaeologists. All of which indicates that from 2500 B.C., countless scribes, priests, and accountants made a living using papyrus paper that was by then a common enough item, which served them well. Then, at the beginning of the New Kingdom, around 1550 B.C., another type of scroll began showing up, this time in tombs and coffins. A copy of a *Book of the Dead*, a guide to the correct path to eternity, was prepared and treated in much the same manner as the mummy they were associated with; consequently, a significant number have survived whole or in part.

More correctly known as the *Book of Coming Forth by Day*, it contained those magic spells needed to assist the soul on arrival in the afterlife. People who commissioned their own copies chose spells they thought most vital, which must have been a gut-wrenching process. Which spells to choose? Would they get it right? Their whole future in the afterlife depended on their choices, and on the availability of paper.

THREE

The Undertaker's Special and the World's First Bestseller

The darkish colored, elongated object lying there between the legs of the corpse had become a thing of fascination to more than one early explorer of ancient Egypt. And it wasn't the obvious mummified body part. Sometimes shellacked or varnished with resin or bitumen, this mysterious object might resemble a foot-long stick of charred firewood, but upon unfolding or unrolling, it is revealed to be a scroll. Nevertheless, it could still be extremely difficult to open and read. If discovered in a tomb or elsewhere, it would hardly be anything to write home about (let alone jump around and shout about); in fact, such things were often left behind by tomb robbers in their frantic search for obvious bounty like precious stones, jewelry, and works of art.

It was only in the eighteenth century when European tourists began showing an interest in these scrolls that they started showing up on the market as curiosities. Sadly, if coated with a flammable lacquer, resin, or bitumen, funerary scrolls not only resembled up-market briquettes, but they could also serve that purpose as well, and were scented, no less. In 1778 an unknown European dealer in antiquities, while haggling over the cost of a papyrus scroll dated 191 A.D., was horrified to see Egyptian peasants set alight some fifty scrolls just for the sake of the aromatic scent of the smoke.[1]

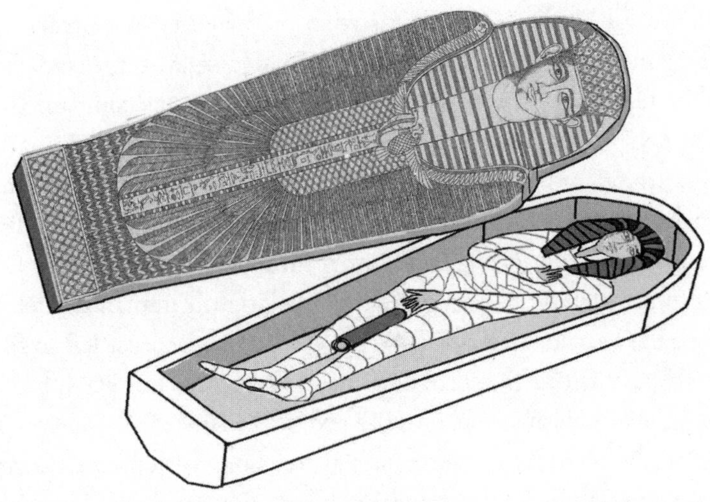

Mummified corpse, Book of the Dead and coffin with feathers on lid (after Mariette and Maspero, 1872 and Wikipedia).

It seems that papyrus has a natural compound in the stem that is akin to incense—Pliny the elder referred to it as "the aromatic weed." Today in Ethiopia papyrus rhizomes are still dried, cut into fragments, and incorporated into the incense mixture used in Orthodox Church services. Burning scrolls produces the same effect. I worked extensively with papyrus plants in Africa in the seventies, and did a great number of chemical analyses for which the dried plant had to be ground up. The scent from the grinding process was distinct and real; my lab reeked of it for months. It is not as noticeable in the upper parts of the stem, flower, or roots, but it increases dramatically in the base of the stem and into the rhizome (the sprout from which the stems grow). A resined, shellacked or tarred scroll would give off an even stronger scent of pine, acacia gum, or bitumen. Whether dealing with fresh material or tightly sealed scrolls, the natural scent of papyrus is distinct. It is missing in ancient sheets or fragments of papyrus dried in the desert air over centuries, since by then it has lost its essence.

Regardless of how interesting it would be to burn such a thing, when you see it lying there entangled in the mummy wrappings, or tucked away under the arm of a corpse, or between its thighs or legs, the first impression is that the owner was desperately afraid of losing it. And who can blame him; his *Book of the Dead* (for that is what the majority of funerary scrolls are) is a guarantee of safe passage on that final journey to the stars. Think of it as the tag that is draped around the neck of the unaccompanied child or elderly person that perhaps you've seen at an airport being led smartly by an airline attendant from one terminal to another, destination guaranteed.

In ancient Egypt, a funerary scroll could take several forms, depending on what you could afford. It might be a brief summary of personal good deeds recorded on a small bit of papyrus paper rolled tightly into an amulet. Or it could be a ready-made or single page scroll with blank spaces left to fill in a name—the first fill-in-the-form document. Or it could be a scroll from 1 to 158 feet in length with as much of the text of the *Book of the Dead* on it as a personal scribe could fit, or one could pay for, along with paeans describing how good a person had been in life and instructions to those along the way about how to help reach the final place among the blessed dead.

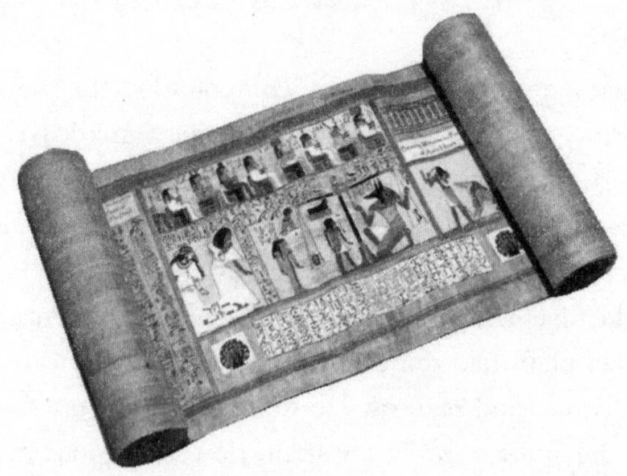

Replica copy of an Egyptian Book of the Dead.

In addition to a papyrus passport, it was also important to have legions of helpers in the afterlife, often in the form of clay or wooden models, and a papyrus canoe or boat or model thereof, to transport your body to its final resting ground and your soul to paradise, otherwise you would have to hitch a ride, which might delay your arrival. In any case, only a papyrus hull would do as a means of transport, for only papyrus held the sacred charm to repel crocodiles in the swamps of the netherworld.

Thus, many of us still have a chance if we were to elect to follow the ancient rites of passage. We all have a place in heaven waiting for us, if we remember to clutch a bit of papyrus to our chest as we expire.

"But," you say, "so-and-so is a Christian!" or of other persuasion. Indeed, according to Sir Ernest Alfred Wallis Budge, mummification came to a close within a hundred years of the preaching of Christianity in Alexandria by Saint Mark. By 220 A.D., thousands of people in Egypt had become Christians. The resurrection of the body of Christ made them hope that the same would happen to them; thus they gradually abandoned mummification and were content to be placed in the ground in their natural state, there to await revivication on the last day. Still, it was difficult to eradicate traces of the old beliefs. Ethiopian and Egyptian Coptic Christians, for example, wrapped their dead in strips of linen or parchment on which were written the secret names of God. Meant to ensure protection in the next world, these wrappings were nothing more than succinct forms of the scrolls of papyrus paper that constituted the Egyptian *Book of the Dead*. They had simply switched Christ for Osiris and cloth for papyrus.

Still, sacredness was a quality among media that was unique to papyrus; it was not shared by pulp or rag paper, linen or parchment in later centuries. So, however much emotion the reader or owner of the prestigious library might feel when they take up a well-loved book, or pass their hand over a rare collection of first editions, the essence of history might be there, but the product of a chemically treated pulp of pinewood, rags, and who knows what is no substitute in the eyes of the gods for the real thing.

Today the Bible placed in the coffin, or the medal depicting Saint Christopher pressed into the cold hands of the corpse, or the recitation of the departed's past and final good deeds at the memorial service in church, temple, or mosque, are all meant to serve in place of the papyrus paper "good conduct pass" used by the Egyptians and early Christians. The Egyptian's papyrus also acted as a sort of AAA guidebook to the unknown, you couldn't go wrong if you followed it. Well, almost . . .

❧

What exactly is the *Book of the Dead*? It is a book most often in scroll fashion that was designed in consultation with priests to ensure that the deceased came alive after death. For the well-off ancient Egyptian, whose life was easy and complete, the afterlife offered a way of continuing this good life forever. For the poor and wretched, it offered relief and a chance to begin again. So, no matter what your station in life was, it was important to prepare for what was to come. Even if someone had to scrimp and save, and live cheaply during earthly life, all available funds could be diverted toward that preparation. A tomb, if one could be afforded, was basic. It was here a soul could come back together with its body in death, and there that individual would regain all functions and go on to enjoy a life eternal.

Ibis-headed Toth, patron god of scribes, helps us prepare our Book of the Dead.

The way to achieve all this was written in the *Book of the Dead*, along with a map to guide, and the user codes and passwords that would unlock the gates and smooth the way. It was possible to go ahead and die anyway and not bother with the preparations, but according to religious tradition, the number of evil gods, spirits, and pitfalls that stood in the way to paradise was such that only the very poor or very foolish went to their grave without a *Book* or at least the most important chapters or verses. The impression had been created and encouraged by the temple priests that they had the secret solutions, they knew how to pass even the most horrific monsters, traps, and terrors. "Think of your worst fear," they probably said, "then multiply that image by a hundredfold and you'll have a small idea of what is in store for you." Which meant that for people like myself, for example, who hate snakes, we would definitely buy into the concept of having a copy of Verse 39, which is a "Spell to Repel Reptiles and Snakes." Once arrived in the afterlife, a guiding spirit could read out the spell that begins, "Get Back! Crawl Away! Get away from me or you shall be decapitated with a knife!"

Another handy spell to have at the ready would be Verse 179 which allows one to "leave yesterday and come into today," during which time a person could reassemble themselves and get all members in proper order, definitely an important procedure to complete before reaching the Hall of Judgment, where one has to look their best.

Lastly, a caution was outlined in Verse 125 that prepares for any surprises, especially those passing the numerous gates on the way to the Hall of Judgment. It is important to be ready with the correct answers to questions that will be called out. Mostly these questions will be posed by the gatekeepers demanding to know their given names, but such demands could also come from door panels, door posts, door bolts, and even the floor itself! All of which will cry out for a correct response. Pity the one not prepared with papyrus scroll in hand for such things.

In time, all personal belongings, amulets, sacrificial foods, and a personal copy of the *Book of the Dead* would be assembled and placed either in the coffin or in some convenient place inside the tomb. In the more spacious tombs or larger coffins, the funerary scrolls were concealed in niches in the wall or cavities inside statues or in nearby boxes.

All of this illustrated the old adage, "be prepared." In modern terms this would mean perhaps an early visit to a mortuary in order to secure the best cemetery plot and a top-of-the-line casket. Thus, when the time arrived to use such things, the trappings of the grave would reflect the deceased's station in life and tell people something about where they stood in society. A hole in the ground and a cheap pine coffin is one thing; a silver casket, marble mausoleum and carefully landscaped plot in Forest Hills is another. Location also provided the most obvious degree of protection, and perhaps the accouterments and trappings seen in King Tutankhamen's tomb provided protection by indicating that the tomb owner was obviously a person of consequence. Tampering with remains or funerary goods could cause eternal damnation. Scrolls of a hundred feet or more in length perhaps also served notice that you were important and thus not to be disturbed under penalty of death.

Once all was in readiness, it remained only to die, after which came the interesting part. The act of embalming would go forward and within seventy days, there would be a well-wrapped, perfumed, and ready body. Only one problem: during the process the deceased would have lost all facility of movement, drinking, reading, speech, and so on. It was imperative therefore to have rituals performed that would reverse all that.

In the Hall of Judgement the heart of Princess Nesitanebtashru is weighed (after Budge 1912).

One important ritual happened immediately before the moment of judgment. This ritual, the Declaration of the Heart, was straightforward. In most *Books* nothing is mentioned of any transgression and the heart of the deceased unfailingly proves cooperative, probably because the priests provide the correct spell, which is:

> Spell For Not Letting my Heart Create Opposition Against me In The Realm Of The Dead: Oh my heart which I had from my mother, Oh my heart which I had upon earth, do not rise up against me as a witness in the presence of the Lord of Things; do not speak against me concerning what I have done, do not bring up anything against me in the presence of the Great God, Lord of the West.
>
> *(Raymond Faulkner, "Ancient Egyptian Book of the Dead.")*

We perhaps wonder if it was ever not so. Was there ever a case when the heart did open up and reveal all to the embarrassment of the owner? Certainly, there must have been those standing by in the Hall of Judgment, former neighbors or old friends, who had to bite their tongues at this moment, proving that there really was a reason why Hank Williams's song "Your Cheatin' Heart" remained one of the all-time hits of country and pop music. He said, when he wrote it in 1953, he was thinking of his first wife as the words came rolling out, "Your cheatin' heart will tell on you." That caught the sentiment just right, a sentiment that apparently has been with us since ancient times. The truth is conceivably more like what Ogden Goelet of New York University offers in explanation, "It is unclear why the heart would wish to sabotage the dead, yet the afterworld was a place where the irrational was a commonplace occurrence. And it is, after all, our irrational subconscious that leads us to blurt out hidden feelings in slips of the tongue."[2]

❧

This influence of papyrus beyond the grave is still with us, as for example, when a papyrus fragment from a funerary scroll called the *Book of Breathing* was the basis for a translation and revision by Mormon founder, John Smith. He called his translation *The Book of Abraham* and published it as such in 1842. Though Smith's translation has been challenged, it did become a part of *A Pearl of Great Price*, which for many years was revered as one of the sacred texts in the Church of the Latter-day Saints.

There is even a connection between papyrus and the modern-day funeral bouquet. The first such bouquet was made from the flowering heads of papyrus, the finely divided strands that made up the umbel that capped the top of every stem, woven into wreaths and embellished with other flowers to be left in the Egyptian tombs as a final touch.

We see then that man could not do without papyrus for four thousand years. It also seems that this plant is still with us symbolically even in our final resting place.

❧

And what of the corpse left lying there with his book between his legs? If we think instead of an old friend laid out at a wake with a gilt-edged Bible resting the same way, which of us, on arriving at the viewing spot, instead of glancing kindly at that old familiar face and perhaps brushing away a tear in memory of Old Tom or Dear Aunt Mary, would scandalize the gathering by suddenly reaching down and snatching their book?

Well, that's what the French artist Vivant Denon did in 1799. While visiting an Egyptian tomb in a temple on the west bank of the Nile opposite Luxor, he was shown a mummy that had been dragged out of its resting place by his Arab guide.[3] At first he hesitated, then he "turned pale with anxiety." He tells us his dander was up and he was going to express his indignation at those who had violated the integrity of this ancient corpse!

He had just finished sketching a relief in that very temple showing a scribe writing when he realized in a flash that "Egyptians must have possessed books!"

So, when he saw the scroll lying in the mummy's hand, he set aside his scruples and seized the scroll, "this sacred manuscript, the oldest of all books in the known world." He then blessed the avarice of the Arabs, "and my good fortune, which had put me in possession of such a treasure . . . I could not restrain a feeling of self-satisfaction in thinking that I was the first to make so important a discovery." Until that date, he tells us that there had been no indication that the Egyptians had had such things.

I suppose we can't blame Denon for this small bit of self-promotion, as he was much more sympathetic to local culture than anyone in the French Army unit that he traveled with: troopers who raped, plundered, and burned given the least provocation. And he had journeyed to Egypt at great expense to himself and his benefactor, Napoleon Bonaparte.

Once he had taken possession of the book he wondered what was written in it, "Was it the history of this personage, the remarkable events of his life? . . . or did this precious roll contain maxims, prayers, or the history of some discovery?" Or, he wondered, was it perhaps "a compendium of Egyptian literature?"[4]

We now know that it was most likely nothing more than another of the myriad copies, or variants of the *Book of the Dead*, the first bestseller of history. As to the exact details of the text, that had to wait, even though the story contained in the *Book of the Dead* had been staring visitors in the face when it had been chiseled or drawn out on the walls of tombs and on the sides and lids of coffins. After 1550 B.C., the text began showing up on papyrus paper scrolls that were rolled up and left with the corpse. The problem was that the Arab occupiers of Egypt and their descendants in the time of Denon had no knowledge of the language. They had been looking at it for hundreds of years, yet they had never understood a single word until 1822 when one of Denon's fellow countrymen, Jean-François Champollion, deciphered the puzzle of hieroglyphics.

Harking back to the moment in question, even if Denon had been able to open the funerary scroll, it would have been incomprehensible to him.

The transition from a sacred message carved on the walls of a tomb deep inside a pyramid to papyrus paper is an important milestone, partly because of the nature of the message.

Much of what was carved on such a wall was instructional, relating how to reanimate and protect the pharaoh during his ascent to the heavens, as well as overcoming the hazards of his nightly journey in order that he might join the gods in his new life when he was reborn.[5] In contrast to this celestial realm emphasized in these *Pyramid Texts*, another set of instructions to guide the royal passage was written out on the lids and sides of Pharaoh's coffin.

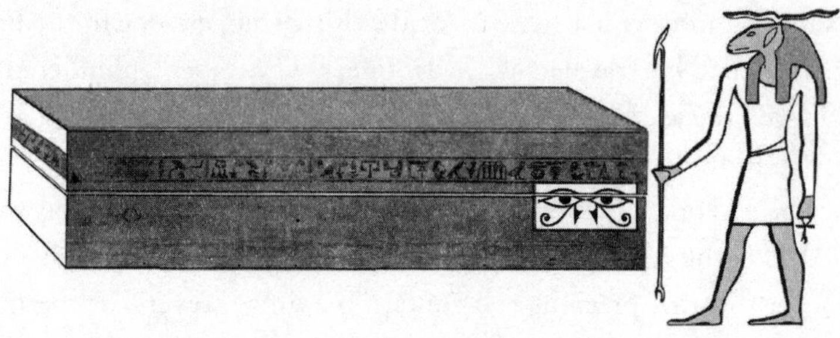

Plain wooden coffin of Princess Mayet the 5-year-old daughter of king Mentuhotep II (2061 B.C.–2010 B.C.) at Deir el-Bahari. Note Eye of Horus ancient symbol of protection through which she can view the Afterlife. (after Wikipedia and Brooklyn Museum, Charles Edwin Wilbour Fund, Creative Commons).

The *Coffin Texts* and *Pyramid Texts* dealt with subterranean elements of the afterlife, places filled with traps and snares, including a judgment of the royal heart, which was to become a pivotal moment later in the *Book of the Dead*.

The next point in the transition from such scenes on the walls to paper came about in the New Kingdom and it happened in a way that I like to think of as a marketing effort, the sort of thing a used car dealer might come up with, an offer that is so good you can't refuse and you wind up with a new, streamlined Honda Accord in preference to an old-fashioned model.

The original wooden Egyptian coffins, rectangular boxes with flat lids and sides, provided surfaces that were very handy and offered plenty of space to write out coffin texts in hieroglyphs. However, these utilitarian, old-fashioned corpse carriers were no match for the new coffins that arrived around 1650 B.C. The new models were "undertakers specials"—sleek, brightly painted, lacquered to a high gloss, and anthropoid in shape (carved or molded to the outline of the mummy's body). They were also decorated with the face and wig of the deceased. The priests who introduced these new models probably had an easy time selling them to the general public.

First of all, they were being used by the royals—a great recommendation. Then came an irresistible selling point: they were copies of the mummy's form, so they could also serve as substitute bodies in the afterlife in case the actual body was lost or destroyed. Still undecided? Then think about the fact that in the old-fashioned boxy coffins, a body was placed on its left side, so its face would be directly lined up with the painted eyes on the coffin's side. But, in the new model, the body is laid out on its back, so that it is looking straight into the face of Osiris when he lifts the lid once the body safely arrives in paradise. The deceased was also often portrayed wearing the Nemes black-striped gold headdress (as shown in photos of the more elaborate coffins) that covered the whole crown, back of the head, and nape of the neck. Two large flaps hung down behind the ears and in front of both shoulders, creating a terrific effect. It was a headdress previously reserved for royalty.

The clincher was the outside of the coffin, which was decorated in a special pattern that wrapped the mummy in wings and clothed it in feathers from shoulders to feet, representing the birdlike nature of Isis and Nephthys.[6] In fact, they were called "rishi coffins" from *risha*, Arabic for "feather." The concept was irresistible that after death you would simply take flight and soar into a heavenly new world.

How popular was the idea? We can gain some indication from the fact that during the New Kingdom, coffins and mummy cases could be purchased ready-made. In place of expensive models carved from sycamore wood, cheap versions were created by molding the container from a papier-mâché-like material formed around disposable cores of mud and straw.

But, this shift in design and the concentration on feathers meant there was no space left for the text and drawings of spells, a problem that was solved by writing out the necessary information and illustrations on a papyrus roll, which was then placed inside the coffin.[7] Once the *Book of the Dead* was thus transcribed as a scroll, the priests and scribes were free of constraint. They could use any and all verses from the old *Pyramid Texts* and *Coffin Texts*, along with an expanded description of paradise, expansive and glowing biographic details of the deceased, and any of the spells, which now numbered in the hundreds.

How many bought a *Book of the Dead* or its variants from 1550 B.C. until the time of Christ? John Taylor of the British Museum estimated that it cost about 1 unit, called a *deben*, of silver (approximately half a year's wages for a laborer). Given the fact that the majority could not afford either mummification or the book,[8] he guessed that less than 10 percent would have owned the world's first bestseller in one form or another. The number of copies of the *Book of the Dead* produced over 1,700 years must have reached over 5 million copies. Not surprisingly, thousands of copies have survived in one form or another because they were sequestered in tombs, which were safe places on purpose.

By comparison, another classic document of the seventeenth century B.C. that should have been a bestseller, as it had wide importance and application, was Hammurabi's Code of Law. It did not fare as well. Written by the Babylonian ruler Hammurabi to establish a series of laws that would ensure that "the mighty not wrong the weak," it never reached the level of distribution that it should have and it barely survived the ages.

Unlike the *Book of the Dead*, the Code affected virtually every aspect of life and society. It even set the cost for surgery; the surgeon was told exactly what he should charge for a minor operation and a major one with different prices for a rich gentleman, a poor laborer, and a slave—all thousands of years before Medicare!

Why did it not reach a wider public? Mostly because unlike the *Book of the Dead*, which was handwritten on paper, Hammurabi's masterpiece was engraved onto a seven-foot basalt stone column, which was placed on public display where its 282 laws could be read. Though written by scribes in Akkadian, the daily language of Babylon, it could then be read only by literate persons in the city, which were limited to males of wealthy families.[9]

Meanwhile, its message was sent out to the country in cumbersome sets of a dozen clay tablets. As important as the message was, its distribution and production was limited by the media employed to publish it. As to survival, only a few tablets are known to exist today along with the original column that sits in the Louvre. Unlike the *Book of the Dead*, it was not left in tombs where its chances of preservation were greater.

FOUR

The Book of the Dead, Guardian of Immortality

Once she came in contact with the outside world, first through expansion and trade and then through conquest by the Greeks and Romans, it was Egypt who influenced the shape and materials of the books of others.

—Leila Avrin, *Scribes, Script, and Books*

To me, the most interesting thing about the *Book of the Dead* is that it is thoroughly Egyptian in origin. After its transition from coffin painting to paper, it was typically produced and sold by priests to Egyptians who could afford it as a scroll.* By contrast, the Bible

* The term "scroll" refers to a blank roll of paper that has been written on.

began life as a papyrus codex (a book made by cutting a roll into pages before inscribing the pages and then sewing them together) and persisted thereafter in bound-book form, the form familiar to us today. The early Christians in Egypt would use local paper, but those in Europe and the Mideast would have had to have their papyrus paper imported from Egypt where the plant thrived.

Since the days of the pharaohs, however, Egypt's wetlands and papyrus fields have been drained and decimated. Even in the summer of 1798, once Vivant Denon had landed in Egypt with Bonaparte's expedition, he saw no papyrus plants anywhere on the Nile, since by then it had been ripped out to make way for food crops. But, at least he could recall what the plant looked like from seeing it in Sicily twenty years earlier, when he spent time there as a young diplomat. Arab traders had planted papyrus there years before and left it to grow wild. While Denon was stationed in Naples in the 1770's and 80's in the service of His Majesty, Louis XVI, he was often engaged in the study of antiquity and wrote an account of his Italian tour. He held a noble title, Chevalier de Non, at this time; it was only after the French Revolution that he took on the more plebian name, Vivant Denon. On tour in Sicily, he looked forward to his trip along the Sicilian rivers where papyrus grows even today. "That celebrated and curious plant . . . I was extremely anxious to see, handle, and make myself acquainted with . . . then in its greatest beauty."

One important conclusion he must have come to in Egypt was that since papyrus had been missing for such a long time, it meant that any papyrus paper that he or his colleagues recovered would have had to come from some ancient source. Denon went on to bigger and better things and in the process, he must have seen many scrolls and pieces of paper made from the plant, but he was left in the dark all his life as to what was contained in the world's first paper book.

In our case, we are lucky because a comprehensive history and interpretation of the *Book of the Dead* was recently assembled in 2010 as a catalog for several major exhibitions including one at the British Museum by John Taylor, assistant keeper of Egyptian archaeology.[1] Taylor's book, "Journey through the Afterlife: Ancient Egyptian Book of the Dead," illustrates the evolution of the *Book of the Dead* text and shows how court authorities, military leaders, and others usurped the privilege from the pharaohs. By then, in the New Kingdom, the idea of the *Book of the Dead* became fashionable and accessible to common folk, though in practice it was still an expensive opportunity, one that only some could afford. Its appeal was that it had been the exclusive right of kings and thus had the royal seal of approval. If it worked for Ramses, it would work for anyone.

Dr. Foy Scalf, head of Research Archives at the University of Chicago Oriental Institute, pointed out that the kings themselves did not bother with paper versions of the *Book of the Dead*.[2] Even the well-equipped King Tut's tomb lacked any funerary papyri.[3] Instead, the royals seemed to have preferred their books drawn, painted, or cut into their tomb walls, coffins, or other objects; all of which must have cost time, money, and patience. For lesser mortals, papyrus paper came to the rescue, and just as a model of a boat would do in place of the real thing, a scroll would serve in place of a costly and time-consuming project of tomb decoration.

Papyrus paper was found to be the perfect medium for writing out the *Book of the Dead* because, unlike tomb walls or coffin surfaces, it could literally be cut and pasted. Adding pictures to the text could be done cheaply and more easily on paper with a reed pen and colored inks. For a while, the linen wrappings used as shrouds were inscribed, especially during the Seventeenth and Eighteenth Dynasties, 1580–1425 B.C. Sometimes during this period, the deceased was provided with two separate books: one on paper and one on cloth. But the flexible, woven-cloth surface was a difficult medium and papyrus paper thereafter came to prominence. In fact, it soon became clear that paper versions of the *Book of the Dead* were serving as the prototype for copying spells onto new coffins for those who insisted on the "old-fashioned" royal tradition.[4]

Embellishing the text with pictures was a boon for those who did not read hieroglyphics; which, according to some, was a significant portion of the population.[5] Each copy was personalized depending on the purchaser's selection. For a price, the priests and scribes would help you organize it. And so a new business was launched. The priests proved that they were essential for the job because they kept up with the continuing research that was almost certain to uncover any hitherto unrecognized danger in the underworld. In concert with the necromancers and soothsayers the priests studid oracles, augury, astrology, and magic signs from nature in order to better understand what might await you in the afterlife.

They could also produce a simple, uniform version that would perhaps do the job cheaply but, in order to be certain, they recommended a tome that was guaranteed to deal with any peril whatsoever, though it would cost you a small fortune.

Papyrus would allow one to get started on the path to immortality. Even if you had yet to buy a tomb, or perhaps would never even be able to afford one, you could at least commission a scroll and have it prepared with care. The finished product would not only show people that you were serious about living on after death, it would also reflect to a limited degree something of your personality.

❧

Once Vivant and his fellow savants from Napoleon's Egyptian expedition sailed away with their acquisitions, and once Champollion had deciphered the hieroglyphic puzzle using the Rosetta Stone, Europe and Britain were seized with Egyptomania. Napoleon and Champollion proved to all that ancient Egypt had been an extraordinary place and still had much to offer the world. As a result, Egypt became a land of opportunity for souvenir hunters and the "Rape of the Nile" began in earnest. Armed with hammers and chisels, amateur and professional collectors arrived to take advantage and follow in the footsteps of Prisse. During the winter of 1889–1890, almost 11,000 tourists visited Cairo, 1,300 of whom went up the Nile. Ten years later, the number of visitors per year increased to 50,000.[6]

Among the visitors in 1887 was young Wallis Budge, an assistant keeper, second class, from the British Museum. He had made a visit to Egypt the previous year when he worked at a dig in Aswan. He came away from that with a large number of cases that he shipped home under the cloak of "military baggage," and was therefore exempt from inspection. In all, on his very first collecting trip, Budge brought 1,482 items home to England, and this was just a start. Is it any wonder that on his scond trip the Service of Antiquities set a police watch over him?

On this second collecting trip, he went by river steamer to Aswan as if to tour the region. Once his escort landed he slipped back on board, stayed in a cabin that night, then sailed early the next morning, arriving in Luxor just as the sun was setting. He lingered in his cabin until nightfall then went ashore and walked quickly through the darkened streets of Luxor, the Mecca of the antiquities trade. Here he meet with some dealer friends. Staying clear of the town police, he traveled across the river in a small boat to a tomb on the west bank where friendly fellahin were waiting. It was all done quickly, efficiently, and in the dark. Arriving at the site, he was offered a rich store of rare objects, among them the largest roll of papyrus he had ever seen. The roll was tied round with a thick band made of papyrus string, and was in a perfect state of preservation. It lay in a niche in the north wall of a sarcophagus chamber with its clay seal unbroken.

In his autobiography, Budge confesses that it seemed like sacrilege to break the seal and untie the cord but, like Denon before him, he quickly overcame his scruples and unrolled a few feet, an inch or so at a time.[7] He was amazed at the beauty and freshness of the colors. In the dim light of the candles and the hot air of the tomb, the illustrated human figures and animals almost came to life. The first scene on the scroll was that of the Judgment of the Soul, from which he knew he had just bought a large and complete text of the *Per-em-hru*, or *Book of the Dead Man*.

The magnificent roll had been written, drawn, and painted for Ani, a royal scribe, "registrar of the offerings of all the Gods, overseer of the granaries of the Lords of Abydos, and scribe of the offerings of the Lords of Thebes." When the papyrus was unrolled in London, the inscribed portion of it was found to be seventy-eight feet long, and at each end was a section of blank papyrus about two feet long.

That same evening, he was also offered a papyrus of the priestess Anhai, a papyrus codex of the *Book of the Dead* written by Nu in the Eighteenth Dynasty and a leather roll containing chapters of the *Book of the Dead*, with beautifully painted vignettes. In one stroke he had come into possession of four rare and extremely valuable objects. What followed next was an adventure as exciting as anything experienced by Indiana Jones, and it demonstrates what separated Budge from the rest of the pack.

On arrival back in town at dawn with his four treasures, he stopped to pick up some tin boxes that he had ordered beforehand, a move that makes one think his acquisitions were not a complete surprise. He seems to have known the dimensions of the "Sacred Four" beforehand. He then went on to a dealer's house for breakfast, at which point he learned that police and soldiers had arrived in town with orders to take possession of every house containing antiquities in Luxor and to arrest their owners, as well as Wallis Budge.

Budge asked to see the warrants and was told that Monsieur Grebaut the head of antiquities was delayed; he would produce them later in the day. Since nothing else could be done, they finished breakfast, after which Budge told the police that he would not leave town and he was therefore allowed to go about his business. Meanwhile they took possession of the house, posted watchmen on the roof, and a sentry at each corner of the building. Then they went to several other houses and did the same.

Among the houses that were sealed and guarded was a small house where Budge had stored his tins containing the precious papyri. This house abutted the wall of the garden of the Luxor Hotel. In this same house were several cases of things that belonged to dealers in town, who used it as a safe place for storage. When the Luxor dealers saw it sealed up and guards posted, they invited the guards to drink cognac with them. Then they tried to bribe them to go away for an hour; but the guards stoutly refused to drink or to leave their posts.

Regarding the hotel, the *Cook's Tourists' Handbook for Egypt, the Nile, and the Desert* of 1897 tells us that "the Luxor Hotel grounds are spacious and shaded, adjoining a farm cultivated to supply visitors with dairy, produce, poultry, sheep, and bullocks. A qualified medical gentleman, a clergyman of the Church of England, and an English lady housekeeper reside in the hotel during winter."

If you were a British tourist intent on staying the winter in Egypt, that information would have been critical, but in the case of the distraught local antiquities dealers, the bucolic location of the hotel had another significance. They went and had an interview with the manager and, according to Budge, the result of their conversation was that at about sunset, a number of gardeners and workmen appeared with digging tools and baskets. They dug under that part of the garden wall that was next to the house and right through into the basement. According to Budge,

> "they made scarcely any noise, and they cut through the soft, unbaked mud bricks without difficulty. Whilst they were digging I watched the work with the manager. It seemed to me that the gardeners were particularly skilled housebreakers, and that they must have had much practice. It appears incredible, but the whole of the digging was carried out without the knowledge of the watchmen on the roof of the house and the sentries outside it. But it seemed unwise to rely overmuch on the silence of our operations, and we therefore arranged to give the police and the sentry a meal, for they were both hungry and thirsty. M. Pagnon, the proprietor of the hotel, had a substantial supper prepared for them, i.e., half a sheep boiled, with several pounds of rice, and served up in pieces with sliced lemons and raisins on a huge brass tray." (E.A.W. Budge, "By Nile and Tigris.")

Budge then tells us that, whilst the police were eating happily, man after man went into the building and carried everything out, piece by piece and box by box, and "in this way we saved the Papyrus of Ani, and all the rest of my acquisitions, from the officials of the Service of Antiquities, and all Luxor rejoiced."

The Papyrus of Ani remains the most famous of all papyrus scrolls yet found and is still the longest one known of the Theban period. Other long papyri are: the Harris Papyrus extolling Ramesses III (Twentieth Dynasty), 133 feet; the Greenfield Papyrus (Twentieth Dynasty), 121 feet; the Papyrus of Nebseni (Eighteenth Dynasty), 76 feet; the Leyden Papyrus of Qenna (Eighteenth Dynasty), 50 feet; the Dublin Papyrus (Eighteenth Dynasty), 24 feet; and the Papyrus of Hunefer (Nineteenth Dynasty) 18 feet.

Unfortunately, many of these early scrolls were cut into smaller sections for ease of handling and are no longer intact. Two of the few long papyri on display are the sixty-three-foot *Book of the Dead* of the priest of Horus, Imouthes (Imhotep) at the Metropolitan Museum in New York, and the twenty-four-foot recently restored scroll of Sobekmose, the Goldworker of Amun, at the Brooklyn Museum (consisting of eight large sections, conservation work was completed in 2011); several are also on display in the Museo Egizio in Turin, Italy. The *Book of the Dead* discovered by Budge and referred to as the Ani Papyrus is still artistically the best example. It dealt with Ani and his wife, Tutu. Ani was more than just a royal scribe, he was also governor of the large granary at Abydos as well as a registrar and scribe of the sacred property of the lords of Thebes, which included keeping track of the temple property in Thebes. His wife was also an important person, being a priestess. Since she is mentioned in the text, presumably Tutu had preceded Ani in death and her mummified body would be waiting in his tomb. In real life the next step after composing his book would be the process of selecting and storing funerary furniture and assembling *shabti* figures, models of the people who would do the daily menial work for Ani and Tutu in the hereafter. The minimum needed would be 365, since the Egyptian year was the same as ours.

The whole process described in the *Book of the Dead* in many ways resembles the rite of the Christian baptism. In fact, when performed for deceased royalty, the Egyptian rituals of purification were known as the "Baptism of the Pharaoh," and ensured that Pharaoh started his new life after death with a pure heart and a clean body.

In the last part of Ani's *Book of the Dead*, Ani and Tutu have entered heaven, a heaven that differed considerably from the heaven or paradise of Muslim, Christian, or modern Egyptian traditions. In place of palatial residences, virgins, angels, soft fluffy clouds, etc., our Intrepid Pair were content to be forever in a celestial papyrus swamp, a marshy place in which all the good times and the most precious things of this life are extended infinitely. It was a haven where the blessed dead and their old friends could regale themselves, and where food and drink of every sort would be provided "in degrees of abundance beyond their imagination." And the Ani Papyrus proves yet again the value the Egyptians placed on the papyrus plant and the swamps it grew in. What greater glory could be ascribed to a plant than to have it next to you in paradise?

According to Taylor, an authority on the subject, the earlier *Pyramid Texts* describe the Winding Waterway, which divides the sky into the northern Field of Offerings and the southern Field of Reeds (or *Sekhet-A'aru*) a place where "the deceased was purified before ascending to the sky."[8] In later *Coffin Texts*, the Field of Reeds became the destination of the deceased and this was carried over into the papyrus paper scrolls, the portable version of the *Book* that found its way into commoners' tombs. It was a celestial marsh similar to the papyrus swamps still found here on Earth. "Here was the abode of the god Osiris, who bestowed estates in it upon those who had been his followers, and here the beatified dead led a new existence and regaled themselves upon food of every kind, which was given to them in abundance."

The ancient drawings of it that appeared in many copies of the *Book of the Dead* has been compared to the Elysian Fields of the Greeks,[9] but Taylor reminds us that the drawings are not maps in the modern sense; they represent imaginary places. Surprisingly, however, they do resemble the watercourses that still flow through the largest papyrus swamps that flourish in Africa today. One glance at the modern areal photos of the enormous papyrus swamps found in South Sudan and the smaller inland papyrus swamps in Botswana tells the story. Their similarity to the ancient drawing of the Field of Reeds with its meandering waterways is striking.

FIVE

Papyrus Paper, Your Ticket to Paradise

Papyrus paper opened up a new path to immortality by allowing common people in ancient Egypt to possess their own copy of the *Book of the Dead*, Anyone who wanted it, and could afford it, could be guided directly to paradise by their papyrus scroll while paddling in their personal papyrus canoe (A small model of a boat left in your tomb served just as well, since it could be converted in the afterlife by magic into the real thing). Once they arrived in paradise and began life anew, they found themselves in the Field of Reeds. Perhaps unspoken in all of this was the fact that this Field of Reeds really did exist at some earlier time, like the Garden of Eden, which is said to have existed in the region of the Tigris-Euphrates River valley within the Fertile Crescent. The Field of Reeds pictured and described in the Egyptian papyrus scrolls may have reflected an earlier time in history when a fertile, green, tropical heaven existed on earth, for which there is now proof. It is known generally as the Green Sahara.

The paleoecology of this region (see insert, Map A) was outlined in a National Academy of Sciences review in 2010, which revealed the astonishing fact that a water world existed in this part of Africa from 8000 B.C. up until about 3000 B.C. An extraordinary region, consisting of the whole of the Sahara, it was interlaced with large, interlinked waterways made up of thousands of rivers, and several lakes, each larger than Belgium.[1] The terrestrial vegetation in the region consisted of savannas interspersed with tree species.[2] A sequence of alluvial fans (fan-shaped deposits of sediment) existed west of the Nile Basin (see insert, Map A) that could well have once been a series of inland deltas, similar to the Okavango Swamps of Botswana. If that were so, they would most likely have been dominated by papyrus, like the Okavango swamps are today. In total, the individual swamps of the Green Sahara would have made up an enormous aquatic ecosystem, ten times as large as the Nile delta—which until modern times was itself a formidable wetland with papyrus much in evidence.

A rough estimate would put this prehistoric wetland at about 12 million acres. A description of it passed down by oral tradition from prehistoric people to the later ancient Egyptians could easily account for the concept of a "Field of Reeds." That it lay coincidentally in the west where the sun died every day and which was the preferred resting place of the dead was all to the good.

The Green Sahara resolved the long-standing mystery of how early man, fish, and other animals moved into, around, and across the Sahara. This lush country was not only a paradise for aquatic animal species—such as tilapia fish, crocodiles and hippos—it was also a haven for papyrus and papyrus swamps, which would have grown in abundance throughout the many aquatic habitats, especially along the rivers that cut their way through the savannas. In fact, papyrus is thought to have played a major role in the diet of one of the early human species, *Australopithecus boisei*, who lived in Africa from 1.2 to 2.3 million years ago. If so, he would have had to eat up to two kilograms of papyrus each day to get by nutritionally.[3]

In later times (after 3000 B.C.), arid conditions set in. But even then, although the verdant countryside had turned to desert, there is plenty of archaeological evidence dating back to the Old Kingdom that indicates Egyptian movement through the desert region. Though restricted to caravan routes, such as the Abu Ballas Trail (see insert, Map A), travelers from the time of Khufu until that of the Romans could make their way west. Once reaching Gilf Kebir (in the far southwest of present-day Egypt) they were allowed a choice. From there they could travel in several directions, including southwest toward Lake Chad.[4]

In the time of Khufu, travel was not easily done along this trail,since water was required at every step and had to be carried, but in the days of the Green Sahara, during the height of the Stone Age. 6,000 B.C., when water was everywhere, expeditions must have been easier. Once in the ancient land of Chad, any members of an expedition would presumably want to explore, or even settle in. The naturalist Sylvia Sikes brought a sailboat to Lake Chad in 1969 in order to survey it,[5] why couldn't the Egyptians have done the same thing in 6000 B.C.?

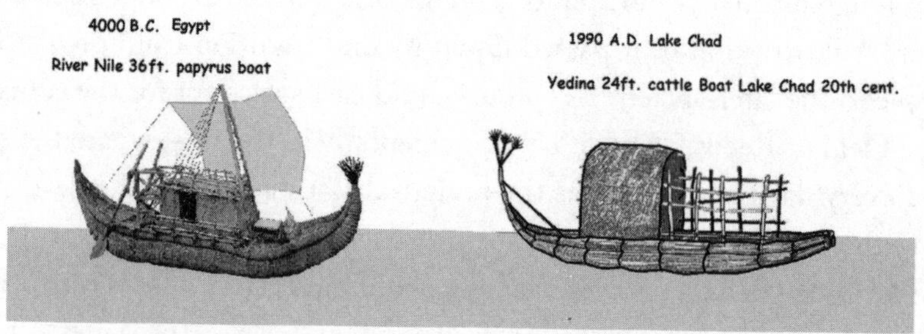

An ocean-going papyrus boat based on ancient lines compared to a modern day cattle boat both built from papyrus from lake Chad (after Konrad 1957 and Wikipedia).

In those days water was plentiful and since papyrus would be growing in profusion on, in, and along the major lakes and watercourses, Egyptian visitors to Chad or local residents could easily have assembled a fleet of papyrus boats, each craft constructed almost entirely from local papyrus. The rope used in the rigging and in the construction of the boat was readily made from dry papyrus stems as was a hull.[6] Even sails could be woven from the flexible skins of green papyrus stems. The only thing that couldn't be made from local papyrus was the mast and the stone anchor, which meant that, since papyrus grew there in quantity, any such expedition would have to bring nothing with them except some very sharp flint knives.

In 2003 the desert explorer, Carlo Bergmann, discovered carved drawings of papyrus boats on rock faces in the region. Dating probably from Khufu's time, they may represent a notion of what went on in earlier days.[7] Of course, in the Green Sahara grasslands also prevailed interspersed between the wetlands. Woodlands were common especially in the south, why not use trees to construct wooden boats? It would have been possible, but the Egyptians only started building wooden boats in the Old and Middle Kingdom (2900–1650 B.C.). During that time in Egypt, wooden ships were being built at a shipyard on the Nile in Koptos, north of Thebes, and then disassembled for transport across the Eastern Desert, where they were reassembled for use in trading on the Red Sea.[8] Wooden riverboats like the famous Abydos boat (75 feet, 2900 B.C.) and the Khufu boat (143 by 20 feet, 2500 B.C.) would not be practical for Lake Chad, as they were slim craft designed to be disassembled for transport around the Nile cataracts and other obstacles. They were built for use in calm water, not for the rough water that could build up on the enormous Lake Chad, which in ancient times was equivalent in size to the Caspian Sea. The first large wave would have shattered a riverboat hull and ended any exploration from the start.

In 600 B.C.the Egyptian Pharaoh Necho dispatched a Phoenician fleet of wooden boats to circumnavigate Africa. But all that was much later. In the time of the Green Sahara in about 8000–5000 B.C., it was possible to use log dugouts in shallow water but wooden boat technology was not yet there and papyrus boats would have to do for travel on the open lakes.

On the other hand, papyrus boats, as Thor Heyerdahl proved so conclusively in 1969, ride well above the waves and will not sink until they waterlog after several months. He found that his *Ra I*, a forty-five-foot, twelve-ton replica of an ancient papyrus boat, carrying five tons of superstructure and cargo, as well as seven crew members, rode high on the water and sailed easily before the wind. If beached and dried occasionally, such papyrus boats should last for years.

By a quirk of fate, the reverse process occurred in 1969 when Heyerdahl, desperate for papyrus boat builders, encouraged two boatwrights to come to Cairo from Lake Chad to build the *Ra I.* There were no papyrus boat builders left in Egypt; they had vanished with the sacred sedge. Thankfully, papyrus boats were still produced on Lake Tana in the upper region of the Nile, and in Lake Chad where there were hundreds of papyrus boat builders living around the lake.

❧

After 3500 B.C. the climate changed, and the Sahara dried out. The extinction of mammals during this period has been reviewed in a paper from NASA in 2014 that tells of the collapse of the whole ecological network (12,800–3500 B.C.)[9] After this point, the desert became the barrier to movement that it is now. And incredibly, this whole story may have been recorded on papyrus paper.

Most likely the rise in use of funerary documents among common people, facilitated by papyrus paper, did not go unnoticed by the Egyptian royals. I would think they must have been appalled when they saw the *Book of the Dead* pass from exclusive use by kings and viziers to courtiers, officers, civil servants, and finally to the general public. Taylor tells us that it became the most popular funerary text in the kingdom. Perhaps viewing this as a trivialization of a sacred text and a loss of prestige, Pharaoh and his viziers had the priests carry out even more advanced and detailed research on the next world, so that by the New Kingdom (1079–712 B.C.) the royals had gained special knowledge, which they then incorporated into a new set of texts known as the *Amduat.*

During the New Kingdom, the *Amduat* was joined by other funerary texts including the *Book of Caverns*, *Book of Gates*, *Book of the Earth*, *Book of the Heavenly Cow*, *Books of the Sky*, *Book of the Netherworld*, and *Book of Traversing Eternity*. Of all these, the *Amduat* (literally, "What is in the netherworld?") remained the oldest and most important of these books.[10]

At first the *Amduat*'s use was restricted, appearing primarily on the walls of tombs of kings and viziers; then from 1069–945 B.C., it ceased to be a purely royal prerogative and, like the *Book of the Dead* (in use from 1550 B.C. to 50 B.C.), it became more widely available. During this time and later, around 945–850 B.C., versions of it were written and drawn on papyrus rolls which were placed along with a shortened version of the *Book of the Dead* in the tombs of high officials, priests, and their wives.

The *Amduat* differed from the *Book of the Dead* in that it described and illustrated the course the sun takes while illuminating the Duat, or world of the dead, during the twelve hours of night. The fascinating thing, according to Thomas Schneider, professor of Egyptology at the University of British Columbia, is that the journey of Ra described in the first three hours of the *Amduat* is similar to the trip one would have taken from Egypt to Lake Chad in the days of the Green Sahara.[11]

He describes a correspondence between the journeys: in that during the First Hour, Ra travels west with the deceased royal personage, toward the sunset in papyrus boats similar to those found in modern Chad and ancient Egypt. They gain access to the underworld through the "western portico of the horizon," a passageway of 738 miles (1260 kilometers in converted units in the text) from the Nile. During the Second Hour, Ra and the deceased enter "the watery expanse of Ra," a region dominated by a gigantic sweet-water ocean. The text also mentions green plants, animals, and the surrounding lands; in the Third Hour they encounter the "waterway of Osiris," which also involves a large water body. Professor Schneider found that in their description of the *Amduat* the ancient Egyptians made detailed references to the vast array of rivers and lakes to the west across the Sahara. It matched the paleo-environment as well as the topographical features of this realm.

The goal of this nighttime journey was to reach the hidden realms of the cosmos, which were characterized by floodwaters and green fields, a landscape evocative of creation and of the Field of Reeds found in the *Book of the Dead*. But in the Fourth Hour of the *Amduat*, Ra, and the deceased pharaoh who travels with him, reach the sandy realm of Sokar, falcon god of the Memphite necropolis at Saqqara.

In the *Book of the Dead*, the Field of Reeds, called *Saket A'aru*, is described as boundless reed fields, like those of a prehistoric earthly Nile delta. The diagram describing the Field of Reeds first appeared on some coffins in the Middle Kingdom (2050 B.C.–1710 B.C.) and according to Taylor is the only true depiction of a landscape in the entire *Book*. The Field of Reeds shown in this diagram is usually placed in the east, where the sun rises.[12] This ideal hunting and farming ground allowed the souls there to live for eternity.[13] In the *Amduat* we see the story of Ra traversing the watery expanse of the west (referred to as *Wernes*). The two books were considered complementary and in both cases we see the ancient Egyptian's fascination with all things wet, especially the lush, floodplains as they existed in the ancient water world of the Nile valley.

Papyrus was the medium in this instance, as well as the message, and, as in the case of papyrus boats and paper scrolls and books, the message could be interpreted either as the word of God, Osiris, or Christ, or it could be seen as an account of how people could travel and trade ideas. Diffusion was possible using the Egyptian and Chadian solution which was to use the local vegetation to build a sail boat or make a book or scroll, either would see you to your destination on earth or in heaven.

Once early Egyptians settled in the Nile River valley, they left behind the arid land of the Sahara, abandoning it to the desert people. In the process, they also left behind a number of cultural parallels. The writer and former Peace Corps volunteer on Lake Chad, Guy Immega found this was especially true in the areas of language, music, musical instruments, cattle, fish and fishing, the use of papyrus, and the waterman's life style.[14] Papyrus-boat building was an obvious carryover, but there may also have been a large influence in the way the local people, the Yedina ("people of the reeds") built their papyrus houses. That seems to be a throwback to the way Egyptians might have built their own huts when they were living in their own water world in 8000–3000 B.C. in Egypt.[15]

On the other hand, it could all be just the reverse. Maybe the ancient Yedina taught archaic Egyptian settlers all about life in and near the water. Maybe they helped them to get started in making use of the swamps that grew so luxuriantly around as well as in Lake Chad, and as well along the Nile, or even showed them how to make papyrus paper. If so, we may owe a great debt to the Yedina, or their predecessors the Sao, for helping at the birth of Western civilization.

In any event, the *Book of the Dead* is key in helping us understand the way the ancient Egyptians saw the world, and how the paper that they invented could serve as an ideal medium on which to record the thoughts of mankind. It also represents a key moment in the democratization of knowledge, something that could not have happened without the inherent advantages of paper—it was flexible, easy to obtain, and cost-effective. As a medium for the *Book of the Dead* and recording the history of the ancient world of the Green Sahara, it was perfect. You could use colored inks applied by brush or pen; it could be cut, pasted, folded and sealed; non-permanent ink could be erased and easily corrected; whereas permanent ink though it couldn't be erased, could be "whited out"; and the needful or thrifty could recycle sheets and scrolls and use them again and again. As a last resort it could be softened and used like papier-mâché to model and form a whole range of objects including a rishi coffin or a mummy case.

Above all, paper lent itself to the new form of writing. The old pictorial form using glyphs had given way to a cursive form of handwriting mostly because it was easy to write this way on paper, and faster, too, to keep up with the exploding demand for paper text.

The Egyptians employed four different scripts for their one writing system. The earliest was hieroglyphics, which was read from right *or* left depending on which way the characters faced. The second script, hieratic, was cursive, meaning that it flowed freely with some characters joined, similar to cursive handwriting of today. It developed almost at the same time as hieroglyphic writing, but it was much faster to write. Unlike time-consuming glyphs, the streamlined characters could also be joined by strokes known as "ligatures." Written from right to left, it remained Egypt's everyday script until about 700 B.C.when a new form of shorthand developed in the south.[16] Promoted by the business world this third script became so prevalent that Herodotus called it by the Greek word for "popular," *demotikos*. As with hieratic, this script was written from right to left.[17] Called demotic, it was an Egyptian cursive that had by now become so changed that there was little similarity to classic hieroglyphics. It lasted until it was replaced by Coptic, a script that dated from the time of Alexander's conquest of Egypt in 332 B.C. This was the Greek version of all three previous scripts: it made use of Greek letters and included vowels.

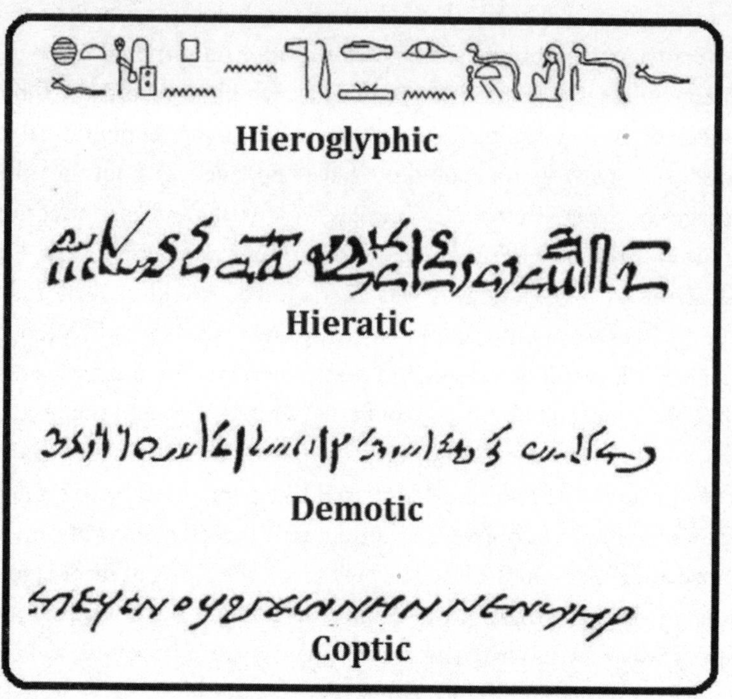

Four scripts compared (after Linkedin Slideshare.net).

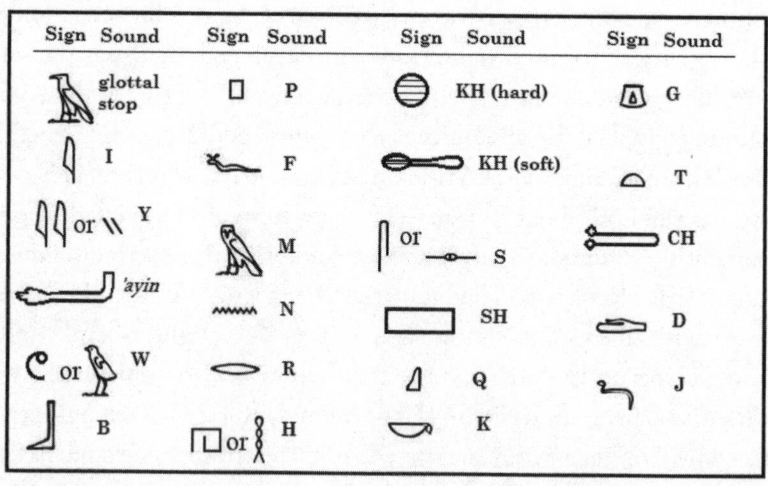

Old form of the hieroglyphic alphabet (after Fischer, 2001).

In appearance, all four scripts were different, but in form, function, and usage they were still just one writing system, which had begun in the earliest days when Mesopotamia's phonetic writing had reached the Nile. Hieroglyphs were born when Egyptian scribes converted the Mesopotamian idea into something unique, a new system that used hundreds of signs. Of these, the most common was a set of twenty-six that represented mostly consonants. Today we know this as the hieroglyphic alphabet," commonly found on the Internet and used by jewelers to trace your name in "Egyptian" on bracelets and necklaces. Though it still lacked most vowels, the hieroglyphic alphabet was a remarkable innovation; it was the first of its kind, and it supplied the forms that were taken for the later alphabets of 2200 B.C., which led to the various Semitic alphabets that became the Latin alphabet we use today.[18]

Stephen Fischer, writer and expert on ancient languages, summarized the process of the development of the alphabet when he noted that writing as we know it may have originated with the Sumerians, but "the way we write and even some of the signs, which we call 'letters,' are the ultimate descendants of ancient Egyptian . . ." According to Fischer, the Proto-Sinaitic script (1850 B.C.) shows at least twenty-three discrete signs—almost half of them clearly borrowed from Egyptian. For example, the depicted object "waves in water,"—*n* in the Egyptian alphabet—became *m*, which reproduced the initial consonant of the Semitic letter *mayim*. Our Latin alphabet's *m* is a direct descendant, still "showing the waves." [19]

Years later in the New Kingdom, the use of hieratic script was confined to documents of value and religious texts, while demotic, the even more cursive form, was regarded by the Ptolemies, the royal Macedonian Greek family that ruled Egypt from 305 to 30 B.C., as some sort of quaint, old-fashioned form of writing. They referred to it as "enchorial" or "native" writing, a reflection of their Greek heritage; they saw Greek in the same way that many today look upon English as the only sensible language for discourse. Little did they realize that in demotic they were looking at the end of a very long cycle where the Greek written language, of which they were enamored, was in fact Egyptian in a modern form. It happened that in another part of the world in Greece during the ninth century B.C., as explained by Johnson, the Greeks took over the Phoenician alphabet, reversed the direction of writing, and changed some signs to vowels in order to produce the ultimate source of the Western alphabet. Since the Phoenicians had borrowed their signs from the Canaanites who had taken theirs from the Egyptians, we come full circle.

"Neither Greeks nor Phoenicians 'created' the alphabet," says Fischer. "Egyptians *distilled* the alphabet from their hieroglyphic system." And, as he noted further, "It is no coincidence that our method of writing at the beginning of the 3rd Millennium A.D. is not too different from that of the Egyptian scribes of the 3rd Millennium B.C."[20]

To my mind, the other extraordinary thing is that in 3000 B.C.and 1000 A.D. handwriting was still being done on papyrus paper, which was still the only easily available medium around.

The complete Western alphabet, that is, one that treats consonants and vowels with equal weight, such as was used in Greek or Latin, now appears to be replacing most other writing systems of the world. Fischer views this as one of the most conspicuous manifestations of globalization. In other parts of the world, the Chinese were developing their own writing, likewise a system that would influence much of the world around them. The earliest Chinese inscriptions from 1400 B.C. displayed a characteristic writing in columns, which made it convenient for writing on dry bones as well as on narrow, yellow-colored strips of bamboo. Thus, while the Egyptians were writing a streamlined script on a light, highly portable medium, the Chinese were carefully inscribing bamboo slips that were then sewn and tied into bulky racks and rolls.

In Egypt the fast form of writing was a godsend to businessmen, accountants, and record keepers who now demanded reams and reams of papyrus paper. Soon letter writers took up papyrus paper and authors and poets matched it to their métier as Egyptian civilization advanced. By the first and second centuries A.D. the funerary document of choice had also been streamlined; it was the more condensed *Book of Breathing*. Its content was short, less than ten lines of the bare essentials, and written in the more fashionable demotic script. These folded, tied, and sealed missals simply listed funerary wishes that encapsulated the bare essentials.[21] These were the last in the long line of evolution of the *Book of the Dead*. Papyrus paper was put to work in the third and fourth centuries A.D. to serve a world that was rapidly turning toward Christian practices.

Scribes

This new combination of pen, ink, paper, alphabet, and cursive writing encouraged the development of a scribal class, which was something new in human history. The historian Herodotus listed them as one of his seven classes of people, distinct from the rest of the population, in fifth century B.C. Egypt.

Young scribes in school. Tomb of Horemheb 1300 B.C. (after Wikipedia and the Osirisnet Project). Note how they are clutching their penholders, each with two inkwells for red and black ink.

Scribes were close to the top of the heap behind only priests and soldiers. They were able to attain this social importance because of their training in scribal schools, the world's first formal educational system. Graduates became members of a professional class whose influence had virtually no bounds. Egyptian scribes could attain great wealth, prestige, and position. And they were distinct from other occupations because they could "put a spin" on theirs. They could promote and help raise the level of respect for their own profession; after all, they had access to documents, historical information, their own personal archives, and mathematical tables. This allowed them to cut and paste or generate new copy or give a new meaning to old text, solve numerical problems, and satisfy current needs. Madison Avenue would pale in contrast.

Before long, no one, not even Pharaoh, went very long or very far without the services of a scribe. It became so respectable a profession that pharaohs prided themselves on their scribal abilities; one, Horemheb, even began his career as an army scribe. Tutmosis II must also have had professional literary training.[22]

The most highly regarded were the priestly scribes, a good example of which was the scribe Ani, the protagonist in, as well as creator of, his famous *Book of the Dead*. According to this book he was, "*. . . accountant of all the gods . . . . governor of the granary of the lords of Abydos . . . scribe of the sacred property of the lords of Thebes.*"

As the historian Paul Johnson pointed out, each department of the ancient Egyptian government had its own special scribes: army scribes, navy scribes, treasury scribes, and so forth, who tended to develop specialized scripts of their own. There were business scribes and accountant scribes, too.

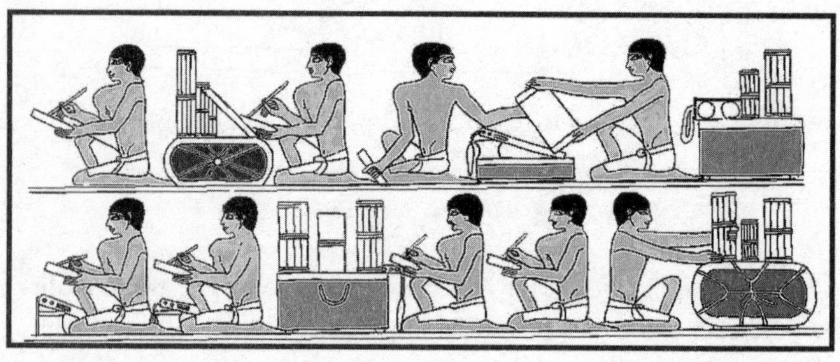

Administrative scribes at work on the estate of Ti, a wealthy member of court (2500–2400 B.C.). Note the stacks of scrolls piling up as work goes forward (after Wikipedia and the Osirisnet Project).

Training a scribe was a serious business requiring long hours and many years, but it paid off, especially for those children recruited from the lowest classes, particularly orphans. It was one of the ways in which a poor man could see his children rise in social status. And so it became a treasured profession. Scribes were fundamental to the propaganda machine typical of each dynasty; in this way, the self-promotion of their calling became easier, and they were quick to take advantage. They advertised the dignity and security of their job and boasted of their exemption from land taxes, military service, and royal calls to work on monuments. Johnson cited many instances of the rewards that were gained, such as, "Learn to write, so that you may protect your own person from any kind of manual labor, and be a respected official." He also made the interesting point that scribes saw beyond the everyday concern of their fellow Egyptians. Knowing that their fellow countrymen attached great importance to "physical" immortality, the scribes made much of "literal" immortality by pointing out that writing perpetuates the memory more effectively than many other forms of human creativity. They pushed the idea that becoming a scribe allowed you to become literally immortal, as noted in a text from 1300 B.C. called *The Satire on the Trades*, "Their doors and buildings have crumbled. No one remembers their mortuary service, their stelae are covered in dirt and their graves are forgotten. But their names are still pronounced because they wrote books. When a man's books are good the memory of he who wrote them will last to the end of eternity."[23]

This particularly applied to the memory of Hordedef and Imhotep, the most venerated of the early Egyptian seers: "They did not make for themselves pyramids of metal, with tombstones of iron. They were not able to perpetuate themselves through their children . . . But they made heirs for themselves in their writings and in the works of wisdom they left behind . . . Wise books were their pyramids and the pen was their child."

Were the scribes right? They must certainly have known as much as anyone about what went on in the tombs before, during, and after the funeral services. In the case of Ani, as far as his friends and family were concerned, he and his wife Tutu had attained immortality by following all the mortuary requirements laid down by the priests. The scribes were now telling them that regardless of all the other measures taken, Ani had really guaranteed his place in eternity by creating a masterpiece in his *Book of the Dead*, which most likely had been assembled by a team of priests and writers. In other times and places, this alone would place him among the immortals; now scribes and papyrus paper ensured that he would live on in the minds of men. Perhaps a much safer bet than relying on your *ba* and *ka*, the soul and spirit-like guardian angels, to promote and protect your everlasting soul.

❧

Needless to say, there rose up a great degree of trust in this new medium; it would last, wouldn't it? The reasoning of the ancient Egyptians was that their scrolls were buried with the dead and thus stayed with them for all eternity. But what of later documents? The Greeks, Romans, and Arabs must have felt their thoughts, words, poems, and tax records were of inestimable value—shouldn't they also be immortalized? Would this new medium match these expectations?

SIX

The Sands of the Nile Give Up their Treasures

> It's amazing that a man who is dead can talk to people through these pages. As long as this book survives, his ideas live.
>
> —Christopher Paolini, *Eragon*

In 1952 workmen digging the foundation for a summerhouse in southern Italy came across the ruins of an ancient church. Digging farther they uncovered a sarcophagus, almost certainly the last resting place of Cassiodorus,[1] the ultimate friend and defender of papyrus paper. A retired statesman under Gothic emperor Theodoric, he wrote a letter to the tax collector of Tuscany in 540 A.D. in praise of papyrus. He was also responsible for eliminating a tax placed on its use.

When the sarcophagus was opened only a few bones were found. Presumably, sometime during the intervening 1400 years, grave robbers had been at work. He had addressed the problem of grave robbing in his own lifetime when, in the name of his King, he demanded an investigation of a country pastor rumored to be rifling through graves and tombs looking for valuables among the blessed dead.

Outraged that "hands which have been touched with the oil of consecration should have been grasping at unholy gains," Cassiodorus perhaps had some premonition that being touched by such hands might also someday be his fate. Yet, according to some, he would be better off by being touched this way. Sir Wallis Budge, who had risen in the ranks to become a long-serving keeper of Egyptian antiquities at the British Museum, thought so. "Whatever blame may be attached to individual archaeologists for removing mummies from Egypt, every unprejudiced person who knows anything of the subject must admit that when once a mummy has passed into the care of the Trustees, and is lodged in the British Museum, it has a far better chance of being preserved there than it could possibly have in any tomb, royal or otherwise . . ."

Would it be too much to hope that in the case of Cassiodorus some memento of his life had survived undisturbed? Of course, the point could also be made that mementos are unnecessary in his case, since here, at least, is one man of ancient times who could rest on his laurels with dignity. Though not the most outstanding figure of his era, he would not easily be forgotten. Unique among bureaucrats for his invention of a form of letter that combined business and pleasure, defender of Gothic rule, loyal public servant in his fashion, protector of history, and guardian of learning in the face of insurmountable odds, he was sought out during his earlier career by the leaders in Rome, Ravenna, and Constantinople to bring some organization to the far-flung empires that they ruled in the Christian Gothic west and Christian Roman east.

He also insured that his worldly fame would endure because he did so much during his life to preserve not only his own books, but all available classical and sacred literature. That was no mean feat, since all around him barbarian forces were at work sacking and burning, and nothing is easier to burn than a book made of papyrus.

Enduring fame for Cassiodorus is one thing; it is a different matter entirely for others. To some it happens by chance: they fall into a cave, turn over a rock, or step out into a sunlit square at just the right moment. To a chosen few, such as Cassiodorus, fame is an entitlement that comes from some natural ability or talent that has been cultivated through training and dedication; they are born to it. But, for most of us, if it comes at all, it is only after a long, hard life of work and constant attention to detail.

And then, of course, who's to know? In the early days, unless it was written down somewhere, there was nothing to impress those who came after you. Because Sappho's poems were once inscribed on papyrus paper, later readers could declare them marked by beauty of diction, simplicity of form, and intensity of emotion. So it was also with Socrates, and his pupil Plato, and in turn, Plato's pupil, Aristotle; even as their thoughts, works and commentaries were being reduced to the fragments of papyrus paper that survive today, they were being marked for enduring fame.

The same applies to early versions of the Bible; they survived on papyrus paper until the time when they could be transcribed to beautifully colored, elaborate parchment volumes for the Christian emperors. Versions of the Koran, Gnostic gospels, and scrolls likewise appeared first as papyrus texts before they could be later lovingly copied and embellished. These sacred writings live on today and reflect the glory of the patriarchs, the apostles, the Prophet, and God because of papyrus. And they also illustrate the fact that papyrus served well those people who counted in history.[2]

But, what of the rest of humanity as it evolved over the last five thousand years? Did the common man ever have a chance at enduring fame? Certainly between the years 3000 B.C. and 1000 A.D. there were hundreds of thousands, even millions of people who committed pen to papyrus paper and thus entered the lottery. As it turned out, they all had at least two chances at fame: one being the substance and character of their writing, and the other being the person who discovered, bought, owned, stole or deciphered their document. Many wrote about the immediate problem that had taken over their lives and wouldn't rest until they unburdened themselves, sought a solution, made contact with a friend, or obtained some satisfaction. Papyrus paper provided them with the medium and the papyrus plant the means, by which they could come to grips with the business of life. In the process, those bits of everyday correspondence often touched on the very essence of life.

Inscriptions cut into stone are as "cold and lifeless as the stone that bears them." On papyrus paper we see something much more lifelike: "we see the handwriting, the crabbed characters; we see the men who wrote them; we gaze into the nooks and crannies of private life, for which history has no eyes and the historian no spectacles."[3]

Today there are many fragments of papyri in existence, the bulk of which belong mainly to the Egypt Exploration Society and are housed by Oxford University in the Sackler Library. The Society owns over 500,000 papyrus fragments, the largest collection of papyri in the world. In the decipherment and translation of these, there still exist numerous chances to provide researchers and professors with at least one small cloud of glory as their reward. The ancient Egyptians would find nothing unusual in this. After all, many of them believed that after death we would eventually all become infinite and immortal.

Of course, conditions applied—a life devoted to good works, a proper burial, and papyrus were the key elements—without which, no matter how adept you were at finance, poetry, writing, or the decipherment and analysis of antiquities, you went nowhere.

Twenty years before Denon showed up in Egypt, a cache of about fifty rolls were discovered in a jar near Giza; these were the ones that were burned to provide a pleasant scent. They differed from the *Book of the Dead* in that they were written in Greek. They represented part of the large repository of knowledge and day-to-day details of ancient Egypt that still fascinate us today. Known as the *Charta Borgiana*, the surviving scroll immortalizes the famed collector Cardinal Stefano Borgia.

The first large discovery of papyri was a collection of 10,000 papyri and some texts written on linen. Found in the Fayum area of Egypt, they were bought by Archduke Rainer in the 1880s. The collection caused a sensation, as Rainier was the richest and most popular member of the House of Hapsburg. The collection consisted of secular, Christian, and Arabic material and was deposited in the Imperial Library of Vienna. Subsequently, it formed the basis for the present-day collection of 180,000 papyri, documents, fragments, and other objects. Papyrology as a systematic discipline is said to date from that time.

Then over a period of six years from 1891–97, the British Museum published an amazing collection of texts translated from ancient Greek. The papyri included Aristotle's *Athenian Constitution*, the *Mimes* of Herodas, the *Odes* of Bacchylides, and some speeches by Hyperides. We are given a taste of how important these four are by historian Leo Deuel in his great down-to-earth treatise on ancient documents, the aptly titled, *Testaments of Time*. Deuel tells us that the *Athenian Constitution* by Aristotle represented the only survivor of a series of 170 articles that Aristotle compiled on various ancient constitutions, a vast study in comparative government. The second item, the *Mimes*, was thought by some to be the greatest literary discovery ever made in Egypt. Totally devoid of poetic magnificence, it consists of eight ancient sitcom scenarios set in iambic meter on the Greek island of Kos, the seat of a considerable culture. As Deuel says, the titles tell all: *The Bawd*, *The Pimp*, *The Women Worshippers*, *The Jealous Mistress*, and so on.

By contrast, the *Odes* were the "purest literature from the greatest age of classical lyrical verse" by Bacchylides, a poet ranked with the likes of Pindar.

The last of this illustrious four, the speeches, is nothing short of marvelous. Hyperides teased the humanists of the fifteenth century who were tasked with the Revival of Learning, the effort that led to the European Renaissance. Only one copy existed in a library in, of all places, Transylvania, before it disappeared in 1545. We are told that Hyperides, like Cicero, the darling of the Renaissance, was a master of legal forensic artifices. Perhaps his speeches provided a foretaste of *LA Law* to Victorian audiences, but because they also revealed the man as well as the age, Deuel felt they were as much history as literature, and were among "the most cherished works returned to life by Egypt."

The person responsible for uncovering three of the four courses of this feast of the mind was none other than our old friend, Wallis Budge, from the scribe Ani's *Book of the Dead* experience. How Budge managed this coup is a story that rivaled all his adventures including the one in Luxor nine years earlier.

I call it "The Affair of the Oranges."

SEVEN

The Affair of the Oranges

Known as Budgie to his friends, Wallis Budge was driven by the Egyptomania collecting frenzy of the 1890s. Over a period of twenty-five years, he acquired 47,000 artifacts from ancient Egypt for the British Museum. In doing so he committed almost every crime in the book of cultural thievery, acts that would be unforgivable today. All the while he thumbed his nose at anyone who lifted an eyebrow; he abhorred what he called the "archaeological Pecksniffs" of his age. In the case of one of the illustrious four papyrus scrolls, he exceeded himself.

As he explained in his autobiography,[1] a dealer friend in Cairo told him that the grapevine had it that a very important work by a fifth century B.C. lyric poet was on the market. Several agents for European museums and three well-known English archaeologists were scouring Cairo looking for it. As a result, the prices for papyri soared.

In November 1896, he made a trip to Egypt specifically to acquire it, despite the fact that everyone who counted said it couldn't be done. They obviously didn't know Budge. By previously carrying off several papyri, including Ani's Papyrus and one featuring Aristotle's work, he had established himself as a master collector, but he had also created enemies. Even his fellow countrymen, the British government officials in Cairo, as well as the expatriate curators at the Egyptian Museum and the Antiquities Service were all dead set on stopping him from lifting anymore items. In his role as curator in the British Museum, Budge was allowed entry and free access to every corner of the British Empire, and so they couldn't stop him from coming into Egypt, but they were damned if he would take anything else out without a permit.

And so the scene was set. The odds were against him, postal authorities and custom agents in Alexandria and Port Said were on high alert, and the police followed his every move. There was only one problem: they were too late. Budge had already outwitted everyone even before the chase began.

It happened that he had bought the Greek papyrus in question a few months back. He had made a deal with Omar, the owner, but since he lacked the funds to complete the sale, he left a deposit and told him to hold the document for him; he'd be back. He did copy out a few lines of the text and sent these to the librarian at the British Museum, who cabled back almost immediately, "The text has been identified and it is of great importance. Buy it, by all means."

Back in Cairo from an upcountry trip, Budge found the sale had become complicated. The Egyptian Service of Antiquities had seen a fragment and word had spread; as a result Omar wanted more money. Budge had to sit with him and bargain for two days and two nights before taking possession, the fact of which leaked out immediately. The Service of Antiquities sent several officials to his hotel to question him, and came away empty-handed. The British consul-general sent him a note telling him to give it up, or else. His answer was to leave Egypt and get back to London as soon as possible. But what about the papyrus?

The papyrus was now known to be a copy of the original *Odes* of Bacchylides, one of the poets of major significance within the ancient tradition of pure Greek lyric poetry, a poet noted for his elegance and polished style. Also known as the "the nightingale of Kos," he was a poet who gave pleasure without demanding effort, "a poet with whom the reader could at once feel at home."[2] And it was not simply a line or two that was involved, but an almost complete version of his work. When it was reassembled at the museum it was found to consist of 1,382 lines, comprising twenty poems, six of them nearly complete. In total, there were over 200 fragments in addition to the three larger pieces. In all, the papyrus was fifteen feet long.

When I read that, I wondered how in the world he would ever get such a thing back to London without detection and without destroying it further. It turns out Budge had a simple solution. He bought a collection of photographic scenes of Egypt in a department store in Cairo along with two cardboard covers, a roll of colorful wrapping paper, and some string. He then cut the larger pieces of this priceless antique roll to fit and placed the pieces along with the fragments between the photos before wrapping the whole package and tying it securely.

His next move was to dispatch his luggage by rail to a friend in Port Said, at the northern end of the Suez Canal, the departure port for those going back to England.

In the morning when he and a helper, Ahmad, boarded the Port Said train, he carried with him the package containing the papyrus, layered now between souvenir photo prints, a heavy overcoat that he used to cover the package, and a crate of two hundred oranges. Just before the train started, two officials came into his compartment saying they had come to take his luggage to the van at the end of the train, and when he said that he had sent his luggage to Port Said the day before, they looked under the seats suspiciously and left. Later, when the train stopped at a switching station, Budge, followed by Ahmad, stepped quickly out onto the platform with their belongings, then boarded a train in the opposite direction that went east to Suez, the port at the southern end of the canal on the Red Sea.

They arrived at Suez when it was almost dark and parted: Ahmad taking the overcoat and the package, Budge taking the oranges. They moved on towards the Customs Office, where all hand luggage had to be examined. Once inside the shed, Budge created a diversion while Ahmad left the station and carried the package and overcoat to the nearby house of Budge's friend. In the Customs shed, Budge's crate was opened, the oranges were turned out and counted, and the officials called upon him to pay fifteen piastres duty, which he refused to do. Bickering to the amusement of the other passengers and loudly exclaiming they were not for him but a gift for others, he distracted everyone while Ahmad slipped out unnoticed.

Budge then paid the fine, which was not much, and left the station loudly directing that the oranges be sent to a local hospital run by the French sisters in town, thereby proving his innocent intentions.

Later around midnight after a pleasant dinner with his friend in town, Budge boarded a steam launch that carried him and Ahmad, as well as his overcoat and package, out to a passenger liner waiting in Suez Harbor to enter the canal. Once through the canal they stopped at Port Said. There Ahmad disembarked and reclaimed Budge's luggage, which was then loaded onboard. While this was going on, Budge remained hidden in his cabin. On being asked where Budge was, Ahmad told the Customs officials he was still in Ismailia and would arrive shortly.

Perhaps they were still waiting, as Budge, the "ninja of the paper chase," disembarked in Southampton a week later wearing a heavy overcoat against the chill and carrying a colorfully wrapped package as he boarded the train to Waterloo Station, London.

❧

Budge left a record; he had probably taken the largest number of items ever removed from Egypt by one man, with the possible exception of Napoleon. Worse than that was his open contempt for the Egyptian Antiquities Service, which left the British Museum with a legacy of scorn that has been difficult to live down. Is it any wonder that over the years they have distanced themselves from Budge and his autobiography?

Late in the Victorian era, professional archaeologists spread out across the hot, dry sands of Middle and Upper Egypt in order to locate and dig up, or buy from local dealers, a considerable number of papyri. In addition to Egyptian funerary documents, classic Greek manuscripts, and the remnants of many early Coptic Christian Bibles, they uncovered business accounts and official and personal records and correspondence.

The story of how Budge "acquired" the Papyrus of Ani in Luxor was the subject of a docudrama on the History Channel, 119 years after it happened. The Discovery film, called *The Egyptian Book of the Dead*, makes for fascinating viewing. The 2006 version is set in the Victorian colonial period in 1887, with flashbacks to ancient Egypt and the story of Scribe Ani, who is played by a young man worried about afterlife. So worried is he that he is already preparing his *Book of the Dead* and the other artifacts that will accompany him to his tomb. The docudrama does a great job animating the monsters and perils that await you in your search for the Egyptian heaven. The story is also told of how the *Book of the Dead* can serve to help us reach what should be our ultimate goal during that final voyage,

Back in real place and time (Luxor in Victorian Egypt, 1887) in the docudrama, Budge is catching hell as the papyri he bought are confiscated by the Egyptian police. In his anxiety over their fate, he believes what his cohorts, the Egyptian dealers, tell him. They claim that the authorities will certainly cut the Ani Papyrus scroll into pieces and sell it piecemeal. Thus, although the film seems to condemn Budge's tomb robbing, it also justifies the role of Budge as a "rescuer of history," because it spurs him on to enlist the help of local housebreakers to steal the scrolls from police custody and escape to England. Next there is a scissors scene at the British Museum showing him cutting the scroll into thirty-seven sections for study. This was a technical necessity for research purposes. The ancient scroll would not have withstood repeated unrollings and rerollings, but to the strict conservationist it must vie with a nightmare created by Johnny Depp in the role of Edward Scissorhands.

During the film, the narrators freely interject their views on how and why Budge was or was not guilty, and they make pronouncements on whether or not he was a thief. Malcolm Mosher, a writer and Egyptologist, felt that the fact that Budge took the scroll out of Egypt was quite normal for the time, and "when one considers all the antiquities that were lost, stolen, and destroyed one can only thank someone, who was a bit of a scoundrel, for having the wherewithal to go in and bribe officials and engage in bizarre behavior because he preserved these things. Also, if he didn't publish as he did, there wouldn't be the interest in Egyptology that there is today." Mosher says, "Budge did more to popularize the Egyptian *Book of the Dead* and the notion of Egyptian afterlife than any other scholar or text."

Zawi Hawass, however, the former head of antiquities in Egypt, stars in the film and, as expected, was quite outspoken in his condemnation,

". . . you can be an honest man all your life but you see something you want and you become a thief. He used his influence and his scholarship to steal many of the antiquities to put them in the British Museum that was not fair. Budge was a strange person with a good side and a bad side, the good side was his publications, the bad side what he stole. His books are very important, I myself read them today. The only bad thing about Budge is that he did steal antiquities."

The British Museum is listed under the credits as one of the organizations thanked by the producers of the film, but they seem not to have played any active part, though several scenes are included inside the Egyptian Rooms. Carol Andrews, who was formerly an assistant keeper and senior research assistant in the Department of Egyptian Antiquities at the British Museum from 1971 to 2000 put in a cameo appearance. In reference to Budge, she said, "You can't look at him from a modern point of view . . . that he's a cultural thief. This is not the way they looked at it in those days."

But he was featured in a newspaper report on "Antica Stealing" in 1903 and was named in a plea that "the only means of dealing with Dr. Budge is to arouse scientific public opinion in England against him and his methods"; these run counter to Andrews's statements. If that is not cultural thievery, it runs very close. And her closing remark that "on the other hand he did sail very close to the wind" doesn't do justice to the scale of his perfidy.

And there remains the cutting of the scroll. According to James Wasserman (author, Egyptologist, and head of the *Book of the Dead* Project), Budge unfortunately cut the original papyrus using the basic yardstick method—dividing it into thirty-seven sheets of relatively even length. "The result was to disfigure the flow of the original scroll." In the preface to Wasserman's 1994 book, Carol Andrews said,

> The original papyrus roll . . . for the sake of convenience of storage and display was divided into thirty-seven framed and glassed sheets, varying in length from 52 cm to 76 cm, the norm being between 65 cm and 70 cm. Budge was sometimes influenced in cutting the roll by what he considered a natural break in the frieze of vignette—even if this led to the text of a chapter

> being on different sheets. At other times the layout of the text was considered of greater importance, and as a result vignettes have been segmented, some even separated from their relevant chapter. Moreover, as the divisions progressed there came points where, unless the sheets produced were to be abnormally short or long, large-scale vignettes were actually cut in two.

Andrews then detailed fifteen of the most damaging examples of this process, a process that was described in the docudrama thus: "When he got it back to the British Museum, he cut it into sections that he could work with. He arranged to have it pasted to wooden boards so that it could be translated. From a technological point of view one can almost forgive him but, on the other hand, he destroyed the integrity of the papyrus forever."

Although we know from his own admission that Budge had no qualms about cutting up priceless papyri such as Aristotle's *Athenian Constitution* and the *Odes* of Bacchylides, the actual cutting and mounting of large papyri was done not by him but by other museum staff, under his supervision. In fact, since his time, so many scrolls have been cut into sections that few examples of intact scrolls or scrolls as scrolls are available in museums today; yet in their time the museum had access to hundreds. Where are they?

If Mr. H. Spencer were alive, perhaps he could tell us. He was in charge of the Egyptian and Assyrian Study Room from 1887 to 1889. I found his report among the museum's correspondence from 1893—at the time Budge was the keeper (the museum's title for curator in charge). To my eyes, what I read next was a tragedy; but for Mr. Spencer it was all part of a day's work. After listing his tasks, which involved rearranging and organizing some 50,000 clay tablets and repairing 1,000 others, he turned his attention to 400 papyrus rolls in the museum's collection, and proceeded to unroll them, cut them up, and mount them all behind glass, including the Papyrus of Ani. There were no alternatives in Budge's day; a glass plate sandwich was the fastest, most efficient way for the researcher to gain access to the material. The immediate and urgent goal was to translate the text, then photograph and archive these unique treasures before someone else did. The result is demonstrated by the Greenfield Papyrus, which was originally an enormous scroll. Its sheer length was so impressive that a photo taken by Budge, now in the archives of the museum, shows a massive roll in end view. Presumably, this was taken just before it was cut up into ninety-six pieces.

Two ends of intact papyrus roll the Book of the Dead of Princess Nesitanebtashru, 6 in. diam., 123 ft. long, Greenfield Papyrus (from Budge, 1912).

The Greenfield Papyrus was created 2,000 years ago for Nestanebetisheru, daughter of a high priest and member of the royal circle. Donated to the British Museum in 1910 by Mrs. Edith Greenfield, the sections mounted under glass languished in storage for 100 years until they were hung in a major exhibition of the *Book of the Dead* put on by the British Museum in 2010. The promise that "complete scrolls will be reassembled and presented in their original form for the first time" wasn't quite fulfilled, as the panels on the wall of the old Reading Room testified. The sad fact is that Spencer was allowed to cut up so many scrolls that an intact scroll is now a rarity. In fact, there are only a limited number of intact scrolls left from the great number that have been discovered. One of the longest scrolls that is still virtually intact and on display is the sixty-three foot *Book of the Dead* scroll of the Priest of Horus, Imouthes (Imhotep) at the Metropolitan Museum in New York.

One thing against the idea of keeping ancient papyrus scrolls on display is that like the Imouthes scroll many are not very colorful. There is nothing to attract the eye of the busy museumgoer. In this regard, the Papyrus of

Ani has an advantage, it has many very colorful vignettes, which may also be a drawback in the future as it is now quite certain that the colors have been fading with exposure to light.

❧

The end result of this extraordinary period of paper chasing was that Budge's arrival in London brought Bacchylides back to life. With about half as many extant verses as Pindar, the poet became one of the best represented of the Greek lyric poets overnight. Budge also introduced the world to Ani the royal scribe, and further advanced the reputations of Aristotle and Herodotus. It was obvious that he would have fitted well with the Florentine book hunters of the 1400s who scoured the world, especially Constantinople and its surrounding environs, for the Greek classics needed to fuel the Renaissance. The Florentines were delighted to have access to the products of Nestorian copyists of the Syrian Desert and the masters of the ninth century in Baghdad, but these were all second- or thirdhand parchment copies. What Budge had acquired were papyrus paper scrolls and books that were closer to the original links with the original authors. His discoveries illustrate well the opinion of Cassiodorus that if papyrus paper had not existed, many an ancient notable would have been reduced to scratching and carving rough letters on bark, an off-putting exercise fit only for primitive man that would keep him further from the immortality for which he were destined.

> Before papyrus paper was discovered, all the sayings of the wise, all the thoughts of the ancients, were in danger of perishing. Who could write fluently or pleasantly on the rough bark of trees, though it is from that practice that we call a book *Liber*? While the scribe was laboriously cutting his letters on the sordid material, his very thought grew cold: a rude contrivance assuredly and only fit for the beginnings of the world. Then was papyrus paper discovered, and therewith was eloquence made possible . . . papyrus paper which keeps the sweet harvest of the mind. (Cassiodorus, 527 A.D. Letters. Book XI, Letter 38)

EIGHT

The Floodgates Open

Following the discoveries in the late 1800s, excitement over papyrus paper died down as the interest of scholars and the public was again diverted toward ancient monuments, temples, and tombs. And who could blame them, when, as in modern times, so much was made of mummies and the fascinating Egyptian rites of the dead. So many activities went forward involving the Sphinx, the Pyramids, and royal tombs that it was difficult for the public to keep track. A good example is the work of Édouard Naville, funded by the Egypt Exploration Society, an organization founded in 1882. Naville, who came from the "old fashioned school," concerned himself with large-scale clearance of sites, indiscriminately turning over whatever rock had been left unturned, much to the disgust of Flinders Petrie, who, though funded by the same group, carried out more systematic and careful research. The situation was made worse by the memory of charred lumps that had been uncovered in a villa outside Pompeii. These were burned scrolls that were too delicate to unroll. They sat mocking classicists starved for more of the ancient literature, since the supply of antique scrolls seemed to have dried up. Then, suddenly, came a series of remarkable discoveries at the turn of the twentieth century, discoveries that again took the world by surprise, discoveries that were of such breathless quality that even the staid, popular leather-bound encyclopedias of the age dared to suggest that "more and exciting finds were imminent." Here at last, the scholars thought, were the long-awaited scrolls that would melt the heart.

The discoveries were made by two remarkable men, Bernard Pyne Grenfell and Arthur Surridge Hunt, who became friends at Queen's College, Oxford while still in their twenties, after mountaineering together in the Tyrol during a holiday. By 1895 they were in Egypt on graduate scholarships funded by the Egypt Exploration Society, near the site of the ancient town of Oxyrhynchus, a prosperous regional capital in the time of Alexander the Great's Egypt. They uncovered an enormous cache of papyrus scrolls close to the surface, almost at the turn of a shovel. We sense the staggering importance and the excitement of their initial find in Grenfell's 1899 report.

> As we moved northwards over other parts of the site, the flow of papyri soon became a torrent which it was difficult to cope with . . . We engaged two men to make tin boxes for storing the papyri, but for the next ten weeks they could hardly keep pace with us . . . At the end of the day's work no less than thirty-six good-sized baskets were brought in from this place, several of them stuffed with fine rolls three to ten feet long, including some of the longest Greek rolls I have ever seen. As the baskets were required for the next day's work, Mr. Hunt and I started at 9 P.M. after dinner to stowaway the papyri in some empty packing-cases which we fortunately had at hand. The task was only finished at three in the morning, and on the following night we had a repetition of it, for twenty-five more baskets were filled before the place was exhausted. (B. Grenfell, 1899)

❧

Since then, eighty volumes of the papyri have been published and more volumes are expected to follow. The items found often consist of fragments, but what fragments! They include poems of Pindar, fragments of Sappho, and diagrams from Euclid's *Elements*. Among the extensive portions are the *Hypsipyle* by Euripides, plays of Menander, and *Ichneutae* by Sophocles. The fragments that bear on Christian history include noncanonical Gospels, the First Epistle of John, the Apocalypse of Baruch, the Gospel according to the Hebrews, early Christian hymns, prayers, and letters, sayings of Jesus, and bits of gospels by Matthew, Mark, and John.

Subsequently, Grenfell and Hunt became the subject of many stories and the basis for characters in a play, Tony Harrison's 1988 *Trackers of Oxyrhynchus*, a modern play about Oxonian scholars and the *Ichneutae* of Sophocles. A revival opened in Leeds in 1998.

Grenfell and Hunt's work has since been carried forward by Professor Peter Parsons, retired from the Regius Chair of Greek at Oxford, and current head of the Oxyrhynchus Papyri Project; under Parsons the focus of the project's attention has changed. Now the study of the social, economic, and political life of the ancient world is foremost. In his book *City of the Sharp-Nosed Fish* he brings that old city to life and has made Oxyrhynchus, if anything, even more important. The very ordinariness of most of its preserved documents makes them most valuable for modern scholars of social history.

After the great caches at Oxyrhynchus were uncovered, attention shifted to rubbish heaps in dry areas in Egypt. Many of the papyri recovered from these places were private documents, written for someone other than us. But, as we know, the unwritten rule that one must never read someone else's mail apparently doesn't apply to archaeologists. It makes no difference to them that some documents—legal briefs, for example—might deal with a case where the original defendant may have lost his case, or been embarrassed by some proceeding and perhaps wanted nothing more to do with that part of his life. The last thing the original owners may have wanted was to have them shown about to thousands of prying eyes. But, they had not reckoned with the mentality of the eighteenth and nineteenth century collectors and the early archaeologists who found it easier and easier to breach the wall of fear that separated them from that final act of desecration.

Hélène Cuvigny, director of research at the French National Center for Scientific Research (CNRS) and noted papyrologist, has pointed out that some of the heaps were as much as twenty-seven feet high, and they were both public and private, containing domestic, industrial, and agricultural garbage, rubble, ashes, rags, discarded objects, and masses of potsherds. She further noted that the papyri that people discarded were not important documents that ought to be kept, like contracts, title deeds, or literary works.[1] Nevertheless, the excavations at Oxyrhynchus show that from time to time, documents and rolls were thrown out in quantity without regard to content. Some of them were still in the baskets in which they had been brought to the dump. Many were systematically torn before being thrown away.

As pointed out by Cuvigny, the work of analyzing a refuse heap is ungratifying, boring, and often academically unrewarding. What then drives the process of discovery? In many instances the workers seem desperate to get their hands on family documents, love letters and such, the means that would allow them to make sense of the day-to-day affairs of these people.

Archaeologists and researchers of ancient documents were equally thrilled with the finds at Oxyrhynchus, though it would be hard to imagine some of them, like the distinguished German scholar Professor Gustav Adolf Deissmann, resorting to the same methods used today by the FBI, paparazzi, and private eyes, glancing furtively over their shoulders while a comrade rifles through trash bags from the homes of the rich, famous, or suspect.

When we look at Deissmann in his biographic photo we see the ultimate distinguished, thoughtful face with steel-rimmed glasses, a dark, perfectly trimmed goatee, a Poirot-like clipped moustache, and an immaculately starched collar. Would this recipient of eight honorary doctorates (from Marburg, Athens, Aberdeen, Saint Andrews, Manchester, Oxford, Uppsala, and Wooster in the USA), and two-time nominee for the Nobel Peace Prize, have joined in with the fervent young Oxford scholars in their fevered search?

According to Deissmann's own words the answer would have been an unqualified yes, if he had been invited. To Deissmann and all the others, it was simply a matter of carrying on a tradition. He came to that conclusion in 1908 when he said, quite simply and clearly,

> the rubbish of ancient cities gives a valuable hint . . . We must regard the masses of papyri from Fayum, Oxyrhynchus, etc., *not as the relics of great archives*, as they were at first thought to be, but as the remains of ancient rubbish . . . where ages ago the discarded files of documents from public and private offices, worn-out books, and fragments of books, and such-like were thrown to await in tranquil repose the unsuspected fates in store for them. (G. Deissmann and L. Strachan, 1908)

He also felt that the papyri from rubbish heaps were of a different character than the papyri found previously.

> The great bulk of the papyri are of a nonliterary character: legal documents of the most various kinds, e.g. leases, accounts, and receipts, marriage contracts and wills, attestations, official edicts, petitions for justice, records of judicial proceedings, and a large number of documents relating to taxes, then letters and notes, exercise books, charms, horoscopes, diaries, etc. etc. The contents of these non-literary fragments are as varied as life itself. The Greek fragments, numbering many thousands, embrace a period of about a thousand years . . . These plain, unpretentious scraps of papyrus come as a stream of new, warm blood reanimating the history of law in the first place, but also the history of civilization in general. (G. Deissmann and L. Strachan, 1908)

In sum, numerous rubbish heaps and innocent-looking mounds in the desert have yielded hundreds of thousands of pages and fragments since 1788, of which 50,000 have been published and generally deciphered. There is a vast remainder still in storage yet to be done.

At one point in 1908, Deissmann suggested that the compilation was long overdue; it was his goal for the near future, as his discoveries were still in progress. In many ways his dream has come true in that the volumes emerging from the Oxyrhynchus Project constitute part of that corpus. More importantly, as Professor Parsons has noted, "When Grenfell and Hunt began to dig el-Behnesa, in 1897, they found a time-capsule of a very special kind. Pompeii preserves a snapshot of Roman life, as it was on one catastrophic day, the buildings and the bodies of those who lived there. Oxyrhynchus offers the converse: not bodies or buildings, but the paper-trail (a trail of paper thrown away by its owners) of a whole culture."

A few of the more interesting examples of professional documents found throughout Egypt are given here simply to show the range of material:

Diaries: The oldest is the collection of pages and fragments of papyrus paper with writing on it found by Tallet and the joint French-Egyptian team in the limestone gallery caves at Wadi el-Jarf, the ancient harbor.[2] These ancient papyri provide new insight into the everyday lives of people in the time of Khufu and his Great Pyramid.

Records: Under Roman rule each district in Egypt was required to have a public depository of records, as well as a depository of property records.[3] All administrative documents were required to be deposited in the public records. In addition, every civil official was required to keep a journal of transactions. One example is the entry from the journal of Aurelius Leonatas from Elephantine in 242 A.D., "after working at the Caesareum on matters of business sat at the office attending to public affairs." This record is authenticated in his own hand as having been read by him. And so it went with duplicates, triplicates, endorsements, and countersignings, each adding another layer of security and trust, and of course, consuming more papyrus paper.

Census Rolls: From 61 A.D. onward at fourteen-year intervals, it was the responsibility of the head of every household in the Roman world to make a declaration stating the house he lived in and a description of the occupants.

Ready-made Documents: Many examples exist of legal or formal documents that were written by one scribe but had names and details entered by someone else. This represents the first use of ready-made documents. The most famous were prerecorded scrolls containing a version of the *Book of the Dead* with blank spaces left to fill in your name, a vital passport to the beyond, and cheap at any price.

Scientific Texts: Among scientific texts, the Rhind Mathematical Papyrus (1550 B.C.) is one of the most interesting. A scroll found in a tomb in Thebes and bought at a market in Luxor in 1858, it is the most valuable source of information we have about Egyptian mathematics. Written by the scribe Ahmes, it is a copy of an earlier work from 2000 B.C. and deals with practical mathematics as well as mathematical puzzles, such as, "Seven houses contain seven cats. Each cat kills seven mice. Each mouse had eaten seven ears of grain. Each ear of grain would have produced seven hekats of wheat. What is the total of all of these?" The answer is a geometric series: 7 houses + 49 cats + 343 mice + 2,401 ears of grain + 16,807 *hekats* (a measure of grain), giving a total of 19,607.

Medical Texts: Two medical texts share the limelight as the oldest and most important descriptions of Egyptian medicine. The Edwin Smith Papyrus is the earliest medical textbook, written in 1700 B.C. it contains much detail regarding trauma surgery, anatomical observations and the examination, diagnosis, treatment, and prognosis of injuries. For its time it is regarded as well done. It also contains a prescription for a wrinkle remover using urea that is still used in face creams today.

The second medical text is the Ebers Papyrus of 1550 B.C., a 110-page scroll that preserves a voluminous record of ancient Egyptian medicine. It contains some 700 magical formulas and remedies, as well as empirical practice and observation. Two remedies to pique the interest of the modern reader are, first, that clothing may be protected from mice and rats by applying cat's fat! It doesn't say how the fat is obtained. The second is a half an onion in the froth of beer, which is considered "a delightful remedy against death."

Legal Documents and Petitions: Last but not least are the thousands of legal documents, account sheets, and contracts that have surfaced, along with divorce papers. A good example from among the Oxyrhynchus collection is the papyrus known as the "Repudiation of a Betrothal," from 600 A.D., to wit:

> I John, father of Euphemia, my unemancipated daughter, do send this present deed of separation and dissolution to you, Phoebammon, my most honourable son-in-law, by the hand of the most illustrious advocate Anastasius of this city of Oxyrhynchus. It is as follows. Forasmuch as it has come to my ears that you are giving yourself over to lawless deeds, which are pleasing to neither God nor man, and are not fit to be put into writing, I think it well that the engagement between you and her, my daughter Euphemia, should be dissolved, seeing that, as is foresaid, I have heard you are giving yourself over to lawless deeds and that I wish my daughter to lead a peaceful and quiet life. (Oxyrhynchus*:* A City and Its Texts, An Exhibition, 2007)

One impression that jumps out at us from the rubbish heaps of Oxyrhynchus and other sites is that the Romans and Greeks used a great amount of papyrus paper. But, though impressive, it still represents only a small part of the total production. Another enormous amount was exported in return for foreign exchange, income that helped support the ruling government, and furthered the development of civilization.

All of which points away from "the sweet harvest of the mind" and more toward the papermaking business, which in ancient Egypt, was one of the country's major industries.

PART TWO

Egypt, Papermaker to the World

NINE

The Birth of Memphis and Paper

Until now our story has dealt with dry regions, places where the first paper would have been preserved, where history was made, and where there was evidence of the great things to which the first paper was destined. We will now turn our attention to the actual production of this first paper.

This takes us from the driest areas to the wettest, since the plant that was used to produce the paper is a swamp plant. Papyrus depends on water to reach its great height (the stems grow up to fifteen feet on average) and is an integral part of delta ecosystems. So we must leave Pharaoh Khufu in Giza and Chancellor Hemaka in Saqqara—both dry places on the western edge of the Nile valley bordering the desert (see insert, Map B)—which makes sense, as both are burial sites where stone mausoleums, pyramids, and deep, dry tombs make preservation possible and provide an ideal base for life in the next world.

Memphis today. View from the ruins toward modern day Mit Rahina (Wikipedia).

The wetlands in which papyrus grew were a world apart. Backwaters and swamps were found all along the floodplain and into the delta, and consisted of all the areas connected by water when the countryside was flooded for months on end every year. Even after the flood subsided, water remained, trapped in pockets and basins. Living in such regions was only possible with water control. Because Memphis was made of mud brick, wood, and reed buildings—stone being reserved for monuments and temples—most of the city would have washed away during inundations were it not for drainage installed early in the life of the metropolis. Drainage was something the Egyptians were extremely good at.

In later years, when hard times fell on Memphis, the dykes and drains fell into disarray, and "Its temples fell prey to vandalism and quarrying. What survived is nowadays buried under a thick layer of Nile clay and covered with modern houses and fields. So today, most of Memphis is lost."[1] The passing of the pharaonic civilization, the rise of Ptolemaic Alexandria in the 300s B.C., and the Arab city of Fustat (later Cairo) in the 600s A.D. ensured its demise. The ultimate insult was levied against the city when Europeans arrived and began asking, "Where is it?" Earlier descriptions gave conflicting views. Looking for evidence of its location in 1799, a famous geographer, Major James Rennell, subsequently known as the Father of Oceanography, created an Egyptian map in England that incorporated all earlier information.[2] He distilled the accounts of many travelers and historians; the result was a map (see insert, Map B) that accurately showed the position of Memphis in relation to the Nile and the Eastern and Western Deserts that dominate the landscape today.

Rennell believed, as did others, that the ancient bed of the Nile River was raised because of sediment. It then overflowed and the overflow followed a new course, a channel carved out by the river in the eastern part of the floodplain. This new bed served as the course of the Nile in Rennell's time and with some changes continues to this day. This division of waters formed an island that became the land on which Memphis was built (see insert, Map B) and with time, the old riverbed silted up. The diversion of water was hastened by man-made channels and dykes, which served to protect Memphis once the land in and around it was reclaimed. These same waterways helped the temple-builders of the city gain access to the limestone slabs of Tura. Once they were developed further, they would also later serve Merer in the time of Khufu to deliver this same stone to the pyramid site.

Even in predynastic days, Memphis was everything that an ancient Egyptian could want, and it was named "enduring and beautiful." It was probably first sparsely settled in prehistoric days (6000–4000 B.C.) then developed further by Menes, founder of the First Dynasty (3100–3050 B.C.), after which, it became the capital city of ancient Egypt. As pointed out by historians, it was in a strategic position to command both parts of the kingdom, south and north, because it lies at the junction of the delta and the Nile valley (Map B, see insert, and Map 2). With its port, workshops, factories, and warehouses, it was a natural regional center of commerce, trade, and religion. Papyrus paper was made in quantity in the wetlands of the delta and the floodplain swamps of the Nile valley and could be brought here for export. The trade route for grain, and products such as paper, began at the port of Memphis and led by way of the Pelusiac branch of the Nile to the large port centers in the eastern Mediterranean.[3] Later in the 300s B.C., the city of

Alexandria would serve the same purpose, and it would be in a better position commercially to exploit the markets. By then Memphis was in decline.

In Memphis in the very early days, circa 3500 B.C., settlers lived on the outskirts of the town in reed huts or in floating homes on skiffs made of papyrus. They included hunters, fishermen, and cattle herders; all people familiar with a marshy terrain. The water world was the focus of their life. They used papyrus stems gathered from the nearby swamps for boat making, weaving, and thatching or, tied into bundles, for all sorts of construction. When used for construction or rope making, the stems were cut then dried. But, often the stems were peeled while fresh in order to obtain flexible strips of green skin from the stems, as seen in a 1400 B.C. tomb drawing in Thebes.

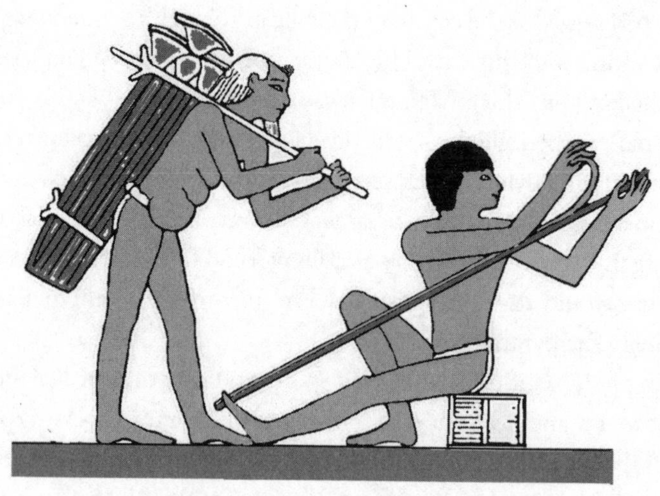

Collecting and peeling papyrus stems
(Tomb of Puyemra, Thebes 1400 B.C. after N. de Garis Davies).

These strips of skin are supple and long and make excellent material for weaving. Mats and baskets were produced this way, as well as woven sails for the thousands of small reed boats that plied local waters. Such papyrus skin is still commonly used for weaving in Africa today. After the stems were peeled, the soft pith at the center of the stem was left over and must certainly have attracted the attention of children sitting there as their mothers weaved. Possibly, as kids do, they began copying their elders and used the long strips of soft pith to make mats of their own. Even more fun would have been squashing the pith mats, after which, if they were left to dry, humankind would have a rough, early form of paper.

The process was further refined by using thin slices cut from the pith, which were laid rather than woven, and then evenly pressed, rather than just squashed. From this process a thin, durable sheet evolved and thus was paper born.

It would catch on quickly once people realized its potential. We see this when the children's father comes home. He is a potter and at work he decorates pots with dark-red painted pictures of animals, people, and boats. Not much of a job, but he is curious and interested in life and in things like the dry, white, feather-light mats his kids left behind on the floor of their simple mud-brick house or reed hut.

This is the day after his wife finished weaving some window mats. Made from papyrus skins, they are finished just in time for the rainy season. He turns the product of his children's handiwork over in his hands. His oldest child wakes from her nap, comes to him, and he shows her how to decorate it using the tools of his trade: a reed brush and colored inks. He is also a recorder for the village chief and must tally the grain that is stored in the village granary. He comes to realize that using this simple mat of papyrus pith is much easier than spending his time scouring the neighborhood for smooth stones, flat bones, shells, or pieces of pottery from his workplace.

Now aware of the potential, and given the inks, pens, and brushes at his disposal, and the great need of priests for records of temple stores and supplies, and that of the village chiefs for agricultural accounts, he improves on it. His career goes forward. He is soon known in the region as a scribe, things begin to look up markedly, and he gives thanks to the gods for his family, his kids, and this new medium, which is now called *p'p'r'*. This name for it meant "that of the pharaoh" or "the pharaoh's own," indicating that any paper in Egypt made from papyrus was the property of the king, since paper manufacture was at that time a royal prerogative, on top of which the plant itself was sacred.

By tradition, papyrus paper was said to have been invented in ancient Memphis,[4] and in time papyrus paper factories dotted the landscape in swampy regions, such as Fayum, the delta, and the floodplain. There were probably many more manufacturing centers in operation than those indicated in Map 2, but these are the ones of which records survive.

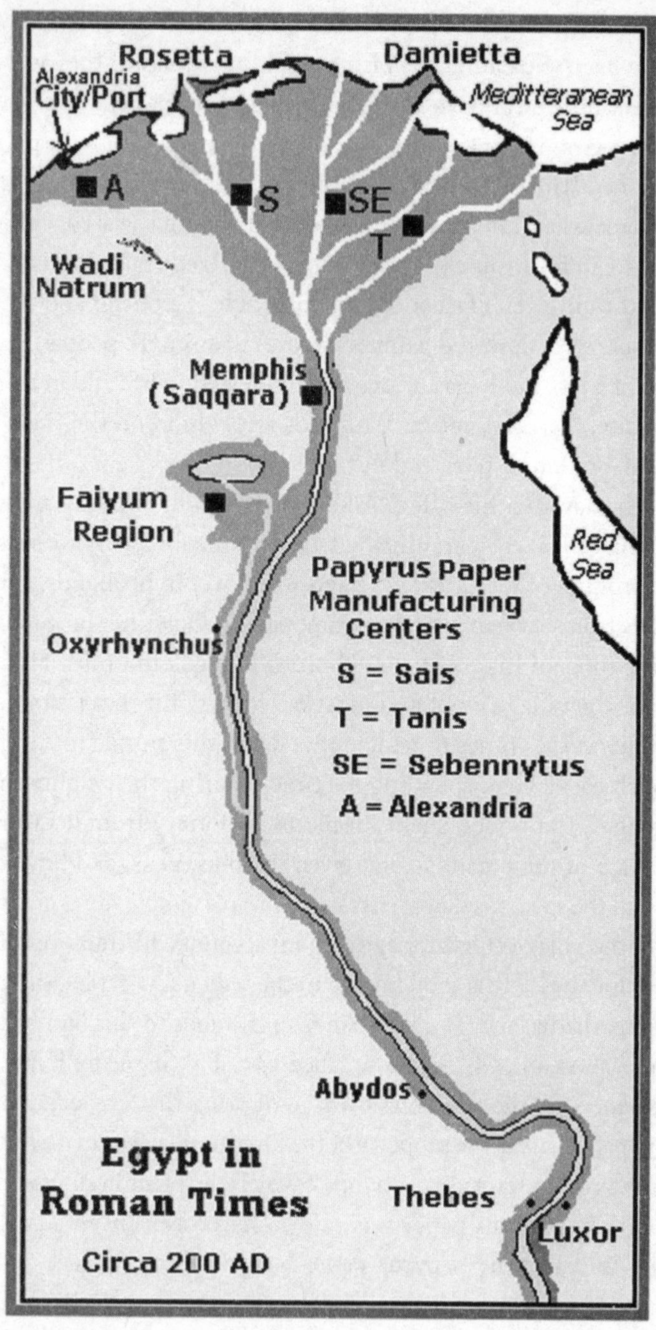

MAP 2: *Egypt in Roman times, showing papermaking centers.*

Once Egypt was taken over by the Greeks, the plant was called *papyros*. The Greek writer Theophrastus uses that term when he writes about the plant used as a foodstuff. When he refers to its use as a nonfood product, such as in rope, baskets, or paper, he uses a different word, *byblos*, or *βύβλος*, which is said to be derived from the name of the ancient Phoenician town of Byblos, a major port where papyrus paper was traded in quantity. One expert thought this was simply another example of calling an item after its place of origin, much like calling a dish "china."

Usage further leads us to the term *biblion*, which meant a book or small scroll, and "bible," the English word for that special Christian book.

No matter when or how all this happened, paper, once invented, would be improved on with every generation as the sheets became stronger, more pliable, and thinner—so much so that there is little difference between the ancient sheets and the modern papyrus paper made from plants cultivated in the shallow waters of the Nile today. The only difference is that the modern paper in Cairo is destined for the souvenir market rather than the stall of an ancient paper seller.

In its own way, a roll of papyrus paper is a sophisticated product, something that did not appear de novo, or by accident, like, say, the invention of fire. Primitive man using a thin wooden shaft to drill a hole in an axe handle drives the point too fast; the wood catches fire and, presto, a dramatic moment happens in history. But with a roll of papyrus paper it is more complicated. Not only must the sheets be fashioned, but the roll of a dozen or more sheets must be joined together in such a way that the joins are as smooth as the made paper.

Interestingly, it doesn't require much skill to make papyrus paper. The better forms and higher grades employ sizing and polishing, and joining the sheets into rolls; perhaps at that stage some expertise is needed, but basically, the making of the paper itself is a simple process and fortunately, the technique was preserved by Pliny in his *Natural History*. Unfortunately, it was this same account that led to a monumental misunderstanding, as commentators and editors wrestled with that same section (xiii: 74–82). Pliny mentions paperworkers in ancient Egypt slicing the inner stem with a "needle." Since modern papyrus paper is most easily made using a razor blade or sharp knife, it remains unclear what he meant. Whatever the instrument was that was used to cut the thin strips, it is still unknown and has driven scholars to desperation since 1492. They have subjected that passage to the minutest scrutiny, much of which is beyond the scope of this book. In order to gain some insight into what can be derived from all the argumentation, and from Pliny's interpretation of the process, we must turn to a specialist. And it happens that one of the best took up the subject, Naphtali Lewis, referred to by many as the "doyen of papyrologists." Lewis was a distinguished emeritus professor at Brooklyn College when I started writing my book of the history of the plant in the early 2000s. He died in 2005; I never met him, but his work is fascinating. His book, *Papyrus in Classical Antiquity*, is an expanded and updated version of his Sorbonne thesis.[5]

He was aware that one of the first things that strikes people about Pliny's description was why he made such a hash of it. Perhaps, as Lewis noted in his book, the answer lies in the fact that there is very little evidence that Pliny actually saw the *p'p'r*-making process. Dr. Hassan Ragab, the founder of the Papyrus Institute in Cairo, did something more helpful than reading about Pliny's account, which was actually re-creating the process in the 1970s.

Dr. Ragab went on to do a great deal of research into the ancient methods of papyrus papermaking, and in 1979 earned a PhD from the University of Grenoble in the art and science of making papyrus paper; meanwhile he brought cuttings of plants from Sudan back to Cairo and started cultivating it in shallow, protected areas of the Nile River. His method of making paper was as close as possible to that described by Pliny and has given birth to many centers in Cairo, the delta, and Luxor where scenes of what might have taken place in ancient time in the papermaking centers of old Egypt are reenacted daily.

In modern times, one of the few working papyrus plantations in the world is the 500-acre swampy plot that was established by the artist Anas

Mostafa in el-Qaramous, a village in the eastern part of the Nile delta in the Sharqia region. Here Dr. Mostafa trained 200 villagers in the cultivation of the plant and the ancient method of papermaking.

The process begins with workers hauling in armfuls of green stems freshly cut from a nearby swamp, exactly as they did in ancient papermaking sites in Memphis, the delta, and Fayum. The sequence for collecting papyrus in the ancient swamps and plantations is well shown in a tomb painting (1430 B.C.) copied by Norman de Garis Davies,[6] which shows papyrus collectors assembling bundles destined for the makers of boats, rope, mats, and paper. In the drawing, the ancient artist also used the scene to show us the ages of man, from a lad on the left pulling papyrus stems into a papyrus skiff, to a gray-haired, paunchy fellow carrying a bundle of stems.

Making Papyrus Paper

1. Green stems are trimmed into pieces about 12 inches long. These are soaked in river water until they are peeled.

2. The tough skin peels easily, exposing the white pith of the inner stem. This pith is then sliced into thin strips with a razor blade.

3. The strips are squeezed to remove excess water then laid parallel, slightly overlapping, to form a sheet.

4. More strips are laid on top at right angles to the first layer. The two layered sheet is then rolled with a rolling pin.

5. The wet sheets are kept under pressure in a press until the papyrus is dry and the strips are fused into a dry sheet.

6. The dry sheets are burnished with a fine clay powder until the surface is smooth and ready to write on.

Making papyrus paper.

The next step after collecting the stems in the swamps is to cut off the tops, the flowering umbels, and the narrow upper stems. The remaining stems are then cut into foot-long pieces and left to soak in large basins of river water. Later they are taken up by another group of workers farther along the assembly line: the peelers. Since the stems are triangular in cross section, the tough skin on each flat side of the stem is easily peeled off with a razor or sharp knife, exposing the white pith of the inner stem. As the peelers work, the peels pile up until they are carried off to be woven into mats, sandals, small baskets, and all manner of handicrafts. The exposed white pith that remains is shaved into thin slices that are squeezed and pressed to remove excess water before they are laid out on a porous mat or matrix.[7] Laid parallel and overlapping slightly, the slices form a sheet. More strips are laid perpendicular and the two layers are rolled with a rolling pin or hammered with wooden mallets to flatten the sheets.

This squeezing or hammering forces water out of the sheet, provides a natural adhesive, and allows the sheets to dry faster. Bridget Leach, former papyrus conservator at the British Museum, pointed out that the natural sap contained in the plant aids the process of beating and pressing to form a sheet before drying. The pressure applied during this procedure fuses the cellulose in each layer together physically and chemically; similar to the way that modern paper is formed. This is yet another way in which papyrus paper resembles pulp paper.[8]

The wet sheets of papyrus paper are laid on linen and compressed between boards, then bound tightly and set aside to dry, usually stacked against some sunny wall in the papermakers' compound. Once dried, the presses are opened and the papyrus sheets are taken out to dry further. We now see a sheet of paper that can be used directly; or, if a finer quality is desired, it can be burnished with a fine clay powder until the surface is smooth.

At this point, the paper can be tested. According to Dr. Ragab, good papyrus paper is quite flexible. In addition to fingering the paper, high quality papyrus paper should be easy to bend, fold, tear, and must remain flexible. This is an indication that the natural juices that bind the sheet and keep it intact have been properly distributed throughout, a condition that only comes about if pressure is used while the sheet is fresh and still wet.

Once fashioned and properly pressed and dried it was very durable, so much so, Professor Lewis tells us, that in ancient and medieval times, papyrus books and documents had a usable life of hundreds of years. Pliny told of seeing papyrus documents that were 100 and 200 years old, and the Greek physician and philosopher Galen told of searching in books that were 300 years old. Papal documents up to 330 years old were handled in 1213 A.D. and there are references in the fourteenth century to papyrus documents from the reign of the Italian king Odoacer (476–493 A.D.).

How was this stability achieved? If there was any secret in the manufacture of papyrus paper it was that sufficient hammering with a wooden mallet, or rolling, or pressing during the early stage was essential. This allowed the strips to adhere to one another and the sheet to stand up to everyday wear and tear. Smoothing of the surface was not an absolute necessity, as it was perfectly easy to write on a freshly dried sheet as soon as it was made.

It should be noted that there are differences between the modern papyrus paper and ancient papyri, as pointed out by Adam Bülow-Jacobsen, former research professor at the University of Copenhagen. Ancient papyri show little or no signs of overlapping of strips. Since overlapping is not mentioned by Pliny, it may not be necessary. Bülow-Jacobsen also pointed out that the modern papyrus paper made in Siracusa, Sicily, though not strongly overlapped, is very soft and pliable; though it still lacks the feel of ancient paper, which is more like good-quality bond paper. On the other hand, modern paper made in Cairo and the delta, though it feels very much like the ancient paper, has marked overlapping, which the ancient material does not.[9]

After the dry sheets were removed from the presses, they could be joined together to form scrolls of twenty sheets (later referred to by the Romans as a *scapus.*) This was done using starch paste rather than glue, in order to preserve the flexibility of the roll. In the final stages of the assembly line in an Egyptian paper facility, large rolls 60 to 100 feet long were sometimes made up on special order. The joins were often so well-made that they have amazed researchers. How was it done? The secret is now out. All the right-hand edges of those sheets to be joined into a scroll were made with a strip missing. The result was a thinner joint once the paste was applied and the seam hammered or rolled. Professor Lewis thought it was astonishing that no one noticed for hundreds of years.[10]

Papyrus was a resource treasured by the kings of Egypt. The plant, and the paper made from it, was viewed as a gift from the gods directly to the pharaoh himself, and all his subjects benefitted. It allowed Egypt to be papermaker to the world for thousands of years while history was in the making.

> Centuries before Alexander's conquest had made the Greeks the masters of the country, Egypt had manufactured papyrus paper by a carefully guarded process . . . and . . . went on to supply the whole Roman Empire. What a wonderful invention, so light, portable and easy to record information on via a reed pen, compared to the more cumbersome or more expensive writing materials, such as stone and metal plates, wooden and clay tablets, or leather. (C. H. Roberts, 1963)

❧

After the roll or separate sheets were made, they were stacked or tied into bundles and sent off to Pharaoh's agent for export. What did the earliest papermakers receive in exchange for their work? Certainly not cash, as the first coinage in general use in the western world was not introduced until 700 B.C. Perhaps they received grain, jewelry, cloth, or other goods from the agents for the crown, or the priests of the temple who often owned and operated large estates and in general acted in the interest of Pharaoh. In Roman times, when money was in circulation, the papermaker was regularly employed and paid by an estate manager.

The question of cost has teased historians of papyrus paper for years. Was it cheap or dear? According to the well-known papyrologist, T. C. Skeat, late keeper of manuscripts at the British Library, this is purely a modern question that no ancient writer ever expressed an interest in. Whatever it cost, it was regarded as essential and so had to be accepted.[11] In order to further resolve the question, Skeat carried out a careful analysis of two sets of records taken from the extensive accounts and contracts written on papyrus and found in the Fayum region (Map 2). One record was from the estate belonging to Aurelius Appianus that was managed by Heroninos

(249–268 A.D.), the other came from a graveyard at Tebtunis (45–49 A.D.), southwest of Fayum.

After careful consideration, he concluded that a standard roll would have cost about two drachma (roughly the equivalent of two denarii).[12] Michael Affleck, librarian at the University of Queensland, tells us that *Xenia*, a very short book written by the Roman poet Martial on papyrus paper, could be bought for only four sesterces in 84 A.D., the equivalent of one denarius. Whereas a more decorative copy of his poems cost five times that. Affleck reckoned the average cost of a book roll to be eight sesterces, which covered the combined value of transcription and one roll of papyrus paper. This is close in value to the two denarii, or two drachmas earlier estimated by Skeat for a full roll of papyrus paper (made up of twenty sheets). A sesterce would be worth about $2.25 today, so the average cost of a book scroll would be about eighteen dollars, while a sheet would be about ninety cents.[13]

Skeat's results did not differ much from an earlier analysis by Lewis, who thought the purchase of papyrus was not likely regarded as an expenditure of any consequence for a prosperous Egyptian, Greek, or Roman. It would have fallen, rather, into the categories of "incidentals" or "petty cash." Lincoln Blumell, assistant professor of ancient scripture at Brigham Young University, makes it clear that for most persons above the social level of a peasant or an unskilled laborer, the use of papyrus for a letter was not regarded as expensive and was certainly not cost prohibitive. And in those days, when it came to letter writing, there was nothing like papyrus paper. Blumell tells us that of the just over 7,500 published letters from Egypt between the third century B.C. and seventh century A.D., about 90 percent are preserved on papyrus.[14]

This is not to say that papyrus paper was not carefully used. When corresponding with their paper suppliers, many an ancient maker of books used *ostraca*, pieces of shell, bones, or broken pottery, the ancient equivalent of Post-its. If a bookbinder would not spare a scrap of paper, ordinary citizens must have thought twice before using it for anything other than important records or correspondence.

And this attitude carried over to copyists who often drafted documents first onto wax tablets (*pugillare*) before transcribing them to papyrus paper.

Luckily, when writing on papyrus, if a mistake was made while washable ink was being used, it was easy enough to sponge it off and start again, a quality that allowed some to take advantage of the situation. Skeat cited the interesting case of Silvanus, a magister in Gaul in the time of Constantius II. Enemies of Silvanus tried to ruin him by obtaining some of his letters, washing off everything except his name and inserting treasonable material. The letters were then shown to the suspicious, paranoid emperor, Constantius II. (Were emperors ever otherwise?) Silvanus, fearing the worst, acted rashly. The forgery was discovered soon after by the imperial court, but too late, the damage was done: Silvanus had been assassinated in Cologne in 355 A.D.[15] To get around this, it was possible to use permanent ink that, once dried, was impossible to remove. Such ink often soaked into the papyrus so that the only way to change a typo was to white it out, which left a telltale mark.

Given the fact that paper was in demand and that in many cases it was also possible to scrub off the writing, why wasn't a major recycling industry taken up? Perhaps, as noted by Skeat, it was because of a sense of caution and suspicion, the same feeling that makes some of us think twice before using something that has been recycled today. In Skeat's view, secondhand scrolls were looked down upon as inferior material, fit only for such things as drafts or scribbling paper. Literary allusions also tell us that the reuse of papyrus rolls by a poet or writer was cause for contempt. Thus, although a number of papyri were reused, an even larger number (75–91 percent) were not and wound up on the rubbish heap after only one use (i.e. written only on one side). They were later found by the likes of Grenfell and Hunt, who noted that they were torn in half before being discarded—they were *not* left there by accident.

Ancient authors were also well aware that any unsuccessful book in those days would be consigned to the fish and grocery markets or the schoolroom as scrap.

TEN

A Gift from the Gods

The plants of Nile arise, a wood without leaves or branches, a harvest of the waters, the fair tresses of the marshes, plants full of emptiness, spongy, thirsty, having all their strength in their outer rind, tall and light, the fairest fruit of a foul inundation.

—Cassiodorus

When we think of modern paper manufacturing today, our thoughts turn to pine. Other plants such as eucalyptus or bamboo, or material such as linen or rag in the case of fine paper, are used in the paper manufacturing process. But the bulk of paper pulp produced in the world today is still derived from softwood pulp made from pine. A walk in a pine forest slated for paper production is a pleasant experience, providing a needle-carpeted, open, resin-scented environment, an environment in which it is even possible to camp or just sit and contemplate.

Not so with papyrus. A good example of how ugly an experience it can be was seen during the 1862 Baker expedition that went right through the enormous papyrus swamp of southern Sudan. Florence and Samuel Baker eventually carved a path through the swamp and achieved their goal: locating the exact course of the White Nile as it emerged from Lake Albert. Later known as Sir Samuel and Lady Florence, they never forgot their first encounter with papyrus. The swamp region they traversed, the Sudd, has remained virtually untouched since the day they left it; it is still a very difficult place to get around in.

A papyrus swamp in Africa.

In such a swamp, papyrus begins its growth on wet mud at the waters' edge where young rhizomes tend to grow over older ones; the whole mass of papyrus, along with a layer of peat, then spreads out over water with the plants rooted in a floating mat. This is possible because the plant is equipped with many air spaces in the stems that provide the necessary buoyancy. On large African lakes or along deep rivers, it will form substantial floating mats, with stems so tall (fifteen feet or more) that it is impossible to look over them unless on the deck of a steamer. Without a map, channel, or guide, it would be a difficult job to fight your way through a papyrus swamp; consequently very few people in the Western world really know what a normal papyrus plant looks like.

The morphology of papyrus is straightforward and typical for a sedge; each upright stem, or "culm," appears and grows upward from the tip of a horizontal stem, or rhizome. The upright stem expands at its top and spreads out into a large tuft of slim, flowering branches or umbels. The base of the stem is closely sheathed in scale leaves, and the umbel at the top of the stem is enclosed in scale-like bracts prior to opening. The stem, which is the part most often used in making boats, baskets, roof thatch, rope, paper, and other crafts, is triangular in cross-section, a distinctive feature that sets the sedges apart from grasses. Collectively, swamp grasses, grass-like plants, sedges, and rushes are all called reeds, and they are among the fastest growing vascular plant species. For example, a modern study of papyrus by a team of researchers on Lake Naivasha in Kenya showed that papyrus stems take only about six months to reach maturity and nine to twelve months to complete their life cycle.[1] The same study showed that papyrus swamps selectively harvested on a twelve-month cycle regenerate completely within the year.[2] In the process, the plant produces on average twenty-two tons of dry matter per acre annually, which ranks it among the highest and fastest producing ecosystems on earth. Reed marshes, for example, those made up of the grass Phragmites, or tropical seagrass beds, produce only twelve to sixteen tons per acre in comparison.

During the time when ancient Egyptian papyrus swamps were common in the delta and in the backwater or swampy regions along the Nile River, the management of swamp plantations in Egypt was a serious business. And that seems appropriate because Egypt during the reign of the Ptolemies was well-managed and economically strong; so much so that Rome was dying to get its hands on it. It is said that the famously rich kingdom was so high a prize that senators and emperors vied with one another to be the first to conquer it. Ptolemy II (known as Philadelphus 283–246 B.C.), even though he had two of his half-brothers murdered and married his own sister, was a superb manager, organizer, and leader. It is assumed that he would have taken an active interest in existing papyrus plantations and there is ample proof that he was mindful of the needs of the paper industry, especially any trade in book scrolls in Alexandria. Under his reign, the plantations, though perhaps not directly owned and operated by the state, would be carefully supervised by government agents.

Collecting papyrus stems for papermaking in a modern tourist plantation. City of Cairo in the background.

The Romans later improved on what he had begun, and in their time carried forward the Greek distinction between wild, or natural, swamps called *drymoi* (singular *drymos*), as opposed to the *helos papyrikon*, or papyrus plantation.

Among the *drymoi* a large one in Fayum particularly stands out, the Great Swamp mentioned by Lewis. Such a swamp would be used to supply village craftsmen, as well as commercial vendors and manufacturers with rope, thatch, canoes, skiffs, and mats. In addition, once Alexandria had developed into a thriving capital city, it, along with other Greek-influenced cities upriver and in Fayum, had baths that were modified to use straw and reeds,[3] an arrangement used elsewhere by the Romans in North Africa, where wood fuel was not easy to come by. The baths were in constant need of fuel, a need that grew even larger with time, so that large quantities of dry reeds were consumed daily.

Although other reeds from other marshes and swamps were available in the Egyptian wetlands, more than likely the easiest and most reliable source of reed would be dried papyrus stems from the *drymoi* where papyrus stems could be harvested and dried in sufficient quantities.

Some historians found it difficult to believe that a single plant species could deliver the quantities needed. In the 1911 edition of the *Encyclopedia Britannica*, an item appeared written by E. M. T.—Sir Edward Maunde Thompson, the first director of the British Museum. He was also the friend and mentor of Wallis Budge. He wrote, "it seems hardly credible that the Cyperus papyrus could have sufficed for the many uses to which it is said to have been applied and we may conclude that several plants of the genus Cyperus were comprehended . . ." He was writing at a time (after 1000 A.D.) when papyrus had disappeared from Egypt and well before the modern studies of the twentieth and twenty-first centuries that show the enormous rate of production that the plant is capable of. We now know that no other species was needed, papyrus was more than capable of providing for the needs of the people, as well as the bath-fire stokers and the papermakers on its own.

As time went on, there would be more and more pressure placed on these swamps even though they were being cultivated as cash crops. Later, with an increase in population and more demand for food crops, farmers were allowed to encroach on the wetlands and the papyrus swamps. At that point, papermakers were probably told to use the harvested stems more efficiently in order to meet production levels. This extended the life of the plant, but did not prevent its eventual demise, which happened in the last part of the first millennium A.D., when the rag paper of Arab manufacture came into its own and papyrus swamps were converted to agricultural land.

ELEVEN

The Monopoly

The technique of papyrus papermaking has always been a simple operation compared to, say, the construction of monuments and buildings; still it was a process successfully kept under wraps, and remained a closely guarded secret since the whole production was considered the property of the pharaohs. Following the arrival of Alexander the Great in Egypt, from 300 B.C. onwards, the royal ownership began to loosen under the Ptolemies. By that point, the royal family, though no longer controlling production, still exerted control over the distribution, sale, and taxation of papyrus paper. After that, the largest change came with the Roman takeover, when the old royal ownership disappeared completely and was replaced by private ownership. The papyrus swamps were now managed like any other agricultural land.[1] Over time, the Romans moved the title of some of the largest swamps into the emperor's *patrimonium* (a fund created to hold the private fortune and inheritance of the emperor's estate), at which point when the land and swamps were contracted out, the proceeds went to the imperial household.

Even when papermaking was privatized, the manufacturing process was not well publicized. Perhaps the manufacturers of paper wanted it that way, and were determined to keep it a trade secret. Even after Pliny published details of the process in 77 A.D. and supposedly papyrus paper could be made by anyone, there was still the issue of getting access to the raw material. As far as anyone in the Roman Empire was concerned, the paper was still only made in Egypt because that was the only place the plant grew in significant quantities.

In this way papyrus paper qualified as a full-blown monopoly and it remained so from 3000 B.C. until it disappeared in 1000 A.D. Compared to other well-known monopolies throughout world history, it was the clear winner. The longest maintained monopolies, such as the Thurn and Taxis family postal service in Europe (578 years); the Tang Dynasty salt commission in China (369 years); the British East India Company (274 years); Standard Oil in the USA (41 years) and DeBeers diamond monopoly (27 years), all pale in comparison. Four thousand years of uninterrupted and exclusive control over production is a clear winner that can never be topped. The rubber, coffee, cocoa, quinine, and banana empires of early days in the American tropics were all broken when rogue planters whipped seeds or cuttings of productive plants and started production elsewhere away from the mother plantations.

With papyrus paper, the only break in the export stream came when Ptolemy II is said to have stopped the export of papyrus paper in an attempt to stifle book acquisition in the city of Pergamum. That Anatolian city was fast becoming a center of Greek learning and stood in direct competition to Alexandria. But normally, production and export went forward inexorably; nothing prevented the flow of paper from the source to the seat of power in Rome, except the occasional riot or political disturbance in Egypt.

Pliny tells us that on one occasion during the reign of Tiberius (14–37 A.D.), papyrus paper tended to be in short supply, which led to the appointment of commissioners from the Senate to oversee its distribution, "otherwise daily life would have been in turmoil." This illustrates the largest disadvantage of such a monopoly, if the supply fails for any reason as it did on that occasion; chaos follows unless the product is rationed as it was in this case by the Roman Senate. To avoid this, there were several attempts to grow papyrus elsewhere[2] but although it grew, it never reached the high rate of production achieved in Egypt in ancient days.

Here then was the one plant in the history of the world powerful enough to stop the Roman Empire in its tracks. In this way, it ruled the world in the same fashion that King Cotton ruled the American South; the demand was met exclusively by the papyrus swamps of Egypt. Whoever controlled Egypt controlled the medium of choice. And it was a big business employing thousands of people, some highly specialized, for the different branches of the industry: cultivating and harvesting the plant, transporting the raw material to the factory, fabrication, sale, and shipment of the finished product.

Why did the paper industry work so well in Egypt? Perhaps because, behind the scenes, a papyrus paper cartel was in operation, as suggested by the historian Strabo in 18 A.D.: "Some persons intending to augment the revenue . . . in many places it (papyrus) is not allowed to be cultivated, and the price is enhanced . . . the revenue is indeed thus increased, though they injure the common use of the plant."[3]

Professor Lewis also saw evidence of a cartel in ancient Roman contracts where pressure was exerted that could only come from such an entity. He felt that only a papermaker's cartel would be able to hold down labor costs and harvest the plant so as to curtail production. The cartel could thus drive up the value of the paper crop, while limiting their liability in the contracts and so protect their income, yet keep the end-user cost of paper within reason.

The cartel must have found it an easy job to keep the price of paper at a profitable level, since from the beginning it cost almost nothing to make. Better yet, it was confined to Egypt. Some papyrus swamps were found in Sicily where a small amount of paper was made in Arabic times for the sultan. It also grew in the Jordan valley and presumably some paper could have been made in the area of the Dead Sea at the scriptorium at Khirbet Qumran. But, the major portion of paper came from the delta where the cartel set the price. And they did this in such a way that papyrus paper always sold below the price of parchment. Even in the third and fourth centuries when papyrus documents were being converted to parchment, papyrus was still two-and-a-half times cheaper.[4]

In the process of making money, the cartel convinced almost everyone for thousands of years that papyrus paper could only be made on the Nile, in their factories, from fresh stems—the growth and processing of which they controlled. That concept has carried forward even today. Thus, when surfing the Internet, you'll find thousands of videos of people making paper from papyrus, virtually all using thin fresh slices taken from papyrus stems, which have been grown in local botanic gardens or tourist plantations in Cairo or Sicily.

What is left unsaid is that if the green stems are harvested, and thin strips taken and dried, they can be used just as easily to make paper at a later date. This was discovered by the modern papermakers in Cairo and at el-Qaramous in the delta. They found that strips taken from fresh stems could be dried and stored for later use. This allowed them to make paper at their leisure, and it runs completely against the notion that only fresh strips from recently harvested plants would do.

The author examining papyrus strips being dried in Cairo.

The original idea was that the juice of the fresh plant was necessary to bind the strips to one another. Even Professor Lewis was convinced that dry stems were of no use in making papyrus paper. He of course was right, since once the stems have dried out they can't be easily sliced. The trick, however, is to take the slices while the stem is still fresh, then dry out the slices and save them, not the whole stems.

In reality, much of the paper made for the tourist trade in Egypt today is made from dry strips. It just happens that the fresh white slices shaved from bright-green stems are more photogenic, and to this day there is nothing like a straight razor being wielded by the shaky hand of a TV presenter to attract the attention of viewers. Dried slices are thus made in quantity and often they're found drying on mats in sunny courtyards. Once dried, they weigh almost nothing and can be baled and conveniently stored until needed or shipped. To make paper at some future date, one need only soak them and they're ready for use. As mentioned earlier, they are available on the Internet, and thus anyone can now make papyrus paper anywhere in the world.

One caution, when using such dried material, more than the usual pressure is required to ensure good adhesion. The ghosts of the papyrus cartel are probably turning over in their graves as I write this, but it seems possible that early papermakers may have known about this method. If so, it would mean two things: that dry strips could be used to tide the ancient papermaker over during a time of crisis and that the papermaker could have had slices harvested and dried in places where labor and papyrus were abundant and cheap, such as in the Nubian swamps of Sudan. Papyrus grows there as well now, as it did in ancient days. The papermakers could have shipped the dried strips north or anywhere else to supplement local papyrus production, say during times of riots when the harvest and processing of local plants would be difficult.

There is no evidence that dry strips were ever used in this way in the old days. Most historical accounts, like the modern videos on YouTube, consider only fresh material, but the possibility is there that dry strips could have acted as a reserve.

One last point regarding the making of papyrus paper in modern times. It is made in large quantities as a souvenir item for the tourist trade in Egypt in Cairo, and the technique used is that developed by Dr. Hassan Ragab, which he elaborated in his PhD thesis. He found that the main reason for bonding between layers is physical, rather than chemical, and occurs during pressing. Despite evidence of starch adhesives and natural gums, Ragab felt that the partially cut cells of one strip mesh and interlock with cells of another strip. Under pressure these strips are forced to merge, their surfaces forming a dovetail-like join at the cellular level. Upon drying, the interlocked tissues undergo appreciable shrinkage and form an even tighter bond, assuring the adherence of the strips. Consequently, in his technique, the dry strips are preferred. If fresh strips are used they would have to be soaked and rolled several times over in order to squeeze out much of the plant sap. His method therefore depends more on pressure to seal the strips into a final sheet rather than natural glues. If natural sap or juices are present they simply enhance the process. The use of thin strips is one of the major differences between papyrus paper and modern rag paper or the early laid paper of the Chinese, which are both made of pulp, not strips, and perhaps led the Victorian Egyptian scholar, Samuel Sharpe, to refer to papyrus in 1862 as "natural paper" versus pulp paper.[5]

❧

One of the few places where papyrus grows outside of Africa is Sicily. It is said to have appeared suddenly on the island, but exactly when and how is not clear. Everyone, of course, is ready with a good answer, most often wrapped in some very imaginative material. The earliest theory of its introduction involves King Hiero II of Syracuse, who is said to have received a gift of plants from Ptolemy II. This is a theory that was subsequently rejected by Lewis, who labeled it a "ghost that refused to be laid" because it has no basis in fact.[6] Also it is unlikely that Ptolemy II, even in a generous mood, would have given up the rootstock of one of the mainstays of the Egyptian economy. Consider the history of other valuable natural products, like cloves and rubber, all closely guarded in their original areas of production in the tropics. One could be shot or hanged if seeds of these trees were found in one's possession.

Even if not true, the theory of Ptolemy's gift remains a very attractive story. However, if I were to take a wild stab at the same speculation, I would choose Archimedes over Hiero II, since Archimedes is the more likely candidate for several reasons. Although he was born in Syracuse in 287 B.C., he went off to receive an early training in Alexandria before returning to live in Sicily from 230 to 212 B.C. He must have already known all about papyrus and the swamps of Egypt, especially those of the delta, and he would certainly have known about paper manufacture and how to organize a papermaking operation outside of Egypt.

Toward the end of his life, together with his friend Hiero II, he played an important role in the development of Syracuse and helped improve defenses during the Roman siege in 214 B.C. At that time, Archimedes applied himself to several of the inventions used to repel the Romans, which helped buy time for the city. The Sicilians held out for two years, but in the end, the Romans took the city and killed Archimedes in the process. The man of "eureka" fame, the same person who invented the water-lifting screw that was so useful for irrigation in Egypt, the catapult that aided in the defense of Syracuse, the pulleys and aerial hooks used to upend ships, and the mirrors used to reflect and concentrate sunlight to the degree that the Sicilians set fire to Roman ships as they sat in the harbor—to such a person the introduction and propagation of papyrus, along with the start-up of a local paper industry, would have been child's play.

It is also intriguing that Archimedes vigorously kept up old contacts in Egypt, and maintained a significant library that must have used lots of papyrus paper. If and when the thought crossed such an active and agile mind, it would have been an easy matter to arrange for cuttings of the rhizomes to be brought to Syracuse, either with or without the approval of the Ptolemies. Once established, within a few years the plants would be ready for use. But there is no proof, and in fact there is at least one large problem with this version of the "ghost"; historical records show that papyrus was first reported from the Palermo region, and only later in the seventeenth century was it said to have been transplanted to Syracuse and beyond.

Another theory is that there was no need to bring papyrus to Sicily at all. According to Professor Luigi Malerba of Bologna, the papyrus in Sicily is a local variety or subspecies of *Cyperus papyrus*, and therefore could have established itself in Sicily on its own from papery wind- or bird-borne seeds. Assuming it did, the problem then arises as to why wasn't it reported earlier in the history of the island.

Another "ghost" concerns the Roman Catholic Church, and the suggestion that its popes had papyrus brought to Sicily in order to have it close to hand. In the old days, the Holy See used considerable amounts of papyrus, and it is said that they wanted to break the monopoly of the infidel Egyptians, and later that of the equally infidel Arabs.

It is interesting that the first indication that papyrus was growing in Sicily came from Pope Gregory the Great, who in a sixth century letter mentioned that it was growing in Palermo in 599 A.D. Much later in 972 A.D., during the Muslim occupation, a merchant from Baghdad named Ibn Hawqal visited the island and described a marshy area near Palermo where "there are swamps full of papyrus . . . Most . . . is twisted into ropes for ships, and a little is used to make paper for the sultan, just enough for his needs."

From this, Napthali Lewis thought the plant could have been brought to Sicily by Arab merchants. It would then have provided a source of paper later used by the papal and Arab chancelleries. This would have allowed them to continue writing on papyrus long after its manufacture ceased in Egypt. According to one land lease in Sicily, at least one swamp was cultivated and used to produce revenue in the twelfth century, and papyrus was growing in Palermo as late as the sixteenth century.

Today in the Museo del Papiro in Siracusa, Corrado Basile produces a fine grade of paper using locally grown papyrus. He does not employ extensive soaking and rolling, and yet produces a very good quality papyrus paper. In fact, it is said to be as flexible and as smooth as the sheets produced in Egypt, though, according to some, it still lacks the feel of the antique material.[7]

TWELVE

Growing and Managing Papyrus for Paper

As mentioned earlier, the largest change after the Roman takeover of Egypt was privatization; many swamps were owned outright and the production contracted out as the swamps became managed resources like any other agricultural land. Three contracts reviewed by Napthali Lewis exist from Roman times and show how papyrus was managed as a crop.

The first was an application from a man named Harthotes in 26 A.D. to harvest papyrus in the Fayum region. The interesting thing about this request is that Harthotes was seeking permission to harvest from a wild swamp, a *drymos*.

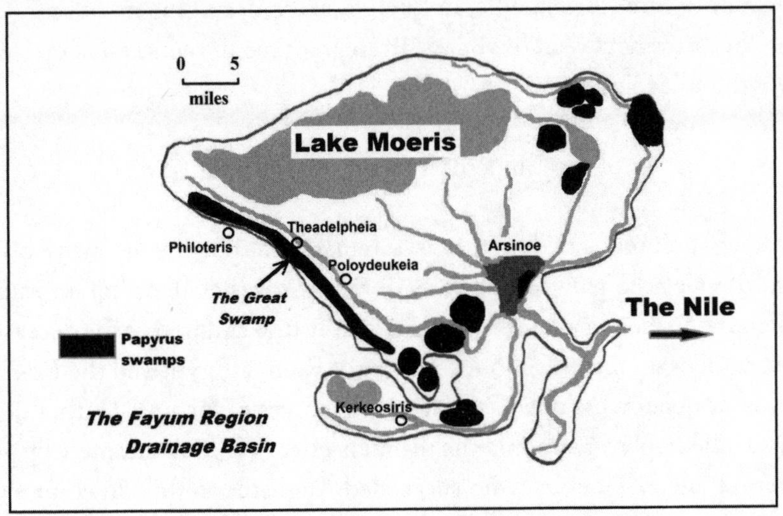

MAP 3: *The Great Swamp in the Fayum Region (after original map from Univ. Leuven Fayum Project, courtesy of Prof. Willy Clarysse).*

Harthotes if successful, would have access to an enormous wetland called the Great Swamp (Map 3). It was twenty miles long and stretched from the ancient Egyptian town of Philoteris northeast to the village of Theoxenis. Since it was about a half mile wide, it amounted to ten square miles or 6,400 acres. His application reads as follows:[1]

From: Harthotes, son of Marres.

To: Aphrodisius, son of Zoilus, contractor of the papyrus holdings of Julia Augusta and the children of Germanicus Caesar.

If I am granted the concession to gather papyrus from the vicinity of Theoxenis to the borders of Philoteris—i.e. reeds and papyrus from the drymos—and weave mats and sell them in any villages of the nome I choose for (the remainder of) the 12th year of Tiberius Caesar Augustus, I undertake to pay four silver drachmas and fifteen obols together with the customary expenses, additional charges, and receipt fees, all of which I will

> pay in three instalments, in Epeiph, Mesore, and the month of Sebastos next year,* if you see fit to grant me the concession on the foregoing terms.
>
> Farewell.
>
> Year 12 of the Emperor Tiberius Caesar Augustus.

Lewis pointed out that this is a remarkable document on its own, regardless of the papyrus harvest, in that it gives evidence of an estate belonging to members of the imperial family (the children of the deceased Germanicus). For the economic history of Roman Egypt and the Roman empire it documents one of the family's sources of income. Germanicus was a major player among the Roman elite. He was adopted by his paternal uncle, Tiberius, who succeeded Augustus as Roman emperor a decade later. He was also the maternal grandfather of Nero. His children, who are indicated as the owners of the Great Swamp included Caligula, Emperor of Rome, and Agrippina the Younger, Empress of Rome. Another owner of the Swamp was Julia Augusta, who is none other than Livia, the widow of Augustus. She was given the name Julia on the death of her husband and was deified by her grandson Claudius, of whom we will hear more in the next chapter.

Another significant detail is the small sum of money offered for the right to gather wild-growing reeds and papyrus stalks over a twenty-mile stretch of marshland. Four silver drachma and fifteen obols would be about fifty-eight dollars today. Presumably there were other swamps in the Fayum region that were used by the papermakers, who paid much more for the right to harvest, as we will see in the other contracts.

The two other contracts describe the workings of plantations, one from 14 B.C. and a later one from 5 B.C. They deal with swamps in the delta that were kept as plantations and illustrate the difference between protected and cosseted swamps and those left in the wild state. The stems of the protected plant were generally superior as well as homogeneous in size. In order to insure that plant stems from the plantations remained in premium condition, Lewis noted that "a whole battery of provisions is clearly

* Months of the Egyptian civil calendar, corresponding to July, August and September.

aimed at maintaining the productivity of the plantation and the quality of the product. Thus, the lessees are obliged to cultivate the plantation in its entirety, neglecting no part of it. Again, they may not sublet but must see to the operation themselves. They must use the proper tools and methods, and must maintain the waterways against blockage or deterioration." Pasturing and watering of animals, common in the wild swamps, was not permitted in the plantations, since the animals would inevitably trample the tall stalks and probably eat the young shoots.

Under the contract, "Woven products could be made from the wild growth . . . but the prime plants . . . destined no doubt for paper-making, were too valuable to be wasted on such inferior uses . . . the bulk of the production was to be cultivated to maturity and harvested at full growth."

He also found the contracts interesting because of the clauses fixing the going rate for hired labor, which was made up of free men rather than slaves, thus eliminating competition for manpower. Lewis pointed out that the paper factories were able to operate twelve months a year because the papyrus plant was harvested year-round. Contracts showed that harvest went on in one case from June to August; in another, daily from June to November; while the lessees of another plantation agreed to pay a rent of 250 drachmas a month in the six months from September to February ($2,250 in modern terms), and more than double that amount in the other six months.

What did they get for their money? In the earlier contract a husband and wife, lessees of a *helos papyrikon*, a proper plantation, acknowledge a loan of 200 drachmas ($1,800) to be repaid a drachma a day; and in lieu of interest on the loan they would deliver to the owner each day, and sell to him at less than the market price, a portion of their daily harvest of papyrus stalks, up to a six-month total of 20,000 one-armful loads and 3,500 six-armful loads of papyrus stalks. This averages out to be some 200 sizeable bundles of stalks daily! The owners could then resell or use this papyrus "interest" at a large profit.

In harvesting, as depicted on the walls of Egyptian tombs, the stalks were pulled up from the rooted base and tied into sheaves, which people then carried away on their backs or in boats. Under the terms of the contracts, Lewis noted that at the end of the first century B.C. papyrus stalks were delivered and marketed in units designated as one-armful and six-armful loads, "a detail which suggests very strongly that the techniques and practices of papyrus harvesting had changed little if at all through the ages."

As to the total harvest, since the above 200 bundles from the contracted swamp were only about 10 percent, a rough estimate of what was taken from the swamp daily would be about 2,000 bundles or about eight tons dry weight. And this was only one of many swamps throughout the country.

In combination, these three documents tell us that from March onward, the yield of papyrus stalks increased, with June through August constituting the major harvest period of the year. The explanation lies, no doubt, in the hydrology of the region. From September to March, the floodwaters of the Nile would be at their highest levels and access to the plants would be more difficult, requiring the use of boats.

Obviously all of the management and production efforts by the Romans were done for a purpose, to provide papyrus paper for a market that continued to expand throughout their empire and beyond. Luckily, they were dealing with a very productive plant.[2]

Professional Papers of All Types and for All Reasons

The amount of paper made from this production was enormous, reaching a peak during the Roman era. By that time, the copying and acquisition of manuscripts went on at major centers of learning. In Alexandria during the reign of Ptolemy II great importance was assigned to the collection of scrolls for the Royal Library, but even this massive undertaking represented only a small portion of documents produced in the world. Under the Ptolemies, books were possibly produced for export along with other goods,[3] and during all of this, some papyrus paper was recycled. Typically, when a scroll was used for the first time, it was written on using the inner surface, or the recto. Once it was no longer needed and not earmarked for the rubbish heap, the scroll could be traded in for one reason or another, or it could be used again by writing on the outside, or the verso. If gums or resin smoke had been incorporated into the ink, the original writing was left because it could only be erased with difficulty. Scraping or scratching the surface could not be done easily without ripping or weakening the paper. One advantage of parchment was that its tougher sheets could be scraped with impunity, which is why it came to be used as palimpsests for school lessons in the Middle Ages, these were the forerunners of the schoolboy slate.

But quite often, the ink used on papyrus was washable, which made the job easier and brings up an interesting point. There was an early belief that drinking the water or beer used to wash away the writing would impart that same knowledge to the drinker! The proof of this theory lies in the story of an early Egyptian prince, who wrote out a copy of the *Book of Magic* by the god Thoth. He then washed the pages with beer, drank the book and captured the magic, or so we are told by the Scottish Egyptologist Reverend James Baikie.[4] In those days, "digesting" a book obviously had a direct meaning.

Even after being written on several times over, old papyrus paper was still in demand for making "cartonnage," a papier-mâché-like material used for making cases, small boxes, or even mummy cases and funereal masks. Since the paper was softened but still used as sheets, not pulped as in papier-mâché, whole sheets could be recovered by soaking the cartonnage and then teasing it apart.

The most famous of these sheets so far are those recovered by Sir Flinders Petrie while digging among Ptolemaic tombs at Gurob in 1889–90. He found mummy wrappings, breast-pieces, casings, and even sandals molded out of previously inscribed papyrus paper. From these items he retrieved, many were important papyri. Eventually published as the "Flinders Petrie Papyri," they were dated from 250–225 B.C. and proved to be of great interest, for they represented some of the oldest Greek manuscripts known up to that time.[5] Mostly an assortment of legal and official documents, wills, official correspondences, accounts and private letters, they also included literary works. Fragments containing Plato's *Phaedo*, lost portions of the last act of a Euripides play, *Antiope*, and even fragments from the *Iliad* of Homer. They fascinated the public and also opened the eyes of other Egyptologists to a previously untapped source of ancient papyri.

The practice of making papyrus paper cartonnage continued through the Roman period when the style of mummy decoration changed and linen again became the preferred medium, especially for headpieces.

In the end many scrolls, loose pages, and scraps eventually found their way to the town dump. Some were uncovered in the heaps of papyri found in 1897–1907 by Grenfell and Hunt. It is estimated that over 70 percent of all the literary papyri so far discovered came from their efforts. But, of the many thousands excavated, only about 10 percent were literary, the remainder were documents, codes, edicts, registers, official correspondence, census returns, tax assessments, petitions, court-records, sales, leases, wills, bills, accounts, inventories, horoscopes, and private letters, which, though humble, have helped generations-worth of scholars piece together the social fabric of ancient Egypt and the early Roman Empire. This proves the adage that even the humblest receipt or letter has value when it is millennia old! It goes from garbage to priceless overnight.

THIRTEEN

The Emperor and the Lewd Papermaker

By the first century A.D., papyrus paper was available throughout the Roman Empire, a market that consisted of the area stretching from Hadrian's Wall in the northern wilds of Caledonia, east to the dry karst plateaus of Cappadocia and the Caspian Sea, south to the lush valley of the Nile, and west to Lixus in the deserts of Mauretania. An empire of over two million square miles surrounding the Mediterranean (*Mare Nostrum*, "our Sea") and comprising a population of almost 100 million people, it had an enormous daily demand for food, drink, and paper. To make things easier, the Romans simply made Egypt a province. In so doing they were formalizing a long-standing arrangement. Egypt had been a major supplier of grain for many years. But even though Egypt was now a province, it was still a major trading partner.

MAP 4: *The Roman Empire in the 1st century (Wikipedia).*

In exchange for luxury imports and raw materials such as gold coins, glassware, olive oil, wool, purple fabric, metal weapons, and tools, Egypt exported gold, linen, glass, painted pottery, papyrus paper, and rope.[1] For years Egypt also sent grain, which fed the ports, cities, and populace of Italy, but grain shipments were essentially a tax in kind sent to Rome instead of money.[2] The amounts rose to more than 100,000 metric tons per year under the first emperor, Augustus.[3]

For many items other than grain, the export business was a two-way street and thrived on finished products in preference to raw materials. Egyptian exporters saw it as an opportunity to export value-added items, a practice that goes on in many countries today as well as it did in ancient times.

The first instance I saw of the value-added principle in action was in Ghana in the 1980s when I was consulting on the environmental impacts of a very expensive dam. Aluminum ore was locally available in quantity and the new hydroelectric facility near Accra was destined to be used to provide the power to smelt the ore. But to make exports competitive and profitable, economists on the project suggested it would be better to export improved or finished products. Instead of exporting ingots, they thought Ghana would be better off exporting aluminum pots and pans.

When papyrus paper left Egypt in sheets or rolls bound for the Roman markets, it represented a marvelous example of the value-added principle. Papyrus paper needed little or no input, unlike grain that was sent raw to be ground into flour by the Roman mills, gold that needed to be refined and recast, or glass and linen that required much initial work, and in the case of producing glass, pottery, and refined gold, fuel was needed in a country where wood was scarce. The kilns and furnaces in Egypt often used chaff, waste from grain milling, dried papyrus stems, and as a last resort local bushes and stunted trees from arid regions.[4]

In the case of paper, it was a finished product that was cheap to make and used local resources that were self-sustaining. It was also a product that was kept under close watch by a cartel of plantation owners who harvested year-round and kept the paper factories operating twelve months a year.[5]

Under Roman administration, Egyptian papermakers were subjected to strict quality controls as paper was now graded against standards set by Rome. The cartel rose to the occasion and produced whatever was necessary, from the high-quality paper of the imperial grades down to the lowest form used as wrapping paper (Table 1). They were so successful through the years that it was even suggested that Firmus, a Moor ruler in Muretania who set himself up as an imperial pretender in 273 A.D. (a position from which he was later deposed), might have been heavily invested in the Egyptian paper trade.[6]

By the time Augustus had taken over the Roman Empire in 27 B.C., the papermaking industry needed to be reorganized and standardized. For thousands of years, Egyptian papermakers had made paper in all sorts of lengths and widths. According to Jaroslav Černý, former professor of Egyptology at Oxford, the papyrus rolls of the earlier dynasties in Egypt were about 12½ inches (32 centimeters) in height, which was the dimension that remained constant; similar to the case when you buy wallpaper where the standard dimension is referred to as the height. The "length" will vary depending on where the roll is cut. With papyrus paper, since the rolls were made of twenty sheets, the width or length of a 12½ inch roll would be about 160 inches. This provided plenty of space for most common writing tasks. If this fell short, paper sheets could be added on as needed. Often the ancient rolls that were 12½ inches in height were sliced into four segments providing four rolls for office use, each 2¼–3½ inches in height and 160 inches long. For literary use, the roll cut in half provided two long rolls, each 6¼ inches in height.[7]

Table 1. Grades of papyrus paper in common use during the Roman period, based on Pliny. Ranked by quality and width of the sheet.* (width of paper in parentheses assumes one *digiti* = 0.74 in.)

1. *Charta Augusta* the best quality formed from the middle and broadest strips of the plant and named in flattery of the Emperor Augustus. But because it was too porous it was ill suited for literary or business use and so was reserved for correspondence. (9.5")

2. *Charta Livia* the next best grade, named in honor of his wife. (8")

3. *Hieratica* formerly the best quality but still considered a good grade of paper. (6.6")

4. *Charta Amphitheatrica* named after the principal place of its manufacture, the amphitheater of Alexandria. (6.6")

5. *Charta Fanniana* papyrus paper re-worked in the factory of a certain Fannius in Rome. Made from the *Amphitheatrica* from Egypt, it was rolled or compressed to make it thinner and so increase its size by an inch. (7.6")

6. *Saitica* which took its name from the city of Sais. (8.7")

7. *Taeniotica* named from the place of manufacture near Alexandria, of uncertain size it was sold by weight. (4-5")

8. *Charta Emporetica* the common wrapping and packing paper. (4")

9. *Charta Claudia* a special paper made in the reign of the Emperor Claudius. (11.5")

10. *Macrocollon* quality paper equal in grade to *hieratica* but much larger sheets. (18.7")

* *Anon., 1911. Papyrus. Encyclopedia Britannica (http://penelope.uchicago.edu).*

Table 1. Grades of papyrus paper in common use during the Roman period, based on Pliny. Ranked by quality and width of the sheet.

With the founding of the empire, the Romans defined the best-quality paper as a sheet appropriately called, *charta augusta*[8] that was said by Pliny to be 9½ inches wide (he never mentioned height). A more diminutive sheet, *charta livia*, one inch shorter, was named after the emperor's skillful, unpretentious wife, Livia, part owner of the Great Swamp in Fayum.

Augustus had many things on his mind in the early days of his realm. He was a busy man embarking on a large program of reconstruction and social reform. Did he know or care about papyrus paper? He was a patron of Virgil, Horace, and other leading poets and interested in ensuring that his image was promoted throughout the empire, thus it is certain that he took an active interest in statues, coins, and perhaps enjoyed the fact that the best paper of his time bore his name.

His stepson, Tiberius, the second emperor, must have acquainted himself with the details of making papyrus paper, since in his time the Senate called attention to supply problems with papyrus paper. Tiberius was very much interested in libraries and thus would have had concerns over the paper that filled them. He built the fourth imperial library as a tribute to his stepfather who died in 14 A.D. The library was in the Temple of the Deified Augustus next to the Augustinian palace on the Palatine Hill. Tiberius also created the position of national librarian, the *procurator bibliothecarum*, and appointed Tiberius Iulius Pappus to the post to oversee all the emperors' libraries.[9, 10]

Claudius, the fourth in succession, seems to have had less interest in libraries, but more in writing. He was a rare ancient scholar who could write about the new empire as well as obscure antiquarian subjects. He even proposed reforming the Latin alphabet with the addition of new letters. Since he wrote copiously throughout his life, including Etruscan and Carthaginian histories, he must have been well aware of the deficiencies in *charta augusta,* the paper that, until then, was considered the best paper bar none. It did not please him; he was upset by what he thought was the high degree of transparency. The paper was so thin the ink showed through. Lastly the sheets were too small.

He thus directed the papermakers in Egypt to produce a paper that was larger in size and thicker. They responded with a two-ply paper that had a groundwork made of second-quality strips over which were laid strips of first quality. In so doing, they produced a paper that was the best papyrus paper of Claudius's day. Another advantage was that it could be written on on both sides, which suggests it had perhaps been polished on the verso by rubbing with pumice stone or a piece of bone or ivory.

Claudius must have been justly proud of this accomplishment. He had commissioned a paper grade famous enough to be placed on Pliny's list, even though the list did not appear until after Claudius's unexpected death. On that list, which appeared in 79 A.D. after Pliny himself had died from asphyxiation following the eruption of Vesuvius, the ten categories were ranked by quality and width.[11] In modern terms, if twenty sheets of 8½ by 11 inch standard bond paper of today were joined in a typical roll, the result would be a continuous piece of paper fourteen feet long that would still only be eleven inches in height. Under Pliny's system it would perhaps be designated *charta moderna*.

Once Claudius's paper was launched, the great paper storehouses of Rome, the *horrea charteria*,[12] would be continuously resupplied with a standard product that would satisfy anyone. But, about the same time, another paper appeared on the market: *charta fanniana*, which rivaled the new *claudiana* because it was just as good, but cheaper. Also, it was the first major paper product ever made outside of Egypt since the beginning of recorded time. No mean feat.

The man who accomplished this was Quintus Remmius Palaemon, called Fannius, a former weaver and slave and later a freedman. He became one of the best-known teachers of his time and in the process, was flaunted as the poster boy of self-improvement.

It seems that as a slave, when he was sent to school with his charges, the children of his master's house, he acquired the rudiments of learning while sitting around waiting to take them home. He soon developed powers of narrative, a style in speaking, and a mastery of poetry, enough so that he became the equivalent of, say, a high school or college English teacher in today's world.[13] After being freed, he was considered one of the most desired teachers of his day. He opened a popular school and managed his private estate with such care that he became a wealthy man.

His largest failings were referred to by the author Suetonius as his "unbridled licentiousness in his commerce with women," and his weakness for "foul indecency."[14] So steeped was he in luxury that he bathed several times a day and he was infamous for his habit of "mouthing" every man he met. All this turned Tiberius and later Claudius against him. They thought he should not be trusted with the education of boys or young men. But he caught everyone's fancy by his remarkable memory and his readiness of speech. The Greek form of his name *Palaemon* meant "the honey eater," which the Romans thought just about summed him up.

He reminded me of several high school and college English teachers I knew who seemed to either know everything about life from real experience or from what they had read (you never knew which), and as a result they took on racy reputations that they may not have deserved.

Was Fannius really that bad? After thinking about all those biographies, films, books, comics, and videos of degenerate Romans high and low throughout history (the names Nero and Caligula come immediately to mind), Fannius's bathhouse antics, kissing males and lewd behavior would seem bland in comparison. It has also been said that he was the object of a smear campaign by Suetonius.[15]

Anyway, Fannius was no fool and he obviously knew his way around. For example, he started a shop selling secondhand clothes for which his experience as a weaver must have been of great help. And soon he had a business empire of his own and an entree into the schools and the writing life, all of which involved papyrus paper. Perhaps his ears perked up when he heard that Emperor Claudius had called for a new type of paper, and with confidence, he probably said, "I can do that."

What was he thinking of? He was not only taking on an emperor, but one that had all but called him a pervert. This could have been a match-up made for reality TV: Fannius, the macho-driven, self-made, wealthy, Donald Trump-like entrepreneur faces the royal emperor, Claudius, who sometimes lunched with plebeians, but was thought to be bloodthirsty, cruel, overly fond of gladiatorial combat and executions, and very quick to anger.

Could Fannius do it? He must have known, perhaps from his days as a weaver, that cloth and paper were sometimes better thought of as living things, because, unlike bricks and mortar, they could be changed, gussied up, even made over until they were unrecognizable.

The old bonnet that gained a second life because of a few artfully placed feathers, or a shawl changed by a dye job was what he had in mind. In the case of papyrus paper, he knew that there was still a lot that could be done even after the paper left Egypt. Perhaps he discovered by experiment, as I did, that papyrus paper soaked overnight becomes quite soft and pliable. It can then be rolled with a rolling pin until it becomes a very thin sheet, thin enough to read through. In my case, I took a piece of modern papyrus paper made in Cairo, cut it into a square exactly 7½ by 7½ inches, soaked it, and rolled it, and within a short period of time found it had expanded to over 8½ inches square, and by then it was thin enough to read the cover of a gourmet food magazine through.

Papyrus paper after rolling while wet lying on a magazine (left), right same, paper after a third layer was added.

Then I soaked up some dry slices, also obtained from Cairo via the Internet, and added a layer to the thin sheet. In adding the new strips, I cut them to the newly increased size, 8½ inches, and did not overlap them. After more pressing, rolling, and malleting I had a three-ply sheet of new paper. And because I had added the new layer in a horizontal fashion (as in the recto side of the original two-ply sheet) I could now write easily on both sides.

Pliny never told us exactly how Fannius did it, but Lewis suggested that a correct reading of what Pliny did say implies that Fannius started with a more common, cheaper grade of Egyptian paper, *charta amphitheatrica*, and added a third layer after making it thinner.[16] In so doing, Fannius would simply have been doing in his workshop in Rome what was being done on occasion in ancient Egypt when a special, high-quality paper was needed. For example, the Papyrus of Ani and that of Greenfield, according to Wallis Budge, were made of three-ply papyrus paper.[17] And, if it was good enough for Scribe Ani, it would also serve Fannius and the rest of the Roman Empire, including Claudius Caesar.

By the time Pliny's list appeared, Fannius, like Claudius, had passed on; but by then Fannius had entered the ranks of emperors, at least to the level of Augustus and Claudius, as namesake for a type of paper. Despite what Suetonius had said about him, he had finally gained a place in history.

FOURTEEN

Taking on the World—and Leaving a Legacy

A wonderful product in truth is this wherewith ingenious Memphis has supplied all the offices in the world.

—Cassiodorus

What was the Roman statesman, Cassiodorus thinking about when he wrote that? The first thing that comes to mind was that he was just stating the obvious that in those ancient days all offices of the world were supplied with paper from Memphis, the once-capital of Egypt. In modern times this is the equivalent of saying that the city of St. Louis, a city on the banks of a mighty river, and surrounding

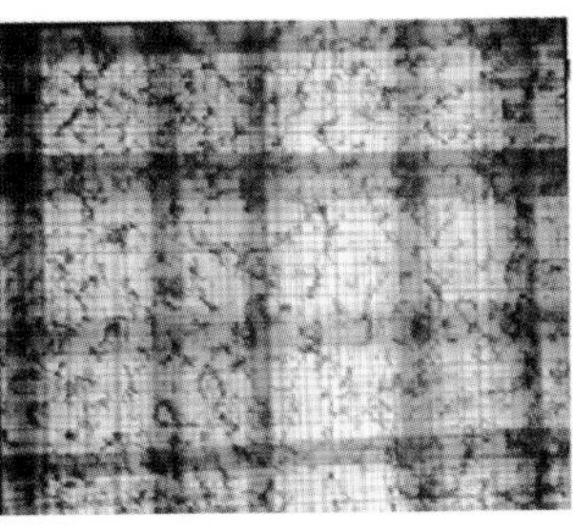

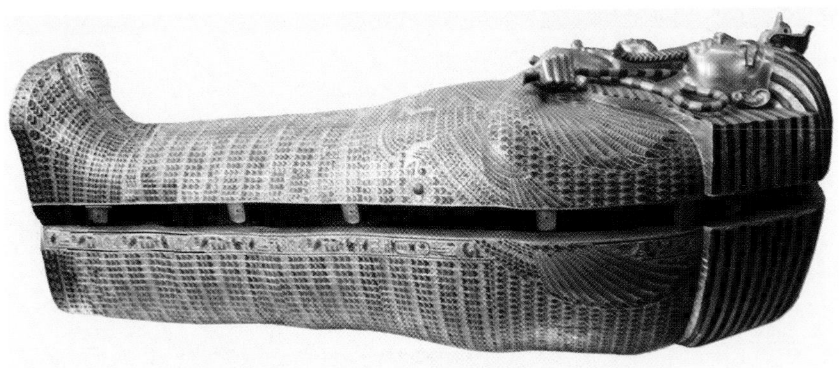

TOP LEFT: Ancient papyrus paper, 1075–945 B.C. TOP RIGHT: Newly made papyrus paper left, backlit on the right (Notice overlaps of strips of pith). CENTER: Book of the Dead of Nebqed, a scribe during the reign of Amenophis III (1353 B.C.), Thebes. BOTTOM: New Kingdom Rishi Coffin covered with drawings of feathers and wings.

TOP: The Field of Reeds from the Papyrus of Ani showing the winding, watery passage through a heavenly papyrus swamp. CENTER, LEFT AND RIGHT: Modern papyrus swamps in Botswana and S. Sudan. BOTTOM: Collecting papyrus from a swamp, Tomb of Puyemra, Thebes 1400 B.C.

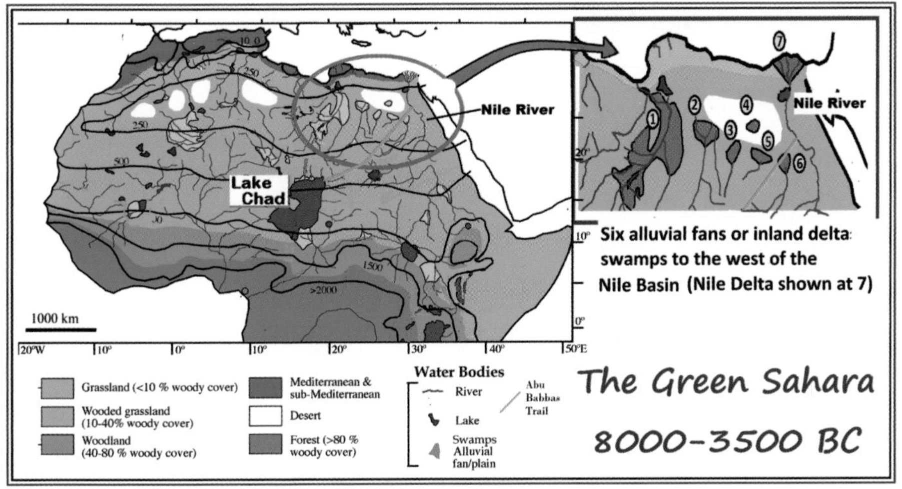

ABOVE: MAP A A vegetation map of the Sahara in prehistoric days 8000-3000 B.C. showing the "fans" or swamps in the region west of the Nile Basin. BELOW LEFT: A papyrus scroll being read in ancient times. The scroll is 20 pages long. BELOW RIGHT: Virgil reading his Aeneid to Augustus and Octavia.

ABOVE LEFT: Harvesting papyrus stems for the tourist paper trade in modern day Cairo. ABOVE CENTER: Cutting a thin strip from a fresh papyrus stem. ABOVE RIGHT: Scroll,replica copy of an Egyptian Book of the Dead. BELOW: Assembling a scroll from sheets of papyrus paper. BOTTOM: Reading from a papyrus paper scroll.

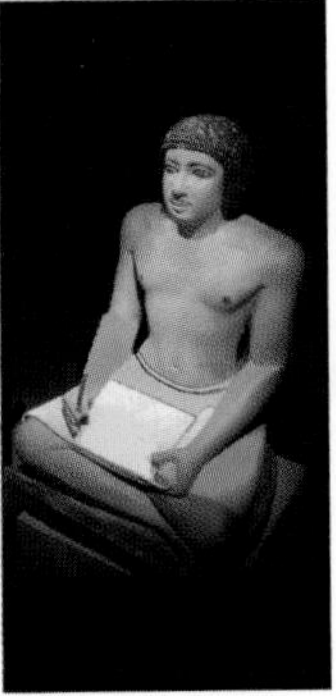

TOP LEFT AND CENTER: A young scribe, no doubt from a well-to-do family, shown in a tomb painting 1350 B.C. offering the deceased a commemorative scroll. He carries his pen holder under his arm while a large bag of scribal equipment sits at his feet. On right is a more traditional pose of a scribe at work. TOP RIGHT: Facade of the Library of Celsus an ancient Roman building in Ephesus, Anatolia, now part of Selçuk, Turkey. CENTER: Replica ancient pen holder and reed pens. Two wells for red and black ink. BELOW: Papyrus book trade–late 48 B.C.–1450 A.D.

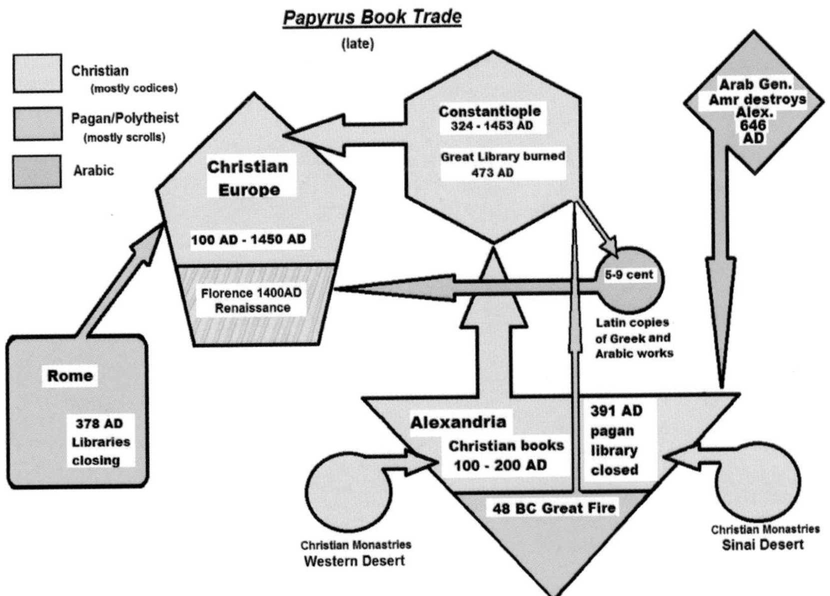

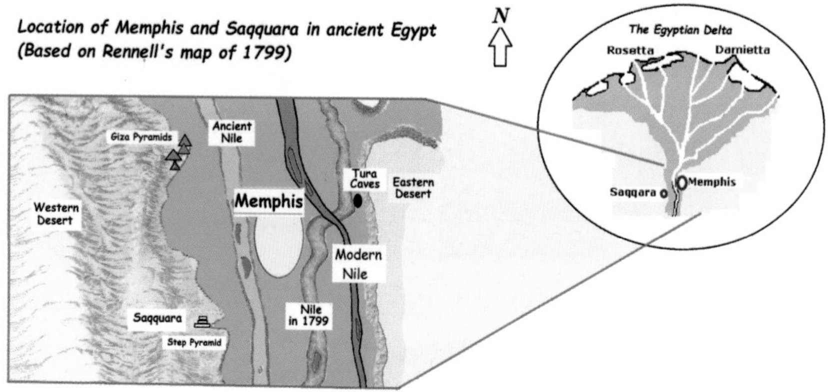

ABOVE: MAP B Location of the ancient Nile and the town of Memphis based on a map drawn by Major James Rennell in 1799. BELOW: MAP C Papyrus paper distribution in Byzantine Europe.

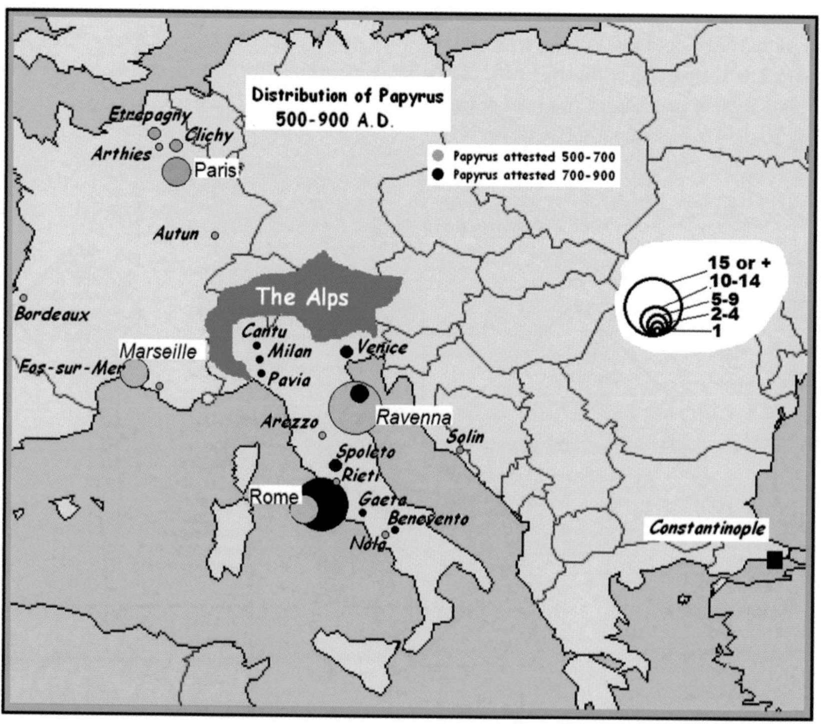

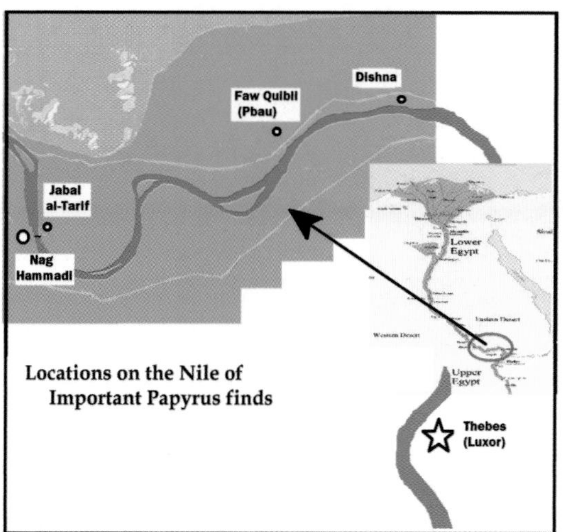

ABOVE: MAP D Location of important papyrus finds in Egypt. CENTER: Modern replica of a papyrus codex. BOTTOM: Papermaking in China, 11th Century A.D.

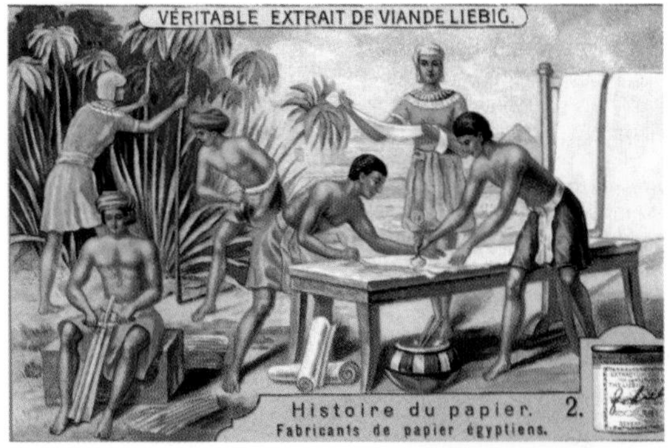

Set of four trading cards from beef extract packets marketed by the chemist, Justus von Liebig in the 1800's showing the four stages of paper evolution.

VÉRITABLE EXTRAIT DE VIANDE LIEBIG.
Histoire du papier. 2.
Fabricants de papier égyptiens.

Papermaking Ancient Egypt

VÉRITABLE EXTRAIT DE VIANDE LIEBIG.
Histoire du papier. 4.
Commerce de papier à Samarcande (Turkestan).

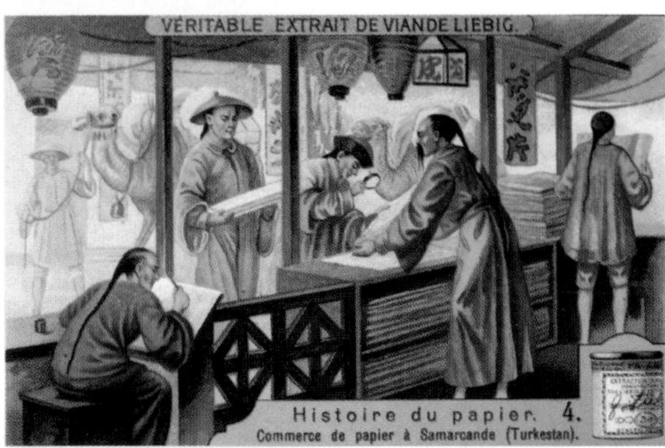

Selling paper in China 700 A.D.

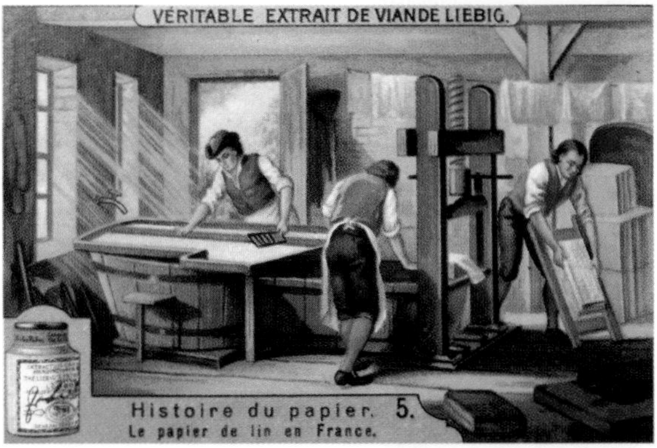
VÉRITABLE EXTRAIT DE VIANDE LIEBIG.
Histoire du papier. 5.
Le papier de lin en France.

Papermaking eighteenth century France.

VÉRITABLE EXTRAIT DE VIANDE LIEBIG.
Histoire du papier. 6.
Fabrication du papier en rouleaux sans fin.

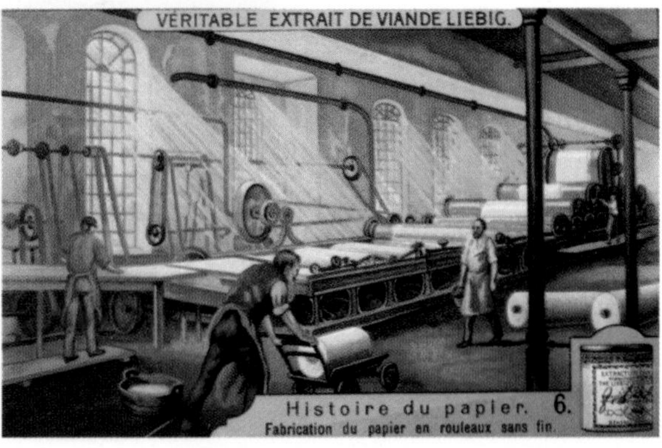

Modern paper mill twentieth century Europe

farms had won the monopoly of supplying paper to the world *for the next four thousand years*! An eye-opener of a statement, if it were true, and a reason for those looking for a financial jackpot to head to that city and make as much inroad as they could into the local paper factories, as well as nearby farms, shipping and businesses.

In Cassiodorus's time, instead of the millions of sheets of letter- and legal-sized bond paper found in the commercial Western world, ancient nations were awash in sheets, rolls, and books of papyrus paper. And it could not have escaped the notice of businessmen of his day that this commodity was made exclusively from a plant that grew only in Egypt using a process that was strictly controlled by the producers. This didn't bother Cassiodorus one bit because in his time, his fellow Romans were the rulers of Egypt and, thus, the owners of the monopoly. However, within one hundred years of his lifetime all that would change, bringing the First Papyrus Era to an end. During those four thousand years, development and paper production went hand in hand as we will see in a brief overview of Egyptian history as follows.

In the Protodynastic Period in Egypt, while papyrus paper was being born, or maybe even because of it, development of the earliest known hieroglyphic writing was in progress. This was Egypt's Bronze Age (ca. 3200 B.C.) when early settlers along the Nile were bent on leaving behind a record along the terraces of the Nile and in the oases. Here they were still busy carving into rock faces in order to record simple stories including the one that the Nile meant life and the desert death. They perhaps had little faith in the new medium even though temple priests and the more advanced settlers swore by it.

With the rise of the First and Second Dynasties in the Old Kingdom (2755–2255 B.C.) funeral practices for the elite centered around the construction of mastabas, which later became models for subsequent step pyramids. Papyrus paper by then had become an essential component of life among the royals who set up shop in the new capital of Egypt that rose in Memphis, where Djoser established his court and ordered the construction of the first pyramid in the nearby necropolis of Saqqara. The Great Pyramids followed as papyrus paper was used by the priests and other officials to record all aspects of state and temple functions as well as the delivery of materials to these massive projects that went forward during this Age of Pyramids.

Egyptians worshiped Pharaoh as a god and, believing that he ensured the annual flooding of the Nile that was necessary for their crops, fell in line with his wishes when he decided to create a centralized government. From this came the extensive powers that he needed to organize and feed the pyramid builders, as well as to provide for the support of a very large crew of specialists, including engineers, painters, mathematicians and priests.

The rising domestic market for ebony, ivory, myrrh, frankincense, copper, and cedar compelled the ancient Egyptians to navigate the open seas. Papyrus paper was a useful tool in keeping track of this expansion, it also provided income as a trade item; it joined gold, grain, papyrus rope and linen in Egypt's expanding list of trade goods.

In its last years the Old Kingdom ended in chaos perhaps brought down by droughts, low river levels, and starvation, once again proving that life could be mean even in a paradise on earth.

After the fall of the Old Kingdom came the rise of the Middle Kingdom and mummies found decorated with magical spells that were once exclusive to the pyramids of the kings. From this point through to the beginning of the Thirteenth Dynasty (2030–1650 B.C.) the delta evolved into the major center of papermaking.

The Seventeenth Dynasty was to prove the salvation of Egypt and would eventually lead to the war of liberation that drove invaders of that period (the Hyksos) back into Asia. In addition to being the commercial and bureaucratic medium of this period, papyrus now became the preeminent literary and historical medium and helped usher in the Egyptian Age of Classical Literature.

Thereafter, from a civilization that was already the product of almost two millennia, the New Kingdom arose like a lotus from the mud. During this period Egypt attained its greatest territorial extent. It expanded far south into Nubia and held wide territories in the Near East. Egyptian armies fought Hittite armies for control of modern-day Syria. This was a time of great wealth and power for Egypt. Some of the most important and best-known pharaohs ruled it and provided proof that Western Civilization was possible. By then Egyptian culture, customs, art expression, architecture and social structure, all closely tied to religion, blossomed into a way of life that remained remarkably stable, changing little over thousands of years.

It was also an age of ascendancy of the written word. Oral tradition using the medium of speech had allowed communication and interpretation of the general meaning of thoughts and ideas, which were passed forward as the essence of history, but paper recorded the exact words and true meaning. Proof of this lay in the fact that by popular demand the *Book of the Dead* on papyrus paper became a commercial success. A great trust in papyrus paper had developed among wealthy people who needed a recorded testimony and a passport in order to attain everlasting life. And their trust was not misplaced, since, as Professor Shaw noted, the ease and convenience of paper to convey information was an overpowering argument for its use. It alone allowed a balance between the horizontal social media and the power of vertical, institutional society, represented by the magnificent temple complexes at Abydos, Karnak, Abu Simbel, and Luxor. This was, after all, the Age of Magnificent Pharaohs, which featured such great figures as Queen Hatshepsut, Thutmose III ("the Napoleon of Egypt"), Amenhotep III, Akhenaten (Amenhotep IV), his wife Nefertiti, Ramesses I, his son Seti I, and Ramesses II ("the Great").

With the rise of Thebes and the New Kingdom (1550–1069 B.C.) came the first real, large increase in production of paper for export. In this respect, the Phoenician city of Byblos was important as it served as a center for the export of paper from Egypt to Greece. In fact, the Greek word for papyrus paper, *byblos*, may have come from the city's name. During the Old Kingdom, Byblos was virtually an Egyptian colony, a relationship reflected in the oldest Egyptian word for an oceangoing boat, which was "Byblos ship."

From there, papyrus paper imports fed the developing needs of the early Greek, Arab, Syrian, Hebrew, and Roman empires. Egyptian contact with Byblos peaked during the Nineteenth Dynasty, only to decline during the Twentieth and Twenty-first Dynasties when Byblos ceased being a colony. This coincided with the end of the New Kingdom by which time Egypt was exhausted and its treasury depleted.

A gradual decline of the Egyptian Empire followed Ramesses III's death. Now came endless bickering, a series of droughts, low levels of the Nile, famine, civil unrest, and official corruption. The power of the last pharaoh of this period, Ramesses XI, grew so weak that in the south Theban High Priests of Amun became the effective de facto rulers of Upper Egypt. The country was once again split into two parts making it an easier task for the takeover by the Libyan kings of the Twenty-second Dynasty.

Libyan. Assyrian, and Nubian rule (945–525 B.C.) was followed by the Persians who had already taken Babylon. Egypt was no match for the Persian king Cambyses who now assumed the formal title of pharaoh. Persians continued to dominate Egypt until 332 B.C.when Alexander the Great was welcomed by the Egyptians as a deliverer.

Following Alexander's death in Babylon, Ptolemy took the title of pharaoh and founded the dynasty that was to rule Egypt for nearly 300 years until the Roman conquest of 30 B.C. During the Ptolemy's reign, a Hellenistic culture was introduced that thrived in Egypt well after the Muslim conquest in later years. Influenced by the great thinkers of ancient Greece the Ptolemies set about making Alexandria the intellectual capital of the world, accomplishing their goal with the aid of the Great Library stocked with hundreds of thousands of papyrus paper scrolls.

Roman rule continued from 30 B.C.until about 325 A.D. when Christian Romans emerged and a Byzantine period flourished until 640 A.D. After which the Saracens invaded Egypt and established Arab rule.

During all that time paper exports continued as the overseas markets grew and paper became essential for growth and development throughout the Western world. Trade in papyrus paper reached another peak during the advent and development of Chinese pulp paper, since papyrus paper was still a valuable export during this period.

Arab control of Egypt as well as the Middle East and southern Europe made it easier for the Arabs to develop and promote rag pulp paper throughout their empire and beyond, eventually leading to a large market for cheaper paper. The decline of papyrus plantations and swamps followed, and a drop off in papyrus-paper production resulted as the use of pulp paper rose during the Byzantine Empire (324–1453 A.D.)

Through all that time, papyrus paper was especially useful in the Western world of business where it was put to good use on the large estates during the Ptolemaic and Roman eras. We see this in the documents discovered from a site near the ancient Egyptian town of Philadelphia. The discovery happened during the winter of 1914 when villagers in Kom el-Kharaba in the Fayum region found a cache of about 2,000 ancient documents, now known as the papyri that make up the Zenon Archives, named after Zenon, the overseer of a large estate belonging to Apollonios, an important financial advisor to Ptolemy II.[1] Sometime around 258 B.C. Zenon, as private secretary, received individuals, managed the household and estates, and looked after the archives of his patron.

The large number of documents found in this cache provided a picture of life both in and out of government in the early Ptolemaic period. Within the archives were letters, appeals for help, reports, accounts, and a few works of art including two epigrams commemorating a hunting dog who died from wounds while saving Zenon from an attack by a wild boar. Zenon retired in 249 B.C. and the farms and holdings of the estate continued operation under other overseers.

The size of the operation can be judged by the amount of papyrus paper used. One report tells us that 454 rolls of papyrus were used by his office in the course of just thirty-three days. At that rate of use, fourteen rolls daily, business must have been clipping along. Papyrus paper was therefore ordered in quantity to meet the need, which created the usual problems of supply and demand.[2]

> Zenon,
>
> Greetings. I suffered anxiety when I heard of your long protracted illness, but now I am delighted to hear that you are convalescent and already on the point of recovery. I myself am well . . . 400 drachmae in silver have been paid . . . for the papyrus rolls which are being manufactured in Tanis for Apollonios. Take note then that these affairs have been settled thus. And please write yourself if ever you need anything here.
>
> Promethion.[3]

And, what happens when things go wrong?

> Zenon,
>
> Greetings. We hear that the boat has sailed past with the papyrus rolls on board! Will you kindly send us the ten rolls which Apollonios ordered to be given us? Give them to the bearer of this letter, in order that we may not be unduly behindhand. Farewell,
>
> Dionysodoros.[4]

By now even those using clay tablets and the cuneiform script of the Fertile Crescent had adapted to papyrus paper, which they imported from Egypt. It is said that this need to change to pen and ink and papyrus was undoubtedly a factor in the Phoenicians' development of their alphabet, one of the forerunners of Greek and Latin characters. As to the plant used to make the paper, *Cyperus papyrus*, the swamps along the Nile were a valuable commodity protected by royal mandate, fed and nurtured by the seasonal inundation of the Nile with its nutrient-rich waters.

Even Shirley Hazzard, the best-selling novelist and writer, found this key role played by papyrus in ancient times extraordinary. In May of 1983, in Naples, Italy, she covered the Seventeenth International Congress of Papyrology as a "Far-Flung Correspondent" for the *New Yorker.* Here she tells us that, "failure of the Egyptian papyrus crop could mean to the Roman world a paralysis of commerce and affairs of state, and suspension of work for innumerable scribes who carried on the enormous labor of transcription."

Papyrus paper would eventually be replaced and the swamplands on the Nile would later be drained, plowed up, and cultivated so that in the time of Napoleon papyrus had disappeared from Egypt. But the plant would continue to grow on in remote places in Africa, just as papyrus paper would live on in the minds and ways of human beings. Why? Because it was the first paper put to such wide use, and it made people in the West accustomed to being able to write things down easily, whether it was household accounts, a shopping list, or government records, as well as books and poetry, etc. Once people got used to being able to record and transmit information so easily, the medium might change, parchment or pulp paper might come or go, but this habit and expectation of writing things down had become a hallmark of civilized life. Thanks to papyrus, humans were never going to revert to stone or clay tablets again for the transcription of the written word.

❧

Many of the early papyrus scrolls were memorials to the skills, patience, and dedication of artisans who knew the value of good papyrus paper when they saw it. The fact that many papyri survived means that papyrus paper, whether freshly made or old, is quite durable if kept under the right conditions.[5] One roll in the Egyptian Museum in Berlin is over 3,000 years old and could still be rolled and unrolled by Wilhelm Schubart who was curator from 1912 to 1937, without the slightest danger to the material.[6] If kept under reasonably dry conditions, it lasts for a very long time, but, once exposed to humid air, papyrus paper becomes perishable and a great deal of effort must then be made to preserve it from destruction by insects, fungi, bacteria, light, and air.[7]

Although most ancient Egyptians were illiterate, many benefited from the manufacture of papyrus paper during the time when Egypt was papermaker to the world. Not only did it provide jobs, it also served a higher purpose as pointed out in the first century A.D. by Pliny the Elder, who said papyrus was also the guardian of our immortality. The thread of history, so often threatened by catastrophic events, was kept whole and intact by saving the literature, thoughts and business transactions transcribed from earlier ages.

With the rise of the Greek state and later Roman Empire, the spread of papyrus paper reached its pinnacle. In retrospect, without realizing it, Cassiodorus's earlier statement about all the offices of the world described a benchmark that was about to be passed in the history of the world. At the time he was writing, papyrus paper was being replaced by parchment in Europe, which, made from local animal skins, did not have to be imported from quite so far. Five hundred years after him both parchment and papyrus would gradually be replaced by laid or rag paper, the forerunner of modern paper.

Laid paper, or linen or rag paper as it is called, was introduced to the world by Arab traders, who knew a good thing when they saw it. They were quick to realize that unlike papyrus paper, pulp paper did not depend on any special plant material. It could be made out of any fibrous material at hand. At first they used mulberry tree bark, flax, or rags, but it was evident that paper could be made out of a large assortment of plant or cloth materials.

What would have happened if rag paper had been introduced in the early days of history? Marvin Meyers, professor of Bible and Christian studies at Chapman University in California and an expert on early Gnostic bibles, made the interesting point that because papyrus is a durable writing surface, if the famous codices found at Nag Hammadi had been written in the third and fourth centuries on pulp paper instead of papyrus, the texts would have disintegrated into dust long ago. On the other hand, the arrival of pulp paper in later days was fortuitous because it was available during the period when the printing press was developed. Its porous nature allowed it to readily take up the special ink designed for printing presses while papyrus did not. Parchment, though still in use, was phased out as it was now too expensive, and so the choice was made and the four-thousand-year papyrus monopoly was broken. But laid and rag paper was able to supplant papyrus paper thanks, in large part, to the paper trade and industry framework that papyrus paper had initially created.

❧

The paper trade in ancient times grew over many centuries. The scale of production gradually rose from nothing to thousands of rolls annually prior to the Nineteenth Dynasty of Egypt (1400 B.C.). Then at the time of Roman conquest (48 B.C.) production grew to millions of rolls.

Leila Avrin suggests that papyrus paper could have been introduced first to the Greek islands as early as the eleventh or ninth century B.C.when the Phoenicians first introduced the alphabet. We know from *The Story of Wenamun*, a text written in 1200 B.C., that Egypt exported papyrus through Byblos, but it was not until after 750 B.C. that Greek expansion, trade, and colonization flourished. Thus, Avrin felt that the late eighth century B.C. would be a more realistic date for the first large-scale, practical use of papyrus in the Greek world.

From then on papyrus was known to be one of the more important Mediterranean trade items, and it would have been quite common in Greece by the early seventh century B.C., as by then the Greeks had established their own colony in Egypt at Naucratis on the Canopic branch of the Nile river, forty-fives miles from the open sea. It was the first and, for much of its early history, the only permanent Greek colony in Egypt. Later, during the Ptolemaic period the Fayum region (Maps 1 and 2) became a popular place for Greeks who made up as much as 30 percent of the population there.

Throughout all of this, the papyrus cartel stood to make a great deal of money, especially as they kept the process secret, which they did until Pliny spilled the beans. Though they continued to do well after that, the market shifted slightly after the time of Constantine (330 A.D.) but continued strong until the tenth century.

> For production on such a mammoth scale—amounting, beyond doubt, to millions of rolls per annum—the papyrus industry must have been one of the biggest employers of manpower in Egypt, perhaps second only to food production. Thousands of workers would be needed, some of them highly specialized, for the different branches of the industry: cultivating and harvesting the plant, transporting the raw material to the factory, fabrication, sale, and shipment of the finished product. (Naphtali Lewis, 1974)

Under the Ptolemies as well as the Romans, information gathering was the norm; the intention was to better manage food production and industries such as papyrus papermaking. It would be important for the managers to know how much raw material was available from day to day in order to keep industries supplied. Though it is something that the Ptolemies probably knew, we are still in the dark about the total amount of papyrus paper and papyrus rope produced or exported. On our part we can only guess. As Naphtali Lewis tells us, "information on the organization of the papyrus industry in Egypt in Greek and Roman times is sparse, consisting of no more than a handful of relevant Greek documents complemented by isolated bits of supporting evidence. The sum total presents us with a chiaroscuro, a few highlights emerging from a dark background of silence."

Using an earlier estimate of the extent of the ancient Egyptian swamps,[8] we can make a rough estimate of the maximum amount of papyrus paper that could have been made at any one time. This is referred to as the "standing crop" and represents a one-time harvest, as when a field of wheat is mown or a forest is clear-cut. From calculations, we can guess that about twenty-five trillion sheets of paper could have been made from this theoretical one-time harvest in ancient Egypt, and it would be worth about $22.5 trillion at current paper prices.

In practice, papermakers were constrained by the owners of the swamps. They were only allowed to cut stems within reason, according to terms that were set out in contracts made at the time the swamps were leased. Since the swamps were money spinners, the lessee had to ensure that he did not overcut or else the swamp would take too long to recover, or might be permanently damaged. From the restrictions and constraints written into the contracts and modern growth estimates of papyrus stems,[9] we can estimate the maximum yield on a *sustainable* basis during Roman times, which turns out to be only about 7.5 percent of the maximum standing crop, or 1,875 million possible sheets per year. This maximum sustainable production was probably never reached, simply because the number of papermakers and reed cutters required was be enormous. My estimate of fifty million sheets per year in Roman times, when paper use and production was at a peak (with a total of 21,250 million over 425 years as shown in the graph (and in Table 2 in the Appendix), is still only a very small percentage of the maximum possible sustainable yield. This would leave enormous numbers of stems for use as fuel for the baths and for the crafts and rope industries.

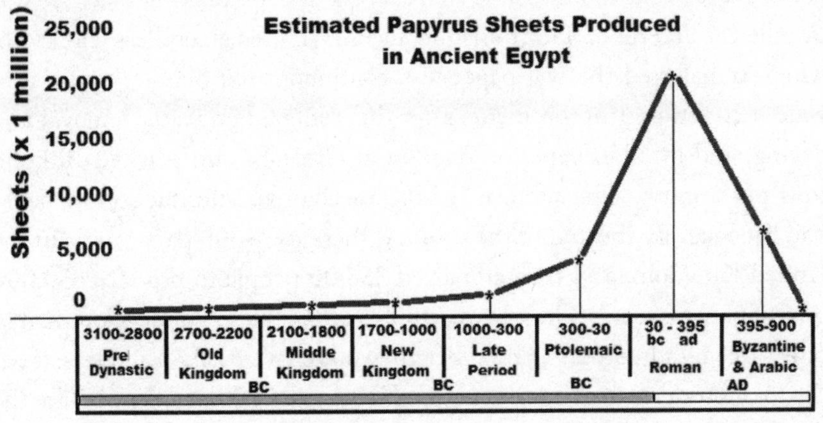

Estimated Production of Papyrus paper in Ancient Egypt.

Unlike food, the market for paper is not directly correlated with the growth of populations, since common people had little use for it. The recurring and ever-increasing demand for paper lay in the world business market. Conversely, papyrus paper was a nonagricultural product that could be exported year-in and year-out without regard to famine conditions. Political disturbances did take their toll, and there were times of disruption in paper exports because of riots in Egypt.

How then does my rough estimate of about 157,807 tons during the four-thousand-year period from 3100 B.C. to 900 A.D. compare to paper produced in modern times? In order to appreciate what it represents, we can compare it to paper production in, for example, nineteenth century Britain. Rag paper was being made by hand in Britain beginning in 1588, using the process invented by the Chinese. This process consisted of pouring a slurry of paper pulp (a mixture of pulverized wood fibers or liquidized cloth rags) onto a fine screen so that the pulp "laid down" on the screen through which the water was drained. Once dry, the sheet of rag paper could be peeled from the screen.

By 1800 there were 430 paper mills in England and Wales, and less than fifty in Scotland, mostly operating a single vat of pulp slurry that was dipped into the paper molds to produce paper by hand.[10] Total annual output on the average was about twenty-three tons per paper mill, or about 11,000 tons in total. The first successful papermaking machine was installed at Frogmore, Hertfordshire, in 1803; it used an endless wire cloth, which transferred the wet paper to a continuous felt blanket to assist in water extraction. Improvements after this centered on water removal and drying, and by 1850 paper production in Great Britain reached 100,000 tons per annum. The pattern for the mechanized production of paper had been set. By the end of the century, there were 300 paper mills in the United Kingdom, and they employed 35,000 people to produce 650,000 tons of paper a year.[11] Thus, by the 1800s, after a period of development of only three hundred years, Great Britain would have reached and far exceed the total production of ancient Egypt (3100 B.C.–900 A.D.), well before the point where handmade methods changed over to mechanized processes.

Today in Egypt papyrus paper is made for the tourist trade. At the height of the tourist market, when tourism surged to 14.7 million visitors in 2010, the papermakers in el-Qaramous in the delta were making about 1,000 sheets a week per family.[12] Given that there were about 200 families engaged over the course of a year, one million sheets were possible from their 500 acres of papyrus plantations, a rate of production that is equivalent to one-tenth of that obtained from 400–900 A.D. under Arab rule.

❧

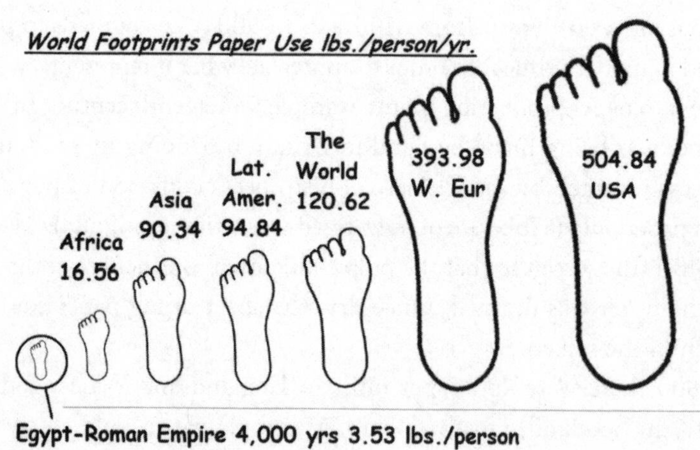

World footprints for paper use, lbs per person per year. (after Statista, 2016).[13]

The footprint of paper usage today compared to that of ancient times makes an interesting comparison. In today's electronic age it often comes as a surprise to find out that an enormous amount of paper is still in use,[14] especially in the United States, which topped the world average in 2010 with a whopping 500 pounds per person per year. This makes the concept of a "paperless world" look like self-deception. It is also interesting to note that the footprint of ancient papyrus paper would not even register unless it was taken in its entirety, thus it is shown as the total poundage used over 4,000 years per person in Roman times.

To the average Egyptian all this would be of little interest, since the most useful thing about the plant was not the making of paper—although the windfall of the paper trade on the local economies was appreciated—but in the multitude of things that could be made from it at no cost. It helped to have the plant close by during a famine or during a cold spell, and it could always be useful around the house for making baskets, mats, and rope. For people living on or near the water it served as a larder and fish nursery; for marsh dwellers it must have been a comfort to have papyrus seemingly everywhere, as papyrus could be made into a mat, boat, or small house. Best of all it was ready, willing, and able to help make the transition to the next life, no matter whether the deceased was rich or poor. Wrapped in a simple, low-cost papyrus mat, or clutching a tiny amulet containing a small piece of papyrus paper, or sealed into a multimillion dollar tomb with a hundred-foot long roll of papyrus paper, the dead were secure and ready to make the voyage thanks to the sacred sedge. To the businessman of the age or the temple caretaker, the paper was a boon; and to the more socially conscious dweller of this ancient world it provided the means to keep up with what was happening. As Tom Standage tells us, papyrus paper enabled people to physically send a message rather than relying on a messenger to deliver it in spoken form. The informal system that had developed now enabled information to penetrate to the farthest provinces within a few weeks at most. He pointed out that news from Rome only took about five weeks to reach Britain in the west and seven weeks to reach Syria in the east.

In ancient times papyrus paper had allowed humans to literally rip the regal prerogative of immortality off the wall. The voices that appeared on paper were those of the gods and the sacred residents of the netherworld.

Now in Roman times came a new evolution, not among the dead, but the living, as merchants, soldiers, officials in distant parts and the general populace raised their own voices. The result was a surge in letter writing on papyrus paper.

Some of these letters circulated information from the heart of the republic within select social circles, others revealed two-way conversations in which information passed horizontally from one person to another. All of which indicated that social networks were developing and civilization was responding.

Best of all was the fact that all of this would be recorded on scrolls and the scrolls in turn would be stored for all time in facilities created just for this purpose. Thus began recorded history and the organization of knowledge.

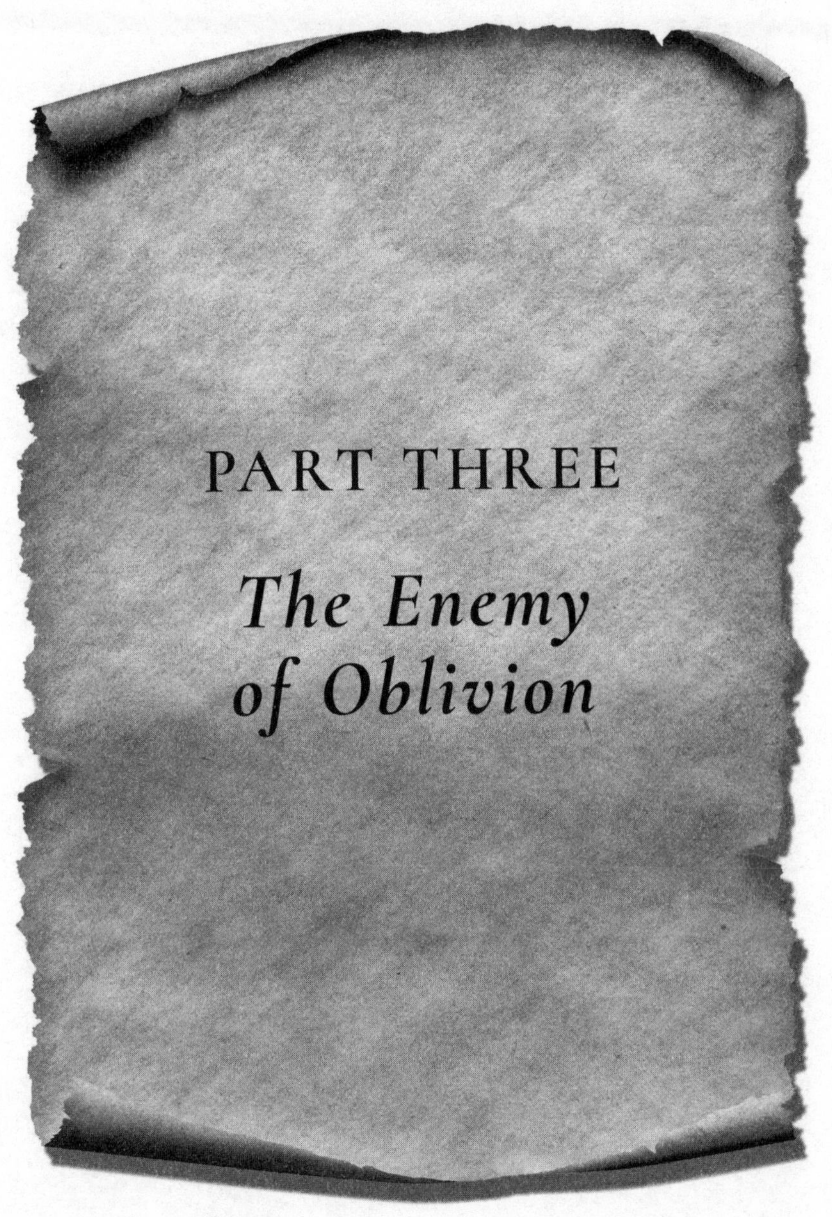

PART THREE

The Enemy of Oblivion

FIFTEEN

Early Libraries, Paper, and the Writing Business

As we have seen with the development of papyrus paper and the advent of ink and scribes, the Egyptians built an enormous business and political infrastructure because of paper. James Black tells us in his 2002 thesis on an Egyptian classic, *The Instruction of Amenemope*, that this effort of building an infrastructure involved the generation of a large body of scribes to "document land allocations and transfers, tax payments, state and temple inventories, administrative decrees, judicial decisions, and so forth. In fact, from present evidence it appears that the use of writing for religious texts and literary compositions was a secondary development; the original motivation for the invention of writing in Egypt—and its primary use in the early centuries—was almost solely for bureaucratic administration and political propaganda."[1] Any religious texts produced would have been of the most fundamental nature. This is a view reinforced by Kim Ryholt, associate professor of Egyptology at the University of Copenhagen, who noted that among the fragments found in the library of a Tebtunis temple in the Fayum region (Map 2), were copies of the Daily Temple Offering Ritual, the basic ritual performed every day in every temple in Egypt.[2]

Ryholt suggested that even though it was routine to the point of being old hat, the keepers of temple libraries zealously protected these texts as if they held secret rituals, perhaps a move guaranteed to safeguard the potency of the magic, as well as to protect the priestly tradition of divination. Keeping such things close to their chests also maintained their edge in the area of medical expertise. The Greeks, for example, found it frustratingly difficult to pry loose the wisdom contained in the famous ancient Egyptian medical papyri from the priests. These were later discovered by archaeologists in the nineteenth century.

The general populace had little practice in writing and reading, so it is no surprise that the evolution and history of the early libraries of the Egyptians clearly supported the priest's need-to-know mentality. Creative thinking was kept to a minimum, the medium continued to be the message and sacred religious scrolls remained as secret as possible.

EdfuTemple in the time of Napoleon and the location of the House of Books. (after a sketch by D. Roberts, 1838).

Since the early libraries served the priests, we can expect that they would keep their books nearby in places of worship. A good example would be the House of Books in the Temple of Horus at Edfu. The remarkable thing about this library is the catalog; that object of desire and pride so dear to the hearts of librarians, many of whom will smile upon hearing that this particular catalog is chiseled on the wall and so is still there today. It tells us that the collection contained books that, among other things, enabled the reader to learn about:

> The smiting of demons, the repelling of the crocodile, the bringing out of the king in procession, knowing all the secrets of the laboratory, all the writings of combat, spells for repelling the evil eye, instructions for decorating a wall, (and) protecting the body, knowing the periodic returns of the two heavenly bodies, and all the inventories of the secret forms (of the god), and all the aspects of the associated deities, which are copied daily for the temple, every day, each one after the other, so that the "souls" of the deities will remain in (this) place and will not leave (this) temple, ever.[3]

The building of the temple was begun in 237 B.C. and finished in 57 B.C. by Auletus, the father of Cleopatra. Thus, exactly ten years before Caesar's arrival in Egypt we find a "house of books" functioning in the same land and at the same time as one of the most famous libraries of history, the Royal Library of Alexandria.[4]

But, what a difference, the Library of Alexandria was fashioned after that of Aristotle and the early Greeks. Aristotle began his library in Athens on his return from Asia in 337 B.C., which coincided with the beginning of his school, the Lyceum. Here he developed a cooperative research program for his students and began collecting books and specimens of interest for the program. Over the years he established a natural history museum and a library of ten thousand scrolls. Aristotle's museum was supplemented by material and specimens sent back to Athens by Alexander the Great, himself a student of the great man.

Alexandria closely followed Aristotle's model with its museum and library, both of which were the delights of the scholars, who loved them. The daily tasks of the copyists, scholars, authors, librarians, and scribes associated with the library was to produce books, catalogs, lists, letters, scholarly papers, broadsheets, announcements, and newsletters. As a result,

Ptolemy II's reputation was made. But since the library lay within the palace grounds, the users were limited to those with royal permission. The general public was given access only to a smaller library in the Serapeum, an imposing temple in the western part of the city.

At the end of Ptolemy II's reign when the library was at its zenith, the 490,000 rolls in the Great Library were supplemented with 42,800 in the Serapeum.[5] Both of these are conservative. Other estimates refer to millions. At the outside there may have been over a million rolls with twenty sheets per roll. Over the almost three hundred years of Ptolemaic rule, the library's holdings would have required a production of about 70,000 sheets per year, an amount equivalent only to less than 1 percent of the annual production of paper under Roman rule. Obviously, the amount of paper used for literary purposes would be dwarfed by that used in the business world, but the production of books was an effort of inestimable worth. The historians, screenwriters and filmmakers Justin Pollard and Howard Reid put this in perspective when they made the interesting point that "other libraries since have held more books; indeed, today the Library of Congress in Washington and the British Library in London hold between them nearly every book printed in the last two hundred years and many more besides. But they are not complete, not least because most of the knowledge of the first thousand years of Western civilization is missing. These were the books that formed the library of Alexandria."

The missing books, the millions of papyrus paper scrolls, along with some codices in later years, vanished, leaving behind only scraps that must now be "painstakingly reconstructed and analyzed by scholars to squeeze out every last drop of information."[6]

The Writing Trade

In the early days of Egypt, if you were at home, thoughts organized and reed pen at the ready, it was an easy task to enter your bid for immortality. A long letter was all that was needed, say, to a friend in Memphis, perhaps someone who was a scribe. Let's call him Serenput, perhaps you might compose a discourse on life in Thebes during the Sixth Dynasty when it was a much smaller city than Memphis. On dying, the letter writer would then confidently go to their tomb knowing that thousands of years later, their letter would be found by an eminent archaeologist, then their scroll would be named after a prominent benefactor before it was cut into sections and placed lovingly under glass in a famous Western museum.

Scrolls being read in which the writing is oriented vertically (After Alma-Tadema's paintings of Joseph's scribe recording grain lots for storage, and Vaspasian reading news from one of his generals. Also the Minerva mosaic by Elihu Vedder in the Library of Congress, Wash. DC).

If this were in the year 2200 B.C., the letter writer would write in Egyptian, but instead of laboriously drawing out hieroglyphs, would use hieratic script, the shorthand version. As with ancient scribes who sat cross-legged with the papyrus paper scroll across their lap, they would hold the unwritten roll of papyrus paper in their left hand and begin writing with their right. Their script would go across the page from right to left as in modern Arabic and many of the earlier writing systems, including early Greek and Phoenician. Since this would still be in the time of the Old Kingdom (2686–2134 B.C.) their writing would go vertically across the page;[7] readers would have read their work by holding the scroll up in front of them.

The American painter, Elihu Vedder, a romantic imagist who illustrated the deluxe edition of *The Rubaiyat* by Omar Khayyam, portrayed Minerva in a mosaic in the Library of Congress in Washington, DC, reading from such a scroll. In fact, the writing is clearly seen laid out in a way that it is vertical to the long edge.

Young readers from Italian wall paintings (after Barker, 1908).

From the Middle Kingdom, 2055 B.C. onward, there was a change in the orientation of writing on most scrolls. The lines were thereafter written horizontally, which meant that a reader could spread out the scroll in front of him rather than holding it up.[8] This is the form you would use if you were writing in a later time. For example, let's say you are living in the period around 231 B.C. you now have to work harder to achieve immortality. You've decided therefore to send an essay to Aristarchus in Alexandria. You have read his book (in scroll form), *On the Sizes and Distances of the Sun and Moon*, and decided he has it all wrong. Your essay will be a rebuttal meant to counter his argument that the earth revolves around the sun. Your hope is that in addition to your work winding up in a museum, your new theory that the sun revolves around the earth will take its place in history. So, this is a substantial document, and you must write it in Greek, even though Alexandria is an Egyptian city. Also you must now write from left to right as in modern Greek, Latin, and English. The text is written on the recto with short lines parallel to the length of the roll and arranged in blocks so that when anyone reads the scroll he can unroll it on a flat surface or across his lap with his left hand revealing from the right, one section at a time.

Your essay is a long one and on page twenty you realize you need more sheets, so you simply paste on a segment cut from a spare roll to finish up. After a while, let's suppose you receive some good news, your work has found its way into the Royal Library! On a visit to Alexandria, you apply for permission to tour the library. You approach the court of Ptolemy V, who is now king. His fifteen-year-old wife, Cleopatra I, will be the first Ptolemaic queen to be sole ruler of Egypt, like Cleopatra VII of Caesar's time. She encourages your visit. The king himself informs you that Aristarchus has been dead for some time and your essay is now famous. His wife invites you to dinner and everyone assures you that no one will ever be able refute your idea that the earth is the center of the universe.

Once confronted with the library's treasures, you are surprised to see scrolls from the early days with writing that ran across the page in a vertical fashion. It was also possible to see in some of the earlier scrolls horizontal writing in long lines that ran the entire length of the roll. This occasioned a great deal of unrolling and rerolling of the scroll.

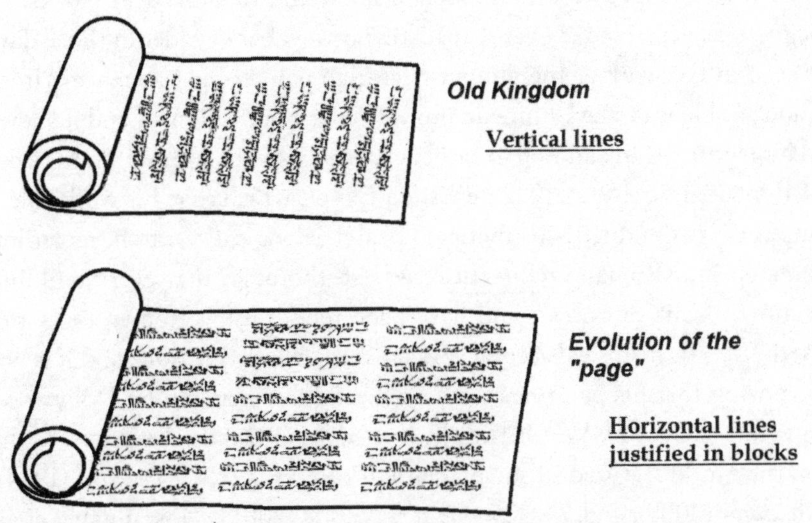

Various ways of writing on papyrus scrolls and the evolution of the "page."

In time, scribes were forced to adopt the method where the writer used short horizontal lines kept within blocks, so that a section could be read in its entirety without so much rolling and rerolling. Once scribes developed the habit of standardizing the blocks of text, they justified their lines closely to the right and left in order to confine the script inside a block about three inches wide. This was called a *pagina* in Latin and represented a regular organization of text that is still the fashion. In English it is now called a "page."

In Roman times, the standard way of reading a scroll was to unroll it on a table or across your lap. When finished, you would leave the scroll wound on the left, just like the old video tapes returned after rental, so the new reader could start fresh with page one and would not have to rewind before using. This method of spreading out a scroll while reading came as a surprise to someone like myself, who remembered watching a scroll being opened by a Roman centurion in the old movies. He would stand majestically in his shiny metal breastplate, short sword and helmet as he unrolled the scroll vertically like a window shade. He then would read the text that had been arranged vertically (that is, across the short axis of the scroll.)

In reality, by Roman times the majority of papyrus scrolls were written with text arranged in a horizontal fashion and organized in blocks, or *paginae*, as explained above. A realistic portrayal of a reader in those days is seen in the work of the famous Victorian painter Sir Lawrence Alma-Tadema. He was a consummate professional, a perfectionist, and it shows in his paintings. In addition to earlier excursions to observe and study places of Roman antiquity, in 1902 he visited Egypt, which gave his work a new impulse. It is said that his meticulous archaeological research, including research into Roman architecture, was so thorough that every building featured in his canvases could have been rebuilt using Roman tools and methods. His historical accuracy was remarkable for his time, and it is not surprising that his paintings were used as source material by Hollywood directors such as D. W. Griffith in *Intolerance* (1916) or in versions of the ancient world featured in such films as *Ben Hur* (1926), *Cleopatra* (1934), *Gladiator* (2009), and *The Chronicles of Narnia* (2005). Most notable of all is Cecil B. DeMille's use of Alma-Tadema in his epic remake of *The Ten Commandments* (1956), where it is said that De Mille would customarily spread out prints of Alma-Tadema paintings to indicate to his set designers the look he wanted to achieve.[9]

In Alma-Tadema's painting *Favorite Poet*, we see a papyrus scroll being read, and it is a correct rendering—the scroll is twenty pages long. The lovely reader has unrolled it and has yet to roll it back up. In another of his paintings, *A Reading from Homer*, we not only see the correct way of opening and reading a papyrus paper scroll in Roman times, but we also see a dramatic presentation by the laurel-wreathed reader, who is reading the contents of the book. He is making Homer's characters come to life for the audience who listen in rapt attention. We see here a great example of the tradition of oral performance that we will hear more about later, a tradition that was an important factor in the early circulation of books.

❧

It is difficult to place ourselves in the position of a copyist or scribe of those days, but by the time of the Romans it was clear that the job was not an easy one. Parsons, on the basis of much experience with the papyri of Oxyrhynchus, gives us a picture:

> These are the essentials: the copyist sharpens his reed-pen, spreads fresh papyrus over his knees, and proceeds to write—somewhere nearby is his pot of ink (soot mixed with gum), somewhere the exemplar from which he copies—on a stand, perhaps, unless indeed someone else dictates it to him. The posture must be strenuous (only afterwards do desks come into fashion) some later images show the left leg over the right, which may explain why in many rolls the columns of writing slope outward towards their base, following the thigh-line. A minor poet depicts the physical suffering of it all: 'my eyes are tired, my sinews, my spine, the base of my skull and my shoulders'. The veteran may end with shaky hands and clouded sight. (P. Parsons, 2007)

❧

Inks and Pens

The ink in your inkpot as you write your letter in ancient times is quite similar to the ordinary ink of modern times. It was mixed by the ancient scribe in one of two shallow depressions on his wooden penholder. The same holder had a deep notch that could hold several reed pens. The holder itself was seen as a badge of the profession and was proudly and prominently displayed in drawings and tomb paintings of scribes. Clutched in their hands or tucked under their arms or thrust inside their waistband or sashes (as in the painted vignette of Scribe Nebqed in his *Book of the Dead*) it declared to the world that you were one of a special breed. It looked like an early form of iPhone and served in a way much like that most influential piece of consumer technology; it was the icon that distinguished the "with it" generation of its day.

The ink used in the wells of the penholder was made by mixing carbon black (soot) with water and acacia gum. The gum was collected from trees growing in arid areas and was the same acacia gum, or gum arabic, that is still in use today as a natural stabilizer and binder for inks, paint, and foods. Ink made from it is very stable and will not fade,[10] but it could still be washed off when a mistake was made or when a sheet or scroll had to be reused. Egg white was occasionally added as a binder, as in some of the Dead Sea Scroll inks.[11] In later years, a mixture of soot and gelatin thinned with water or vinegar made up the ink called *atramentum* by the Romans.

These washable inks could be made more stable and waterproofed by the addition of mordants, such as alumina, or binding components such as burnt resin, dextrin, gum tragacanth, albumen, or wax. David Carvalho, a noted expert on ink and handwriting, tells us that permanent inks could be made using a combination of soot obtained from resins, or resinous woods, mixed with gelatin and oils, egg white, or glue. Some of these mixtures resulted in a close approximation of the indelible ink used in ancient India.[12] "India Ink" of the fourth century B.C. was made of burnt bones, tar, pitch, and other substance, such as shellac. This last added by the Chinese made the ink so tenacious that it was unwashable once dried. We know that some scribes used inks of this nature because of the examples that exist where the writer obviously gave up trying to erase a document and turned to the verso side in desperation.

To apply the ink Egyptian scribes wrote with a thin reed, the stem of the rush *Juncus maritimus*. Cut on a slant, the point was then chewed to form a small brush tip.[13] The reed stylus came into use in the time of Alexander. Made from the stem of the reed grass *Phragmites aegyptica*, it was trimmed and pointed with a split nib, as with a quill pen. This made for faster writing, especially when cursive script was involved. It also signaled a change in papyrus paper because the stylus required thicker paper, which the papermakers were happy to provide.[14]

With this change in pens also came a change in ink, which can be seen in documents from 252–198 B.C. onwards. By then papyri inscribed using the Egyptian soft pen and carbon-based ink were being replaced by Greek papyri on which a water-based metallic ink was applied with the reed stylus.[15] The metallic ink used at this time was different from the iron gall ink used in later centuries.[16] Traces of these earlier metallic inks were identified in burnt papyri from Herculaneum dating from 79 A.D. The X-rays used in the study of the charred rolls found that the ink used, though still carbon based like the earlier inks, now contained substantial levels of lead and copper.[17] Since the papyrus documents concerned were about 200–350 years old at the time of the eruption of Vesuvius; this meant that these water-based metallic inks were used in place of the ancient Egyptian ink probably by the third century B.C.[18]

The largest change in ink came about much later, at about the time when papyrus paper was being replaced by parchment. It was then that *encaustum* came into its own. This was an ink made by boiling gallnuts to obtain a dark-brown liquid tannin. Although the exact date of the transition from *atramentum* (carbon based) to iron gall ink (*encaustum*) is unknown, it can be safely stated that by the end of the Middle Ages, iron gall ink was the primary ink.[19]

In later times vitriol, a metallic sulfate, was added and the ink became so powerful that it would occasionally eat through parchment, leaving a space where the original letter was.

With the advent of printing, Johannes Gutenberg found that neither the earlier soot-gum-water version of the Egyptians, nor the metallic inks of the early Greeks and Romans, nor the later gall ink that became popular for use on parchment, could be used for printing. All of these inks were water-based and thus pooled on the metal typeface, blurring the letters on the pulp-based paper that Gutenberg was using. As a result, in the fifteenth century, a new type of sticky, thick ink had to be developed for printing. Gutenberg designed one for his presses: an oily, varnish-like mixture of soot, turpentine, and walnut oil that is still in use today.

Gum Arabic–A Second Monopoly?

This brings us to a second item exported from Egypt that became an essential and prized commodity, and for which there would be a steady and growing demand in the ancient world. I speak here of the African ink component acacia gum, also known as gum arabic, a crystalized gum that excretes from cuts made in the branches of *Acacia senegal* trees. These trees grow in many places in Africa and even on the Indian subcontinent, but most of the world's gum arabic comes from Sudan, where a thick belt of the trees stretches from one end of the country to the other. This gum has been an item of commerce from as early as the twelfth century B.C.

Gum arabic ready for grinding (Wikipedia).

It was collected in Nubia and exported north to Egypt for use in the preparation of inks, watercolors, and dyes. Herodotus, writing in the fifth century B.C., mentions its use in embalming in Egypt. In later days, other trade routes may have taken it through Phoenician, Berber, and Greek hands, but like papyrus paper, the main avenue of transit would be through Egypt.

Scribes all over the world valued it as an emulsifier and stabilizer. When added to soot and water, it brought the two components together so well that the ink flowed easily from the pen. It also helped the ink attach firmly to the paper surface, rather than pooling, as would happen with water alone.

To produce this ink, the crystals of gum arabic would be ground into a powder, which dissolved readily in water; then, once the soot was added, the ink formed and could be used directly or dried into small blocks and sold by weight.

Gum arabic was sold on its own for other uses. It is a natural emulsifier and is still in demand; pharmaceutical companies use it to keep medicines from separating into their component ingredients, and a dab of gum arabic makes newspaper ink more cohesive and permanent. It is also a common emulsifier used in soft drinks, including Coca-Cola. Sixty thousand tons are used annually.

The extraordinary thing is that since it is still shipped primarily out of Sudan, the legend grew that Osama bin Laden owned a significant interest in its production in that country, and therefore one should boycott products using it. Dana Milbank in the *Washington Post* described a press conference held at the Washington Press Club in 2007, when Sudan's ambassador to the United States threatened to stop exportation of gum arabic if sanctions were imposed. Brandishing a bottle of Coca-Cola, he said, "I can stop that gum arabic and all of us will have lost this."

Eventually, the State Department issued a release stating that while Osama bin Laden had once had considerable holdings in Sudanese gum arabic production, he divested himself of these when he was expelled from Sudan in 1996.[20]

In summary, with the power of these two plant-based products combined, papyrus and gum arabic, paper and ink evolved. This filled the need of people to write, keep written records and record ideas. There was also something about a beautifully inscribed roll of paper that must have captured the fancy of the human mind. Picture, for example, the excitement and joy of the modern high school or college graduate as they raise high that scroll that testifies to their achievement. Generally tied with a colored ribbon, it puts us in the same league as the numerous, wealthy, book-loving Romans, who thought the owner of any well-inscribed papyrus scroll must be a person favored by the gods.

SIXTEEN

A Library to End All Libraries and the Sweet Smell of History

Papyrus paper which keeps the sweet harvest of the mind, and restores it to the reader whenever he chooses to consult it.

—Cassiodorus

By the time the Romans arrived in Egypt to take control, there was an unlimited supply of papyrus paper on hand, ink as good as the fountain pen ink of today, scribes and clerks standing by, and in Alexandria a heritage of learning, as well as one of the largest libraries, all there for the asking. The stage was set for the next great leap forward in global cultural advancement, which would begin with the arrival of Julius Caesar.

Caesar, the conqueror of Egypt, landed in Alexandria in 48 B.C. with 4,000 legionnaires in pursuit of Pompey. He gained control of the docks and boat landings in the harbor, but the Egyptian navy kept control of the basin and access to the sea. In order to clear the harbor and open his supply lines back to Rome, his first act was to prepare several fire ships. These were ships loaded with combustible material that were sailed out by skeleton crews toward the enemy fleet and set afire. The crews jumped over and swam ashore just before the ships collided with and set fire to the enemy ships.

Alexandria, fire is discovered in the Library (Hutchinson's History of the Nations, 1910).

Crowded into the harbor as they were, the Egyptian fleet was quickly engulfed in flames fanned by a stiff northerly breeze. The wind blew flaming material onto the docks, which were laden with heaps of dry material ready for export. From there, the fire spread to surrounding buildings and the Royal Library, which unfortunately had been built close to the harbor. All of the scrolls, which contained the records of 3,000 years of history, went up in flames and were gone within hours.[1]

It must have given off a fantastic aroma as we recall that papyrus contains something akin to incense, and that Pliny referred to it as "the aromatic weed."

Some called it the greatest act of vandalism ever committed and blamed Caesar for setting the fire. They cite the fact that he never mentioned the destruction of the library in his memoirs as proof of a guilty conscience.[2]

Throughout all this Cleopatra would have stood horrified watching the momentous work of generations of her family burning away while Caesar sniffed. Being a politician and an army man the whole experience may have meant less to him, but the extraordinary thing was that this incident planted a seed in Caesar's mind. If Alexandria had benefited so from a library, would Rome not benefit from one as well? Perhaps he had heard that among the scrolls that went up in flames were almost certainly copies of Ptolemy's biography of Alexander, the godlike conquering hero who served Caesar as a role model. Being a consummate politician, he may have been attracted to the idea that he could make practical use of a concept that Alexander, Aristotle, and Ptolemy had begun. If knowledge was power and libraries a focus of such power, then why not make provision in Rome for such things? In addition to books and buildings, he probably visualized entertainments that would appeal to the *populus Romanus*: including public readings, lectures, and seminars.

The Great Library burns and chaos reigns (from Thomas Cole's Destruction—The Course of Empire, N.Y. Hist. Society, 1836).

As Professor Ewen Bowie, emeritus fellow of Corpus Christi College, Oxford, noted in his excellent review of *Libraries for the Caesars*,[3] Julius Caesar's objectives in establishing a public library must have included maintaining his beneficent image in the eyes of the people and offering the population of Rome something that the major players in late Republican politics, with private libraries in both their town houses and villas, had never offered. Once conceived in Alexandria, Caesar launched his concept of public libraries when he returned to Rome, but was assassinated before any progress could be made.

As for the Royal Library in Alexandria, it survived and with time came back, and what an extraordinary place it must have been. Justin Pollard and Howard Reid captured the tone of the place in their book of *The Rise and Fall Alexandria*. The library was "the single place on earth where all the knowledge in the entire world was gathered together—every great play and poem, every book of physics and philosophy";[4] and all this on papyrus paper.

Alexandria occupies a point of land on the shore of the Mediterranean Sea that encloses several harbors. Though Alexander founded the town and was buried there, it wasn't until after his death in 323 B.C. that his general, Ptolemy I, arrived and built a city that would remain the capital of Egypt for the next thousand years, and become one of the cultural capitals of the world. Lionel Casson, late professor emeritus at New York University, ascribed much of the intellectual aura and reputation of the city to the nature of the first four Ptolemies, all of whom insisted on having leading scholars and scientists as tutors for their children.[5]

It must also have helped that before leaving Macedonia the first Ptolemy (later titled Soter or "savior," by the people of Rhodes), had taken great pains to acquire the corpse of Alexander, his childhood friend. In those days whoever had the body of the ruler who had just passed, held the future as a legacy, since, at the time of his death, Alexander had no heir. His only son was born after he died.

Ptolemy, intent on building his own kingdom in Egypt, could afford to snub the imperial regent and the rest of Alexander's entourage, since he was encouraged on all sides by signs and portents regarding Alexandria; the city he would develop. Soter's goal was to start his own dynasty and do his own thing rather than succeed to the Macedonian empire; so, once the city had been laid out and the first settlers had populated the early buildings, he set out to attract the best and the most talented people to his new capital. Thirty years after Alexander's death, Soter succeeded.

One of the most attractive institutions in his new city was the museum. Built in about 299 B.C. and founded as an institute of advanced learning, it featured a roofed walkway, an arcade, and a communal dining room where scholars routinely ate and shared ideas. In addition to private study rooms, residential quarters, lecture halls, and a theater, it also housed the library, which along with the museum became "the cradle of modern science, of rhetoric, philosophy, medicine, anatomy, geometry, geography, and astronomy, [and] greatly influenced Rome, the other pole of the Mediterranean basin."[6]

In time several of the city's most distinguished thinkers served as librarians or counselors and advised on acquisitions. In addition, there were, as Pollard and Reid pointed out, a "host of geniuses who walked and talked, debated and denounced, read copiously, and finally set pen to paper in the great library and museum attached to the royal palaces of Alexandria."

Among these were Euclid, the father of geometry; Archimedes, mathematician, physicist, engineer and philosopher; Galen, the greatest doctor and physiologist of the age; Claudius Ptolemy, the father of both astronomy and geography; Apollonius, the author of *Jason and the Argonauts*; Eratosthenes, the first man to measure the circumference of the earth; Aristarchus, the first to envisage a heliocentric solar system; Plotinus, a founder of Neoplatonism; Clement of Alexandria, a father of Christian theology; Arius, perhaps the first great Christian heretic; Philo, the radical Jewish theologian; and many more.

Ptolemy Soter died in 283 B.C. at age eighty-four and left a compact, well-ordered realm, a fitting climax to the end of forty years of war. In 289 B.C. he made one of his sons, Ptolemy II, coregent, who, following a smooth transition, further developed the library. Called Philadelphus, he was an army man, historian and shrewd diplomat. He declared himself pharaoh soon after establishing the library and thereafter ruled over an expanded kingdom. His son, Ptolemy III Euergetes ("Benefactor") was also a great administrator and collector and continued in his father's footsteps and spent lavishly to make Alexandria the economic, artistic, and intellectual capital of the Hellenistic Greek world. The rule of Euergetes's not-so-great son, Ptolemy IV, marked the end of Ptolemy power. Eventually the arrival of Caesar and the Romans brought the dynasty down and changed Alexandria forever.

❧

In addition to being a major port and thus having access to books from around the world, Alexandria had the advantage in that it was the main outlet for the only source of paper in the world. At that time, papyrus paper ranked second only to grain as a major export. We see how important it was in an account by Dio Cassius, a Roman consul and noted historian, who wrote that during Caesar's fire "the storehouses of grain and books of the greatest number and excellence were burned . . ."[7] Some have suggested that the books referred to were simply old records kept in storehouses in the port, one of the busiest places in the world. But if so, why use commercial buildings that must have been prime real estate? We have already seen the disdain with which old records were treated. Torn in half, they were carried to the town dump, hopefully to be quickly disposed of so that prying eyes would never discover any tax frauds, minor or major.

Assuming instead that the storehouses were holding paper rolls for export, we have grain and papyrus ranked together in the port commerce. It was also possible that Dio was referring to an even more valuable commodity, inscribed rolls; that is, copies of books stored in these dockside buildings and intended for export. The Ptolemies would not have been above making money by exporting such things.[8]

It is tantalizing to wonder if the rolls in the warehouses were as blank as those in Hemaka's tomb three thousand years previously. Sadly, this also indicates what little progress we've made in understanding the papyrus paper industry of the day.

The Royal Library

Strabo, the Greek geographer, said later that the location of the new city was perfect. It was by the sea, not far from the plantations of the delta, and the very productive grain fields of the Nile valley. A 1521 map of Alexandria by Piri Reis, the Ottoman admiral and geographer, shows the walled city with plantations of food crops marked by palm trees to the west in that part of the delta where extensive papyrus swamps and paper factories would have been in production a thousand of years before. In fact, on his triumphal march from Pelusium to Memphis, Alexander must have passed by acre after acre of papyrus plantations. Once he established himself in Memphis, the old capital city, he was sure to realize the importance of papermaking and that he had just conquered and now ruled the only source of writing paper in the civilized West.

MAP 5: *Sixteenth century map of Alexandria showing plantations east of the city as indicated by palm trees.*

Once the capital shifted to Alexandria—and in later years, once it became a Roman port—a large harvest of papyrus stems would be taken each morning from these same delta plantations. A large portion of this harvest, once dried, would be fed into the boilers of the city's baths, which had been modified to burn reeds rather than wood. Even more impressive was the daily production of paper that fed the ever-growing markets of the world, all of which, like the daily shipments of grain, would pass through Soter's new city. Books became the concern of the Ptolemies early on and they acquired them in great numbers from booksellers in Athens and Rhodes. Casson tells us that in their effort they commissioned agents to buy everything and anything, especially older book scrolls that were close to the originals.[9] Legions of Greek slaves were trained up as copyists and put to work copying books in foreign libraries as well as back home in Alexandria in the Great Library.

Having noticed on some occasion that ships passing through the port often carried books, either for trade or for ship's officers to pass the time, the Ptolemies order these seized. The originals were then catalogued and copies sent back to the ships before they sailed. Books were also copied while they were on loan, the most famous example being the original definitive texts of the plays of Sophocles, Aeschylus, and Euripides. These were kept by the city clerk in Athens until Ptolemy III borrowed them against an enormous deposit, fifteen talents, which was the equivalent of millions of dollars. When challenged for their return, he sent back a deluxe set of copies on papyrus paper and forfeited the fine.[10]

The object of the Ptolemy effort was to make Alexandria the repository of every book ever written, thereby securing the title of the "best and only." They also intended to provide the greatest tool for research ever assembled. From early descriptions of the library it is evident that they were well along the road to achieving their goal, and with holdings of over 490,000 books they were in excellent shape when Caesar dramatically brought all progress to a halt.

Sunset on the City

Just as Alexandria and the Royal Library had grown so spectacularly over the years, even rebuilding itself robustly after the initial fire, its decline was a spectacularly slow, dismal wasting, which included an attack by Aurelian in the 270s A.D., a decree followed by a crusade of vengeance by the Coptic Pope Theophilus in 391 A.D. and finally total destruction during the Muslim conquest of Egypt in 642 A.D. But, as early as the third and fourth centuries, Athenaeus wrote that in Alexandria, books, libraries, and the collection in the museum were by then just a memory. The reasons for this decline in the holdings in Alexandria are many but it did not help when Emperor Diocletian had the early Christian books in the library burnt in 302 A.D. In addition, he had Egyptian technical books thrown into the fire as well.[11] Another large factor was the movement to transfer reading material from papyrus scrolls and codices to parchment, which had begun in a big way by 325 A.D. under Constantine the Great. The books of interest then were the Christian works being produced in Constantinople, not the pagan ones languishing in the Alexandria collection. Another factor was that Rome now had its own libraries, thanks to Julius Caesar. In addition the new center of interest for leaders, politicians, intelligentsia, and theologists had shifted to Constantinople where the first Imperial Library had opened. Luckily, as we will see, there was a selective system put in place in Constantinople and pagan classics were saved systematically. By then Rome and Alexandria were just "so yesterday."

The end was complete when the Great Library was leveled in the seventh century. At that time Amr Ibn al-Asi, the Arab general who conquered Alexandria in 642 A.D., sought advice from his leader, the Sultan Umar, about what to do with the hundreds of thousands of papyrus scrolls in the library. Umar gave him the following famous advice, "If what is written in them agrees with the Book of God, they are not required; if it disagrees, they are not desired. Destroy them therefore." It is said that General Amr ordered the papyrus book rolls distributed among the bathhouses of the city where they provided fuel for the boilers for the next six months.

The Library of Alexandria was superseded in later years by the Imperial Library in Constantinople started by Constantius II, son of the Christian Emperor Constantine, which became the last of the great libraries of the ancient world.

Papyrus paper seemed doomed to the same fate as the Library of Alexandria in that its production had reached its zenith and by the third century B.C. was also on the decline. It was slowly being replaced with parchment, which was not subjected to the cartel economic system that controlled papyrus paper. But, before Pharaoh's treasure sank completely, it was to experience one last burst of glory, as when a sunset sends out an explosion of light just before the orb dips below the horizon.

The new religious movement, Christianity, had arrived in Alexandria on the heels of the Apostle Saint Mark and this incited a burst of religious zeal, during which papyrus paper came to be used for Bibles, first in scroll form, then later in bound versions, codices that were the forerunners of the modern book. During the transition, which spanned a period of about three hundred years until 300 A.D. and until the Imperial Library in Constantinople got underway, the world had to make do with Roman libraries and Roman books that were evolving during this time.

SEVENTEEN

The Romans and the Book Trade

> (My book) my monument shall it be, and raise its head over royal pyramids . . . and the long lapse of immemorial time. I shall not wholly die."
>
> —Horace, *Odes (Carmina)*, 3.30

The scraps, scrolls, and pages of papyrus paper that were conserved and analyzed in the Western world in modern times now show a clear historical progression of literature from 3100 B.C. until the tenth century A.D. But when this story originally unfolded, it was more like watching a movie played backward, since before modern times, say back in the 1700s, anyone looking at this same history would have the impression that the early book trade and the history of papyrus paper began and ended with Rome, which was far from the case. The impression was created because the oldest examples of papyrus paper dating from earlier centuries resided in the archives of the Catholic Church and almost all were written in Latin. In fact, the Romans appeared late on the literary scene. Their world turned on military arts and agriculture. It was not until 240 B.C. when the playwright Livius Andronicus produced what is generally regarded as the first known works in Latin, two plays adapted from the Greeks, that Roman literature began.[1]

Meanwhile, in life and education, the Greeks before them could draw on a literary tradition that went back to the early writings of Homer, Hesiod, Aesop, and the lyric poets, which would have been written down on papyrus paper. It seems to have come as a surprise when some charred papyrus scrolls were dug up in Herculaneum in Italy in 1752 were found to be mostly written in Greek. This offered a clue that the Greek writing world had been built on papyrus paper, a picture that became clearer when more Greek-inscribed scrolls and fragments were uncovered in Egypt in 1778 by early travelers. Now came the realization that there must have been a healthy export trade in papyrus books over the years. Loveday Alexander, emeritus professor at the University of Sheffield, noted that there was evidence as far back as Xenophon's *Anabasis* (370 B.C.) of scavengers finding cases of books washed up on the Black Sea coast, clear testimony to the existence of a papyrus paper book trade.

Even after the Roman takeover of Greece (146 B.C.) Roman literature remained in many ways a continuation of Greek literature and many educated Romans still read and wrote in Greek. It took several centuries before Latin became a dominant factor in the literature of ancient Rome, but when it did, the Roman golden age of classical literature blossomed. Said to have begun with the first known speech of Cicero, it ended with the death of Ovid (81 B.C.–17 A.D.) From the thousands of papyrus fragments that have survived we can assume that millions of books existed during this period. Also, assuming the Romans would have organized and managed the recording, production and distribution of these books, and assuming they would have operated along the same lines as in the modern world, several authors suggested an extensive publishing industry existed. However, publisher, editor, and journalist Rex Winsbury feels they have it all wrong.[2] It was just wishful thinking.

He set out a good argument that there was no publishing industry as we know it today, no distribution, promotion, or sales driving a process based on making money. He notes that the market for written material in Rome was just too small. Many people still could not read. As a result, Roman authors were more apt to have written a book but only so that it could be read aloud. Some writers, called "Euphonists," cherished the sound of poetry over prose. Professor Alexander also points to the lively tradition of oral performance in the early circulation of books. He noted that in the second century A.D., Lucian speaks of an audience hearing the latest histories read. Here we hark back to Alma-Tadema's *A Reading from Homer* that showed this in such a dramatic way.

Thus, in Roman times the audible book was favored over the written text because it was cheap, if not free; only a few copies were needed and it allowed listeners to be educated without ever learning how to read or write! As a result, there was little money to be made from writing; most likely authors in those days looked at their creations as a means of gaining status in this life and the next, which meant they had to make a living elsewhere. Meanwhile their books would serve them as memorials, cheaper perhaps than a tombstone or statue in a public square, but it portended a mean life at best.

Is this any different from today? Alison Flood tells us in the *Guardian* that the median income for a book author in the tweny-first century is $16,200, which is well below the salary required to achieve a minimum acceptable living standard in the United Kingdom.[3] The best advice to an author then as now would be, "Don't quit your day job."

In Roman times books were thought of as great gifts, either to a friend or a library where they would perhaps be read out for the entertainment of others. The size of the audience would become the measure of your immortality, and in this way Homer, though not a Roman, would rank as the model for all eternity.

With the distribution of the content of books done aurally, and not for commercial gain, the production of physical books in Roman times centered around libraries. Libraries had copyists, the ubiquitous Greek slaves, who could faithfully copy out a book. The alternative was to buy a scroll from a shop or a peddler, in which case you had to have your wits about you because the scrolls so offered were often of poor quality. Anyone interested in a good read would be better advised to exchange book scrolls with friends or library staff who had access to authenticated scrolls. This reliance on the real thing brought the libraries and their staff and patrons into exchange programs where lists of holdings were traded, and copies organized among the literate elite.[4, 5]

Professor Alexander illustrated how this production of books went on among social circles of like-minded intellectuals, who were themselves often the main vehicle for the transmission of texts. In the process, once the desired papyrus scrolls had been located, copying went forward. The role of the bookseller in all this was almost incidental. He was clearly useful as an extra potential source for scholarly books, but, as Alexander pointed out, what was central, and primary, was the expectation that books were for sharing.

All this is well illustrated in the example she gives taken from a papyrus letter from Oxyrhynchus. This letter, sent towards the end of the second century A.D., describes a circle of literati exchanging notes on how to procure originals and get copies made. Some of their comments and instructions were made in two footnotes in different hands. Footnote One reads: "Make and send me copies of Books Six and Seven of Hypsicrates' Komodoumenoi, Men Made Fun of in Comedy. For Harpocration says that they are among Polion's books. But it is likely that others, too, have got them. He also has his prose epitomes of Thersagoras's works On the Myths of Tragedy."

Footnote Two instructs the reader of the letter further, in that (also according to the writer's source Harpocration, a Greek author and grammarian), "Demetrius the bookseller has got them. I have instructed Apollonides to send me certain of my own books, which you will hear of in good time from Seleucus himself. Should you find any, apart from those which I possess, make copies and send them to me. Diodorus and his friends also have some which I haven't got."

What was interesting to Alexander was the way in which this scholarly elite intersected and interacted with each other and with patrons, wealthy people who could provide a social framework for scholarly communication. The opportunity provided to an author was important; in this way he gained an entrée into different social networks within the great houses of republican and imperial Rome. In addition, he could promote his work by giving oral performances to the patron's own peers, or by handing out presentation copies of his books. The author's work would thus find a permanent place in his patron's private library where it would be available to anyone who wished to read or copy it.

As the exchanges between libraries widened, and as the opportunities for travel presented themselves, the book trade extended throughout the empire. This process of production and acquisition of books between libraries was self-perpetuating in that the book lists and bibliographies circulated by librarians served as advertisements. Copyists were then charged with searching out the listed scrolls and copying the texts.

As the Christian era loomed, books increasingly became a symbol of cultural power and were thought of as strengthening the Christian movement,[6] which caused leaders like Valens, an earnest Christian emperor of the eastern half of the Roman Empire in 372 A.D., to attach four Greek and three Latin copyists to the library staff at Constantinople,[7] a cost-effective move to strengthen the library, since the cost of producing book scrolls using copyists could not have been much. And the cost of papyrus paper, which did not change during thousands of years, was not excessive. As Skeat showed, one scroll was worth about two drachmae. Obviously, the cartel was still keeping things well in hand.

At about this point papyrus scrolls were being converted to parchment codices, a transition that the Romans did not find easy since, as Winsbury pointed out, the scroll was treasured by the Romans in preference to the codex.

The scroll was treated as a prestige item in Roman society that would be difficult to replace entirely with the new codex format. It would be hundreds of years before the changeover was complete.

An empire-wide trade in papyrus books now developed between libraries (as shown in the diagram on the next page) along with a parallel commercial market for literary scrolls. All of which encouraged scribes to ply their trade privately and sell their products to bookshops.

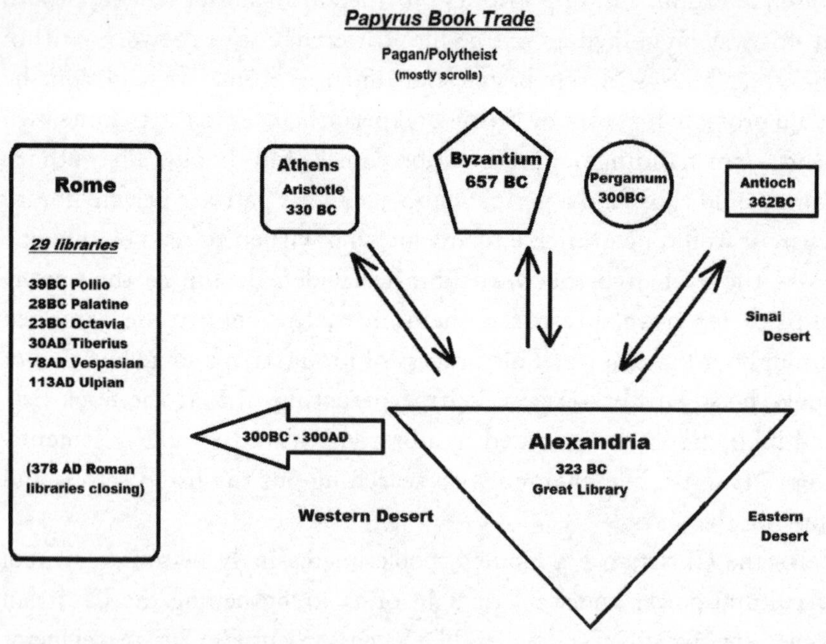

Papyrus book trade—pagan and polytheist (mostly scrolls).

Book stores were known from the early days when Socrates mentioned that books were available in the market in Athens in 399 B.C. By the second century B.C. Alexandria, Rhodes, Brindisi, Carthage, and Athens had all become renowned for the production and export of book scrolls.[8] The most famous booksellers of the day were those located in the large shopping centers of old Rome. In the Forum, for example, Romans could buy books on the Argiletum, opposite Caesar's Forum where you could find Martial's favorite bookseller, Atrectus. His shop could be recognized, says Winsbury, by the doorposts which were covered with the names of poets so that you could work out quickly whose works or books were to be found inside as ready-made copies on the shelves of the store, that is, "a sort of shop-window point-of-sale advertising." Deluxe editions of Martial's own works were available there, "in good presentation copies," for only five denarii each.[9] Need more books by Martial? Try Secundus down the street:

> Lest you wonder, reader, where my book is sold,
> Or waste time looking, I'll be your trusty guide:
> Go to the shop of Secundus, the freedman of learned Lucensis,
> Behind the Temple of Peace and the Forum of Minerva.
> —(Martial, *Epigrams*, 1.2.5–8)

Martial was one of the few writers who could live by his pen. His publishers in Rome owned large numbers of slaves who were trained to be neat and rapid scribes. Fifty or a hundred of these slaves could write from the dictation of one reader, and thus an edition of a new volume of his *Epigrams* could be produced with great rapidity and at very small cost.[10] But, as successful as he was, he hardly made enough to live on.

Galen, one of the greatest physicians of antiquity, commented in the second century A.D. on the fact that the Sandalarium district near Vespasian's Temple of Peace contained the largest concentration of booksellers, but he questioned whether the copies they sold of his work (on papyrus scrolls) were accurate and true. A prolific writer, he prepared a register of titles of his authentic works in order to ensure that medical students of his day or anyone interested could check titles offered against his detailed list, a list that in his case numbered more than fifty titles.

It was considered wise when dealing with the likes of Atrectus and Secundus to bring someone with you who could judge the quality of the copy. Consider the famous door-to-door book salesman that Dius described,[11] who in 150 A.D. stopped by Julius Placidus's place to offer him six scrolls for sale. Julius rejected the lot, buying only some separate pages. Better perhaps to buy from a reliable dealer such as Pomponius Atticus. This was the wealthy friend of Cicero who decided to compete with the Roman booksellers by maintaining a staff of Greek slaves who would copy manuscripts and sell their work, presumably at a cheap price. In this way he could provide the public with trustworthy copies at reasonable cost.

Once acquired, and assuming the right climate prevailed and that the librarians controlled insects and physical damage, papyrus book scrolls could last for hundreds of years. Most of the rolls in the library of the Villa dei Papiri in southern Italy were 120–160 years old at the time the Villa was destroyed. The collection also contained a significant number of scrolls about 200 years old and even a few 350 years old,[12] the equivalent of today owning books dating back to the 1600s.

❧

Looking back over the Roman period, in addition to a great void created by the paucity of surviving literary texts, there was also a lack of knowledge about what must have been an extensive use of industrial paper. We cannot therefore know the exact role of paper at the time, but, like the Roman army and the supply of grain, paper must have been one of the important items holding the empire together. No matter what the leadership and command qualities were of the leaders in Rome, Constantinople, Milan, or Ravenna, no matter how much the *denarius* was worth, or how many new ones were produced, or the nature of laws passed that affected the outlying provinces, they were as nothing if the leaders could not communicate their wishes to the far-flung regions of imperial rule and record births, deaths, and other vital statistics.

Perhaps the first newspaper, the *Acta Diurna*, served this purpose. Carved originally on metal or stone, it was later recorded by scribes on papyrus paper. It was said to be a record of the proceedings of the Senate and is mentioned by contemporary writers as a regular official medium for transmitting news. Cicero, for example, thought of it as a source of city news and gossip about marriages and divorces; and it was sent to subscribers in distant cities and sometimes read out to an assembled army.

One consequence of papyrus paper becoming so widespread was that as more and more documents arrived in cities throughout the Empire, archives had to be created. Many of the incoming documents were of a standard nature; for example, census forms that were completed at village or provincial level that included information on land ownership, animal or human counts, or anything of interest to a Roman prefect. Since they were standard forms, sheets could simply be pasted, one after another, into the appropriate roll. Each form would be marked as a separate item and numbered in the top margin with a file reference of say, "roll 10, sheet 19."[13] This was especially useful for keeping track of data that came in on a regular basis. A single roll could then run to 400 items and more; and could build to a length of at least twenty-three feet. Such files could be tightly rolled so that a thirty-foot roll would have a diameter of about three inches. But, as Parsons has pointed out, it would have required a brisk wrist to check item number 300, and any repeated process of scrolling through would put a strain on the pasted paper joins within the rolls.

And so the official archives grew into a mountain of papyrus paper that rose right in the heart of Rome. The extent of the archives is appreciated in Suetonius's description of the Great Fire of Rome in 64 A.D. when many of the books held in Rome's libraries were destroyed. But, as related by the Australian historical author, Stephen Dando-Collins, a number of the records held in the Tabularium, the massive 140-year-old state archive on the lower slope of the Capitoline Hill overlooking the Forum, were removed to safety by the city fathers.[14]

These rescued records, all handwritten papyrus scrolls, ranged from the *Acta Senatus*, the verbatim record of every word spoken in every single session of the Senate since the late Republic (made possible by the invention of shorthand by Cicero's secretary, Tiro), copies of every edition of the government newspaper the *Acta Diurna*, the private, unpublished letters and memoirs of Augustus, and the memoirs of Nero's mother, Agrippina.

All of this would be of great use to Suetonius when he came to write his biographies of the twelve Caesars half a century later. Which all goes to show that papyrus was doing its job providing the medium that allowed life to go on; a function that only worked if it was kept away from fire, a lesson that the Roman emperors seemed incapable of learning.

EIGHTEEN

Roman Libraries

In order to appreciate the impact of papyrus paper on the daily life of the Romans in a more familiar setting, we could take a trip to my favorite library. This is a library that no longer exists, but when it did it was a bit different from the ordinary community or regional public library that many of us are used to. Not only was it located in Rome; it was situated on the south of the Coliseum inside the compound of the Baths of Caracalla. Another odd thing is that it lies mostly in the open space of the ruins.

On my way to Africa years ago, where I would begin my work on the ecology of the papyrus plant, I stopped over in Rome, where I saw a performance of Verdi's *Aida*, a production that used to be staged in the Baths of Caracalla. The original opera had been commissioned by the Khedive of Egypt to celebrate the opening of the Suez Canal in 1869; so I thought this would be a great introduction to the early days of Africa and Egypt. It was first performed in Cairo and played for years in Rome where the ruins of the Baths evoked the ancient temples of Egypt. Little did I know as I watched the live elephant and dromedaries trooping across the stage that I was within a stone's throw of a place where, at the height of Rome's glory, hundreds of scrolls were kept, all inscribed on papyrus paper made originally in Egypt.

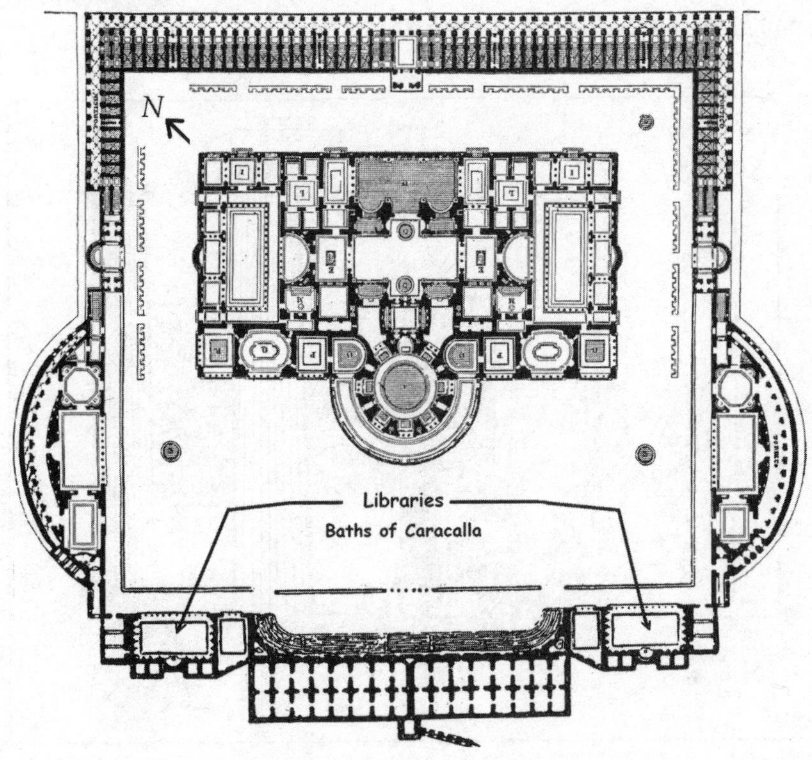

Plan of the Baths of Caracalla showing the two libraries.
(after Giuseppe Ripostelli, The Thermae of Caracalla. Rome, 1914).

I have since returned to Rome and on occasion walked by the most southwestern end of the ruins to gaze fondly on the remains of the walls of this library, trying to recapture the mood of those days.

Dedicated in 217 A.D. in the last year of the reign of the notorious Caracalla, the baths were the largest in Rome at that time. A trip to my library meant you had to gain entrance to the baths. Even so, visiting the library back then would have been a notably different task than visiting any library today. In ancient days, when you were tired of reading you could take a quick dip in a cold or hot bath, or work out in two gyms, take a run around the sports field, or have a snack, a massage, or a nap—or all three—in a private room. Lockers, food, drink, even the occasional lecture and other entertainments were available. There were two reading rooms, one for Greek and another for Latin scrolls, both were roomy places that occupied the southern ends of the bath complex.

A Roman library with book scrolls, readers and a caretaker (after Wikipedia).

On a visit there we would pass by the columns of the courtyard and perhaps enter the Latin room first where we would see statues in niches. At a minimum there would be one of Minerva the goddess of poetry, wisdom, and virginity. Lining the walls would be more niches or wooden cases with hundreds of scrolls stacked inside. Jacalyn Spoon, publications assistant at Cornell University, tells us that niches did not appear in Greek libraries and their appearance in Roman libraries might be traced to Caesar being influenced by the library at Alexandria in Egypt. In Egypt the niches served as shelves, wood being scarce and costly, it was cheaper to leave spaces between or simply cut a niche in the thick local limestone blocks that made up the walls. She found that in Rome the niches averaged twenty-four inches deep, more than enough to accommodate the longest roll.[1] On the other hand, George Houston, professor emeritus of classics at the University of North Carolina at Chapel Hill, is having none of this; he argues that wooden cases must have been present, if not in every library, at least in the large imperial collections. Such cases or, *armaria*, would present an impressive display of cabinetry as befitting such buildings.[2]

Papyrus scrolls "books" being stacked in an ancient library (note each scroll has a label). (after Fourth century A.D. Roman relief).

Casson likewise sees armaria taking up the spaces designed for them in Trajan's Ulpian Library.[3] He suggests the wooden nature of the cases would have protected the book rolls from moisture that would have been inevitable in walls of stone. The cabinets in that library would have contained something like 20,000 books. Assuming armaria were used in the library dedicated to the Roman Senator Celsus in the ancient Greek city of Ephesus (now in Turkey), Houston estimated that that library held up to 10,500 scrolls.[4] He also made the point that some of the book cabinets must have been substantial, as we are told that one Fannius Caepio (not our

Fannius of honeyeater fame) hid in one during an assassination attempt on Augustus. Caepio was subsequently caught and executed.

The most popular scrolls, those used daily, would be stored conveniently in *capsa*, a book container that looked like a large hat-box (as shown at the feet of Clio in the frontispiece). Capsa also served as scroll carriers for travel. For the most part such scrolls would be simply rolled up without handles. Carla Schodde, historian and Latin scholar in Melbourne, Australia, found most scrolls of the Roman period lacked wooden handles from a quick survey of Roman sculpture, frescos, and the carbonized scrolls from Herculaneum. Perhaps they were reserved for the more elaborate, high-end editions created in order to occupy a permanent place in an elegant private library. Schodde concluded that wooden handles would be too cumbersome for scrolls that had to be brought with you on a long voyage. When it came time to pack, wooden handles would be a nuisance if you were stuffing scrolls into a capsa.[5]

In our case, if we were using my favorite library, we'd write out the titles on ostraca, the shards of pottery mentioned earlier, which would be passed to the library staff, who were well-versed and well-trained Greek slaves. While they searched out our volumes, we'd find a place to sit and wait or go about our business at the baths. In private homes, book scrolls were simply stored loose on open shelves or left in earthenware jugs. When they were on the shelf in a library, they would be kept in a scroll box, or *scrinium*. Several scrolls could be stored together with a title tag at the end of each and possibly a handle or center stick, called an *umbicus*.

Private libraries became fashionable in the more sophisticated Roman villas and palatial manor houses where a room or two would be set aside just for papyrus scrolls in magnificent cabinets. And what scrolls! Beautifully finished connoisseurs' editions, inscribed on the finest quality papyrus paper, smoothed with pumice, rolled onto center sticks that had been anointed with cedar oil to discourage insect pests, and fitted with *cornuta*, ivory, or ebony handles. The whole would be wrapped in a red-dyed parchment sleeve tied with red leather thongs and perhaps silver labels attached.

Such ostentatious trappings were missed by Ovid, who would send his poetry home on plain scrolls from his place of exile outside Rome, lamenting that the rolls were "unadorned, as becomes the book of an exile. In your misfortune wear the garb that befits these days of mine."

Imperial and Private Libraries

In addition to standardizing papyrus paper, privatizing the industry, and vastly increasing papyrus paper's use, the Romans also set up "public" libraries to accommodate new holdings and archives. These impressive institutions were erected toward the end of the republic during the expanded program of building that accompanied the beginning of the empire.

As we saw earlier, it was Julius Caesar who broached the idea of the first library in Rome. Some say he did this in a fit of remorse, since it was his fault that the Great Library in Alexandria had burned down. But because of his execution by Brutus, et al., the honor of building the first public library fell to one of his allies, Gaius Asinius Pollio in 39 B.C., who in the words of Pliny was "the first to make men's talents public property."[6]

Set up in the atrium of the Offices of the Censors on the Aventine Hill, south of the Palatine, this first library was said to contain a large collection of books on civil law and general culture following a wish of Caesar's for the consolidation of works in these areas of study.

Though it was called a "public" library, the people who used it were members of the literati who, when they referred to "public access," had in mind an exclusive public made up of people like themselves.[7] Such libraries were more accurately called imperial libraries because they were housed in buildings built by imperial fiat, such as in temples, federal office buildings, even palaces. What then was their function? Matthew Nicholls from the Department of Classics at the University of Reading felt they were designed from the outset with an ostentatious public function in mind, part of a wider program of cultural display in Emperor Augustus's new Rome. They were meant to serve as magnificent backdrops for cultural activities of various sorts, events such as readings by popular authors that involved lots of people.[8] Excess books, archives, and scroll copies that were not needed immediately were stored in nearby storehouses, which were among the buildings burned down in the fire of 192 A.D.[9]

Pollio's library was followed by two libraries established by Augustus, who in 28 B.C. built the Temple of Apollo on the southwest side of the Palatine Hill to commemorate his victory over Antony and Cleopatra in the Battle of Actium. He included a Greek and Latin reading room among the buildings. This was the second public library in the city. Winsbury suggested that it was in fact built to house books that were part of the loot Augustus confiscated from some of his generals who found themselves on the outs. At that point he may have had "a lot of books to put somewhere."

The third library in Rome was that erected by Augustus inside the Portico Metelli located between the Tiber River and the Capitoline near the Theater of Marcellus. This portico was built in 146 B.C. by an army commander who fought in the Macedonian wars. Architecturally, it was one of the most beautiful buildings in Rome.[10] At the center were the Temples of Juno and Jupiter, among the first marble temples built in Rome. When Emperor Augustus rebuilt the portico between 33 and 23 B.C., he dedicated it to his sister Octavia and it was known from then on as the Portico of Octavia. It included the Library of Marcellus, which was commissioned by Octavia in memory of her son, while her brother, Augustus, completed the large popular theatre nearby, also in honor of Marcellus that became the largest and most important theater of its time.[11]

We see in all this activity that libraries, and the papyrus scrolls deposited in them, had risen to a new level of sophistication, almost an obsession with those interested in creating these "Temples to the Book" or "Sanctuaries of Paper." It is important to note that they were built in proximity to a place of worship or palace of a patron god or deified hero. Presumably the link between books and immortality was becoming more apparent, especially when we see that Octavia chose such a thing as a memorial for her son. This is a statement in itself, as she was an extraordinary person. One of the most prominent women in Roman history, she was respected and admired by contemporaries for her loyalty, nobility, and humanity, and for maintaining traditional Roman feminine virtues. Called Octavia Minor to distinguish her from an elder half-sister, she was the fourth wife of Mark Antony; their marriage was severely tested by Antony's abandonment of her and their two children in favor of his lover, Queen Cleopatra.

Antony divorced her in 32 B.C. but only after she had supplied him with men and troops in 35 B.C., to be used in his eastern campaigns. Octavia returned to Rome from the East following Antony's suicide in 30 B.C. and became the sole caretaker of Antony's children from her own marriage as well as his pervious ones. Her undying love, however, was reserved for her firstborn, Marcellus. Emperor Augustus also adored him and when Marcellus died unexpectedly of illness in 23 B.C., Augustus was thunderstruck. Octavia was disconsolate; she never fully recovered and retired from public life. The popular poet of the age, Virgil, added the name of Marcellus to the very end of the list of illustrious future Romans whom Aeneas sees in the underworld in the *Aeneid.* Several verses in Virgil's epic recount Marcellus's life, connect him back to his illustrious ancestors, and lament his tragic early death.

When Virgil recited this part of his work during an audience with Augustus and his sister, it caused Octavia to faint with grief. Revived only with difficulty, she later sent Virgil 10,000 sesterces, a very generous token of respect for what he had done.[12]

The whole scene is captured for us in a painting by Jean-Baptiste Wicar, a French historical painter, where we see Virgil reciting as he holds on to one scroll of papyrus paper, while several others stand ready on a nearby table. The scene is perhaps taking place in the Latin room of the new library commissioned by Octavia. Urged on possibly by Pollio, a great supporter of Virgil, the poet is following the popular mode of reciting from his books, memorializing himself, as well as his works and his patrons, and commemorating Octavia's son and the medium that made it all possible, papyrus paper.

The Library in the Portico of Octavia burned in 80 A.D. and was restored, probably in 90 A.D. by Domitian. It burned again in a second fire in 203 A.D. and was again renovated, this time by Septimius Severus and his son Caracalla in ca. 200 A.D. in honor of Caracalla's great-grandmother.

The portico was used as a fish market from the medieval period up to the end of nineteenth century. This role is remembered in the name of the annexed church of Sant'Angelo in Pescheria, or "the Holy Angel in the Fish Market," perhaps even a reflection on Octavia, a saint and an angel by any measure. The building, which lies in the *rione* (or district) of Sant'Angelo, represents the center of the Roman Ghetto.

❧

All three of these early Roman libraries stayed open and in operation for years. After the time of Caesar and Augustus, the next imperial library, was built by Tiberius near the colonnade around which he built his palace, the

Domus Tiberius.[13] He built another in the Temple of the Deified Augustus (37 A.D.) as a tribute to his stepfather who died in 14 A.D. Vespasian continued the tradition of building libraries with one next to the Temple of Peace in 71 A.D. That temple lasted all of 120 years, after which it burned down in 191 A.D.[14]

The greatest enemy of these ancient libraries seems to be fire. Presumably the dry paper rolls and wooden cabinets were easy to set alight. Even if precautions were taken inside the library, fires could break out in the neighborhood, which was always a problem because of the close quarters inside the city. The Great Fire of Rome in 64 A.D. caused terrific losses to the book collections and archives of the time. This fire destroyed the Palatine Library in the Temple of Apollo and was later followed by a fire in the library of the Portico of Octavia in 80 A.D. In 192 A.D., during the reign of Commodus, a fire destroyed the Temple of Peace together with many warehouses and storehouses in the Via Sacra, in which the overflow of the local imperial library was stored. A warehouse of papyrus paper, or *horrea chartaria*, was also located here and must have contributed significantly to the blaze.[15]

The two rooms of the Ulpian Library straddling the Column of Trajan in ancient Rome (Wikipedia).

The most impressive Roman library of all, the Ulpian, was established by Trajan in 113 A.D. as part of his Forum. The sumptuously appointed Greek and Latin rooms spanned the area on either side of his famous column. Two enormous rooms (each sixty by eighty feet) provided matching, two-storied temples to books, the rooms of which were paved in granite and marble from Egypt and Africa, with columns and walls of variegated marble. Green marble was used liberally throughout, as the color was thought to refresh the eyes.[16] The thousands of papyrus paper scrolls rested in white-marble niches lined with citrus wood and ivory decorated cabinets, a luxury and elegance that befitted the pharaoh's own as well as immortalizing an emperor.

The Ulpian lasted many years and was followed by the libraries of Domitian, Hadrian, and Severus, all of whom followed the imperial tradition; by the fourth century A.D. there were twenty-nine public libraries in Rome. They were supplemented by at least twenty-four others throughout Italy and more in other parts of the empire, such as the Grecian provinces, as well as Asia Minor, Cyprus, and Africa. The imperial libraries served the Empire well. Michael Affleck, librarian at the University of Queensland, summed up their usefulness when he noted that the Palatine Library ended its life when destroyed by fire in 363 A.D.—a lifespan of nearly 400 years. The Ulpian Library of Trajan built in 114 was still operating in 456 A.D. He compared this to the two most significant library collections in the world today, the British Library and the Library of Congress, both of which are infants in comparison, having been in existence for only a little more than 200 years.[17]

Though they were powerful reminders of Rome's literary ideals, these enormous imperial library buildings served more like archives, record offices, or meeting places than libraries as we know them. One emperor used his as an audience hall, a place to hold meetings of the Senate, and receive foreign ambassadors. It was practically an extension of his house. The Ulpian served as part of the state archives along with the Tabularium, which was the Public Record Office.

Though imperial libraries were well founded, several researchers have pointed out that Romans preferred to work in their private libraries or those of their friends. Private libraries had been in existence well before public libraries appeared on the scene. The idea that books were worth taking as loot occurred about the time General Paullus returned from his conquests in Macedonia in 167 B.C. He brought home the contents of King Perseus's royal library, which he presented to his sons, who were fond of letters. Pompeius Strabo took many manuscripts during the sacking of Asculum in 89 B.C., and later still, Sulla, the Roman general and statesman, while master of Athens (86 B.C.) seized the remains of Aristotle's library, and just as Ptolemy had taken the body of Alexander back to Egypt, Sulla brought home Aristotle's great *corpus* of knowledge. Aristotle, who by chance had been Alexander's tutor, affected the minds of men so gravely that perhaps some felt that just being close to the Master's books and his works would allow the greatness to rub off. In any event while they were housed in Italy, and until they finally went missing, they were much in demand.[18] Sulla, well-read, intelligent, and fluent in Greek, a sign of education in Rome, obviously knew what he was doing, as he shortly became dictator of Rome.

Lucullus, the remarkable and skillful conqueror of the eastern kingdoms, returned to Rome with so much captured booty that it is said the whole could not be fully accounted. He poured enormous sums into private buildings and patronized the arts and sciences lavishly, transforming his hereditary estate in the highlands of Tusculum into a retreat house for scholars and philosophers. He stocked the library there with loads of papyrus scrolls acquired during his conquests in 70 B.C. It was this family library that was the noted exception to the policy of privacy at all costs. Lucullus's library was thrown open to men of letters, including the Greek literati of Rome. "Accordingly his library and the neighboring walks were much resorted to, especially by Greeks" who would "pass whole days together, happily staying away from their other duties."[19]

Lucullus, Cicero, and Atticus set the fashion and many followed. Tyrannion, a Greek grammarian who organized Sulla's and Cicero's libraries, is said to have had 30,000 volumes of his own; Varro, the Roman scholar and writer, had a large collection; and Sammonicus, a savant and tutor to Caracalla, left one of his pupils, the young Gordian, no less than 62,000 volumes.

And so the idea grew that rich men could profit by furnishing their libraries with something other than chairs and tables. By then perhaps a library was as much the signature of affluence as in modern times, when we occasionally hear about a large house with a library in which the owner has never set foot.

The average library in ancient days held 30,000–100,000 scrolls; of these, the number of complete works might be less. Consider the writings of just one of the most prolific of the ancient philosophers, Epicurus, whose entire production filled 300 papyrus rolls. His longest single work, *On Nature*, took up thirty-seven rolls. Thus, a large number of scrolls might represent only about 20,000 complete books, not much in comparison to modern libraries.

Stocked with shelves, niches, and cabinets containing thousands of scrolls, the imperial and large private libraries were bilingual with two reading rooms, mostly because the Greek classics were still in vogue; many lesser Greek documents had yet to be translated, and wealthy Romans, even if they couldn't read Greek, were terrific snobs and would attach a certain hubris to being seen as bilingual.

Our library in the Baths of Caracalla is not in the same league as the large Roman libraries with their stately porticos, colonnades and restricted admittance, but it was a lot easier to get into. Admission was free, although the bath attendant received a copper coin called a *quadrans,* the equivalent of less than a penny. It also opened at sunrise, as did the Ulpian, but it was not in an ideal location since the reading rooms were oriented to the southwest so the light was not as good as it could be, the better libraries had rooms facing east to catch the morning light. Locating the library with eastern exposure also helped preserve the papyrus scrolls, since the morning air from that direction was drier. That, and sunlight itself discouraged the insects and dampness that ruined the books.

Another problem with our library in the baths was that it was close to the water intake and reservoirs. Luckily, the baths are covered with vaulted roofs, so the humidity was less of a problem. The sound of hundreds of bathers echoing throughout the large open halls of the main baths would have been a real headache but for the fact that our reading room was located some distance from the main area where people congregate.

Libraries located in baths and gymnasia were kept going by donations and perhaps subscriptions from members. In 275 B.C., Ptolemy II presented the city of Athens with a gymnasium and the people were ordered by popular mandate to increase its library holdings by a hundred rolls each year, while prominent citizens were expected to provide 150 rolls or 200 drachmas.[20]

In the early days, one inscribed roll was perhaps worth slightly more than two drachmas, but this changed by the time of Cicero (106–43 B.C.) when dealers pushed up the cost of the finished book scroll. Cheap copies could be had in Rome from Cicero's wealthy friend Atticus, who was producing the equivalent of the first Penguin Classics of history. But still, even though the scrolls in the bath libraries would probably not be of the highest quality, it would take years to accumulate a decent collection. Quick copies of the classics, satires, and gossipy journals of the day and ordinary material by the minor authors would be dashed off and well thumbed. So we can't expect too much as we sit waiting for our scrolls to arrive.

If we intend to make notes as we read we are most likely going to use a palimpsest notebook, a collection of small leaves of parchment that acted as a scratchpad or better yet a wax tablet, the *pugillare* that was in common use throughout the empire. In that case the writing, quick notes and dictation, could simply be smoothed over to start anew once transcribed to papyrus. But it might still be a while before we get to the final stage of our work. Meantime, perhaps we have dallied too long as the light is fading, or perhaps you've spent too much time in the baths.

"Can't we just take a few of these home?" you ask.

It was possible to do that, but remember: the fine for not returning on time could be quite steep. There was no such thing as a dollar or two as today. Spoon tells us that in one library in Athens a patron who would not return an original ancient text was punished with a fine of fifteen skilled slaves! Hoping to appease the librarian he sent the library a copy of the original, apparently to no effect. So, we had better make plans to return to the library some other day, and look forward to the time when libraries will be better equipped. We know things will change because John Willis Clark, in his 1901 classic, *The Care of Books*, tells us that in 538 A.D., when our mentor Cassiodorus started his religious brotherhood in southern Italy, he provided his library with self-supplying lamps to enable readers and copyists to work at night, careful always, we hope, to extinguish all open flames before they retired for the night.

But all that was yet to come, during our visit we are lucky to have had as much daylight as we did.

Now for dinner and a good night's sleep before we leave for Pompeii.

NINETEEN

Those Precious, Tender-hearted Scrolls

I've passed through Pompeii on several occasions, and in every case found myself looking over my shoulder, wondering what or who might be following me or lurking in the ruins. If there is any place on earth where ghosts roam unfettered, it must be there. Ever since the eruption of Vesuvius in the summer of 79 A.D., it has been a quiet, almost eerie place, like a large cemetery in which the dead are only partially interred. The scariest part is the Garden of Fugitives with its plaster casts on view of people frozen in death throes. Who could ever forget the expressions on the faces of these vaporized bodies, or the remains of food left on the table on that fateful day?

Prior to the eruption, it was a prosperous, thriving resort town with luxurious villas positioned to take advantage of the natural beauty of the place. The Bay of Naples close by is unrivalled in its scenery and sunsets, the warm waters of the hot spas fed by volcanic hot springs brought droves of wealthy Roman tourists to the local art galleries. The construction business blossomed as vacation houses sprouted and nearby towns grew. Julius Caesar, Augustus, Cicero, Tiberius, Caligula, Claudius, and Nero all had summer places on the bay.[1]

In the seaside town of Herculaneum, which lies between Pompeii and Naples, the residents heard a tremendous explosion late one afternoon. With that warning, they made their way down to the boats in the harbor; thus, when the town was excavated hundreds of years later, few corpses were found in the houses or streets of Herculaneum, unlike the bodies strewn about in Pompeii where people had been caught in the streets. Sadly, however, in Herculaneum many were found trapped on the beach. When the boats left the docks, hundreds were left behind. People who were too late, too poor, or too weak were huddled in the ancient boathouses where their corpses were uncovered in 1981.

Following the eruption, the town was then engulfed in pyroclastic clouds of hot gas and glowing dust along with tons of glowing ash. At that point, a great number of residents probably wished that they had, like the locally adored poet Philodemus, gone elsewhere.

> Melicertes and his mother, sea-blue queen of the deep,
> Leucothea, goddess against evil,
> And dancing Nereids, and waves, and Poseidon,
> And Zephyrus eek of the gentlest breath,
> Be good and bear me clean over the big swells
> Safe and sound to the sweet shore of Piraeus.
>
> —*(G. Economou, 1987)*

Late the following day, heavy rains commenced and the ground was soaked for three days until mudslides flowed down the flanks of Vesuvius covering the town and the villas with a deep blanket of ash, rock, and mud, and bringing a silence that lasted many years. In 1709 well-diggers uncovered evidence of buried marble sculptures, and in 1738 the military engineer Roque de Alcubierre began excavations for the King of Naples, Charles III. Numerous sculptures, murals, and remnants of buildings were dug up as over ninety bronze and marble statues were recovered.[2] Early reports from the site that told it was still contaminated with poisonous volcanic gases after many hundreds of years made excavators leery of further work; but by 1750 a long, narrow passage had been hacked below the sixty-nine-foot ash layer, and King Charles and his wife, the Queen Consort Maria Amalia, encouraged the excavations.

Over time they decorated one whole wing of their summer palace in the nearby town of Portici with artwork from Herculaneum. Ten years later, Alcubierre transferred his interest to a neighboring site that had been identified as Pompeii. He charged his assistant Karl Weber with drawing up a plan of the Herculaneum excavation. Weber's plan included the remains of a large villa called the Villa Calpurnia that had once belonged to Lucius Calpurnius Piso, scourge of Cicero and father-in-law to Julius Caesar. Piso was one of the richest Romans of his day. In 1752 word came that 250 rolls of papyrus had been found in that villa. Subsequently, it became known as the Villa dei Papiri.

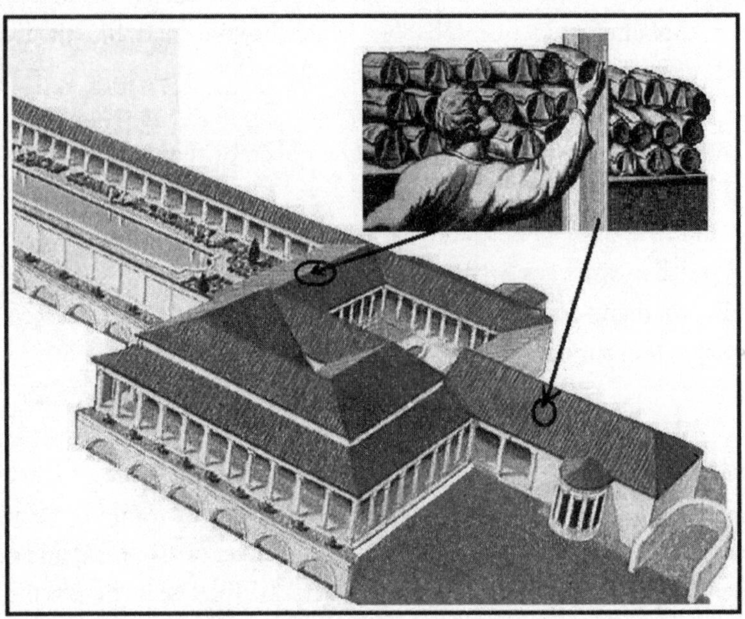

Villa dei Papiri with the location of papyri found, some stacked on shelves. (Dr. M. Capasso, with permission).

The announcement in Europe of the discovery of ancient books was treated as extraordinary news. By then the Enlightenment was in full swing; people had begun reading extensively. Philosophy, the science of reason, was being devoured and digested, leaving behind an enormous appetite. Original and new books of the ancient Greek and Roman philosophers were exactly what were needed, perhaps accompanied by a few small volumes of delightful and meaningful ancient poetry or prose. Many thought the works of Virgil and Livy would be forthcoming. Until then, other than the old papyrus church documents in Latin and occasional fragments from Egypt, papyrus paper had been considered history, and the plant itself had been forgotten. In fact, it was only in the following year 1753 that Carolus Linnaeus (Carl von Linné) got around to giving it its official Latin name, *Cyperus papyrus*. But he was in no doubt that it was a thing of the past, since a colleague of his had traveled the length of Egypt in 1752 and found that it had disappeared.

The news from Herculaneum unleashed a torrent of interest. Then came the details, the objects found resembled nothing more than lumps of coal. It was announced in *Philosophical Transactions*, the science journal of the Royal Society of London that year that yes, they were ancient papyrus paper books, and yes, there were hundreds of them, but sadly, they had been "*turn'd to a sort of charcoal, so brittle, that, being touched, it falls readily into ashes.*"[3]

Back in Naples, realizing that the world was looking over his shoulders, Charles, who was a conscientious collector, formed an Institute that would record and look after those items that could not be transported to his house. It was here that the charred scrolls were deposited under tight security. The enormous interest from the public forced him to keep the excavations highly controlled. No visitor, of which there were now hundreds, was allowed to use a pencil, the equivalent of today's proscription, "No photos, please!"

The first attempts to read the rolls began under the direction of Camillo Paderni, an Italian artist and newly appointed head of the Institute. He simply cut several lengthwise down the center like so many cucumbers, and was astounded when they fell apart and crumbled into black dust. Next, the Duke of Sansevero, a personal friend of the king and a budding alchemist, tried his luck. Judith Harris describes the results in her book,

Pompeii Awakened. He soaked several in a pot of mercury and the scrolls dissolved completely.[4] Then came a Neapolitan philologist who was convinced that strong sunlight would vaporize the ink and leave behind an impression against the charred surface that could be read. Disappointingly, exposure wiped out both the ink and the impression. Rosewater was tried next, which was a disaster but left the rolls smelling better than the next treatment tried by an Italian chemist using "vegetable gas," a dreadful odor (think rotting cabbages) that drove everyone from the room, including the courtiers and ladies drawn there to witness the first readings of the words contained on these precious rolls.[5]

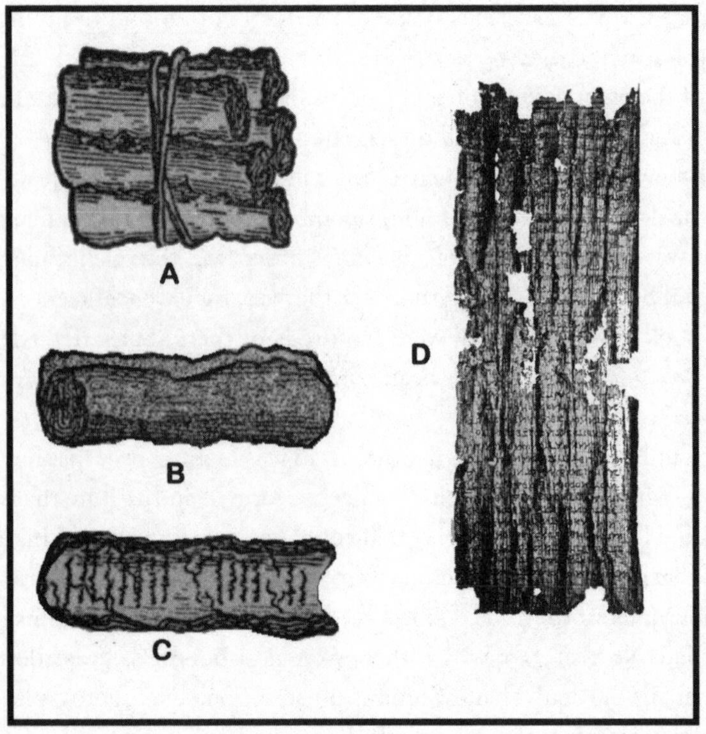

Charred scrolls: A-tied for transport; B-single scroll; C-split open; and D-unrolled (after Barker, 1908).

All of these efforts were to no avail; the learned world would have to wait. And so they were left sitting on the edges of their chairs.

Finally, an expert, Padre Antonio Piaggio, a calligrapher from the Vatican, was called in. Because of his two callings as a monk and a calligrapher, who, by necessity must work with care and attention, Piaggio's slow and patient attitude incensed the impatient Camillo Paderni, who needed immediate results. The Institute, now his responsibility, had begun, in his own words, "under straitened circumstances." It would never succeed if it were burdened by what he called these "useless things," which contained "no element of noble erudition." Besides that they were "torn" and "impossible to repair." To the horror of Padre Antonio, Paderni continued to slice, poke and pry at the rolls, while the saintly monk built and perfected a machine.

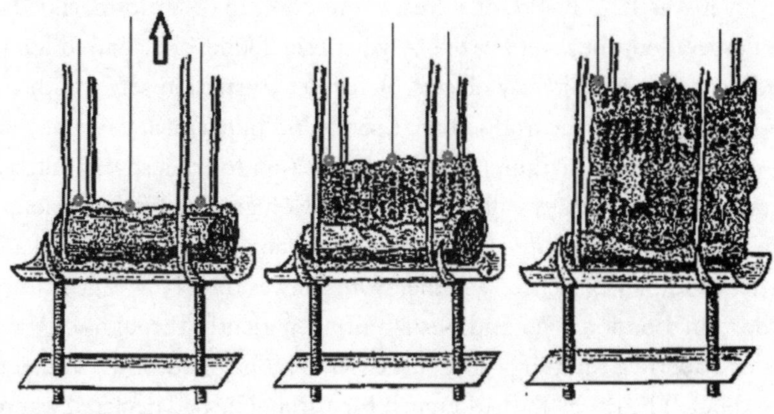

The monk Piaggio's machine for unrolling charred scrolls (after Barker, 1908).

Described as a marvel of its day, it was equipped with slender silk threads gummed gently to the fragile ashed remains of papyrus that it lifted with care from the surface of the rolls, which had been moistened with a special liquor. This delicate film was unrolled onto a membrane to support it. He could unroll a few millimeters during the course of a whole day, a full scroll would require four years. Padremi tore his hair out, there was nothing to do but wait.

And so, in a classic rerun of the race between the tortoise and the hare, Piaggio won, but as usual in such cases, his exasperated boss Paderni made the first announcement and therefore received the credit. In 1755 he let the world know that the Greek writings on the papyrus scrolls "favored the writings of Epicurus."

In 1793, three years before he died, the first of Piaggio's work was finally published and the world learned that after forty years of waiting, there were to be no manuscripts of Virgil or lost books of Livy. Instead everyone had to be content with an essay on music by Philodemus, a follower of the Epicurean school of philosophy; though it miraculously saw the light of day after seventeen hundred years, this was poor fare for the starving. As Professor James Porter of University of California Berkeley pointed out in his elegant essay, "Hearing Voices: The Herculaneum Papyri and Classical Scholarship," the original expectations of discovery had been shared by an entire generation. Their search for books, or at least manuscripts in codex form, ended in utter desperation; they were dazed by what they found, the charred lumps defied description as literary objects. A further frustration set in with the news that many were the works of the Epicurean Philodemus, the same man who rejected classical culture! There was a reason for this special interest in Epicureanism by the wealthy upper-class Roman elite of the region; it offered them "a compelling alternative to the chaos of political turmoil and the stress of urban existence." In other words, it was their New Age culture.

Those in London who had been waiting patiently through all those years of Paderni's fumbling now turned away. They had other things to think about. The newly formed French First Republic had declared war on England and by the end of 1793 the Reign of Terror had started.

The work in Naples waited until Reverend John Hayter arrived in 1800. It continued from there under the direction of people using methods based on hands-on experience and research. Still, interest remained high enough to look further, dig deeper, and probe more extensively, a sentiment voiced by William Wordsworth who wrote in 1819:

O ye, who patiently explore
The wreck of Herculaneum lore,
What rapture! could ye seize
Some Theban fragment, or unroll
One precious, tender-hearted, scroll.

Despite their disappointment, the Western world never ceased longing. Today we are encouraged further by the great strides in our understanding. The art of multispectral scanning of the carbonized papyri, the building of a replica of the Villa dei Papiri in California by the Getty Foundation, the organization of official research into antiquities, and the museum at Herculaneum all help. In addition, an inspired effort at research funding and two and a half centuries of media attention has kept the interest of the general public focused on the prospect of finding, "One precious, tender-hearted, scroll . . ."

It also helps that two best-selling authors maintain a long-running interest in the charred papyrus scrolls. The concerns of Shirley Hazzard and Robert Harris are well known. Hazzard devoted columns to the rolls in her August 1983 *New Yorker* story on papyrology, as well as a *New York Times* story on Herculaneum in 1987, and her coauthored 2008 book, *The Ancient Shore*. Elsewhere, she has called attention to an eighteenth century trade whereby the king of Naples bartered some of the Herculaneum papyri for live kangaroos; presumably an equally rare and valuable commodity in those days.

Alexandre Dumas used this incident in a historical novel, *The Neapolitan Lovers*, where he had Ferdinand IV trade with the English envoy to Naples, Lord Hamilton (the husband of Lady Hamilton, the famous mistress of the celebrated Admiral Nelson) and hoping that Lord Hamilton "has not deceived me in saying that the kangaroo is a rare animal, I hope, or I shall regret my papyri. They were found at Herculaneum. Hamilton, an amateur of that sort of old rubbish, saw them; he spoke of the kangaroos, and I told him I wanted to try and acclimatize some. So he asked if I would give the London Museum as many rolls of papyrus as the Zoological Gardens there would give me kangaroos. I said, 'Bring over the kangaroos as quick as you can!' Yesterday eighteen arrived, and I have given him eighteen papyri."

One of the protagonists, an English banker, says, "Sir William has not made a bad bargain, perhaps he has got Tacitus' panegyric on Virginius, his speech against the pro consul Marcus-Priscus, or his last poems." It worried the king that he had indeed made a poor bargain, the rolls he gave up might have contained a classic. But we now know better. King Ferdinand can rest in peace, since the chances are 99 percent that the British Museum scrolls, if ever unrolled, will reveal nothing more precious than more essays from our old friend Philodemus.

Hazzard's patience wears thin when it comes to the question of why the remainder of the ancient library and possibly thousands more papyrus scrolls are left to languish under the lava beds, not far from her beloved Naples. In this she joins Robert Harris who, following the success of his 2003 novel *Pompeii*, increased the pressure to uncover the remaining parts of the Villa dei Papiri.

Robert Fowler, professor of classics at Bristol University, in an interview in December 2013 with Robin Banerji of the BBC pointed out that near the room where many of the original scrolls were found, and on the same level, is a section of the villa that has never been dug up.[6] There is also a range of well-furnished rooms with views out to sea, and Fowler remains hopeful that the villa could yet yield a trove of ancient scrolls. But the Italian authorities are reluctant to permit further excavation, arguing that this would be disruptive for residents of the modern town of Ercolano, built literally on top of Herculaneum. They also point out that 300–400 of the original rolls remain unread.

In the meantime, Harris and Fowler keep up the pressure by reminding everyone of the possibility of another big eruption of Mount Vesuvius, which might end our chances of recovering anything else forever.

In summary, the conclusion after many years of research seems to be that the villa was not only a holiday home, it was also a *mouseion*, a place to show off Piso's collection of literature and art, especially sculpture. As to the scrolls, most are philosophical works in Greek, many by Philodemus, but other works have been found including a comedy in Latin by Caecilius Statius called *Faenerator*, or *The Usurer*, about a young man who borrows money at high interest to get his girlfriend out of the hands of a pimp.

❧

Another extraordinary result of the interest in the Herculaneum story was the decision by the wealthy financier and philanthropist J. Paul Getty to build a replica of the villa in Malibu, California. Working from the original plans drawn up by Karl Weber in the eighteenth century, the Getty Villa was built and opened in 1974 and became part of the Getty Museum complex. Getty, who died in 1976, never visited the villa.

Stephen Garrett, architect and former director of the Getty Museum,[7] tells us that J. Paul Getty had a clear view about what he wanted to achieve in doing this. "He wanted a person that came there to get some idea of what a villa way back 2000 years would actually have felt like."

In the same spirit of what it must have felt like walking around the original villa in ancient Italy, the thousands of papyri were as much an integral part of the scene as the gardens that are now so nicely re-created in Malibu. As James Porter said, "One of the great virtues of dealing with papyri is that they help us view documents of classical history as objects and not only as texts."[8]

As far as I can see, the replica of the villa is incomplete. It lacks a reproduction of the library, or a reading room, or even a book storage cabinet that would be close to the original places in which papyri were found. We already have a fictional description from Robert Harris in his book as to what the rooms looked like. Would it be too much to hope that someday a major museum would re-create a library of papyrus scrolls? As far as I know, such a thing does not exist. Such a display would overcome one difficulty that has arisen: today there is a paucity of intact ancient scrolls. Of the millions upon millions extant between 3000 B.C. and 900 A.D., only a few are found intact today. In museums such as the British Museum, there are a few small, unrolled scrolls from tombs. Thousands of intact scrolls were acquired in Victorian times (400 at the British Museum alone), but virtually all were cut into pieces and mounted under glass for study. Today many of these are left in storage, another reason why a small library of intact replica scrolls would be an attractive exhibit. Indeed, re-creating the Epicurean library of scrolls from the original villa would give the modern day papermakers of Egypt a chance to perfect and widen the scope of their work. Many of the papermakers in Cairo, Luxor, and the delta have access to fresh papyrus as well as tons of dried strips. Beside their expertise, artists and materials are readily available to re-create what is needed.

TWENTY

Saving the Day

Papyrus paper which keeps the sweet harvest of the mind.

—Cassiodorus

It was not the best of times. The Roman Empire was crumbling under the advance of barbarian hordes. Poor weather conditions prevailed, the most severe and protracted short-term episodes of cooling in the Northern Hemisphere in the last 2,000 years caused crop failures followed by famines that allowed a weakened population to be ravaged by a terrible plague, a disease that killed thousands daily in Constantinople from whence it would spread worldwide.

Within fifty years almost 100 million people would die from this disease as it swept across the civilized world in an epidemic that would empty the cities. Throughout the land ignorance prevailed. The mass of people could neither read nor write. Education and learning had retreated to the seclusion of the monasteries as books were being burned faster than they were being produced and darkness settled over the West.

In the midst of this desert of the mind, several oases stood out: Caesarea in Palestine, Hippo on the Algerian coast, and Aelia in Jerusalem. And, in southern Italy, on the sunny coast of Calabria at Squillace sat the Vivarium, a monastery and library on the estate of Cassiodorus that took its name from the local fishponds. Located near an abundant stream on a little hill immediately overhanging the sea, it looked out toward the rising sun.

Aptly named for a place where fish were kept alive, it would also serve to help keep the flame of learning lit. One of the most ambitious and important enterprises of its time, it was an undertaking intent on turning back the tide, the effort of one man to preserve, expand, and exalt Christian intellectual culture.[1] The man who started it, Cassiodorus, was a thinker and writer, and also one of the world's most famous librarians. Shortly after founding the center, he ensured it was well supplied with manuscripts and maintained a staff of bookbinders employed to "clothe the manuscripts in decorous attire." He also provided his readers with self-supplying lamps to light their nocturnal studies, and sundials by day and water clocks by night to enable them to regulate their hours. And what better environment for this scholarly enclave than the solitude of a country cloister, whose silence was broken only by the song of birds and the murmur of surf from the Ionian Sea as it lapped the shores below?

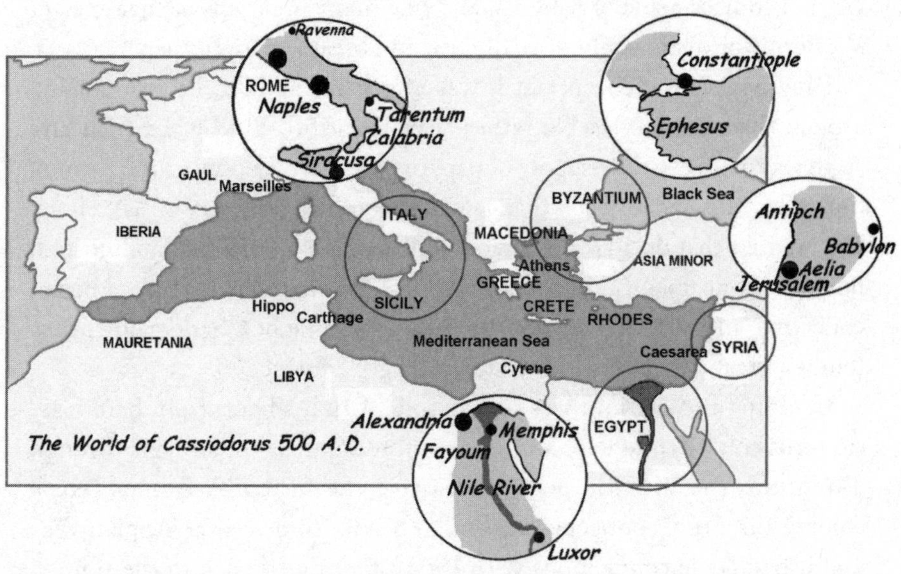

MAP 6: *The world in the time of Cassiodorus.*

Cassiodorus had served Theodoric the Great in Ravenna, then moved on to the Justinian court in Constantinople until his retirement in 554 A.D., when at the age of sixty-five he returned to his Italian retreat. In addition to several cartloads of books, he also carried with him the reputation of a man of proven character. A Christian scholar, Roman statesman, and writer, he would live on in peaceful isolation, dying at the age of ninety.

His staff probably turned out to greet him on the day of his arrival. His thirty-year sojourn had sharpened his thirst and he would throw himself into, among other things, collecting and producing books. Undoubtedly, a number of the books he had already acquired would be made of parchment, but not many, since the price of parchment and vellum had become such that complete copies of a vellum Bible cost as much as a palace or farm. Just one parchment volume of a cosmography cost King Alfred the Great of England an estate of as much land as eight ploughs could till.[2] In Bavaria an illuminated missal was exchanged for a vineyard, while a monastery used a missal to buy a large piece of land.[3]

If Cassiodorus went in that direction, he would soon be out of resources. So, the major portion of the documents in his collection would be handwritten codices made of papyrus, and like many librarians of that ancient Western world, he would virtually live and breathe papyrus paper.

Papyrus was not cheap, but it was affordable and ideal for producing a book that was serviceable rather than beautiful. But by the fifth and sixth centuries even the supply of papyrus had become erratic; the turmoil caused by wars and invasions had taken their toll on trade as well as welfare. We are told that during this period between 550 and 750 A.D., almost no non-Christian manuscripts were recopied, so that when scholars began collecting and copying classical books in the time of Charlemagne, they found a great part of Latin literature had gone forever.[4]

Luckily the Vivarium was on the sole of Italy's boot, from here Cassiodorus could arrange for a reliable supply from Egypt perhaps through Tarentum, the thriving port just east of the instep. A former Greek colony, Tarentum connected the Ionian Sea to Rome via the Appian Way and it had trade connections with Egypt that dated back to the time of Ptolemy II.

During all his many years in the imperial government, Cassiodorus had developed an affinity for papyrus. In those days he had drafted, written and copied thousands of documents, letters, notes, books, and reports. Papyrus paper had rolled off his desk for at least forty years. He also was a rare specimen in that he knew the papyrus plant better than most people. Unlike many of the writers, historians, and geographers of his day (and of ours), it is obvious that Cassiodorus had actually seen the plant growing in nature.

How do we know this? In his writings he never mentions any travel to Egypt, or the other places in Africa where it grows. We have a clue in a letter he wrote to a tax collector fifteen or twenty years earlier, in which he expounds on the subject of the plant, its history, and its importance, and he does this in such a way that we know this man has been there. We also have another clue in the fact that at the time of his birth, his father was the governor of Sicily.

By chance, papyrus grows luxuriantly in only two places outside of Africa, in the Jordan valley and in the swamps of Sicily. In both places, the plant yellows during the winter, a sign that it is at the furthest extremity of its growth zone. But in both places the plant does well enough to be used for the production of mats by local farmers. We know also from a letter from no less a figure than Pope Gregory the Great that papyrus was growing in Palermo during the sixth century, and further from a merchant Ibn Haukal who traveled there from Baghdad in 972 A.D. that it was still being used to make rope as well as a small supply of paper for the sultan, "just enough for his needs."[5]

From the family estate at Squillace, where he was born, Siracusa in Sicily is only a distance of about one hundred miles, an easy journey for a governor's son by land and sea. The brilliant blue rivers of the historic city of Siracusa have always attracted tourists. In earlier days the city was called Syracuse, a name that comes from the Greek *sirako*, referring to the nearby swamps and marshes. The region, which is topographically flat, would have papyrus swamps scattered throughout the river floodplains, and it is not far-fetched to think of Cassiodorus traveling there as a young man before he was quaestor at age seventeen or consul at age twenty-four.

What would he see?

In a papyrus swamp in Africa (Denny, 1985).

First impressions of papyrus in its native habitat differ on many points except one: the flower, or umbel. Here we can refer to a great description of the flowering head by Guy de Maupassant in the 1800s standing perhaps on the same spot as Cassiodorus stood in 500 A.D., or where I found myself one day in the twenty-first century. He could not get over the resemblance of the flowering head to that of human hair "round clusters of green threads, soft and flexible . . . heads that had become plants," an impression reinforced by the local peasants who called papyrus *parucca* or "wig."

For de Maupassant, it looked like a forest of quivering, rustling, and bending hairy heads, a strangely enchanted ancient body with an enormous mane of thick and flowing hair, "such as poets affect." Cassiodorus was not far off calling them, "the fair tresses of the marsh."

Another point about papyrus is that most people take their impression from the thin-stemmed, weedy little plants that grow in pots of wet soil in water gardens or in ponds in temperate botanical gardens throughout the world, not realizing that in nature each upright stem appears from the tip of a horizontal stem, or rhizome, and grows upward of fifteen feet. Then the very top of what Cassiodorus calls its "seamless stem" expands and spreads out into a large tuft of slim, flowering branches: the umbel, or "hairy tress" that sways and flows, following the slightest breeze.

Papyrus served as a major natural resource in the Nile valley, and it also served on the other side of the world in places where Roman legionnaires were on the march. They spoke and wrote Latin throughout their new European colonies, and in doing so brought about an interesting development. Latin, as becoming for an official language, had to be used in written and spoken language. All official transactions, notices, signs, census reports, etc., had to be written and passed along in this language. In effect, the colonizers, like the Goths and Visigoths that sacked Rome, were forced to speak it even as their own barbaric languages withered on the vine. Pen, ink, and papyrus paper were always at work keeping spoken Latin alive by allowing it to be written out, a usage that eventually led to the five modern Romance languages that evolved from Latin between the sixth and ninth centuries. Again we have papyrus at work as a medium helping to ease the way of man into the modern world.

In the end, the literature of Greece and Rome survived, but barely. During the Renaissance, scholars rediscovered just seven remaining tragedies by Aeschylus, seven by Sophocles and nineteen by Euripides, while ancient sources show that originally Aeschylus wrote between seventy and eighty, Sophocles wrote 120, and Euripides wrote ninety. Compared to what we now know of these writers' oeuvre, this is a survival rate of only 10–20 percent.

Without the durability of papyrus paper and its position as the medium of choice for the great writers of antiquity, all might have truly been lost with the advent of the Dark Ages.

In addition to keeping the legacy of antiquity alive, papyrus paper also played a key role in the transmission of news; something Julius Caesar once again played an unwitting part in.

TWENTY-ONE

Media One Makes Its Mark in the World

"What's new?" It is one of the basic human questions. Whether through curiosity, or boredom, or because they think it will help them, people have always been eager to learn the latest developments.

—John Gross, *New York Times*, 1988

One way to find out the answer to the question "What's new?" among the educated ancients whether Egyptian, Greek, or Roman was to write a letter, usually on single sheets or small rolls of papyrus paper. This was a reality for thousands of years. We know this from seeing what came to light after researchers combed through the mountain of papyrus paper found in the trash heaps at Oxyrhynchus. That cache, according to Parsons, produced "a huge random mailbag of letters."

Another interesting collection is described by Roger Bagnall and Raffaella Cribiore, professors of history and classics at New York University.[1] They examined women's letters dating from 300 B.C. to 800 A.D., including several letters from the Zenon Archive (260–256 B.C.) mentioned earlier. They make the point that the letters are the one genre in which women are definitely expressing themselves on their own behalf and not through some male acting on their behalf. The immediacy and sense of direct access to the personal lives of the letter writers who lived several millenia ago account for part of their appeal.

Since Egyptian women always had a strong social position—and were better off than women in any other major civilization of the ancient world—it is not surprising that the earliest letters dealt with petitions and they complained forcefully about entitlements due to them and their families. The women involved were not shy about how their concerns could be addressed. One letter from a woman beekeeper implored an official for the return of a donkey, while another, Mrs. Haynchis, who operated a village beer concession wrote to Zenon, pleading for the return of her daughter. She complained about Dimetrios, a local who prunes, tends, and cultivates grapevines. He has decieved her daughter into thinking they will be living together. In reality he already has a wife and children. Before she left, her daughter managed the shop and was a great help to Haynchis in her old age. She therefore asked Zenon's help.

While most of the letters were from women of the top part of society, people of modeate or substantial wealth who discussed problems relating to estate management, property issues, hiring servants and stewards, and money matters, some letters were from women of modest means. The most common reason for writing was to assure people that you care about, and who care about you, that you were alive and well. Next in importance were announcements of arrivals and transfers of goods or people, then followed queries regarding the state of domestic affairs and petitions. Less often was there any warmth of emotion or personality in these letters. Scandal, sex, romance, as well as politics, and major historical events were rarely mentioned.[2] Often written by a third party or scribe and signed by the sender, they are a far cry from the meaty, prosaic, and often-florid letters of the Victorian and Edwardian eras. Still, the letters show us what people thought was most appropriate and important in their lives. The fact that they were written on papyrus was the one thing they had in common, along with the fact that but for the letter itself, we would never have heard of the writer.

Once written, the sheet of papyrus was folded or rolled, then squashed flat and tied and sometimes sealed; following which it was addressed and sent off. Officials sending letters by imperial post could expect prompt service. Suetonius tells us that young men, in the time of Augustus, were stationed at short intervals along the military roads, and later were sent in post-chaises to speed dispatches along.[3] On good roads in Italy, messengers in a vehicle supported by changes of animals could achieve speeds between fifty and eighty miles a day, deliverymen on horseback rather more. Cases of same-day delivery are recorded even when the distance covered was over 120 miles.[4]

Private mail, by far the most common type of post, was sent by letter carrier. These carriers were active and trusted messengers functioning as the representative of the sender; often they were expected to answer questions about the letter or its content, thus they had to be people who could, if necessary, expand on the author's meaning, a practice that was honed to a fine degree by the followers of Christ.[5] In the days when letters from the disciples and Apostles were sent out, the carrier became even more important as he was a means by which the Word could be spread and conversions made, while maintaining a degree of security and secrecy, often needed in the early days of the church. Oral reading and additional oral messages publicized and confirmed that the message was bona fide and also confirmed the sender's authority. In which case, the recipients would be more likely to carry out any church directives contained in the letter.

Those with an education often relied on form letters found in manuals on how to write letters. One such book, a papyrus scroll by Demetrius, appeared in 270 B.C. and described four different kinds of writing that could be used, plain, grand, elegant, and forceful.

Most letters required only a single sheet of papyrus paper. Single sheets could be had from scribes who would cut a piece from a roll or would even write the letter on the roll and cut it afterward. In their book, *Women's*

Letters from Ancient Egypt, Bagnall and Cribiore noted that ancient letters sometimes mentioned the author paying for sheets, even half sheets, so retailers must have cut up rolls in order to have sheets available for sale. It was possible to use pottery, shells, or bone for a letter, but, of the just over 7,500 published letters from Egypt from between the third century B.C. and seventh century A.D., about 90 percent are preserved on papyrus.[6]

The "multiple letter" evolved in order to economize, in which case several letters were inscribed on the same sheet or roll to be delivered in the same neighborhood by a letter carrier who was charged with delivery of each in turn. Perhaps he did this by cutting off each letter or reading out the message much like the singing telegram is delivered nowadays, while the hard copy would be given to the last, perhaps most prestigious, person on the recipient list.

These early letters provide us with many examples of how papyrus paper helped establish two-way systems that passed information horizontally from one person to another along social networks. Information could also be delivered vertically from an impersonal central source such as the *Acta Diurna* literally a "daily gazette" that acted as the first newspaper. It appeared around 131 B.C. during the Roman Republic and was originally carved on stone or metal and mounted in public places like the Forum Romano. At that time the *Acta* published the results of legal proceedings and outcomes of trials. Then in 59 B.C. Julius Caesar was elected consul, at which point Suetonius tells us his first act was to order that the proceedings of the Senate should be compiled day by day and posted in the *Acta*. This was a masterstroke that resulted in a large change in the way news was handled.

> The Senate . . . met behind closed doors and released the details of debates, speeches, or votes only when it wanted to. Mandating the publication of a brief summary of its proceedings each day was therefore a handy way for Caesar to highlight the aristocratic senators' opposition to his populist policies and subtly undermine the Senate's mystique and authority. Caesar's aim was not to make Roman politics more open and democratic, but to undermine the Senate and further his own ambition to become Rome's absolute ruler. Only by concentrating authority

> in the hands of one man, he believed, could Rome's chaotic politics be tamed. (Tom Standage, "Writing on the Wall: Social Media—The First 2,000 Years.")

Mark Pack, on his blog *The Dabbler*, pointed out that Caesar, by converting the *Acta* into a tool for his own use, created a communications marvel; well before traditional newspapers, the Internet, before computers, before even electricity, the *Acta* delivered the news! In the process it showed the world how Caesar could make use of available technology to get the right information into the right hands.

First, he allowed the *Acta* to mix dry official news, such as the latest election of magistrates, with news of human interest, such as notable births, marriages, and deaths, or strange omens. Second, he spiced it up with interesting human color. In our day, we'd use a cat video; in Caesar's day the *Acta* reported an unusually loyal dog that refused to abandon the corpse of its executed master. When his corpse had been thrown into the Tiber, the dog swam to it and tried to keep it afloat, a great crowd assembled along the river to view the animal's loyalty.

Caesar also learned early that if you want to influence what people think about, you don't leave it to others to do all the communication; or as Mark Pack put it, "when someone tries to dazzle you with the wondrous newness or fiendish technicalities of a communications medium, remember that the basic principles remain much the same."

Another large innovation that helped Caesar make better use of the *Acta* was the availability of papyrus paper. The state took care of the initial publication of the *Acta* and posted it in the Forum on wooden boards but made no attempt to copy or distribute it. That was left instead to the *Acta's* readers and it wasn't long before scribes made it their business to copy the latest issue and deliver multiple copies on papyrus to paying customers within the city and the provinces, where they were further copied, eagerly sought after and extensively read. This avidity to read the news reminded some that keeping in the loop for them had become a matter of life or death. Not knowing what was happening on a day-to-day basis among the Roman power elite might bring you to the point of committing an irreversible error of judgment.

The power of social gossip to kill can be seen in the death of the illustrious, politically savvy, orator and insatiable letter writer, Cicero. He came from a wealthy municipal family and all his life viewed it as a dangerous thing to be out of the loop, but he was completely taken by surprise when Caesar was assassinated in March of 44 B.C. He wasn't present, but during the assassination Marcus Brutus called out Cicero's name, asking him to restore the republic.

As an enemy of Antony, Cicero became a popular leader during the period of instability that followed. He was looked upon as a spokesman for the Senate, while Antony, as consul, remained leader of the Caesarian faction, and unofficial executor of Caesar's will.

Cicero began to play Octavian against Antony by praising Octavian, declaring that Octavian would not make the same mistakes as his father. Cicero's plan to drive Antony out failed. Antony and Octavian reconciled and allied with Lepidus to form the Second Triumvirate. Cicero was caught in 43 B.C. leaving his villa in a litter going to the seaside where he hoped to embark on a ship destined for Macedonia. They cut off his head and, on Antony's instructions, his hands; the very hands that had penned on papyrus paper the fiery, damning tirades against Antony called *The Philippics*.

Cicero's hands were nailed, along with his head, to the platform called the Rostra in the Forum. Then, according to Cassius Dio, Antony's wife Fulvia (the third of his five wives) took Cicero's head, pulled out its tongue, and jabbed it repeatedly with her hairpin in final revenge against Cicero's power of speech. But, even as the executioners struck, they must have realized that Cicero would live on after death. His over 900 letters on papyrus paper assured his immortality. Years later it was clear that many of these for one reason or another had vanished. In the spring of 1345 the scholar and poet, Petrach, discovered a collection of Cicero's letters that is often credited with initiating the fourteenth century Renaissance. These same letters provided the impetus for researchers looking for ancient Greek and Latin writings, but more importantly Cicero's letters provided an example. Letter writing became perhaps the most popular medium of Humanist literature.[7] Why? Because Cicero's letters contained such a wealth of detail regarding the leading lights of his time, the follies of the politicians, the weaknesses of the generals, and the machinations of the government so that little was left to the imagination. His command of Latin prose and his humanist reputation brought him many illustrious admirers among the Catholic Church Fathers such as Augustine of Hippo. Thomas Jefferson named him as one of a few major figures who shaped American understandings of the common-sense basis for the right of revolution.

In his letters he typically did not mince words; in a letter to Cassius in the spring of 43 B.C., eight months before his death, he exults, "With what zeal I have defended your political position, both in the Senate and before the people . . . and although we have not yet had any intelligence either of where you are or what forces you have, yet I have made up my mind that all the resources and troops in that part of the world are in your hands, and feel confident that by your means the province of Asia has been already recovered for the Republic. Take care to surpass yourself in promoting your own glory. Good-bye."[8]

If we skip ahead to the sixth century A.D. to the time of Cassiodorus, who was another prolific letter writer, we see he also used papyrus paper. In his case, he applied his talents to help promote himself during the bloody and murderous period of the 520s, a time when a split occurred between the ancient senatorial aristocracy centered in Rome and the new adherents of Gothic rule at Ravenna, and continued to worsen. That was also the period when Boethius, the reigning *magister officiorum*, or head of all the government and court services, was sent to prison and later executed. By some accounts he was beheaded; by others, he was clubbed to death. According to another version a rope was tied around his head and tightened till his eyes bulged out, then his skull was cracked. In addition, for good measure, his father-in-law's head was put on the block within a year.

Throughout all of this, Cassiodorus survived. He accepted advancement in 523 A.D. as the immediate successor of Boethius, who fell from grace after less than a year as *magister officiorum*. Cassidorus went on to become *praetorian prefect* for Italy, effectively the prime ministership of the Ostrogothic civil government. He kept his head and used his letters to protect himself and promote his ideas and work. The forthright style and brash, honest manner of Cicero was not for him. Cassiodorus adopted a chatty, friendly style of writing; he mixed homilies, anecdotes, and parables with business topics. Papyrus paper and pen always at hand, his voluminous correspondence lacked the historical information people hope for today: dates, figures, names of men, and places were frequently omitted, perhaps sacrificed in order to preserve an elegant, open style.[9]

Proof of the value of his approach lies in the fact that he did not die until aged ninety, whereas Cicero was assassinated at sixty-four. Anyone reading Cassiodorus's letters today would have no trouble identifying him as a man born before his time. He is the epitome of the blog writer, the spinmeister who has mastered the art of writing a chatty web page, in which he carefully avoids all concrete details of the troublous time in which he lived. Cassiodorus left out anything that might in any way offend Goths, Romans, or Byzantines, while lavishing praise on those princes who were killing one another. He also polished and elaborated his monarch's thoughts, leading some to suppose that the king's nobler sentiments about his rule are all attributable to Cassiodorus.

In his case his letters were not meant for a general audience or, like Cicero's, for a circle of close friends and relatives. Cassiodorus directed his to people employed like himself in the civil service, or government agents and managers appointed by the king. He intended his letters to be models for the future, his aim being to demonstrate how to avoid pitfalls and dangers, and above all, how to get by. So in one case, we have Cicero trying to restore the republic and change the world; and in the other, Cassiodorus is showing us how to survive by hacking the system. Both were abetted and supported by papyrus paper, the medium on which Cassiodorus wrote his letters and the medium that provided for the newspapers, books and numerous handwritten documents in circulation that kept him and everyone else in the loop.

The Holy Internet

Standage notes that early Christians were unusual in their heavy reliance on written documents. In addition to preaching, teaching, instructing, and debating, they wrote letters on papyrus paper by the thousands, and they eagerly sought out and treasured the collected works that came their way that eventually made up some of the books of the New Testament.

Compared to the other Apostles and disciples writing letters, Paul was the most masterful. He recognized the value and usefulness of the social media system of his day, and he took advantage of his status as both a Jew and a Roman citizen to minister to both Jewish and Roman audiences. In the process, he founded several churches and traveled a great deal as an official, an entrepreneur, a preacher, and a pilgrim. Along the way, he left countless directives, comments, arguments, and advisories to guide the flock when he was not there. He also sent letters by the thousands in all directions by trusted letter carriers. His letters are the earliest surviving Christian literature. A large part of the New Testament, fourteen of the twenty-seven books and seven of the epistles are ascribed to him or his followers. He became "the most influential letter writer of antiquity, overshadowing even Cicero."

The Reverend Michael Thompson, lecturer in New Testament at Cambridge University, points out that Paul made use of the closest thing to an information superhighway in the ancient world: the grid of Roman roads and shipping lanes that made travel far safer and easier than it had ever been. Thompson calls it the Holy Internet and credits Paul with seeing the potential in it for bringing disparate elements of the church together. Standage also makes the point that Paul's influence was such that "his letters are still read out in Christian churches all over the world today—a striking testament to the power of documents copied and distributed along social networks."

About 9,000 letters written by Christians survive from antiquity, proof that they were a community of letter-sharers and also proof that Paul's methods were working and their prayers of support had been answered.

As a young man, Paul was an avid Christian hater. He probably cheered while standing in the crowd watching Saint Stephan being stoned to death. "At last," he must have thought, "someone is taking action against these tiresome Jesus-followers."

Saul, as he was originally called, was a tentmaker, a Pharisee, and an educated man. He spent years in Jerusalem and was on his way to Damascus when he experienced the vision of Jesus that drove him to convert to the new religion. From then on he was known as Paul the Apostle, and he became as avid a Christian as he had been against Christ. He set the tone, completely embodying the concepts of celibacy, divine grace, salvation, and rejection of circumcision in place of baptism. Above all, he espoused the written word—especially the gospel and epistle—to spread the word and the teachings of Christ. After he met James, the brother of Jesus, and Peter the Apostle, he went out and converted Gentiles. This helped make Christianity a universal religion. He was beheaded in Rome, under Nero, in about 67 A.D.

Thompson reminds us that written messages to a Christian community in those days were delivered with a power and immediacy that was far more gripping than text on a computer monitor's screen or on a printed page of today. Thus the news of Mark's Gospel, the first of the four to appear, would have moved even faster once Paul picked it up and passed it on. The hubs of his networks in Rome, Jerusalem, Antioch, and elsewhere were ideal for spreading the Word the way he wanted it spread.

But, one may ask, what would have happened if papyrus paper were not there? Suppose in the first century a disease attacked the papyrus plantations and the plant ceased to be available to the papermakers. Where would the early Christians have been without papyrus paper?

"Parchment," someone might suggest. Possibly. According to Herodotus parchment, made from untanned sheep skin, had been used since the fifth century B.C., but even in the early years of the Roman Republic, it would have required great skill to come up with a consistently high-grade product. If Christians had turned to parchment to help drive the spread of their good news, it would have required a sizable outlay of money, which was never in large supply among the early believers. And the question looms why didn't people turn to animal skins earlier? The answer of course was that a cheaper alternative was available in papyrus. Farmers killed their animals for meat. Their skins, horns, hooves, etc., were looked upon as frosting on the cake and sold for what they could get. What would have happened if they were forced to reverse the process and slaughter animals for their skins? The classical scholars Colin Roberts and T. C. Skeat thought a parchment industry on a scale adequate to serve the needs of the ancient world would have required many years, perhaps even centuries, to work out the details by trial and error.

To build up and train a sufficient labor force that was spread over the length and breadth of the world and eventually provide for the uses of the early

Christians would have cost much time and money. An interesting point is the fact that Paul, for one, would probably not have been affected by such things; as a partner in a tentmaking business he seems to have had connections in the business world where the cost of paper or parchment would be viewed as simply another necessary business expense. He also seems to have been quite capable of raising funds whenever money was needed, whether it was for famine relief or to help the poor.

❧

All the while papyrus paper was being used for letter writing, it was also used in other ways, some of which were to have great effects on the movement of news in the future. One item in this regard was the advent of pigeon post, the earliest forerunner of airmail.

Pigeon Post, the Twitter of the Ancient World

The carrier pigeon has been used for short messages since the time of the Egyptians. Since a bird was used, the text had to be kept within limits; thus it was writ small using a fine-pointed reed pen on a small scrap of papyrus paper. The process smacks of the original form of Twitter with its 280-character limit.

Serial messages could be sent by carrier pigeons much as they are today on Twitter: short posts that made up a longer text once the individual messages were put in final order. In ancient days, however, serial messages could be a risk as one or more birds might be intercepted by hawks along the way.

The earliest reference to the pigeon being used to carry messages dates back to 2500 B.C. in Egypt.[10] Later in the New Kingdom, pigeons were routinely being used to deliver military communications. They also sent birds in the four cardinal directions to announce the ascension of a new pharaoh and the arrival of the Nile flood.

In the time of the Greeks, pigeons were used to announce the results of the Olympic games to the various city-states and later, Julius Caesar utilized them to relay messages back to Rome from his military campaigns.

During the Roman Empire, they helped ships alert their homeport of the ship's arrival. The role of papyrus paper was crucial in that the very first bird sent aloft could not be loaded with anything but a lightweight, highly portable medium that could be easily cut into small pieces.

In 43 B.C. Aulus Hirtius, a consul and friend of Cicero, set out to help Decimus Brutus, one of Caesar's assassins, to fight his way out of Mutina (now Modena) in northern Italy. Though Hirtius died in the effort, he succeeded in making Antony retreat. During the battle, according to Pliny, Hirtius used carrier pigeons in order to communicate with Decimus Brutus who "in that way was informed of everything, especially after he set food in certain spots and taught the pigeons to alight there."[11]

Once again small pieces of papyrus paper were the key.

By the time of the late Crusades, pigeon-post papyrus paper had been replaced by a thin, light rag paper called *waraq al-tayr*, or "bird paper" used by the Mamluk sultans and attached to the pigeons' rigid feathers that were not used in flight. In this way the Saracen rulers in Cairo could receive daily reports from their far-flung provinces.[12]

Illuminated Scrolls and Illustrated Books, Newspapers, and Magazines

Another item of interest in which papyrus paper played a key role involves the evolution of the illustrated manuscript, the illustrated newspaper, and the magazines of our times.

In his essay on Herculaneum and the books that the Victorians found there, Porter commented on the disbelief of some scholars in the eighteenth century that the scrolls found in ashed form were books. They thought that unless the object was in codex or volume form, it could hardly be anything more than say, a contract or deed, or more likely some sort of ancient census roll, which meant that the Villa dei Papyri would prove to be nothing more than an ancient public records office. It came as a shock to such people to find out, as we have seen, that not only did early books exist in scroll form, but that they contained illustrations, drawings, and even catchwords written in colored ink, all of which can be traced back to the Egyptians. Later, copyists in Alexandria (mostly Greek artists), were exposed daily to illustrations drawn in bright colors by Egyptian artists and scribes, and they couldn't help but be influenced.

The illustrated manuscript therefore evolved in the same way that Greek columns evolved, from early Egyptian papyriform models. In the case of the scrolls and later codices, the Egyptians used red ink to highlight important names and dates and they incorporated drawings and colorful figures directly onto the papyrus paper surface, a surface that lent itself to the use of colored ink, paint, and freehand drawing. It was easier to do this on this new medium than on other media available in ancient times. Thus, the copyists of Alexandria, producing illustrated scrolls using these ancient papyri as prototypes, started a trend that eventually led to the popular tradition of illuminated manuscripts in the West and East from the time of Constantine onwards.

The oldest extant colored illustrations in a book are appropriately drawn on a fragment of papyrus paper from a fifth century A.D. Greek codex. This painted page was discovered in Egypt in 1904 by J. de M. Johnson, while he was working for the Egypt Exploration Fund in Antinoe, a town 125 miles south of Fayum. The plants shown are lifelike images of two common herbs: comfrey, *Symphytum offinale*, with its black, turnip-like tuber, and mullein, *Verbascum thapsus*, with its green rosette of wooly leaves. The anonymous artist of this page, which is now referred to as the Johnson Herbal, has been much maligned by modern authors, blogsters, and Wikipedia, who all mistook the rosette of mullein on the facing side for the common herb comfrey. Comfrey with its black, turnip-like tuber does appear, but on the *reverse* of the page where it showed up in a very life-like painting.[13]

It is even suggested that illuminations first done on papyrus paper and inspired by the Egyptians' *Books of the Dead*, evolved into the drawings, etchings and art paintings on canvas of later times. "Only fragments of such illustrated texts remain, principally from the early centuries of Christianity. Because classical literature was depicted in Hellenistic and Roman mosaics and wall paintings, it is assumed that illustrated scrolls were the prototypes, or models for painting and sculpture, as well as for later Byzantine and European illuminated manuscripts."[14]

In other words, papyrus and the Egyptian scribe conspired to be the forerunners of the illustrated book and many other art forms of the Western world. As a model, the *Book of the Dead* must seem like a far-fetched forebear of the world's first illustrated weekly news magazine, the *Illustrated London News*, which appeared in May, 1842; but the fact is that illustrated news had to start somewhere. Why not the ancient Egyptian scroll? Or, as Sir Francis Bacon once said, "In conjecturing what may be, men set before them the example of what has been, and divine of the new with an imagination preoccupied and colored by the old."

For the next part of our story we must shift again to the Christians who were the last major users of papyrus. It was their search for a new and better way of keeping their early Bibles safe and sound, yet available to their target audience, the masses, that led to the evolution of the papyrus codex and eventually, the modern book.

TWENTY-TWO

The Last Bastion, the Church of Rome

After Egypt became a Roman province, it was clear that the new leaders, republicans though they were, were no different from earlier conquerors. The Romans' first duty was to ensure a continuous supply of goods to Rome, and that was that. The differences were clear from the start when the emperor did not grant provincial Egyptian leaders control over military resources, as was the usual custom in other parts of the empire.[1] In place of power and responsibility, the Egyptians were given an abundance of Roman landlords and rich businessmen who bought up farms and plantations to be worked by the readily available cheap labor. This added another layer to the large number of foreigners, mostly Greeks left over from the earlier conquest by Alexander, who were firmly entrenched at all levels of Egyptian society. They set the standard for any Egyptian anxious to climb the socioeconomic ladder; Egypt was still Hellenized even though it was a province of Rome.[2] To top it off, Egypt had its share of retired former legionnaires, Roman citizens that were therefore exempt from many of the taxes and levies imposed on the locals. It was obvious that as the newest addition to the imperial dominion, Egypt would be farmed and milked in more ways than one.[3]

Alexandria itself was changing. With its great libraries and museum, and plethora of scholars and thinkers, it was still a world-renowned center of thought and philosophy. With its mix of population, rich, poor, men and women, street-wise evangelizers and highbrow theologists, and its history of contrariness, argumentation, and learning, the city was a perfect place for early Christianity to evolve. And because the Alexandrian Christians had an unrivalled access to an unlimited supply of paper, they were ready to record anything that transpired. Of course, when those in defense of the new creed met those in opposition, conflict was bound to happen. So, when Christian blood was spilled in Alexandria, no one was surprised. There followed a long history of persecution during which Christians, pagans, and Jews each had their turn. For Christians, it began with the martyrdom of Saint Mark in 68 A.D. and the purges that followed, ordered by Septimius Severus in 202 A.D., Decius in 250 A.D., Valerian in 259 A.D., and a fanatical crackdown in 296 A.D. under Diocletian called the Great Persecution, which was the last and most severe persecution of Christians in the Roman Empire. In 303 A.D. the Tetrarchy—consisting of four emperors, Diocletian, Maximian, Galerius, and Constantius—issued a series of edicts rescinding the legal rights of Christians and demanding that they comply with traditional Roman religious practices. This "Reign of Martyrs," began a period of slaughter that did not end until 311 A.D. with the ascendancy of Constantine.

Conditions then shifted in favor of the Christians, especially on that momentous day, February 27, 380 A.D., when Emperor Theodosius I enacted a ban on all pagan practices. Effectively, this law established Christianity as the official religion of the Roman Empire. All other religions were heretical, including those Christians of different persuasions, such as the followers of Origen, who were hunted down in Alexandria by the new patriarch of the city, Theophilus. The Eastern Orthodox Church still commemorates the 10,000 monks slain during Theophilus' paranoid campaign.[4]

In 391 A.D. all pagan temples were finally closed and pagan cults banned. This act also served as a license to begin the slaughter of Jews in 417 A.D. carried out by the Patriarch Cyril.

The Codex

The triumph of Christianity within the course of two or three centuries was a remarkable happening. The pendulum swung from the persecuted to the righteous dispenser of mob justice as the underground movement rose to take on the mantle of imperial rule. In the deep folds of that mantle were the tools that allowed the revolution to take place: sacred texts, codified and hammered out in the streets and back rooms of Alexandria, Rome, and any other place touched by the Apostles and disciples in the dissemination of the Word.

From the beginning, the new interest in Christianity and the wave of Christian literature that followed demanded a new form of presentation. The codex, a cheap, compact alternative to scrolls, was exactly what they were looking for, and they took to it with a vengeance. In later years, parchment became fashionable for books, but in the early days when the Bible first emerged, the books of which it was composed, up until the fourth century, were mostly written on papyrus and always in codex form. Papyrus accounts for over 88 percent of all the early codices found to date.[5]

Several methods were open to make a papyrus codex; the earliest method to be adopted was simply to cut the required number of sheets from a roll, lay them on top of each other, then fold the whole pile. This produced a single, huge "quire" which, if the sheets numbered sixty, for example, would result in a codex consisting of 120 leaves (or if both sides of each "leaf" are counted, 240 pages.) It seems an exceedingly cumbrous and inconvenient format, particularly as the inner margin was often very narrow, but it was quite common in the earlier period. Later methods required that each sheet be folded separately, forming a succession of small quires consisting of four sheets folded to form eight leaves, or sixteen pages. Once sewn and laced together, this method allowed the new codex to open flat—a great improvement. Used today for most modern books, it is still referred to as a "codex binding" and remains a throwback to the days of the pharaoh's own sacred sedge.

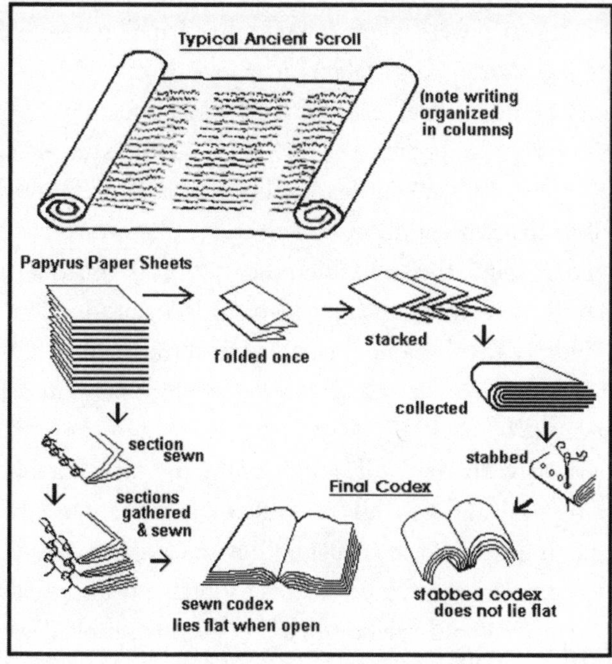

Evolution of the codex and the book (after Johnson, 1973).

At this point in history there may have been many who did not see the codex as anything more than a simple copybook or notebook. To a first century Roman it meant a collection of wooden tablets, each page a wax tablet or *pugillare*, held together along one edge by cords. This constituted a "block" or "codex" from the Latin *caudex*, or trunk of a tree or block of wood. In Martial's day the wooden leaves could be replaced by parchment, some of his books were produced this way, but in scroll-crazy Rome it was still a novelty, a notebook that served as a new tool for the busy man about town. Among people who still valued the papyrus scroll as the definitive text, these first codices were considered simply a handy notebook useful for drafting text for a book in scroll form.

On the other hand, there were those who wanted to convert their scrolls to this new compact form. In that case, they wanted something more than a simple scribe writing out copy in a bound volume. The process involved is well illustrated in a publication by Pope Gregory the Great. In Constantinople, before becoming pope, Gregory preached a series of sermons about the Book of Job, which were taken down in shorthand on wax tablets. Then the text was transferred from tablets to papyrus rolls, thirty-five in all. After Gregory became pope in 590 A.D., the scroll texts were transferred and condensed into six parchment codices. This illustrates the concept described by Richard Clement, dean of libraries at Utah State University, who reminds us that while the parchment codex that evolved was certainly a desirable end-product, the wax tablet, the papyrus scroll, and the papyrus codex all played important and integral parts in its production. Thus the parchment volumes that became the hallmark of the medieval library often represented the end products of an evolution in which papyrus paper played an important role.[6]

In comparison with the traditional scroll, the new notebook format provided more space and less bulk as well as a more contained format. At the same time, it facilitated the consultation and reading of a specific passage, all of which were significant factors for public readings at important Christian ceremonies and celebrations. People then moved on from the notebook to the more book-like codex, which happened, as Tom Standage noted, when Christians saw a value in having something with a larger capacity. "They were . . . happy to abandon the traditional view that codices were for notes, and that real documents should be written on scrolls. This view is also supported by the fact that Christian texts had distinctive formatting right from the start. Rather than the traditional 'river of text' of a Greco-Roman document, which lacked punctuation, paragraph marks, and spaces between words, Christian documents had large letters to indicate the beginning of each paragraph. They also had marks to separate words, along with punctuation, section marks, and page numbers. All this made Christian texts much easier for ordinary people (as opposed to specialist lectors) to read aloud. So the switch from scroll to codex may be just one aspect of a wider abandonment of Greco-Roman literary customs."

Even after the switch to the codex format, writing on the reverse side was still not easy unless the verso had been polished. Early writers were forced to write against the grain in order to make use of this new resource. This problem was later solved when Egyptian papermakers produced special paper for codices to make writing on both sides easier. Still, the copyist could no longer simply add on to a codex as with a roll, one had to estimate more precisely the length of the finished work. But Christians needed more books for less money and were quite willing to suffer these disadvantages. On the other hand, pagans, those Egyptians, Greeks, and Romans still of non-Christian persuasion, continued to prefer scrolls. In a way the codex helped to distinguish Christians from pagans, a quality that the Christians would probably have encouraged.

Skeat considered the question of economy,[7] since the copyist could now write on both sides of a codex page, whereas the roll only allowed the use of the inside (recto), it has been suggested the early Christians converted to the codex form because they got more paper for their money, which perhaps meant they would use every square inch on the page. But when he analyzed the codex pages he found no attempt to economize; some of the Gospel codices could just as well have been written on a roll using the same amount of papyrus. He found one codex that was noted for its lavish use of papyrus, the text occupied only 30 percent of the total page area, leaving 70 percent blank. Thus, he concluded that wherever papyrus may have been regarded as "expensive," it was certainly not in the field of book production.

❧

Taking on the codex form later proved to be a wise choice because a codex Bible survived abuse, and its contents were better protected. Because it was flat, there were no air spaces to collapse like in a scroll. Consequently, from the fourth to the eighth century, papyrus codices gained such wide acceptance that many religious texts formerly in scroll form were converted to codex form.

During the early confrontations with the Roman Empire, the papyrus codex became a weapon loaded with the new teachings of Christ and the Apostles and more easily concealed in times of threat than a bulky pile of scrolls. It was a handy, compact way of providing answers at impromptu meetings, which were often held under illegal or clandestine circumstances.

In order to further define the early codex format, Gary Frost, conservator emeritus at the University of Iowa's main library, coined the term, "the African codex model," which he shrewdly observes "was produced in Africa as an evangelistic medium for service throughout the Roman Empire. That the papyrus codex is better suited for travel and open country reading while the scroll is more easily read in interior library settings may speak volumes in explanation of the emergence of the codex among early Christians."

Frost also helps us to see how the codex format resembles similar modern technological developments in the book trade and compares the codex to the paperback. It seems that the codex and the modern paperback have no rounding or backing, that is, no shaping of the contour of the back of of the book. The binding has a rectangular shape, so that the resulting book shelves like a videocassette or DVD case. Its all-paper construction, equitable leaf attachment, attachment of covers as if they were outer leaves, and a flush trim of covers and pages to the same size are all perennial features of the paperback and the codex.

Certainly papyrus was up to the task, as Lewis noted, earlier suggestions that papyrus pages in a codex would be more exposed to damage and would tend to ravel at the edges has been shown to be illusory. Everything in a codex depended on the paper used and for this, papyrus turned out to be a good choice since, as Lewis also noted, during the whole of an immense period of time from 3,000 B.C. to 900 A.D., the method of manufacture of papyrus paper changed very little, except for a very gradual decline in quality. All the evidence indicates that in its original state, papyrus was at least as durable as the best hand-made paper of ancient or modern times, if not more so. Documents from Ravenna written in the fifth century A.D. have survived to modern times without any of the benefits of present day conservation techniques.

> Papyrus produced by the ancient factories had, and retained for years and years, the following qualities: it was white (or slightly colored), flexible and durable, and its surface was shiny and smooth. It was not for lack of these qualities that papyrus gave way to parchment and paper, but because these other materials

> were better able, with the passage of time, to meet the needs and conditions of different times and places for carrying the written and eventually the printed word. (Naphtali Lewis, 1974)

According to Roberts and Skeat, papyrus document production reached a turning point in the third century, when the codex achieved parity with the roll. By the fifth century A.D., the roll barely accounted for 10 percent of the market, and in the sixth century it vanished as a vehicle for literature, and with that ended the great Roman love affair with scrolls. Thereafter, the codex form remained unaltered for more than a thousand years, until the twin developments of rag paper and printing transformed it into the book of today.

For businessmen and the recorders of public records, the scroll or individual sheets remained the mainstay, mostly because they were easy to use: you simply started writing on them. With a codex the pages were laid out, written on, then assembled and stitched, procedures that were accepted in the book trade, but not in everyday commerce.[8]

Until the rise of rag paper in the tenth century there were no cheap alternatives. Parchment and vellum (the finer form of parchment) were expensive, making up 23–38 percent of the cost of a book.[9] Later they became the new vehicles, but papyrus continued to be used for books and even had some illustrious fans, including Saint Augustine in the fifth century, who apologized for sending a letter to his wealthy friend, Romanianus, written on vellum instead of the more usual papyrus.

As Frost has pointed out, once early Christians got into the book business, they found that it was a blessing in disguise, because the codex became a new tool of communication as well as a mechanism for forging social solidarity. A codex could enable "distance learning" and thus spread ideas beyond any central control and beyond any parent literature or culture. In sum, papyrus, the great vehicle by which the Egyptians reached the afterlife, the reed that had supported the Roman Empire, and by which the Jewish prophet was saved in a papyrus basket as baby Moses, was now instrumental in the spread of Christianity.

TWENTY-THREE

Constantinople and the Long Goodbye

Our mentor, Cassiodorus, lived most of his life in an Italy that, by the sixth century, had become a backwater. The Roman Empire of his time was a shell. The Goths, Huns, and Vandals had emptied the coffers, burned the libraries, trashed the archives, and taken control. A superb and diligent bureaucrat even at a young age, Cassiodorus went to work for the Goths when he was thirty-eight and rose rapidly in their political system. He had great connections under the old regime, where his father had been the governor of Sicily and Calabria, and his grandfather a tribune. Cassiodorus knew his way around and how to get ahead. Professor James O'Donnell, librarian at Arizona State University, historian, author, and authority on Cassiodorus, referred to him as a man who had an "aptitude for compromise with power," and also "a great seizer of opportunities," he was someone on the side of change and innovation.[1]

In Ravenna under Theodoric the Great, the Ostrogoths greatly appreciated his literary and legal skills. As Christians, they had taken over the reins of government, and with that came a nightmare, an enormous legacy of documentation, everything connected with the business of church as well as state. It all seemed to require written responses of a lengthy and careful nature. Snowed under by this avalanche of papyrus paper, it helped that they had a man who embraced the task. His appointment as praetorian prefect for Italy effectively made him prime minister of their civil government and he was often entrusted with drafting significant public documents. He kept copious records and letter books concerning public affairs, all on papyrus paper, which he, like Saint Augustine, felt was one of the world's greatest inventions.

Cassiodorus and a papyrus codex (after Gesta Theodorici 1176).

His boss Theodoric was so swayed by him that in due course he removed the tax on paper, which Cassiodorus thought to be a fine moment in the history of government. By 534 A.D. the people had a great supply of papyrus paper in Italy and it was tax free, thus, "a large store of paper . . . laid in by our offices that litigants might receive the decision of the Judge clearly written, without delay, and without avaricious and impudent charges for the paper which bore it."[2]

What a man! And remarkably cool-headed as the Goths continued their wars, beheadings, tortures, and all manner of blood-spattering incidents. If one were to read only Cassiodorus one would never suspect they were anything but a docile church-going flock.

Following the death of Theodoric's young successor, Athalaric, in 534 A.D., and Justinian I's conquering of Italy in 540 A.D., Cassiodorus left Ravenna to settle in the new seat of power, Constantinople.

In Cassiodorus's day, Constantinople was a walled city surrounded on three sides by water. It reflected wealth, power, and protection and, like Rome, it was built on the rising ground of seven hills that provided then, and now in present-day Istanbul, spectacular views of the Bosporus. A chain could be placed across the Golden Horn estuary so as to cut off further boat traffic in order to protect the flanks of the city.

It was the largest city of the Roman Empire and of the world, and so its emperors no longer had to travel between various court capitals and palaces. They could remain in this Great City and send generals to command their armies as the wealth of the eastern Mediterranean and western Asia flowed to them.[3]

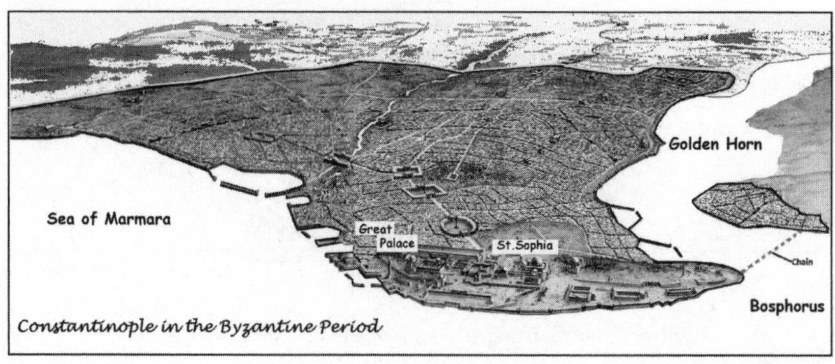

Aerial view of Constantinople in the Byzantine period (after DeliDumrul–Wikipedia).

In the eighth century A.D. the Theodosian Walls (double walls with a moat) kept it impregnable from land, while a newly discovered incendiary substance, known as "Greek Fire," squirted under pressure allowed the Byzantine navy to destroy Arab fleets and keep the city safe.

Grain arrived regularly from Egypt, spices and exotic foods came from India, grapes and wine from local vineyards, while produce from extensive gardens and abundant local fisheries was brought into the city daily. This supplemented vast quantities of stored provisions, while the Lycus River that ran through the city provided abundant fresh water to many underground cisterns and reservoirs. Constantinople was thus famed for its massive defenses, and though besieged on numerous occasions, it was not taken until 1204 when it was sacked by the army of the Fourth Crusade.

As for paper, Nicolas Oikonomides, the illustrious Byzantine scholar, noted that papyrus from Egypt was still being imported into Constantinople by the shipload in the tenth century. It was regarded as the choicest of materials.[4] He pointed out that although parchment was being used to make new books, and to transcribe older papyrus codices, it was still quite expensive. It made up almost a third of the cost of a book. Also, the supply of parchment was seasonal, since slaughter of the animal mostly involved the sheep, and happened at a particular time of the year, and it was not always of the desired quality. There were frequent shortages in Constantinople, especially in the winter months. Papyrus paper could be ordered in large enough quantity so it could be stored as well as used to satisfy daily needs. Michael McCormick, in his concise economic history of the era, *The Origins of the European Economy*, points out that the papal chancelleries of the 840s A.D. had so much papyrus paper in reserve that one piece was at least thirty-eight years old from the day it was made in Egypt until the day it was used.[5] To the east of Constantinople, stored papyrus paper served the Muslim governments equally well. According to historian Matt Malczycki, the caliphs in Baghdad around this time kept tabs on papyrus paper in their storehouses.[6]

So, throughout the world, from Anglo-Saxon England to Baghdad, and until the tenth century, papyrus served everyone's everyday needs and more; this situation did not change even after 794 A.D. when an Arab paper mill was started up in Baghdad.[7] The mill used the new Arab improvisation on the Chinese method, a process that involved the pulverization of linen rags in order to make a slurry of pulp, and the pouring of this slurry onto frames for drying. The laid rag paper produced this way was cheap but, according to Oikonomides, it was not very strong. Chinese paper was made out of wood fiber, such as mulberry bark, but the earliest paper made in the Muslim world was made of linen rags, which turned out to be a useful idea, as the flax plant was grown and linen cloth made in quantity in Egypt especially under Fatimid rule (969–1171). The new rag-paper industry would thus be a natural adjunct to the large linen-weaving industry. The most interesting part of this story is how the Arabs, after latching onto the Chinese process and changing it, now had a use for their recycled linen waste left over from their cloth industry. For hundreds of years, they manufactured all three in Egypt: papyrus paper for the Christian world, rag paper for the Eastern Muslim markets, and linen cloth in quantity for everyone.

Constantinople found itself directly in the path of development of rag paper on the one hand and parchment on the other; yet papyrus continued to be used for ordinary everyday business. It is no wonder that Oikonomides tells us that up to the ninth century, the imperial secretariat preferred papyrus for important documents, such as the famous "Saint Denis Papyrus." In this letter, Emperor Theophilus sought help from the Franks in turning the tide of Muslim forces in the Mediterranean, perhaps a prelude to the Crusades.[8]

With the end of the first millennium came a change in Europe. It was no longer economical to transport papyrus northward across the Alps. Though Italy was awash in papyrus paper (see insert, Map C), the new kingdoms north of the Alps throughout Frankland and as far as Northumbria had to look elsewhere, and they did so. These kingdoms did not have the historic trade ties with Egypt that Rome did. And perhaps also they were following the example of the village priests and curates who, even if it was an expensive process, stocked their local church libraries with codices made of vellum and parchment. Thus the new rulers of western Europe turned to a locally produced medium for their everyday needs and said goodbye to papyrus.

Further north in Europe and England, the supply of papyrus diminished until it reached the vanishing point, and here we see what happens when Pharaoh's treasure was at the end of its rope. As in modern times when we live far from the grocery store, we just have to make do. In the outer fringes of the Roman Empire in northern England, just south of Hadrian's Wall, we find ourselves in a Roman fort called Vindolanda living in a military colony of Belgic Gauls in 100 A.D. surrounded by people they referred to as those "wretched little Britons."[9]

Although papyrus paper still arrives with the monthly dispatches, and scrolls of the *Acta Diurna* reach us periodically so that we are still informed as to what is happening in the world, there is less and less paper included in the supplies that are sent to the fort. Now that the major source of paper is far away, we must learn to use what is available locally. In the other parts of Europe, the trend would be to start up a parchment industry; here the military establishment is a small enclave, a fort surrounded by forests not like the monasterial infrastructure of elsewhere. Anything needed for our daily existence that can be made of wood is a blessing. The commanding officer assigns a noncommissioned officer with woodworking skills to provide writing materials. That person decides not to turn to the inner bark of trees, as did earlier Romans; this is where *liber* of ancient days, the word for bark, comes from. The Latin word for book comes from *liber* (and the later English word for "library"). He looks instead to the light-colored wood of local trees: the so-called sapwood of birch, alder, and oak.

After cutting down a suitable tree, he saws out a block of wood approximately the size of the final half sheet (about 8 by 3 ½ inches); then, along the surface of the grain of the wet wood, he passes a nine-inch wide, very sharp, iron blade—perhaps contained in the frame of a large block plane. Very soon he has a pile of wide shavings about one millimeter in depth that will serve in place of paper. He treats them further by drying them under a weight so they won't warp. Then, after a light sanding, he has a supply of small sheets that can be used for everyday correspondence as well as the needs of the army.

Daily and weekly accounts must be kept, work rosters, interim reports, lists of day-to-day needs, and daily checks on men and material have to be recorded. All this is done on what is referred to today as a "tablet," though perhaps it is more rightly named "wood paper," since it was used in place of paper, served the same purpose, and probably when first made was as flexible as stiff bond or postcard stock.[10]

The value of these postcard-size sheets lay in their use as interim material. Larger official reports, which became part of the official archive at regional level, were still drawn up on papyrus paper scrolls; but for all else the sheets of wood were more than adequate.

Discoveries since Vindolanda, especially in the fort and town at Carlisle at the western end of Hadrian's Wall, show that these tablets were in wide use, and there is evidence that they were well-known in the Roman world. The third century historian Herodian, describing the death of the Emperor Commodus (180–192 A.D.) noted that the assassination was caused by the discovery that the emperor had made a list of proscribed persons, "on a writing-tablet of the kind that were made from lime-wood, cut into thin sheets and folded face-to-face by being bent."

This is part of the picture of what a well-oiled and bureaucratic machine the Roman army was, and it is also further demonstration of how such a small number of ingenious, resourceful men could be used to police and control a wide frontier.

❧

South of the Alps, as McCormick explains, the Roman church offices and the papal registry followed Saint Augustine and Cassiodorus in their preference for papyrus, which was "part of the conservative symbolic culture of papal power." In other words, the demand for papyrus paper in Italy was based on the same kind of sacred church liturgical and bibliographic traditions that called for lead seals for documents (*bulla* in Latin, hence any important church manuscript became a "bull"), special handwriting, prose rhythms, sacred ties, and foldings, all to the glory of God, the church and the pope. One of these traditions demanded that documents of the early popes had to be written on papyrus, and so, in the papal chancery, papyrus was used to the exclusion of other materials, even though alternatives were available in parchment and vellum.

Another factor influencing the decision of the church's preference for papyrus over parchment may have been security. The fact is that writing normally will adhere firmly to parchment or vellum and ordinarily cannot be erased by rubbing or washing; but even a tenacious ink like that made of iron gall can be removed. Because parchment is very durable, a thin layer can be scraped off the writing surface. This practice was put to use in teaching where the term "scratch pad" in the Middle Ages meant a palimpsest. This was a parchment used in the fashion of a schoolboy slate; any practice writing was simply scratching off to begin again. In the early Middle Ages parchment was even recycled by washing away the original text using milk and oat bran.[11] With the passing of time, the faint remains of the former writing would reappear enough so that scholars could discern the text (called the *scriptio inferior*, the "underwriting"). In the later Middle Ages the surface of the parchment was usually scraped away with powdered pumice to prevent this reappearance of the ghost of the original text, yet irretrievably losing the writing. Hence the most valuable palimpsests today are those that were overwritten in the early Middle Ages.

None of this applies in the case of papyrus, if a permanent ink was used, scraping would leave a hole or scar, making it difficult to falsify a document. This was also a factor in the preference of some caliphs for papyrus over parchment. How could they be certain that their subjects or the person addressed in a letter or decree would receive the real thing? In this they were not alone: the popes also had the same problem. In both cases they were reluctant to give up the use of papyrus paper. Parchment was okay for books, but not for their letters or official documents.

At that time, the term "papal bull" included many things: encyclicals, decrees, notices, and pronouncements of all types. The earliest were written on very large sheets of papyrus, though smaller copies were often made on parchment. A French writer of the tenth century, speaking of a privilege obtained from Pope Benedict VII (975–984 A.D.), says that the petitioner who went to Rome obtained a decree duly expedited and ratified by apostolic authority; two copies of which, one on parchment, the other on papyrus, he deposited in the archives on his return.[12]

It boggles the mind to think that papyrus, the sacred reed of the pagan Egyptians, was now equally blessed and revered by the Catholic Church. And it remained special until the ink dried on the last bull known to have been written on papyrus in 1083 A.D., the *Typikon* of Gregory Pakourianos, the noted Byzantine politician, military commander and patron of the Chuch. By then, Europe had turned to parchment for its needs and the church followed suit. Thus, in the late twelfth century, Eustathius of Thessalonica complained of the "recent" disappearance of papyrus.[13]

In the Muslim East, improved forms of rag-pulp paper eventually became the preferred medium, thanks to fact that it had a more uniform surface, could be written on both sides, and more easily made into a book, so that the last Arabic document on papyrus in 1087 A.D. existed side by side with Arabic manuscripts on laid paper that survived into the eleventh century.[14]

The Great Library and the Book Trade

The Great Library of Constantinople was set on course to become the rival of the libraries of Alexandria and Rome, with the difference that it would be Christian from the start. To help it on its way in 361 A.D., Emperor Julian appointed a staff of seven copyists under the direction of a librarian. The library also profited from the interest of the statesman and philosopher, Themistios, who served under a host of Byzantine emperors, Constantius, Julian, Jovian, Valentinians I and II, Valens, and Theodosius I, and was made prefect of the city before he died in 388 A.D.

The important thing from the point of view of world literature was Themistios's effort to preserve the work of the early Greeks. As a famous non-Christian and Greek himself, it took all of his enormous power of persuasion to save the pagan classics, since by this time the church had become more hostile to the study of pagan books, some of which were still written on papyrus scrolls.

After the Great Library of Constantinople had been burned during a fire that broke out in the city in 477 A.D. under Emperor Basiliscus (an incident that reminds us of Julius Caesar and Alexandria), it was restored and enlarged. It then commanded a considerable team of calligraphers and librarians who made such a stalwart effort that by the time of Cassiodorus's arrival, the library was said to contain over 100,000 volumes.[15]

The Role of Fire

As libraries evolved, they seemed to be haunted at every turn by the specter of fire. If papyrus was the enemy of oblivion than fire was the ally. It is easy to see how in the first libraries where papyrus rolls were stored, the dry, flammable scrolls were ideal fire starters with their lightweight rolls that harbored air spaces. Later libraries of parchment volumes and books made of rag paper fared no better. A list of notable library fires[16] cites examples from the beginning of paper-based archives with the destruction of the Library of Alexandria (48 B.C.), fires in the libraries in Rome (64, 80, 192, 203, and 393 A.D.), as well as in the Library of Antioch in ancient Syria (364 A.D.), the Imperial Library in Constantinople (477, 726, 1204 and 1453 A.D.), the destruction of the Library of Nalanda in India (1193 A.D.), the Birmingham Library in England (1879) which caused extensive damage (only 1,000 volumes were saved from a stock of 50,000), and the fire of the Duchess Amalia Library in Weimar, Germany (2004), where an 850,000-volume historic collection suffered severely with a loss of 50,000 volumes destroyed and 62,000 severely damaged.

Even the Library of Congress suffered from fire damage first at the hands of the troops of the British Army in 1814, and again on December 22, 1851, when a large fire destroyed 35,000 books, about two–thirds of the Library's collection and two-thirds of Jefferson's original transfer. Congress appropriated $168,700 to replace the lost books in 1852 (worth $5,000,000 in today's money.)

The causes of these fires vary from arson to the sun's rays focused through a magnifying lens setting fire to leaflets, as happened to a library in Northam, England. Wars and revolutions take an enormous toll, as in the firebombing of the Egyptian Scientific Institute in Cairo in 2011. The Institute was established in 1798 by Napoleon Bonaparte as the Institut d'Égypte with the aim of promoting scientific advancement in Egypt. The fire centuries later caused great damage; 140,000 books were lost, almost 70 percent of the 200,000 volumes.

Obviously open flames from early reading lamps were to be avoided, but one of the largest factors throughout the history in library fires has been the innocent attempt to keep down mildew. Realizing that papyrus scrolls exposed to damp would soon be lost to mold, librarians placed much emphasis on library designs that increased the flow of fresh air into the collections. It turned out that flames were then drawn from floor to floor by this airflow, thus ensuring the relatively easy destruction of a whole library rather than a small section.

Among all the newly developed technologies introduced to prevent fires in libraries, the most important seems to be closing off airflow openings and using air conditioning to reduce mold.

The Spread of Ancient Books

Library fires occurred in Constantinople in 726 and 1204 A.D., and finally in 1453 when the city fell to the Ottomans. These, along with the numerous blazes in Rome and Alexandria took a terrible toll on world literature, but still, as Knut Kleve, the Norwegian classical philologist reminds us, the efforts of people like Themistios, the Ptolemies, the book-loving emperors, both Roman and Byzantine, and thousands of early librarians, administrators, scribes, and philosophers, were not in vain. During their time, visitors from the provinces came to these great libraries to consult the works that had been put in place, and they took away copies that were recopied and treasured, and the thread of history was thus kept intact.

Many of these recopied scrolls, codices, and indices would wind up in the smaller but impressive libraries on the periphery of the ancient world, in Hippo, Caesarea, Cirta, Arethas, Herculaneum, Pompeii, Nisibis, Aelia, Cappadocia, Mount Athos, Squillace, Evegetis, Patmos, Sicily, and on and on. In Egypt, thousands of small and large monasteries developed in the Eastern and Western Deserts. These "Desert Fathers" were the models for later monastic orders in western Europe. In these remote, arid region, as we will see in the next chapter, texts were copied, and recopied. This is summarized in the diagram showing book trade in the Christian era (see page five of color insert). Compared to the earlier diagram of the Roman era it is obvious that enormous changes had been wrought.

The Christian era culminated in a simultaneous demand in Europe and the Arab world for the same works. These works were being translated into Syriac, Hebrew, and Arabic for the East, as well as Latin for the West. The work done in the older monasteries of Egypt and the newer ones in Europe demonstrated the effects of Cassiodorus's philosophy, which was outlined in his classic guide for monasteries and universities, a popular book called *Institutiones Divinarum et Saecularium Litterarum* or *Institutions of Divine and Secular Learning*. It became one of the important schoolbooks of the early Middle Ages. In it he made a winning argument for a well-rounded education, and for the copying and production of books not simply as the duty of a subordinate, but as a life experience. He loved books and scriptoria, but outside his own libraries he must often have felt that he had landed in a world of gnomes. It would be many years before it became clear that it was his example, along with the direct involvement of Pope Gregory and Saint Benedictine, which caused the production and preservation of books to become an integral part of western monasticism.[17]

Today we are indebted to the labors of the monastic copyists for practically all that survives of the secular and sacred literature of antiquity. In the next chapter, we will delve into the way papyrus paper helped them serve this purpose, particularly in the first monasteries which, by chance, were located in Egypt and luckily close to the major source of paper.

Elsewhere in the world, literacy, book production, and the Roman economy declined as new waves of barbarians descended on the civilized world in the sixth century. Booksellers in Rome must have begun clearing their old stock and taking on used books, which were now becoming a rare commodity. To supply this need, Professor Avrin tells us that books—now mostly codices—were being forged and then buried, to make them look old. Plundered manuscripts from Italian monasteries, and whatever remained of great private and public collections, were showing up in the markets.[18] Ecclesiastical and royal shoppers from the monasteries of England and the Carolingian court spread out in a buying spree; the needs for texts were beginning to grow as at about this time the teaching function that medieval monks performed was being transferred to the first universities. But by then the medium that allowed it all to happen, papyrus paper, was only a memory.

Old is Gold, and When is Forgery a Sin?

One of the consequences of the decline and final disappearance of papyrus paper was the fact that old papyrus paper became quite valuable, almost a treasured commodity, because new paper was no longer being made. Then in the Middle Ages, the unthinkable happened. According to Father Herbert Thurston, an English Jesuit priest and prolific contributor to the 1908 *Catholic Encyclopedia*, papal and other documents were being fabricated in a very unscrupulous fashion. As a result, he felt that a number of early documents in church libraries were not only open to grave suspicion, but were plainly spurious. He also emphasized that the motive for the forgeries was often not criminal. Many of the perpetrators were prompted by the desire to protect monastic property. Title deeds were often lost, misplaced, or illegible, a circumstance that left the peace-loving fathers open to persecution and extortion. They might have to pay overlarge sums in order to get their charters reconfirmed, or worse: ambitious clerics, anxious to exalt the importance of their own house, might blackmail the fathers into providing credentials less than impeccable in origin.

Take the Abbey of Saint Benignus at Dijon. The abbey church was built in 511 A.D. and rebuilt in 1325, and became no less than the famous Cathedral of Dijon, a French national monument and final resting place of the Burgundian duke, Phillip the Good. Hardly a place to harbor malpractice. But Father Herbert pointed out two papyrus papal bulls in the abbey library, professed to have been addressed to the abbey by Popes John V and Sergius I and accepted as genuine, that have since been proved to be fabrications. They were made out of a later bull from John XV addressed to the abbot in 995 A.D., one half of which was blank. Someone literally cut the bull, divided the resultant sheet in half, and used the venerable paper in a most unchristian manner. Father Herbert was at a loss, however, as to why a papal bull would be forged either in this case or at any other time.[19]

The monastery of Saint Denis is another case. Situated in a small town about four miles north of Paris, it is the burial site of Saint Denis, the first bishop of Paris. In 630 A.D. King Dagobert founded the abbey for Benedictine monks, and his successors further supported it until it became one of the richest and most important abbeys in France. So important was it that Christ himself was supposed to have assisted in person at the consecration of a new church at the abbey, which was commenced in 750 A.D. by Charlemagne. The abbey thus figured prominently in the history of France and, for several centuries, its abbots were amongst the chief seigneurs of the kingdom. During the Crusades, the abbot of Saint Denis acted as regent of France whilst King

Louis VII was absent. Joan of Arc hung up her arms in the church in 1429.[20] Again, who would think anything but good of such a place?

According to Patrick Geary, historian at the Institute for Advanced Study in Princeton, New Jersey, nineteen historically important papyrus paper documents exist today in the archives of Saint Denis, but at least three others were known to have existed in the seventeenth century, including a forged donation of King Dagobert, a forged bull of Pope Stephen II, and a forged *Confessio Genechiseli*. Also, he notes that a bull of Pope Nicholas I is either a ninth-century forgery or at least a copy that the papal chancery agreed to authenticate with a lead seal, or *bulla*! This indicates that higher ups also played the game!

What drove them to it? One thing, of course, was the Vatican's insistence on the use of papyrus paper for its important documents. This meant that those libraries with numerous scrolls were the most desirable places to look for old paper. In fact, Geary tells us that during the eleventh century, forgery became such a venerable tradition at Saint Denis that the forged works served as models and "without exception, the other documents survive only because, at a time when supplies of fresh papyrus were unobtainable, they became the raw material on which the diplomas and bulls needed . . . were written."[21]

And so it went until the present day when a 1½ by 3 inch piece of papyrus paper surfaced in 2012 and Karen King, professor at Harvard Divinity School, announced that the fragment contained the words, "Jesus said to them, 'My wife . . . '" The subsequent claim that it was a forgery put the fat in the fire. But it was not the first time that the idea has come to us that Jesus was married with children; about fifteen years ago readers of *The Da Vinci Code* knew about Jesus's wife as a revelation, not from the Fathers of the Church, but from Dan Brown. Two hundred million readers of Dan Brown have already said, "I knew it!" They would have no problem believing in this scrap of papyrus. To them it was the real thing.

What made the document unusually appealing was the authenticity of the news release, from Harvard no less, and from a King. It was even blessed with a sacred name that made it hard to dismiss.

But for me the moment of truth came with the mention of papyrus. In which I saw that once again McLuhan was proved right: the medium really is the message. Why? Because all the experts examining the scrap of paper declared it authentic—the paper that is. Anyone carbon dating the scrap or physically scrutinizing the material would have to say, "Yes, it is an eighth century document." Even the ink looked old according to AnneMarie Luijendijk, professor of religion at Princeton University, who said, "We can see that by the way the ink is preserved on the papyrus."

Since then, the ink and paper have been both proven to be real;[22] that is, really ancient, it was only when other experts looked at the Coptic script that they spotted a fake. A lengthy analysis by Alberto Camplani of Rome's La Sapienza University (cited by the Vatican), and studies by Craig Evans of the Acadia Divinity College, Professors Francis Watson of Durham University and Leo Depuydt of Brown all suggested that it is a modern text reassembled from phrases taken from well-known Coptic texts and inked onto a scrap of ancient papyrus paper.

The Vatican jumped on it with both feet in order to squash the idea, because Catholic Christian tradition has it that Jesus was not married, and, since his Apostles were men, women cannot be priests. The idea that he was married to Mary Magdalene and had children could spell a great deal of trouble. But years ago, it was in fact members of the church who did just what the writer of the *Gospel of Jesus's Wife* did—forge papyrus documents for a purpose, not for money!

Probably from before the time the fragment was made, members of the Church of Rome have been creating forgeries. Does this excuse the fact? Not at all, said Father Herbert, who stated that, "No doubt, less creditable motives—e.g., an ambitious desire to exalt consideration of their own house—were also operative, and . . . lax principles in this matter prevailed almost universally . . . !"

So where are we who were taught not to cast the first stone unless we can show a spotless record, a past free of blemish? According to some, the *Gospel of Jesus's Wife* is as valid as any of the documents in the New Testament, even if was written yesterday. They would say that the mysterious author of the *Gospel of Jesus's Wife* has done us a favor unconsciously, and in the process, he or she used a method not unknown to the church in the distant past.

For believers, this new gospel provides, "a glimpse into an otherwise occluded moment in the evolution of Christianity . . ." And, according to Tom Holland of the *Guardian*, "a reminder of how effectively religions have been able to manufacture for themselves, in defiance of messy reality, a streamlined and authorized past."[23]

Oh, papyrus.

TWENTY-FOUR

End of the Road and the Battle of the Talas River

The Battle of the Talas River was just that, a battle. Some have tried to make it into a turning point in history, the point where the secret of making Chinese paper from rags or wood pulp was uncovered by the Arabs, who went on from that point to develop paper the way we know it today. The story goes that in the summer of 751 A.D. on the banks of the Talas River near the border of present-day Kazakhstan and Kyrgyzstan, a Chinese army under the leadership of a Tang Dynasty general was defeated by the forces of As-Saffah, the founder of the Abbasid Caliphate. Some of the soldiers captured were found to be skilled in making Chinese paper and were thus spared. Thereafter papyrus paper met its death, along with 8,000 Chinese warriors.

Jonathan Bloom, the Boston College expert on the paper from this time tells us that too much is being read into the event.[1] It wasn't as if the

Arabs were seeing or hearing about Chinese paper for the first time. In his great book, *Paper Before Print: the History and Impact of Paper in the Islamic World*, he notes that Chinese paper was already present in the area before the time of the battle. In fact, Bloom feels that paper was already being used in Samarkand (in present-day Uzbekistan) and probably had been made there decades before the battle.

So, after winning the battle of the Talas River, the Arabs were undoubtedly more intent on other things, such as the development and use of the resources of the region that they had conquered. Following the death of the Prophet Mohammad and the rise of the caliphates, a vast empire had been created especially during the reign of the Sultan Umar who became the caliph of the Rashidun Dynasty in 634 A.D.

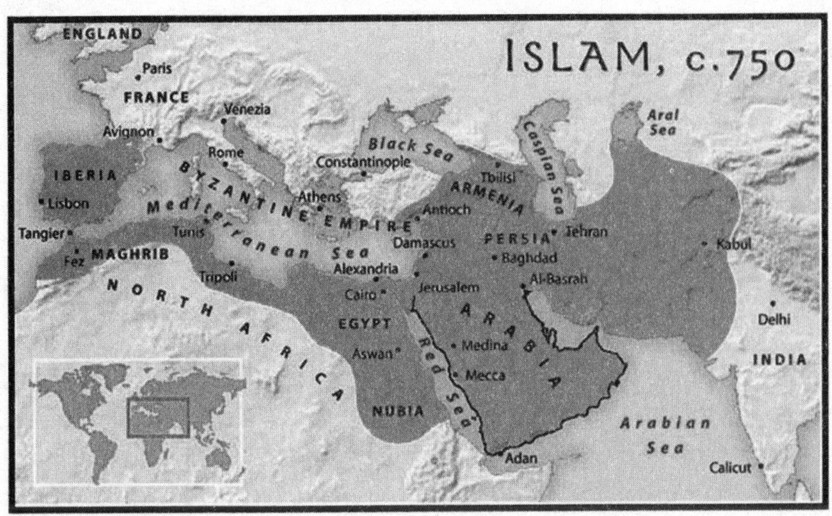

MAP 7: *The world of Islam 750 A.D. (after The Muslimah Feed–WordPress.com).*

At his death ten year later, this empire would include Iberia (most of Spain), present day Iran, Iraq, Arabia, Syria, Egypt, Lebanon, Israel, Jordan, the Caucasus, large parts of Turkey, much of Central Asia and Pakistan.

Sultan Umar was one of the most powerful and influential caliphs in history. We previously met him when he sent General Amr Ibn al-Asi to conquer Egypt. After arriving in Alexandria in 642 A.D., Amr sought guidance from Umar about what to do with the hundreds of thousands of papyrus scrolls in the Great Library. He ordered Amr to destroy them.[2] Other than this disdain for the secular written word, he was an expert jurist known for his pious and just nature.

Thereafter Egypt was ruled by governors acting in the name of the righteous caliphs whose capital remained in Damascus. For our purposes, the most interesting aspect of Sultan Umar's rule was that not only did he now control an enormous empire, but also, like Alexander and the Romans, he sat on top of the entire production of paper for the Western world, which was still a valuable commodity since papyrus paper exports continued unabated during the Arab takeover. It certainly filled a need in the Islamic world where, even before their Golden Age, the business of running an empire and the increased use of commercial paper, archives, and records meant that a large and growing market for papyrus was still there. The amount of paper needed was as great as it had been in the old Roman and Byzantine empires. By owning the source, the Arabs had not only cornered the market, but were also in an excellent position to meet any and all of their own needs.

This situation did not change when Umar's Rashidun Dynasty gave way to the Umayyad Caliphate (661–750 A.D.), which allowed merchants and scholars to travel easily through western Eurasia, expanding their knowledge and commercial bases further. Also, Mohammed's teachings insisted on literacy for all. In all these activities papyrus paper stood ready to help.

Then in 749 A.D. the Ummayads were overthrown by the Abbasids, and the first caliph of this new regime, as-Saffah, established Kufa as the new capital of Islam. This ended the dominance of Damascus, which had lasted for centuries. One of as-Saffah's first undertakings was to confront the Chinese at the Talas River. Not long after the successful outcome of that battle, his brother al-Mansur came to power. Al-Mansur moved the capital again, this time about 110 miles north of Kufa to the new city of Baghdad. A few years into his reign he toured the royal stores and decided to keep an overabundance of papyrus paper on hand. He worried that if they ran out, his scribes would have to write on some material with which they were "unaccustomed."[3]

After al-Mansur, the Islamic Golden Age arrived and was carried forward and magnified under the reign of al-Rashid from 786 to 809. His

House of Wisdom in Baghdad became the active center of a global effort to gather and translate all of the world's classical knowledge into Arabic. It especially targeted the sciences, medicine, mathematics, and astronomy. Some of this enlightenment had an unintended effect when it was transferred to the West and kindled a rebirth of learning that eventually led Christian Europe out of the dark ages and into the Renaissance.[4]

All this meant transcribing books onto parchment, but also it meant more and more use of papyrus in commerce and letter writing. Interestingly, parchment was used relatively little for early Islamic books. Johannes Pedersen, late professor of Eastern languages at the University of Copenhagen, felt that the reason why is that parchment was an expensive material. Papyrus was always a cheaper alternative, but it was not until after the conquest of Egypt by Islam when the papyrus industry was taken over by Muslims that papyrus became an article in everyday use by those writing Arabic. We know that papyrus paper was known in Arabia in the time of the Prophet (ca. 630s A.D.) because of a statement in the Koran that certain revelations were written on papyrus, and because Allah says to the Prophet that even if he sent down a book of papyrus for his adversaries to hold and feel, they would still reject the revelation (Koran–Sura 6: Ayat 7.91).[5]

Of the many thousands of Arabic papyri that have come to light since that time, Pedersen noted that the bulk consisted of official correspondence, legal documents, ledgers, tax receipts, and so forth. There were some literary fragments, but very few. He also tells us that there were caliphs who preferred papyrus to parchment for their correspondence because, although it was easy to scrape away writing on a parchment page, it was impossible to make erasures on papyrus if permanent ink was used, and by that time Arabic scribes were using inks made of vitriol and gallnuts, which was as permanent as you can get. This insured that the caliph's missives remained true versions of the original.

The rapid growth of Arabic literature, which began to gain momentum from about 800 all over the far-flung world of Islam, generated a demand for writing materials in unprecedented quantities. During this time (ca. 900 A.D.) Pedersen tells us that parchment, papyrus, and rag paper were all in use. By this time also, Chinese paper was being made and became readily available. Under the Arabs this pulp paper was being made using their method, mainly with linen rags in place of plant fibers. Though its quality was being improved daily, its use was still limited. Perhaps al-Mansur's reluctance to let go of papyrus reflected a more general feeling of "Let's wait and see."

So, throughout the world, from Anglo-Saxon England to Baghdad, and until the tenth century, papyrus still served an everyday need, and this situation did not change even after 794 A.D. when the first Arab paper mill was started up in Baghdad. During this time of transition, papyrus paper was still prized as a writing surface, so much so that al-Mu'tasim, the Abbasid caliph who founded his new capital of Samarra on the banks of the Tigris River in 836 A.D., went to great trouble to bring papyrus papermakers from Cairo to help establish the industry there. But after the decline of Samarra in 949 A.D. and the improvement in Arab rag paper, which was now cheap and in demand, the caliph's effort became moot. Also by now, the Arabs had begun to give up on the propagation of papyrus as after four thousand years the manufacture of papyrus paper in Egypt, and the greater cost it now demanded compared to this new alternative, was no longer worth it.[6]

Chinese Paper

The process of making paper in China, like so many discoveries that changed the world, was based on a simple process; the process was so simple that you might wonder why it had not been discovered earlier. The invention of pulp paper is often said to date from the description of the process by Cai Lun, an official attached to the imperial court during the Han Dynasty in 105 A.D.[7] Prior to that time, from the early Shang (1600–1050 B.C.) and Zhou (1050–256 B.C.) dynasties, documents were written out on bone or bamboo strips sewn and rolled up into bundles that were heavy, awkward, and hard to transport. Silk, the alternative medium, was normally too expensive to use on a routine basis.[8]

Cai Lun's account gives credit to the paper wasp or hornet for being the true source of pulp paper. The Asian paper wasp queen uses her mandibles to scrape bits of wood fiber from fences, logs, or even cardboard. She then breaks the wood fibers down in her mouth, using saliva and water to weaken them as she flies to her chosen nest site with her mouth full of soft pulp. From this she constructs water-resistant nests made of gray or brown papery material. In larger nests, she builds a few cells in which she lays sterile eggs, which hatch to produce workers who continue building the paper cells while she busies herself with other matters.[9]

In ancient times if someone decided to try their hand at the process and by chance produced an early form of pulp paper, they would have had to duplicate the mastication performed by these insects. More importantly, they would also have had to simulate the next step, in which the wasps shape the mush into six-sided cells, or, in the case of a hornet's nest, to spread the pulp out in thin layers to dry, eventually building a large nest the size of a rugby ball. In any event, this may have given an early pulp papermaker the idea, the result of which was the paper recently found at Dunhuang in Gansu Province where a 2,000-year-old piece of pulp paper was discovered inscribed with legible handwriting that dates from 8 B.C.[10]

This early pulp paper was made from the paper mulberry tree, *Broussonetia papyrifera*, the inner bark of which was pounded and mixed with water to produce a paste like that made by the wasp. Chinese papermakers sometimes added cloth fiber, for which purpose they collected old fishnets, rags, and hemp waste, all of which had to be pounded into a pulp; but chiefly their paper was mainly made of wood or plant fibers.

After much pounding, stirring, and cooking, the pulp obtained would be poured out and collected on fine bamboo screen-molds. The slurry was then allowed to settle into a matrix that was peeled off the mold and pressed or further dried, then polished to form the actual paper. The whole process was scaled up in Chinese paper factories so that thousands of sheets could be produced each week.

Although the use of paper by the Chinese became widespread for writing and block printing by the third century, it was also used for wrapping and, in the royal households, as facial tissue and toilet paper. An Arab traveler to China once wrote of the curious Chinese tradition in 851 A.D., "(the Chinese) do not wash themselves with water when they have done their necessities; but they only wipe themselves with paper." Some exclusions were in place; earlier, in 589 A.D., the Chinese scholar-official Yan Zhitui wrote, "Paper on which there are quotations or commentaries from the Five Classics or the names of sages, I dare not use for toilet purposes."[11]

The Arabs knew that the use of rags rather than wood fibers would make a better quality paper. Then they found that speeding up the pulverization process by using water-powered mills not only improved efficiency but also improved quality. Since their mills were built over slow-flowing, shallow river water, the water wheel for the mill had to be built in a horizontal fashion and powered by water from a reservoir.[12] The result was a large daily production of paper that exceeded their greatest expectations.

Arab paper was further improved by the use of sizing; that is, a coating that improved and hardened the surface. Sizing was especially used in Egypt during the Fatimid rule (969–1171 A.D.). It consisted of adding liquid starch to the new rag paper during or after manufacture.[13] Starch is still used today to make paper less porous; 1.7 million tons are used annually by the US paper industry.[14] These improvements made rag paper very attractive, and even while papyrus paper was still in use for commerce and letter writing, and parchment for the production of the Koran in codex form, rag paper became the medium of preference in Arab states for everyday use.

The earliest dated example of Arab paper is a letter written in 874 A.D., followed by a contract from 900 A.D., and a receipt from 909 A.D.[15] An analysis of the documents held in the Erzherzog Rainer Paper Collection in Vienna (mostly paper found in Egypt) showed the steady displacement of papyrus paper by rag paper. From 719–815 A.D. there are thirty-six dated documents all on papyrus paper. From the following century (816–912 A.D.) there are ninety-six documents on papyrus paper and twenty-four on Arab rag paper. From the tenth century (913–1069 A.D.) only nine are on papyrus paper and seventy-seven are on rag paper, the last one in the collection on papyrus dates from 936 A.D.[16]

A hundred and seventy years after the introduction of Arab paper, in 1074 A.D. the first paper mill to produce rag paper in Europe was built by Muslims in Spain near the Jucar River. This mill employed thirty workers and used a hammer mill powered by a water wheel to pulverize the rags. After that paper mills were built in Rome, Auvergne, Nuremberg, and finally, in 1490, in England, almost 700 years after the first appearance of a mill in Baghdad.

Kilgour ascribes this slow advance of rag paper to its poor quality. Even in the fourteenth century the cheaper versions were fragile, had a rough surface and "drank" water-based ink. This may be why in the markets of

Cairo by 1035 A.D., vegetables, spices, and hardware were being wrapped in rag paper, which was more pliable than papyrus, and could be looked upon as a "throwaway."[17] Carter, late professor of Chinese at Columbia tells us of a Persian traveler, writing about 1040 A.D., who recorded with surprise how "the venders of vegetables and spices in Cairo were furnished with paper in which everything that they sell is wrapped." The paper used was of a cheaper variety, one that incorporated rags from a macabre source, as Carter discovered from a physician in Bagdad, writing a century later, who revealed the source of this wrapping paper used by the grocers: "The Bedouins and fellahin search the ancient cities of the dead to recover the cloth bands in which the mummies are swathed, and when these cannot be used for their clothes, they sell them to the factories, which make of them paper destined for the food markets."

But quite soon things would change again as papermakers in the Arab world realized their paper had to conform to the needs of the European market. It seems that the complaints of the Europeans of the poor quality of this new paper had nothing to do with the actual substance, since the Chinese, Arab, and Persian calligraphers from 800 A.D. onward had no problems with their paper. In fact, they preferred the soft finish of the paper produced from their own mills. The Chinese used brushes and their own ink, which worked fine, while the Arab and Persians used reed pens that also worked well. The cause of concern in the West lay in the quill.

Paper Finish and the Quill

With papyrus paper the ancient Egyptians had used reed brushes, while the Greeks and Romans had made do with reed stylus pens. The quill first appeared in Seville, Spain, and became the preferred writing instrument from 600 to 1800 A.D.[18] Suffice it to say that Europeans found writing with a quill pen was not only convenient but allowed faster writing, which seemed suited to the times, thus there was no problem during the transition from papyrus to parchment. Even when hand-cut goose quills became the primary writing instrument, the hard finish typical of both parchment and papyrus paper made writing easy and spoiled the scribes. It was only when the point of the quill hit the soft finish on the surface of a piece of the early Arab or Chinese paper that the trouble began.

In the West, scribes, authors, publishers and copiers were still scratching their heads as to whether or not to use this new medium when the Italian papermakers began turning out a hard-finished paper that won them over.

By the thirteenth and fourteenth centuries the Italians had taken over the paper industry. They did this by using gelatin size, a thin, watery solution that when dry helped seal the paper finish. Rice-starch sizing used by Chinese and Arab papermakers was not available to the Europeans, and the wheat starch that they were using smelled bad and attracted molds and insects in the humid parts of Europe. The Italians got around this by using a gelatin size that gave paper the hard finish ideal for quill pens. They also used improved pulping methods made possible by building their mills in fast-water areas of Italy, rather than the slow-moving rivers of the Arabs. The result was that Italian paper became better, cheaper, and more available in quantity. It was preferred over Chinese paper, as we learn from a story Jonathan Bloom recounts about an English administrator with the East India Company in Patani, India in 1614, who pleaded with his London office to replenish his supply of paper because, "for want of paper all our books are kept on China paper, having not so much other as to write a letter to Your Worships: I therefore entreat Your Worships to remember us with books, paper and ink of which we have great need, the cockroaches eating the China paper." Bloom also quotes Adam Olearius, ambassador for the Duke of Holstein to Persia in the seventeenth century, "Goose-quills . . . would be too hard for their Paper, which . . . is very tender."

In the Muslim world, the Arabs and Persians were forging ahead using their own production: often fine, white paper, sized, and in plentiful supply made in Egypt, Iran, and Damascus. They even devised assembly-line methods of hand-copying manuscripts so they were able to turn out far larger numbers of books and editions than any available in Europe for centuries.[19] As a result, in the Middle Ages, Arab libraries grew to enormous size while the libraries in the West remained modest. In the 1300s A.D. the library at the Sorbonne had only 1700 books.[20] By the tenth century in the Islamic world, Cordoba had seventy libraries, the largest of which had 600,000 books; the library of Cairo had more than 100,000 books; while the library of Tripoli is said to have had as many as three million books before it was burnt during the Crusades. As many as 60,000 treatises, poems, polemics, and compilations were published each year in Al-Andalus in Spain, (which was still under Arab control).[21]

The contents of these Islamic libraries reflected the advantage of the Arab world. First, they had commandeered the papyrus market, then they had moved on to pulp paper and tried to monopolize that. While they were forging ahead, the Europeans were left saddled with parchment and circumscribed by quill pens. They seemed in no better a position than the Chinese had been in the early days with their bamboo slips.

All this would change in the 1500s with the advent of printing, an invention that the West would take up with a vengeance. Also, at that point Europeans began making paper at the same rate as the Arabs. Until then, the Arabs' new medium did for them what papyrus had done for the Western world years before, it gave them a leg up at a time when Islam seemed poised to accomplish its universal mission. But history has a way of thwarting expectations; this time, the thwarting came in the form of the Mongol invasions of the thirteenth century, followed by the Crusades, thus the devastation in the Middle East that led to a slow retreat of Muslim power and Islamic influence throughout the rest of the world.

In time their new books on paper were copied by Christian monks in Muslim-Christian border areas, particularly Spain and Sicily, and from there the translations would make their way into other parts of Christian Europe, especially into book collections in monasteries that were small but numerous. Upwards of 500 monasteries in England by the end of the Middle Ages led some to estimate that a total of 300,000 volumes were then held, by which time books printed on paper had begun to appear in place of handwritten tomes, thanks to Gutenberg.

In Egypt, papyrus lost ground in more ways than one. The swamps of the delta and the backwater areas along the Nile were drained and planted with grain, other food crops and linen—linen that in turn supplied and advanced the new trade in rag paper.

TWENTY-FIVE

The Mystery of the Disappearing Plant

Behold, the Lord rideth upon a swift cloud, and shall come into Egypt . . . and shall set the Egyptians against the Egyptians, city against city and kingdom against kingdom . . . and the rivers shall be wasted and dried up . . . the paper reeds . . . shall wither, be driven away, and be no more.

—Isaiah 19: 4–7

I was amazed to read this prophecy in the Bible. Although the timeframe referred to by Isaiah dealt with that part of the Old Testament that took place in the eighth century B.C., during the takeover by the Kushites, he seemed also to be predicting what would happen in a relatively modern age. He could have no inkling of the final disappearance of the "paper reed" that happened just prior to the time of the Crusades, also he could not be aware that the final blow leading to extermination would be delivered by man, rather than God. Also, if his prophecy were fulfilled in later times, as it was, there would never be any doubt that he was referring to a plant so important that before its demise, it had influenced the economic and aesthetic well-being of the Western world.

Its disappearance happened after the Arab occupation of Egypt, but not immediately. As we saw above, papyrus paper was still in production in Egypt until the tenth or eleventh century.

During the period from the start of the Arab occupation in the 600s A.D. until the arrival of Napoleon in 1798, a period of over a thousand years, Egypt had changed. For one thing, the population had grown to ten million. Agriculture remained the mainstay of the economy, yet during the intervening years, papyrus had gone missing, and the worst part was that its absence was not remarked upon until French scientists began asking around in the late 1700s. They asked in vain, though papyrus was well known in many languages. In Arabic it was called *bardi*; in Greek, *papyrus*; in Latin, *papyrum;* and in Hebrew, *suf.* In Kiswahili it is still known most appropriately as *ndago mwitu* ("the people's sedge").

Before taking up the reasons for its disappearance, it might be of interest to know what the ancient papyrus plant of Egypt must have looked like. According to botanists familiar with Egyptian flora, the original plants of the Nile valley must have been similar in size to those found today in the equatorial region of central and eastern Africa, and specifically in southern Sudan; in other words, the papyrus plants of ancient days were from a robust and vigorously growing stock as befits one of the fastest growing vascular plants known to man. When the slender stems each topped by a fluffy flowering umbel reached maximum growth potential, they were tall, fifteen feet or more.

We can also infer that they were robust from indirect evidence; the width of the dried slices of pith used for making paper in those early days in Egypt indicate that at least some of the plants were of a hefty size. For example, in two scrolls of papyrus paper found in Fayum (ca. 300–500 A.D.) the slices of papyrus incorporated in some of the sheets were 8–9.7 centimeters (three to four inches) wide.[1]

When first reported in modern literature, these findings were met with disbelief, since ordinary strips used in modern papyrus paper made for the tourist trade normally average one to two inches. But, if we assume the plants growing in ancient days were as robust and similar in growth as African plants that reach fifteen to eighteen feet in height, often with a base diameter of six inches, slices could easily be obtained that would measure in that range, even accounting for shrinkage during drying when the paper was made.

Sir Wallis Budge also reported that the paper used in the manufacture of the Scribe Ani's *Book of the Dead* was made of plants that were at least 4.5 inches in diameter.[2] Likewise, some of the strips used in making the paper for the Greenfield Papyrus were taken from a plant that was at least four inches wide.[3] This indicates that along the Nile River in Egypt, in the heyday of papyrus, the size and weight of stems would be similar in range to what is found in equatorial Africa today.

Although papyrus is a robust plant, it is also a swamp species and amphibious, therefore it is very susceptible to any drying out or drainage of the local landscape. It would also suffer if the Nile River water became more saline. Unfortunately for papyrus, during the first millennium A.D. in Egypt the most obvious changes to occur in the Nile valley were increases in drainage and salinity. As a result, the wetlands of the delta were affected early, and the papyrus swamps that grew there in profusion began dying back, leaving behind small isolated clumps of papyrus that existed well into the 1800s, when conditions changed even more drastically and the last vestiges of the plant vanished.

We can see this reflected in reports from 900 A.D. onward by visitors to Egypt who commented on the state of the papyrus growing in the Nile marshes. The merchant Ibn Hawqal in 969, and the travel writer Ibn Gulgul in 982, both reported that papyrus, though present, was no longer in abundance.[4] Later, the French naturalist, Pierre Belon noted in the 1540s that papyrus was still growing in Egypt, as did the Italian doctor and botanist, Prosper Alpinus, in 1580, but the impression one gets is that it was no longer easy to find.

The famous Swedish explorer and botanist, Fredrik Hasselquist, did not see the plant in his travels of 1749–50. In 1790 James Bruce wrote that papyrus was still hanging on in Egypt, and in 1820–1821 Baron Heinrich de Minutoli, a Prussian army general, found it growing but only in a few places in the Nile delta and northeast of Cairo. Finally, the distinguished French botanist Gustave Delchevalerie referred to its complete extinction in Egypt in 1897, with the exception of a dozen plants brought to Egypt from the botanical garden in Paris in 1872.[5]

❧

In prehistoric times and later, when the early residents went about their first efforts at basin control, the river banks were too steep and the rush of water too strong for any plant growth in the main stream of the river. Papyrus was relegated to patches of waterlogged soil, shallow swampy areas left in depressions and ravines after the floodwater receded. It was tolerated, perhaps even encouraged, in the backwaters of the floodplain because it was useful to have it nearby to provide raw material for things around the Stone Age house. Later distinctions were drawn between wild and plantation swamps, but both became just another component in the course of floodplain agriculture where the chief occupation remained food production. During the period of Roman conquest and occupation, enormous levels of agricultural production were achieved in the delta and the Fayum region. Production levels were so great that large grain boats were employed to carry the surpluses to Rome.

Modern Egypt is still an agrarian-based economy. If you fly along the Egyptian Nile today you'll see the flat green aspect that is typical of irrigated schemes, with dusty brown riverbanks and a floodplain blanketed by a man-made haze, a haze that comes from water evaporating from flooded fields, a weary vista broken only by the sight of corrugated roofs of houses or storage buildings, isolated palm trees, and the occasional urban landscape of a modern town or city.

If you had made the same flight in ancient times, as the plane passed over the floodplain on its way to the delta, the land would still appear clothed in green, but the farms and croplands would be interspersed with willow thickets and verdant patches of natural marshes and swamps. And as the plane dipped lower, you'd also see what is missing today, the large areas covered by the fluffy umbels of the sacred sedge, a sight that would certainly be dear to the heart of the ancient Egyptian.

Some ecosystems are more resilient to change than others; some are so sensitive that they seemingly change overnight. Aquatic ecosystems are among the latter, of which papyrus's natural ecosystem is an outstanding example. In the Nile valley, the flora of seasonally flooded basins began to change as soon as the first irrigation ditch was dug. We know that such projects got underway early. In fact, one of the first historical "documents" is a stone macehead found by Frederick Green and James Quibell in 1898. It was found along with the Narmer Palette in the main deposit in the temple of Horus at Hierakonpolis, an ancient city between Luxor and Aswan. The macehead is referred to as a "document" because there is a story written on it, which shows an early Egyptian king, Scorpion II, ceremoniously opening a new irrigation ditch in circa 3000 B.C. He is depicted with pickaxe raised while an attendant stands by with a basket to catch the diggings. Above them, rows of papyrus plants are positioned almost as if they were looking on, perhaps in apprehension.

This is also one of the earliest representations of papyrus, and, as the late Helene Kantor of the Oriental Institute in Chicago pointed out, the papyrus plants shown are stylized.[6] They appear springing from two superimposed ground lines more as representations rather than as hieroglyphs. This could perhaps be taken as a suggestion that in the early days, these plants were being singled out for special treatment; that is, they were being kept apart as hunting preserves or places to live in as part of the Floating World.[7] Community development and public works in the days of Scorpion or during the Dynasty of Narmer (or Menes, the first pharaoh, 3100 B.C.) involved the elevation of village areas by mounding and the digging of canals. This would put the residents of places, such as Memphis, above the flood level while they built up the main banks of the river into levees. Presumably this heaping up of the soil went on whenever they were not busy building pyramids and temples.

In those early days, groves of acacia, tamarisk, Egyptian sycamore, and Egyptian willow were encouraged in regions close to settlements and on floodplain farms in order to assist in stabilizing the soil that had been heaped onto levees and the banks of early irrigation canals. These trees are aggressive water users, so they helped in drying out the land: all actions detrimental to wetlands and especially swamps. Dikes and canals were a well-established part of the landscape by the time of the Ptolemies and the Romans. Covered with grass and small trees to strengthen them and most likely with a chariot road or footpath running along the top, the embankments served as roadways during inundation. At that time of the year, the river was guided into channels and flow was contained, while breaches made in the bank, intentionally or unintentionally, allowed the water to rush out into the floodplain creating immense shallow lakes six feet deep on all sides.

The Loss of the Plant and the Swamps

Often in the modern world, when rivers lose their native fauna and flora, especially when plants disappear along the waters' edge, the usual culprits are salinity and changes in river water quality and, beginning with the twentieth century, pollution. In the case of the Nile valley, during ancient times the water did not radically change in quality until the changeover from basin to perennial irrigation, something that didn't begin until the first barrages were built in the delta from 1843 through to 1930. In the main river, water quality stayed within reason until the Aswan Dam was built in stages from 1899 through to the last high dam phase in 1970.

Prior to the 1800s, changes in salinity and sediment probably didn't happen to any large measure because of the enormous quantity of water passing through the system. For example, until 1904 two-thirds of the Nile water that entered Egypt from the Sudan was poured into the sea, along with a major share of the sediment load. So much water came through that it flushed the system and kept the water fresh and potable along the length of the river. Proof of its freshness? All Alexandria drank water directly from the Nile at its mouth from 323 B.C. until 646 A.D., a period of one thousand years.

During that time there must have been small or temporary changes in water quality due to geological effects, erosion of upriver substrates, and cataclysmic events or storms. Low-water years must also have brought a concentration of salts and silt in the water due to evaporation. But until the 1800s, Nile water changed so little that it could not be a major factor in the disappearance of papyrus from the delta and from other floodplain swamps during the period prior to 1000 A.D. If there were any chief culprits, they must have been physical and economic factors, especially those that led to clearance of the swamps for food crops during that period.

Once the Arabs conquered Egypt, papyrus was still plentiful and papyrus paper was still in production, and they made a great deal of money off the sale of papyrus paper until they developed rag paper, at which point they walked away from papyrus leaving it to its fate. From then on, during a period of 800 years lasting from circa 1000 A.D. until the arrival of Napoleon in 1798, the population of Egypt exploded while agriculture expanded exponentially to meet the increased expectations of the Arab overlords, who now controlled Egypt.

For the Arabs, clearing papyrus swamps would not be a difficult job. The process is repeated daily in many places in Africa where papyrus swamps are still being reclaimed. Unlike clearing a forest or an acre of brush, there are no stumps or deep-rooted masses of vegetation to pull up. In their attempts to force a path through the swamps, the early European Nile explorers, with their river steamers, resorted to cutting and chopping their way if all else failed. They made the job difficult because they approached floating papyrus swamps head on. From the water's edge it is very difficult to cut through a tough, fibrous mat that sinks under your feet, making it a horrendous job in the typically hot, humid, insect-infested atmosphere. No wonder they often came to a standstill, frustrated by this tall, green barricade.

The African farmer comes at a papyrus swamp in a different way. He approaches from the land side during the dry season. By then the older stems have died back. He simply walks into the solid mat and starts slashing the soft green shoots, which are left to dry. After a while the whole is burnt, and the ashes are left on the newly exposed swamp soil to enrich it further. Then the shallow-rooted papyrus rhizomes are rooted up from the light organic peat, soil is dug up from the edges or under the shallow parts of the plot and mixed with the peat. The old rhizomes are heaped along with other debris to form berms along the edges of the plot. These berms will later act as dams to allow for the controlled flooding of the plot during the flood season. Within a short while, the farmer is growing a crop of cabbages or other plants that he knows will survive on the new land he has reclaimed where a swamp used to be.

In ancient Egypt, clearing the swamps on the Nile obviously took place first along the riverbanks at boat landings. Later, more extensive clearings would be needed whenever wharves were built. These riverbank areas were widened and raised over the years, which involved clearing of the local vegetation. Later, as villages became towns, then small cities, or major building sites for pharaonic monuments, papyrus along the waterfront and surrounding floodplains would be further cleared, relegating it more and more to areas away from settlements. This initial clearance was not done hastily because some demand for papyrus for use as a fuel was still there, and the need for papyrus for household crafts did not diminish until the time of the Ptolemies. By then other natural products, such as cloth, leather, palm trees, and wood, had replaced the use of swamp products. Its use as fuel was taken over by the byproducts of grain milling. Chaff, often mentioned in ancient farming accounts as the source of energy, was used in pottery kilns and bakery ovens. Once it was clear that papyrus was of use only for paper and rope making, more and more of the swamps were probably allowed to go under. Still, that left large areas in the delta and Fayum where the bulk of paper manufacturing was concentrated.

Economically, the paper industry was not affected by the diminution of swampland, since the papermakers became more adept and more efficient at their trade. During this period more and more control was exerted over the plantations by the papyrus papermaking cartel. Over time the interest of the cartel became the only reason for the survival of papyrus. When Egypt was conquered by the Arabs in 639 A.D., papyrus paper was still being produced and exported, but during the next 300 years, the protection offered by the cartel would vanish, and more and more of the rich swamp soil would be converted to cropland.

Also it did not help that ancient landowners had grown accustomed to the idea that cutting back on production might make papyrus more valuable. As suggested by Strabo in 718 A.D. "they do not let it grow in many places, and because of the scarcity (so created) they set a higher price on it and thus increase the revenues, though they injure the common use of the plant."[8] So, in the early days of Arab occupation, swamps that were quite capable of being brought into paper production may have been allowed to stay fallow, or been cleared and converted to other crops.

In the case of papyrus, unlike other crops, clearance is often a one-way street. The habitat and structure of papyrus swamps depend on the organic peat substrate, a natural substance that is in delicate balance. Once cleared or drained, peat is more difficult to re-create, and without it, plant growth is more difficult. So, the clearance of swamps as a market ploy by the papyrus paper cartel may have played a large role in its eventual demise.[9]

Clearly the Romans preferred and encouraged privatized industry, but privatization meant less control over the natural resource base. Swamps taken out of service may never have recovered. Under the Arabs between 600 and 800 A.D., Egypt was again rich. And, while it was also closed off to the West during that period, population numbers rose and the need for land rose as well. Population estimates vary widely for ancient Egypt; it has been set at only one million at the beginning of the pharaonic period (3500 B.C.) Later, in the time of the Romans (30 B.C.) it was five million.[10] Despite the rise in population, or perhaps because of it—after all, population is a main driving force behind agricultural production—Egypt once again became an attractive target for conquest.

In the old days, the most notable conquerors of Egypt were the Libyans. Then Assyrians and Nubians, were followed by the Persians, who had already taken Babylon. Egypt was no match for the Persian king Cambyses who now assumed the formal title of pharaoh. Persians continued to dominate Egypt until 332 B.C. when Alexander the Great was welcomed by the Egyptians as a deliverer. After this came the Romans, then the Arabs. Later it was the turn of the Crusaders representing Christianity. They tried conquering Egypt early in 1096 A.D. to no avail. They returned in 1219 and landed in Damietta in order to fulfill the purpose of the Fifth Crusade, which was to capture the Egyptian stronghold at Damietta, and then take Cairo as well. They took Damietta by the end of 1219, but spent all of 1220 waiting for the arrival of reinforcements. In the end, they advanced but were driven back to Damietta where they evacuated in 1221 and ended their effort. From that time on, papyrus was no longer a factor in the development of the Nile valley.[11]

Perhaps we shouldn't be surprised that by the year 1000 A.D., in the Egypt created by the Arabs, no one would have mourned the passing of papyrus. After all, like the Greeks, Persians, and Romans, the Arabs were never intimately involved in the history of the plant. They knew it only as something used to make rolls of writing paper. They did not grow up with it in their backyards as the early Egyptians did. They certainly had no plans to walk beyond this world into a swampy paradise known as the Field of Reeds, even if they were to be invited there by the likes of Hathor and Isis. Their visions of the afterlife were, and still are, of a different sort: visions in which a papyrus swamp would not figure.

In ancient times papyrus was well established in Africa, but the extent and height to which it grew was not appreciated until the Victorian explorers arrived. As they trudged forward into the swamps of eastern and central Africa, often fighting their way through papyrus in order to survive, they came to understand the full effect and implications of what a high rate of growth can achieve for a plant, especially one that had little competition until the arrival of modern man.

Today all other countries of the Nile basin—Sudan, South Sudan, Ethiopia, Uganda, Kenya, Tanzania, Burundi, Rwanda, and the Democratic Republic of Congo—have substantial natural growths of papyrus. Egypt, in a historic twist of irony, is the only exception.

Small relict wild stands have been found in Wadi Natrun and Damietta,[12] and in 1969 Hassan Ragab brought papyrus plants to Cairo from Sudan and cultivated them there in shallow areas of the Nile River in small patches. This isolated cultivation is what serves as a source of material for the paper used in the tourist trade today.

TWENTY-SIX

The Pharaoh's Own Conquers the Vatican

The armored car with a police escort, lights blazing, sirens hooting, and whooping, sped noisily along the back roads of the city. Fortunately for the residents there were several direct routes that skirted the city center and led away from the Bodmer Library in the Cologny enclave of Geneva, Switzerland. The same roads stayed well away from the Lake Geneva waterfront. Disruption in that area was thus kept to a minimum.

Once over the Rhône River, the cavalcade drove on at moderate speed to an exit that took them along the Route de Pré-Bois from which they passed into a high security section of the Geneva airport where they lurched to a sudden halt.

The Swiss have experience in such things, so the police escort and private security agents equipped with automatic rifles that jumped out and surrounded the armored car raised few eyebrows. It was all second nature to a city used to the transport of large sums of cash, gold, or *objets de valeur*. Still, some employees at the airport must have been surprised to see the container being manhandled up the steps into the passenger cabin of the small chartered plane. Whatever it was, it was obviously too precious to be trusted to the baggage compartment.

Inside the aircraft, enough seats had been removed so that a space was created that allowed the guards complete access and visibility.[1] They had to have a clear view of the container at all times. Once they were satisfied, they settled back and the plane taxied out onto the runway. It was airborne within minutes.

Regardless of their confidence in handling such things, based on past experience, the authorities at the airport knew that anything could happen at any time, which is why they gave a collective sigh of relief when the flight finally took off and quickly passed out of Swiss air space into France as it winged its way onward to the Eternal City. Inside the plane the guards stayed on alert for the entire hour and a half required to get to Rome.

Their arrival at Fiumicino-Leonardo da Vinci Airport was an entirely different matter than the operation in Geneva. First of all, one whole part of the chartered cargo section of the airport had to be sealed off to the public until well after the event. On landing, the package was transferred under the eyes of a new set of armed guards to a waiting van. A motorcade formed up consisting of this van sandwiched between two Italian police cars and four motorcycle police outriders. Once clear of the airport the fast-moving, blinking, hooting entourage was tracked overhead by a helicopter. The chopper was necessary to guard the airspace above the convoy as it traveled through the outskirts of Rome into the western approaches of the city. Any James Bond-type maneuvers or interventions would be ruled out.

They sped along on the Via Aurelia to where it joins the Viale Vaticano then onto the Via Pio X that took them into the parking lot of the Vatican Library, now cleared of all vehicles. Pulling to a stop at the front entrance, the container with its precious cargo was carried directly to a vault room for inspection by Cardinal Jean-Louis Tauran, librarian and archivist. As he stepped forward, we can only imagine his feelings, as with the greatest of trepidations, he snapped open the sealed latches on the container to reveal the contents.

What was in this container that had been treated with such extraordinary deference? What had demanded an entourage expensive and worthy enough to satisfy any head of state of any major world power? It was nothing more than two-dozen sheaves of papyrus paper.

It was a small homely bundle that is now considered to be the most precious item ever owned by the Vatican Library. The auspicious date of this codex's arrival was November 22, 2006, the day when the Bodmer Papyrus XIV–XV, containing the Gospels of Luke and John, was actually delivered to the Vatican.

At that point, according to the Catholic News Service, the papyrus paper sheaves were subjected to the ultimate obeisance, as Cardinal Tauran invited the pope to "come in person to the Library to meditate, if I may say so, in front of that which can be considered a true relic . . ."[2]

Dating from between 175 and 225 A.D. this codex includes the oldest extant copy of portions of the Gospels as well as the oldest transcription of the Lord's Prayer. It had been bought and donated by Frank Hanna, the American entrepreneur, merchant banker, and philanthropist. In appreciation, the codex was renamed the Hanna Papyrus. After receiving the package, the cardinal took a few special pages directly to Pope Benedict's private apartment. Everyone involved now believed that this bundle of papyrus paper had come full circle and the text contained on it had been brought back to the church, back to its proper home. The Vatican accession was a small part of a large cache of papyrus documents found over a period of time in the Dishna region near Nag Hammadi.

The first part of the Nag Hammadi discovery appeared in 1945 when a local Egyptian farmer, Muhammed Ali al-Samman, found twelve leather-bound codices in a large earthenware vessel. They constituted fifty-two classic and religious texts written in Coptic; about 1000 pages of papyrus paper in all. The place concerned, Nag Hammadi, is a town on the west bank of the Nile at the north end of the large bend in the river above Luxor (see insert, Map D). The codices were eventually collected by the Egyptian Department of Antiquities and deposited in the Coptic Museum in Cairo.

In a way, that part of the Nag Hammadi story illustrates how discoveries of ancient papyrus documents should turn out, since the finds were kept together and deposited in a responsible way. Research into these volumes can then be focused on questions like: what was the exact date they were written, or where was their place of origin, or what events or people were involved with their production? This is in contrast to what happened after that, when more volumes were discovered in a place called Dishna. Professor Marvin Meyer of Chapman University in California provided an excellent summary of these subsequent discoveries.

Spurred on by the hope of uncovering more codices, possibly even the remains of a library or scriptorium, archaeological excavations were begun and continue to this day. The diggers had cause for great expectation since it happens that the town of Nag Hammadi was in an area of Egypt that had a strong Christian presence in the fourth century. The region is today rife with the remains of the earliest monasteries, the very first monasteries ever built. When I first heard that from someone whose life has been devoted to the study of the early history of Christianity, I found it difficult to believe. "Didn't monasticism begin in Europe?" I asked, incredulous. I soon learned that it started in Egypt, and according to tradition it began with Saint Anthony, the first Christian monk.

Born in Egypt into a wealthy family in 21 A.D., he received the call at age thirty-four, gave away his possessions, and made his abode in a small cave in the Eastern Desert, deep in the Red Sea Mountains southeast of Cairo. He attracted thousands of followers and disciples, but they often found solitary life difficult. It was another Egyptian, Abba Pachomius, who developed the idea of having Egyptian monks live and worship together under the same roof. (His name "Abba" evolved into the term "abbot," the traditional head of a monastery.) Like Anthony, he was an Egyptian convert to early Christianity. Pachomius established his monastery in 318 A.D. on the eastern bank of the Nile not far from Thebes (the Greek name for Luxor). His second was founded in 330 A.D. at Pbau (now the modern town of Faw Quibli, Map 7), a place where he later spent much of his time.

Along with the Pachomian monastery at Pbau, a monastic church was built; the basilica was completed in 459 A.D., by which time it was the center of a thriving Christian community. Caves in the region today contain ancient Egyptian signs and symbols, as well as Coptic Christian graffiti added later perhaps by the monks of Pbau.

In 1952, not long after the Nag Hammadi discovery, another papyrus cache was found in Dishna, a town twenty miles east of Nag Hammadi on the opposite bank of Nile not far from Luxor. The documents in this cache were thought to have originated in a scriptorium at Pbau and were all that were left of the library of the Pachomian order. They contained Coptic letters of Pachomius and early Greek copies of the Gospels mixed in with Gnostic texts and works belonging to the *Corpus Hermeticum* and even a partial translation of Plato's *Republic*.

James Robinson, who served as professor emeritus of religion at Claremont University in California, suggested that these codices might have been buried after the church condemned the use of noncanonical books in 367 A.D. "When the Pachomian monks heard the stern words of admonition of the holy archbishop, they may have thought of the books of spiritual wisdom in their possession, books that could be considered heretical, and they determined to dispose of them. Yet they simply could not bring themselves to destroy them, so they gathered them and hid them safely away, to be uncovered on another day . . . buried by the boulder at . . . Jabal al-Tarif."

This collection was later known as the Dishna Papyri, and unlike the Nag Hammadi codices that ended up in the Coptic Museum, the documents in the Dishna collection were passed from surreptitious hand to surreptitious hand with odd lots being sold off whole or in part. The famous wealthy collector, Martin Bodmer in Switzerland, bought sixteen of the codices and three of the rolls, all of which joined the 150,000 works in eighty languages in his collection in Geneva. Other volumes went to the Chester Beatty Library in Dublin and further material wound up in Barcelona and at the Universities of Mississippi and Cologne. In later years, as we saw above, part of the Bodmer cache was even presented to the Vatican.

And what of papyrus paper? In this respect, the monasteries and their libraries were ideally located. They had landed right in the heartland of papyrus paper production.

Although the bulk of paper used by the monks may have come from the delta north of Memphis, the swamps all along the river throughout the Nile valley could easily have provided for their local needs. Once the papyrus paper was laid out and pages copied by the monks in the scriptorium, they would be folded, sewn into quires, and then collected into finished codices ready for leather covers. This process in the Egyptian monasteries probably closely resembled that of Cassiodorus one hundred years later in his Italian enclave at the Vivarium in Squillace; and like the production there, the main component available for the books would be papyrus sheets, still the most easily available and a most reliable source of paper in the world.

It's true that parchment was available; Professor Meyer suggests that the cattle from the monastery probably provided the leather for the covers and thongs used to protect the volumes. They could just as well have provided parchment and vellum in small quantity, but cost and trouble involved in such an effort held the monks back. Perhaps in years to come those in authority would demand parchment be used, especially for important codices. We know that in the Bodmer collection in Switzerland, of the thirty-five books eventually collected from Dishna and mostly produced in these same Egyptian monasteries, only three were written on parchment.[3] For practical purposes all the Nag Hammadi codices and the major share of the Bodmer books and scrolls from that region show that the monks used papyrus paper extensively.

The limitation of these early codices was explained by Sever Voicu, of the Vatican Library.[4] He tells us that Bodmer Papyrus XIV-XV (the gift delivered with such fanfare and now called the Hanna Papyrus) originally consisted of thirty-six sheets that had been folded and placed one on top of the other to make a codex of seventy-two leaves or a total of 144 pages. This shows that the codex form used by the monks, although it provided much more room than the classical papyrus scrolls (one codex would equal seven full scrolls), had a tendency to split along the fold, especially if the number of sheets exceeded fifty. Thus, he concluded that a codex of this kind could only contain a little more than two Gospels. It's true that the new acquisition is the oldest example of the text of the Gospels of Luke and John being bound together, but why, Voicu asks, did it not contain all four Gospels? The answer he informs us is that the other two Gospels, one each by Matthew and Mark, wouldn't fit.

He concluded that, since all the lists of the Gospels begin with that of Matthew, one must presume that another volume was also made and is now lost, which contained the Gospels of Matthew and Mark. He further noted that, "Translation of the papyrus showed that the versions of the Gospels of Luke and John found in our Bibles today reproduce almost exactly the words of those Gospels as transcribed just over a century after they were first written: God's words to us have come down to us intact."

Yet again we have the word of the divine transcribed on papyrus the list of which includes Moses, Muhammad, Christ, Osiris, Thoth, and many of the Roman deities and gods of the Greek pantheon.

❧

During the period in the 1940s and fifties when the Nag Hammadi papyri and the Dishna papers were being uncovered, another find captured the attention of the world: the Dead Sea Scrolls.

Initially found by a Bedouin shepherd, Muhammed edh-Dhib, in several large earthenware jars in the region of Khirbet Qumran on the northwest shore of the Dead Sea, they were written in Hebrew, Aramaic, Greek, and Nabataean-Aramaic between 408 B.C. and 318 A.D. More scrolls were discovered following this initial discovery. In all, there were eleven caves that from 1946 to 1956 gave up a total of 930 different texts, mostly on parchment, though some (131) were on papyrus.[5] They were often so fragmented that, to date, thousands of small pieces still exist that are the subject of continued research.

During the lectures I gave promoting my earlier work on papyrus, I was often asked about the Dead Sea Scrolls. They remain probably the most famous modern finds known to the general public. People wanted to know why so many were written on parchment? "After all, wasn't this, as you tell us, the Age of Papyrus?"

I would explain that in most other Judean desert sites papyrus paper makes up the majority of finds[6] and the paper used was most likely obtained as a trade item from Egypt. The scarcity of papyrus paper at the Qumran site remained a mystery.

The most intriguing idea connected with Qumran seems to me to be the archival library concept recently outlined by a team of scholars who are specialists in the Dead Sea Scrolls, Professors Sidnie Crawford and

Cecilia Wassen, who in 2016 presented a case that the settlement contained a library where the Essenes studied, read, and copied manuscripts. The Essenes would then have used the series of nearby caves as residential archives, [7] much like modern museums and libraries use ancillary buildings to house their overflow in places where researchers can still have access to the volumes. A case in point is the Library of Congress that maintains three large facilities in Washington, DC, and one in Virginia.

The team bolstered their theory with several observations, the most important being that the bulk of the scroll collection, that is, 580 of the total 930 documents, was in Cave Four, a cave that has anchor holes cut into the walls presumably to hold dowels that in turn would support shelves on which the scrolls could be kept. They considered the Dead Sea Scrolls were simply the remains of a library and archival complex of the Essenes. Their propensity for reading and communal organizational structure was well known, and this provided the team with a compelling analog to the library of Alexandria and its scholarly community.

Crawford thought that the main library was in the settlement at Qumran where several rooms were available, especially those with niches in the walls along with a high bench that may have been a support for shelving. She concluded that the caves served as residential library archives where Essene scholars lived and worked on the collections. In the caves she saw an effort to preserve, store, and keep everything. Here there were multiple copies and multiple editions of major works, scriptural, nonsectarian and sectarian, some of which were two centuries old in the last decades of the community's existence. Included in the archives were tiny scribal exercises of interest to nobody except possibly the trainee scribe himself. In the caves there were also extremely esoteric works, which would have been of interest only to a few highly trained master scribes. There are even Greek texts, only of interest to an inhabitant with specific training in that language, such as the person living in Cave Seven.

Thus, the Qumran collection has all the hallmarks of being an archive with a master library in the main settlement. This would also allow the cave residents to live and work on the collection whose purpose was "to function as the archive of the wider movement to which the Qumran community belonged, as well as the library for the residents at Qumran, and it was collected and tended to by the professional elite scholar scribes attached to the community, some of whom resided in the caves for that purpose." And there is no reason why later documents could not have been added to the cave archives even after the Romans destroyed the main settlement.

The Essenes were a religious community of Jewish priests who flourished from the second century B.C. to the first century A.D. They had escaped Jerusalem because they held theological differences with mainstream Judaism concerning diet, oaths, celibacy, and the role of sacrifices. During excavations of the ruins, archaeologists found remnants of their primarily male community, including baths, cemeteries, a scriptorium with inkwells, and a ceramics workshop. The pottery made there was chemically similar to that found housing the Dead Sea Scrolls, suggesting a positive link between the pottery in the caves and this Jewish monastery.[8]

The Essenes perhaps cultivated their isolation; it must have worked in their favor to remain secluded. If so, they may have discouraged outside contact with any caravan trade that could have delivered papyrus paper if desired. This meant that they purposely put themselves in the same position as Chinese communities in Asia, or Europeans north of the Alps, or the auxiliary Roman soldiers in the fort at Vindolanda.

Once removed from the source of papyrus paper, no matter where you were in the ancient world, the official community and general public would have to rely on local products, like parchment or vellum made from local animals, or bamboo slips, or tablets of wood veneer made from local plants.

In the case of Qumran, there seems to have been an extensive freshwater system including a dam in the upper section of Wadi Qumran to secure water that was brought in quantity to the settlement by an aqueduct. As I mentioned before, the possibility is there that they may even have cultivated papyrus. The plant is known to have grown in the Mideast in swamps, wadis, and riverbanks, and it has grown wild in the Jordan valley for the past 5,000 years.[9] Since dried papyrus stems could supply fuel for their baths and pottery kilns, as well as provide for the production of a small amount of paper, it could have easily served a purpose in the Qumran settlement. The Essenes could have used it in limited quantities. After all, even though the majority of the texts were on parchment, 15 percent were written on papyrus paper, and who knows how many more vanished during the intervening 1600 years.

Parchment Makes its Way

The Dead Sea Scrolls bring up the fact that earlier Jewish writing is assumed to have been done on papyrus, but only a few examples of this remain. Leila Avrin, late professor of history at Hebrew University, observed that Hebrew tradition assumes that the Torah was copied by Moses onto a scroll in 1200 B.C. Presumably this scroll was made of papyrus paper, since Moses wrote it on Mount Sinai, which is located in the southern part of the Sinai Peninsula that was even then part of Egypt, a place where papyrus paper was the most common medium. Since there is no historical evidence for Moses and the events related in the Torah, there is no reliable way to know the time when Hebrews switched from papyrus to parchment scrolls for their religious books.[10] Following Jewish tradition, parchment scrolls are still today copied from one to another so that today there are examples hundreds of years old, such as the 800-year-old Sephardic Sefer Torah from Spain.

Of course, in Qumran they made parchment and vellum from any available animal, provided it was allowed in the dietary lists named in the Old Testament (Deuteronomy 14:4–5) including the ox, sheep, goat, deer, gazelle, roebuck, wild goat, ibex, antelope, and mountain sheep. This ruled out ruminants like the horse and camel, because they don't have two digits on their feet, just one semicircular horn, so they don't "divide the hoof."

As time went on, even though it was more expensive and more troublesome to produce parchment, it became an attractive alternative to papyrus paper throughout the Western world, as it seemed a better technology for the future. Books made of parchment held up under heavy use, and history was approaching the point where the need for a resilient, sturdy surface was attractive. Until then the world had been satisfied with papyrus paper, a relatively cheap and useful writing surface. In the future, parchment itself would suffer as the expansion of trade, government bureaucracy, the growth of intellectual pursuits, the spread of ideas, and the extension of literacy, led to a point where parchment would be put aside. It became too slow and expensive to make in the face of fast-growing needs. At that point, rag-pulp paper was waiting to be taken advantage of.

The best-selling author Mark Kurlansky took this moment as proof of how society develops technology to address the changes that are taking place within it.[11] This would be just the reverse of what he calls "the technological fallacy," the idea that technology changes society rather than the reverse. His point is that as societies evolve and develop, a need arises. In this case there was a need for cheap and easy writing materials. Thus, papyrus paper came into being when the need arose. It was then used for thousands of years before the need arose for a local product such as parchment, and later the technological innovation arose that resulted in rag paper made from pulp.

The Scrolls Live and Think for Themselves!

Riyad Fam, a goldsmith living in Dishna, was very much involved with the acquisition and sale of the Bodmer manuscripts. Robinson tells us that at one point, Fam acquired a very long roll of papyrus. One night in his house in Dishna, he placed the roll on a table where he intended to unroll it and see what was in it, but he found it too difficult to unfurl. It began to crack the minute he tried. This was the result of being kept under extremely dry conditions in the arid caves where, over the last 1600 years, even the very small amount of natural moisture normal to a sheet of paper had been lost. To resolve the problem, Riyad, after determining that the writing did not dissolve, immersed the roll in a bucket of warm water, following which he found that the papyrus paper could be easily unrolled.[12]

He was briefly distracted from the paper now lying flat on his desk. He carried on with some other task and later turned back to the scroll to continue his examination when he was shocked to find it had rolled itself up! He was stupefied. Here was an ancient papyrus paper document with a mind of its own. Certainly it had its own "memory"; perhaps it even had had its fill of the modern world. The message it passed on that night was clear to Fam, "That's enough for now, take a break and leave me alone." Would that Mr. Asabil, who we will meet in the next chapter, had taken that advice.

TWENTY-SEVEN

The Road Back

Greed had driven Mr. Asabil to New York, the Promised Land of antiquities trading. He landed at JFK in the spring of 1984, and appropriately carried in his suitcase an antique worthy of the trade: a priceless manuscript made of papyrus, an ancient Coptic Gospel wrapped in newspaper. His first name was Hanna, not to be confused with the American philanthropist. He had smuggled a codex out of Egypt and had previously asked as much as $3 million for it, an unheard of fortune in those days, a price tag that showed to what lengths avarice would lead him.

Father Gabriel, a Coptic priest from New Jersey, had agreed to help him and had already made an appointment for Hanna with an important dealer in Manhattan. In the course of that transaction, Hanna dropped the asking price to $1 million, still a significant amount for a document of suspicious origin. But it made no difference: the deal fell through. Hanna then had a friend drive him out to Long Island to find a place to store the manuscript while he waited. He could afford to wait; he was certain that in such matters time was on his side. Or was it?

They drove east toward Jericho, a name that must have made him think he had entered the original Land of Goshen. Just west of Jericho was Bethpage, a Long Island town named after a Biblical village on the road to Jerusalem, the place where Jesus mounted the donkey that he rode triumphantly into the Holy City. Hanna may have thought this was his triumphal entry; he was entering the American market and he was certain that despite his recent disappointment in Manhattan, he could still sell the Gospel for a great deal of money because the dealers in the United States were wealthy and eager, and while looking over the manuscript in the Manhattan gallery, the experts who had been called in obviously thought it was a significant find. Perhaps they would pass the word and, in their anxiety to have it, they would snap at the bait. He was certain a client would turn up sooner or later; meanwhile he would stash the manuscript and fly back to Cairo.[1]

After driving around for a while, they found a bank that Father Gabriel had told him to look out for. It was in a strip mall in the distinctly non-biblical town of Hicksville. There they found a bank clerk who had been recommended by the priest and who assigned safe-deposit box Number 395 to Asabil, into which he placed the document, locked it, and flew home to Egypt. It lay there for sixteen years.

For many years I lived on the North Shore of Long Island and on several occasions went through Hicksville; you can't miss it on the Long Island Railroad because it's still the main junction for the Northern and Southern Shore lines. Hundreds of commuters get on and off at the Hicksville station going in and out of New York.

I was just beginning to take up my studies in the biology and history of papyrus, but even in those years, if I had been asked, I would have advised Hanna or anyone else not to leave the Gospel anywhere on Long Island. The percent relative humidity there ranges from average highs in the sixties up to the eighties and beyond and, with a summer temperature range of 50 degress Fahrenheit to over 102 degrees Fahrenheit, the Hicksville area becomes a pressure cooker in the middle of summer. Even in an air-conditioned building, Box Number 395 would not be impervious to the moist air, and with time it would become an incubator for all sorts of papyrus-eating fungi, insects, and bacteria.

The story of the Gospel of Judas is well told by Herbert Krosney. His exciting book, *The Lost Gospel*, contained a detailed account of the quest, discovery, and subsequent history.[2]

It is a codex from the third or fourth century, originally of sixty-four papyrus paper pages that contained several other documents in addition to the Gospel of Judas. The pages are all sewn together into what Krosney calls, "one of the greatest discoveries in Judeo-Christian archaeology." Yet when it was later taken from the Hicksville bank box, it was hardly recognizable.

Ancient papyrus left in dry tombs or placed in earthenware jugs buried in the hot, dry, sands of Egypt will last for thousands of years. Once brought out into the moist air of northern cities such as Geneva, Switzerland, or New York City, they begin disintegrating. Scrolls or codices kept in a moderate environment, just slightly on the dry side, will survive quite well, so well that papyrus scrolls of earlier centuries were strong enough and pliable enough to be written over in later centuries or rolled and unrolled.[3] As long as a certain low percentage of moisture is contained in the papyrus paper, it remains flexible and tough, but when excessively dried it shatters, or if moistened it becomes moldy or is eaten away. Unless it was conserved and restored, the papyrus codex left in the box at Hicksville would soon have deteriorated beyond all hope of repair.

Hanna's second trip to JFK was made in 2000 at the urging of a Swiss antiquities dealer, Frieda Tchacos Nussberger. She had decided that it was time to get the document out of the hands of Hanna (which was a pseudonym, his real name has never been disclosed). A short, stout man with a goiter in his neck and a chain smoker, when he first carried the Gospel to the United States in 1984 he was forty and unmarried. He had subsequently married and through the intercession of his wife, accepted Nussberger's new, lower price. Perhaps he was now aware that the cost of repair and conservation would exceed his original asking price but even he was not prepared for the deterioration that had gone on inside the safe-deposit box.

When it was opened, "Hanna's face turned pale with shock," said Krosney. "The stale air was filled with the odor of rotting papyrus. The manuscript had deteriorated significantly . . . it was in miserable condition."

In 2004 it was announced that the Gospel would be returned to the Coptic Museum in Cairo, which had agreed to accept it after it had been restored, which happened in 2009 and was the most famous repatriation of a papyrus artifact ever. This feat was accomplished by Tchacos who transferred the manuscript to the Maecenas Foundation for Ancient Art, based in Basel, Switzerland, a foundation that later teamed with the National Geographic Society and the California-based Waitt Institute for Historical Discovery to restore, translate, and publish the Gospel, with the agreement that all pages would eventually be housed permanently in Cairo.

The key to the project was the interest of the National Geographic Society, which, according to Terry Garcia, National Geographic's vice president for Missions Programs, provided the Maecenas Foundation with "the necessary resources to restore and translate the documents." In exchange for which, they acquired the intellectual property rights to the document. One of the NGS's conditions for funding the restoration was that the papyrus codex be returned to its country of origin.

There were several reasons for this papyrus book being returned; one was that it was illegally smuggled out of Egypt, often a point disregarded in the fast-talking, fast-moving global antiquity market, but as it turned out, the codex was found to be quite a famous document, and thus became a hot property in more ways than one. And with the then-head of antiquities, Zahi Hawass, on the trail of such things and quite willing to make a legal stand, it required a braver than usual museum director to keep such a thing.

The second reason it was given back was that it was disappearing, it was in such delicate condition that every curious collector and papyrologist who opened the covers to look at it, or turn its pages, or just unwrap the newspaper it was wrapped in, took a toll. It crumbled as they watched. And because of the extraordinary cost of restoration, private dealers would not likely be interested. Conservation, restoration, and imaging are extremely expensive undertakings, best done by qualified institutions, meaning that the document could no longer remain contraband; it would have to be brought out into the open and made public.

The Judas Gospel as it was called, is an interesting case beyond the fact that it was repatriated after restoration. It is also an example of the destruction that can be wrought when an antiquity is "rescued" by private individuals motivated by profit. The philosophy of Wallis Budge and others, such as the dealers and traders in Dishna, that they were "rescuing history" doesn't work if the antiquity is a papyrus page made delicate by being kept under adverse conditions. In the hands of a dealer who is not an expert, it could be lost forever.

On the other hand, the international effort to rescue the codex by making use of new technologies showed the advantages of having major organizations involved in restoration. It also helped that the object concerned could be restored to at least some level of its former self, making repatriation an attractive proposition.

Meanwhile, how are museums to deal with repatriation of antiquities, especially those made of papyrus? Today millions upon millions of fragments exist almost always in delicate condition and often in need of restoration, the cost of which is prohibitive; it involves the use of techniques such as transmission electron microscopy, Raman spectroscopy, radiocarbon dating, UV scans, multispectral imaging, and X-ray fluorescence scans, as well as standard manuscript restoration, cleaning, and translation. Is it any wonder that restoration programs often cost more than the initial price paid for a manuscript?

The Judas Gospel project was also an example of how repatriation could work, essentially by having a willing dealer act as broker and a foundation provide a base of operations so that a consortium of restoration experts can be assembled for the purpose. Most importantly, a major organization would have to be found to provide funding under conditions that were agreeable to all parties, including the stipulation that the restored object go back to the country of origin.

In the future, however, it would be more desirable to see some of the major technical work and management of such a program carried out in the country of origin as much as possible, even though it might require more time and effort, it is still worth it. Many of these countries already have facilities in place and are carrying on programs and acquiring experience. In Egypt, papyrus restoration programs are going forward in the Museum of Islamic Art in Cairo, and in the Restoration, Conservation, and Microfilm Centre affiliated with the Books and National Manuscripts House and Bibliotheca Alexandrina in Alexandria. The Laboratory of Papyrus

Conservation at the Egyptian Museum in Cairo under the directorship of Sayed Hassan helps deal with almost 30,000 papyrus items in the museum. Also, an old friend of mine, the Italian conservationist Dr. Corrado Basile, vice president of the International Institute for Papyrus (Museo del Papiro) in Siracusa, Sicily, is partnering with Egypt in a project, "aimed to preserve the papyri for the long-term, not just to restore them to be looked at now," according to Basile, who is also helping restoration efforts underway on papyri owned by the city's Greco-Roman Museum and the Alexandria Library.

In summary, not only is the proper restoration of cultural relics like papyrus codices and scrolls ethically the right thing to do, it is vital to the preservation of world cultural heritage. The history of the world, and our modern understanding of thousands of years of history, after all, would have been vastly different without them.

Which brings us at last to global development and the role of ancient paper. To understand what part paper had to play we could look at the technical side and compare it, for example, to the wheel, which gave rise to everything from transportation to modern day machinery and almost everything in between. Most people would say that because of all that, the wheel is a key element in global technical development. But, what of global *cultural* advancement? There the role of the wheel diminishes. Writing might be a better candidate, except for the fact that it is not an element in the sense intended; it is more an act or process. When inscribed on a rock surface, it transforms the stone into a "document," but one that may be monumental in scope and size. It is perhaps the ability of paper to bring such a "document" to life that qualifies it as a key element in cultural advancement.

The word advancement implies momentum, and it was the move away from messages painted and carved on rock faces that made the difference. Once the move was made to papyrus paper—a mobile, flexible, portable new medium—it never stopped. This was a pivotal moment in world history; we were set free.

Trust in papyrus paper became possible once it was clear that it was capable of lasting if kept under the right conditions; it was durable and, unlike parchment, erasures of permanent ink on paper could be detected.

It was also comparatively cheap, made from what was an inexhaustible supply and very handy, which was why the Christians took to it for the production of their most cherished writings, such as the Bible. Soon it gave rise to collections stored in libraries, new institutions that reminded us that knowledge was power and that libraries were a focus of such power.

People in the ancient western world became accustomed to being able to write things down easily, whether it was household accounts, a shopping list, or government records, as well as books and poetry, etc. Once people got used to being able to record and transmit information so easily, the medium might change, parchment or pulp paper might come or go, but this habit and expectation of writing things down became a hallmark of civilized life—thanks to papyrus. Humans were never going to revert to stone or clay tablets again for the transcription of the written word. In other words, we are what we are not in spite of paper, but because of it.

Epilogue

The Road Ahead

At the meeting it was obvious they were suspicious. The Egyptians had never met anyone like Thor Heyerdahl before, and it wasn't because he was Norwegian; his companion at the talks, Peter Ankar, the Norwegian ambassador to Egypt, was well-liked and easy to fathom. Perhaps it was because it was a hectic time in Egypt. The 1969 War of Attrition was in progress. At the bottom of the steps of the government building in which they were meeting, a barricade had been erected, characteristic of wartime Cairo, with sandbags stacked in front of all the windows.

Egypt was mounting a springtime offensive in the Suez. Large-scale shelling was going on along the Suez Canal, extensive aerial warfare and commando raids were in progress daily, which meant perhaps that they were at a point where they might need friends, and another Scandinavian might help, much like Gunnar Jarring the Swedish diplomat who had been charged by the United Nations to find peace that year in the Middle East.

At least they knew where Peter and Gunnar stood, unlike this whacky Norwegian archaeologist.

"You want to rope off a bit of desert behind the Khufu Pyramid to build a papyrus boat?" the thickset Egyptian minister asked in disbelief. He adjusted his horn-rimmed glasses and looked at Thor with a questioning smile. He glanced half dubiously at Ankar who politely smiled back as he stood erect and white-haired beside Thor, as "a sort of pledge that this stranger from the north was in his right mind."[1]

Thor was asking to violate the sacred ground on which stood the tombs of the pyramid builders, a place that according to Zahi Hawass was protected by a curse. "O all people who enter this tomb, who will make evil against this tomb . . . May the crocodile be against them on water, and snakes against them on land."[2]

Mohammed Ibrahim, Egypt's director of antiquities, died in 1966. His successor Gamal Mehrez, director of antiquities who was present at the meeting, had been plagued with dreams of death, and then while going to a meeting in Cairo on King Tut's treasure, he was hit by a car and died instantly. Three years after Mehrez's meeting with Heyerdahl and Ankar, during a loan of King Tut's death mask to London in 1972, Mehrez himself slumped to the floor dead at fifty from circulatory collapse.

Thor was asking permission from people with such memories and fears fresh in their minds. They finally agreed to allow him to cordon off an area and set up a tent, a camp, and a boat-building site, but only if he swore that he would not dig in the sand.

Present at the meeting was a man in his late fifties, Hassan Ragab. Early photos show him as a handsome young Basil Rathbone type, with a dark, clipped military moustache that turned gray in later life. Ragab had brought cuttings of papyrus back from Sudan and established plantations and an institute in Cairo where he made papyrus paper for the tourist trade. At the meeting he was the most qualified to judge Thor's project. Would it work? Would it sink? If so, how would that reflect on Egypt? It was, after all, a very public undertaking, and while the boat was being built, tourists would be visiting the site, which lay near the Khufu's Royal Boat Restoration project close by to the pyramids.

Like the other high-ranking Egyptians, Ragab was suspicious at first. In the papyrus plantations that he had started on the Nile, he knew that if fresh green stems were cut and tied into large bundles, they would be very heavy. A boat made of that may not sink, but it would not float easily. Thor explained that he was not talking about using green stems; he would use dry stems in which air could be trapped when they were tied tightly together in bundles. He had done a great deal of research on reed boats and knew it could be done. Ragab, an engineer as well as a diplomat and military man, was satisfied and Thor's project went forward, but perhaps Ragab learned something else at that meeting besides the basics of reed boat construction. He was good at book learning and admired academia, but it must have been obvious to him that he had just received a lesson in public relations from a master.

If you are going to deliberately attempt to manage the public's perception of a subject, this was the way to start. Thor had used the meeting to good effect. The day he set foot on the sacred ground of the pharaohs the fame and press coverage would begin, and the minute he announced that he was having tons of papyrus shipped from Lake Tana in Ethiopia to Cairo it would be news. Why? Because papyrus had not grown in Egypt for over a thousand years? Or was it because a papyrus boat had not sailed on the Nile for twice as long? Or was it simply because papyrus, plant of ancient days, was again playing a crucial role?

Whatever it was, Ragab saw the cameras clicking and whirring, and he realized as a result that the plant that he had fallen in love with was again on the front pages of the world press because of this Norwegian. It was a lesson he would never forget.

A former engineer, general in the Egyptian Army, cabinet minister, and ambassador to China, Italy, and Yugoslavia, Hassan Ragab had by then retired from active government service, and the previous year had founded his institute in Cairo devoted to the history and manufacture of papyrus paper. He called it the Papyrus Institute and he eventually came to know practically everything about papyrus that could be known. While in China as ambassador, he had seen a small family operation where laid-pulp paper was manufactured by hand, a process not very different from the method used 2,000 years earlier during the period when China invented the process of modern paper production. That gave him the idea. "It occurred to me," he said, "that if we could set up something like that in Egypt, perhaps it might become another tourist attraction."

Hassan Ragab's original Papyrus Institute, a houseboat on the Nile, 1973.

He went on to do a great deal of research into the ancient methods of papyrus papermaking and in 1979, earned a PhD from Grenoble in the art and science of making papyrus paper; meanwhile he also cultivated more cuttings of papyrus from the plants he had brought from Sudan and expanded his plantations in shallow, protected areas of the Nile River.

He died in 2004 at age ninety-one, but by then his plant cuttings and papyrus paper initiative had evolved into a modern industry. Today in Cairo, Luxor, and the delta thousands of sheets are made and sold to tourists, a production similar to that of ancient days when Egypt was the major center for the production of papyrus paper in the civilized world.

❧

Ragab was a great believer in making museums "come alive." We first met in 1973 when I was on tour in Egypt; by then his papyrus paper project was just beginning to turn a profit and he looked forward to expanding the Institute. His goal was to create a "living museum," a concept that was all the rage then. The major museums of the world in the seventies were in a terrific hurry to jump on the same bandwagon. I imagine it was, and still is, difficult for museums to come up with innovative exhibits, though they've made great strides: witness the Metropolitan Museum in New York, the Smithsonian museums in Washington, the British Museum and the Victoria and Albert in London, and the Louvre in Paris. They go to extraordinary lengths to breathe life into the past. And the new museums—the Holocaust Memorial Museum, the Museum of the American Indian, and the Museum of African American History and Culture in Washington—are all designed from the beginning to address the issue of "living history." This is obviously the way of the future.

"For me Williamsburg still has the edge," Ragab said, referring to the trade and small industry boutiques at America's largest showplace of living history. "I want to transport the viewer back into an ancient world and to allow them to mingle with the craftsmen, let them look over the shoulders of the ancients to see how they did things. You Americans are good at that." In his new facility he decided that everything must be there, "From Pharaoh on down, the papermakers, scribes, weavers, potters, artists, all in their proper place."

Around the time I first met Hassan, there was already talk about re-creating the great Royal Library of ancient times in Alexandria. The new library was finally built and dedicated in 2002 at a cost of $176 million with the support of many nations. Dr. Ismail Serageldin, a former vice president of the World Bank and an accomplished writer in economic development and biotechnology, was appointed its first director.

The library's design features a cylindrical building, set in a pool quite near the sea and a gridded glass roof sloped downward until part of it disappears below ground level. A spectacular structure, it accommodates an ambitious international program, including a library that can hold millions of books; specialized libraries, conference centers, and research facilities to restore manuscripts. The library also serves as one of the external backup archives for the global Internet. As part of a joint program with the Internet Archive, the library received a donation of five million dollars and a collection that includes: 10 billion web pages spanning the years 1996–2001 from over 16 million different sites; 2000 hours of Egyptian and U.S. television broadcast archives; 1000 archival films; 100 terabytes of data stored on 200 computers.

The new Library in Alexandria (Wikipedia).

It should be noted that the new facility was built from scratch using modern ideas and concepts, since we have no idea of what the original looked like. But now because of advances in 3-D imagery and digital reproduction, existing documents, antiquities, and even buildings, no matter how large or small, can be replicated almost exactly.

A case in point are the tombs of Egypt. Sharon Waxman in her 2008 book *Loot* remarked on the tomb of Seti I in the Valley of the Kings—a marvelous, incomparable work of art, with its twenty-foot ceiling and bright colored wall paintings—but it is not an easy place to get to and today it is closed to the public because of the risk of damage to the artwork.[3] No one can see or photograph it, except by special permission. Waxman pointed out that after it was discovered by Giovanni Belzoni in the early 1800s, he had the bright idea of re-creating the rooms and putting them on display. He hired an Italian artist to make wax models that could be reconstructed as full-scale models in London. "He opened it as a tourist attraction and business endeavor in 1821 at the Egyptian Hall in Piccadilly and charged an entrance fee. The exhibit was such a hit that it lasted a full year. It is worth considering in our age of modern technology. Can't we build a replica and invite everyone in? Constructing the same sort of model today would be easier and more faithful to the original. It would open up access to the wonders of ancient Egypt and could travel the world or sit permanently near the Valley of the Kings. In short, perhaps Seti could be brought to the people if the people cannot be brought to Seti."

Thankfully, someone is listening. Adam Lowe, a former painter who runs the Madrid-based restoration workshop, Factum Arte, built a replica of King Tut's tomb in Egypt, which according to Daniel Zalewski, features director of the *New Yorker*, was the most heralded digital facsimile yet made.[4] Lowe now intends to take on a replica of Seti I's tomb.

❧

Hassan Ragab was enthralled with the idea that the Alexandria Library would be rebuilt. "That library, as you may remember, held hundreds of thousands of volumes of papyri—until Julius Caesar burned them. We can't restore all of them, but there are more than 40,000 papyri still in existence today (under glass or in storage) and once we can get some of the originals and copies of others under one roof, we'll have a nucleus. That assumes, of course, that by then we will have begun to make papyrus on a large enough scale—and we will, we will."

That was in 1973, and back then it was only a dream; now in the twenty-first century it could become a reality. The days are gone when the papyrus plant was lacking and technicians nonexistent: the papyrus papermakers in Cairo now have the means and the skills. A good example of what could be done at the village level is the story of papermaking in the delta, where papyrus plantations on a 500-acre swampy plot were established in the seventies by Dr. Anas Mostafa. Dr. Mostafa trained 200 villagers in the cultivation of the plant and the ancient method of papermaking. At the height of the tourist market early in this millennium thousands of sheets of papyrus paper were being made here. There is also a capability for illustrating papyrus sheets with silk screening, 5,000 sheets per week can be done.[5] What is needed is a link between the papermakers, the library, and the museum world, and a global effort to re-create in major museums what the world of scrolls looked like.

The papermakers and artists are ready, willing, and capable of re-creating a large enough number of scrolls to allow at least one corner of any major library to be used to play out the ancient drama of papyrus paper in the time of the Ptolemies.

Such an exhibit could also re-create the environment of an early age with readers, researchers, and thinkers wandering in and out of the facility, with ready access to real scrolls of papyrus paper inscribed with the classics that could be rolled and unrolled with impunity. The touristic possibilities of such an exhibit are impressive.

Aside from the re-creation of such a library of scrolls and bringing back to life the world of ancient scholars, another benefit of the papermaking industry in Egypt would be the replication in a detailed manner of special scrolls, such as the case in 1989 when the McClung Museum at the University of Tennessee in Knoxville commissioned an exact replica of the first three feet of an original papyrus scroll, the Papyrus of Kha. This papyrus is an edition of the *Book of the Dead* similar to Ani's Papyrus, and was likewise found in Thebes. It belonged to the ancient builder, Kha and his wife Merit and is dated 1386–1349 B.C. It was 52½ feet long and is today in the Museo Egizio in Turin. The replica depicts the deceased Kha and his wife before the great god of the dead, Osiris, and, according to Evans "in twenty years the colors of the replica have not faded and the papyrus copy is still in excellent condition." The facsimile was done by Antonio Basile, of the Museo Didattico del Libro Antico in Tivoli, Italy. Antonio is the brother of Corrado Basile, the founder of the Instituto di Papyri in Sicily, one of the few places outside of Africa where papyrus grows naturally. Corrado, a pioneer in the restoration, repair and re-creation of antique papyrus paper has worked with the Egyptian Museum and the International Papyrus Institute in Cairo. His goal is to help restore the 30,000 ancient papyri in the museum's collection.

Luckily the technique for creating facsimiles has grown by quantum leaps with the introduction of digital methods. The newest techniques avoid the problem of replicas painted by hand, which record only the details that the copyists notice; they have no scholarly value. Also helpful is the fact that several photographic facsimiles of the Ani Papyrus have been available for many years on paper. The first appeared in a British Museum edition in 1890, the latest was printed in 1978 by ADEVA (Akademische Druck-u. Verlagsanstalt, Graz, Austria) on thirty-seven pages. A more sophisticated edition appeared in 2018, produced by CM Editores in Salamanca, Spain. This latest facsimile is an expensive limited edition of 999 copies made from the original color photos and printed on modern papyrus paper on thirty-seven pages. One drawback of all of these facsimiles is that they represent thirty-seven separate sheets rather than a complete scroll. Perhaps it would be possible using techniques devised by Adam Lowe to print an entire seventy-eight foot scroll intact. In replicating the King Tut tomb, for example, he used a very accurate "warts and all" method that involved modifying an enormous Epson printer so that it could make repeated passes over a gesso-like skin in perfect registration. The skin was then put in place on walls built for the purpose in Luxor. Lowe is also unusual in that he makes a great effort to incorporate Egyptian personnel and facilities into the project. He is training Egyptians in his scanning methods in his Madrid workshop, and plans to set up a digital-fabrication studio in Luxor. The moment is approaching where a facsimile of the complete seventy-eight-foot roll of Ani's original book can be printed on native papyrus paper by Egyptians, much like Ani's team of scribes did when they produced the original over 3000 years ago.

The immediate goal of such an initiative would be to supplement the exhibit of ancient scrolls visualized by Ragab for the Alexandria Library, or a similar collection in the Getty Villa dei Papyri, or any other museum interested in the history of ancient Rome or Egypt. In addition to a collection of scrolls similar to those in the ancient libraries, a mobile exhibit could be mounted that would use the new Egyptian-made scrolls to be placed inside of, or attached to, a flexible plastic medium. This would allow them to be used in a free-form manner inside any viewing space and would get away from the large problem of having to display such documents on a wall. Often a bare wall is a rare and most coveted item in a modern museum.

Rolled in part or whole, it would also show the public what scrolls are all about, much like the case of the Bayeux Tapestry and the British facsimile that has been on view since 1895 in Reading. It could be an effort equivalent to Heyerdahl's highly publicized Ra project where he produced a replica of a papyrus boat, but this time the project would feature the return of the ancient papyrus paper industry to Egypt. Egyptologists from all over the world could be involved, assisted by a multinational team of experts who would simulate not just the effects of ancient Egyptians on the people of other lands, but the world of papyrus paper from the time of the New Kingdom until the time of the Roman and Islamic Empires, when papyrus paper was the principle medium in use.

Another advantage of the techniques used by Lowe in Egypt is that facsimile scrolls could be made in multiple copies, enough to use in any available space in the old or new Cairo museums, as well as in national museums in countries worldwide. A flexible medium would allow the scroll to be "free formed," or wrapped around or through any collection. It could be paired with smaller "living" mini-exhibits, as in the new museums, or, in a darkened room it could be highlighted with sequential spotlights in a mini sound and light show. The possibilities are endless.

Papyrus-making crafts, papermaking, the history of writing, art, manuscript illumination, restoration and research on ancient papyrus scrolls, along with hands-on and visitor involvement activities, and so on, could all be put in place and supplemented with some or all of the thirty-seven panels of the original Ani scroll on loan from London to Cairo or elsewhere. The originals could finally be taken out of storage and shared out and incorporated into the "living" exhibits from the start. The intention would be to have the original scroll become a useful resource for participating museums in Africa, Asia, the Middle East, and the Americas.

Other centers of Egyptology would be encouraged to join in; France, the United States, Germany, Italy, Austria, and the United Kingdom could participate in the program by duplicating or borrowing the exhibit on their own as they wished. The Papyrus of Ani would be ideal for this as it is one of humanity's earliest and finest spiritual treasures. The exhibit would highlight the papyrus paper industry, explaining and reliving its history and illustrating how it affected the world in the way that Marshall McLuhan imagined, where the form of the message determined the ways in which that message was perceived. In the ancient days of papyrus paper, the scroll had far-reaching sociological, aesthetic, and philosophical consequences, to the point of actually altering the ways in which the ancients experienced the world, just as later papyrus pages in the form of a codex influenced the Christian world. In the case of papyrus, the medium was the message, and it was a medium that changed the way people lived their lives and went to their deaths.

That is the story that would be illustrated by the Papyrus of Ani, and shared not just by Egypt and England, but by the world. In the process, Wallis Budge might even be pardoned, forgiven and possibly even thanked, for starting something he never intended.

❧

The way ahead was illustrated to me one day in New York. I had a few hours to kill, the Metropolitan Museum was close by, and so I decided once again to visit the Egyptian Great Hall, which is always a treat. Once through the hall, I started through the galleries and caught myself thinking what a shame when I saw the large colorful Egyptian frescoes lining the walls.

Having just read Brian Fagan's *The Rape of the Nile*, I recoiled at the thought that someone had cut these wondrous works off the walls of Egyptian tombs. Even though they were well mounted and obviously cared for, like Vivant Denon, I felt the gall rising as I thought of the crime involved. Then at the end of the gallery before passing on, my eye caught a small sign that read Facsimile Wall Paintings.

I stopped cold in my tracks. Facsimile! I couldn't believe it. But after going back and looking as closely as I could, without arousing the suspicions of the guards, I had to concede there wasn't a piece of purloined plaster in sight.

They were drawings on paper!

Did any of my fellow viewers notice? Were they disturbed by the fact that these were facsimiles? As far as I could tell there wasn't a jaundiced eye in the house. For the next ten minutes as I watched hundreds streaming by (the gallery is on the way to many other exciting displays), I saw quite a few pass with only a glance or two, but many stopped, looked and snapped photos, some sat and consulted their printed guides, and some sat and admired the paintings with satisfied looks on their faces.

I realized then that it was an extraordinary exhibit, and, despite my ill-founded suspicions, to all intents it was the real thing.

How was this done? It turns out that the story behind the Facsimile Collection of the Met is as exciting as the collection itself. It begins with the artist couple, Norman and Nina de Garis Davies, already in residence in Egypt when they were joined by a third artist, Charles Wilkinson, who later became an emeritus curator. A student of the Slade School in England, Wilkinson was recommended because of his abilities in tempera painting. Also, as he noted in one of his books, active service in WWI had left him, at twenty-two, "none too strong physically." It was felt that "the climate of Egypt would do him good." It must have helped, as he lived to be the last surviving member of the expedition and died at age eighty-eight.

Once the museum's Egyptian Expedition had been granted a concession to work in the tombs at Thebes on the west bank of the Nile opposite Luxor, all three settled down to work in the early 1900s. One problem that arose immediately was that permanent, accurate copies of the wall drawings could not be easily done. Existing photographic means were inadequate. Photos alone would have been too artificial. Neither would watercolor sketches do, as existing pigments were too transparent. The solution was found by Francis Unwin, Norman's assistant, who discovered that egg tempera would closely duplicate the original earth colors of the ancient paintings.

I realized later that this was the reason I was taken in. I had grown too used to the fake colors used in gaudy copies on postcards, and now on the Internet, which led me to reject reproductions. Having seen original paintings in Egypt, I thought I knew the real thing on sight. It turns out in this case that it wasn't only the paint that did the trick; it was the skill of the artists.

We have one description from Nigel Strudwick, a specialist in Egyptian art at the University of Memphis on how it was done. When, for example, Nina was "painting a male figure wearing a white robe through which the body color is partially visible, she would paint the background, apply a solid area of color for the body, overlay it with the white for the robe, and draw the red-brown outline, cleaning the figure up, as had the ancient painter, by application of further background color."

She also developed a way of including damaged sections by painting them in. She did this in such a way that it captured the texture and the composition of the gaps and holes. Even the cracks in the original wall that are so common to the original wall paintings were carefully rendered, so much so that they seem three-dimensional. The result of their effort is a collection of 350 wall drawings in the Metropolitan, all of which are valuable records. In those cases where the originals have disappeared, from one cause or another, the drawings have become priceless as the only remaining record. In sum, the de Garis Davies had made an elegant case for facsimile tomb paintings. Recently the same case was made for ancient papyrus paper when the new Museum of the Bible opened in Washington, DC.

It was at this time I decided to leave aside the complexities of exhibiting very long rolls of papyrus paper and turn my attention to the single sheets found in ancient letters and early codices. Here I struck gold. The Museum of the Bible had opened to great fanfare in Washington, DC, in 2017 and, I thought, this was only right as, after all, the Bible as a subject of historical research has to be a crowd-pleaser. Even more interesting was the media reaction, in which this museum was said to be "the most technologically advanced museum in the world, offering an unbeatable combination of interactive entertainment, scholarly investigation, and historical exhibition."[6] The *Washington Post* declared that it would "set a new standard for how this country's museums fuse entertainment and education," and it does so "in a way that many visitors will probably find more compelling and accessible than the dense cultural stew on view at the Smithsonian's Museum of American History."[7] The *Post* also pointed out that the museum uses the "master narrative" idea of history, "that there is one sweeping human story that needs to be told, a story that is still unfolding and carrying us along with it . . . It is an exciting idea, and an enormously powerful tool for making sense of the world."

I was encouraged to think that this museum was the answer to my prayers since, if there were any place that papyrus paper would be taken seriously, it would be here. Obviously there has been so much original material lost over the last two thousand years that it makes the remaining fragments and pages of papyrus relating to the early Christians rare and very valuable. Proof came as I passed through the pair of awe-inspiring forty-foot bronze panels inscribed with Genesis 1 that flank the front entrance. Immediately inside the vestibule, I saw an illuminated blow-up of some papyrus paper pages. Several large glass panels were in place showing Psalm 19 from the Bodmer Psalter, an ancient papyrus prayer book used by third century A.D. Christians. This is a psalter the publication of which in 1967, according to Professor Albert Pietersma of the University of Toronto, was nothing short of sensational for scholars interested in such things. Not only is this manuscript the most extensive papyrus of its kind discovered to date, but its text, even apart from its immense value for the reconstruction of the Old Greek, presents us with a Greek psalter as it was used in Upper Egypt in ancient days.

Further along on the third floor, I was pleasantly surprised to see the extensive use of papyrus facsimiles in the museum's permanent exhibit called, *History of the Bible*. On display were eleven original ancient papyrus pages or fragments including five pages of the famous Bodmer Psalter. Alongside these were seven facsimile items including an eleven-page facsimile codex, all of which fitted seamlessly into the story that was being told.

An important point made by Professor Pietersma was that scholars such as those using the museum's facilities, are much indebted to various editors and the Bodmer Library who have helped in the production and circulation of complete and excellent facsimiles, since this "enables one to obtain first-hand information and to correct the edited text where necessary. It also makes it possible to reassess the restorations compiled by editors which, upon reexamination, can sometimes be improved upon."[8]

Under the soft lighting in this special room, a room devoted to the earliest part of Bible history, we can almost hear the Christian copyists scratching out the Word and calling out for fresh pages of paper—papyrus paper—as they press forward on their pathway to glory.

Acknowledgments

Special thanks to Jacqueline Flynn at Joëlle Delbourgo Associates, who reviewed and commented on my earlier drafts. Also, I owe a large debt of gratitude to Jessica Case at Pegasus Books for believing in the book and providing encouragement and common-sense advice when it was needed. I'm not an Egyptologist, but several years ago I took a course of video lectures called "The History of Ancient Egypt," one of the Great Courses produced by the Teaching Company and given by Bob Brier, senior research fellow at Long Island University, which inspired me to take an interest in ancient Egypt. And so thanks to Professor Brier I began a long journey back into the antique history of papyrus.

Helpful sources for the technical and historical information about papyrus paper are Professor Naphtali Lewis's classic book *Papyrus in Classical Antiquity*,[1] and "Papyrus," an essay written by Bridget Leach and John Tait.[2] Leach, lately retired from the British Museum, is one of the foremost conservators of ancient papyri and Professor Tait is emeritus professor of Egyptology at the University of London. Both provided me with helpful information regarding the existence of intact papyrus scrolls. Another important source of current information on papyrus paper was *The Oxford Handbook of Papyrology* (Oxford University Press, 2011) edited by Roger Bagnall, emeritus professor of ancient history at New York University.

Of great help also was *Ancient Libraries*, the compendium of everything worth knowing about ancient libraries edited by Jason König, Katerina Oikonomopoulou, and Greg Woolf (Cambridge University Press, 2013) and the most recent information on the Egyptians' *Book of the Dead* found in *Book of the Dead: Becoming God in Ancient Egypt*, edited by Foy Scalf (Oriental Institute of the University of Chicago, 2017).

In this book I also draw upon my own research on the plant from which ancient paper was made. Most of that work took place in Africa in the 1980s and perhaps would never have amounted to much if I had not gotten a small research grant from the National Geographic Society that was renewed several times and for which I am thankful. I also doubt if this book would have been written without the patience, help, and guidance of my wife, Caroline, to whom I am eternally grateful.

Thanks also to Dr. Ilona Regulski, curator of Egyptian written culture, Department of Ancient Egypt and Sudan at the British Museum; Professor Willy Clarysse, University of Leuven, Belgium; Dr. Günter Dreyer, German Archaeological Institute, Cairo; Myriam Krutzsch, restorer of Papyrus at the Egyptian Museum, Berlin, Germany; and various fellow members of the American Society of Papyrologists for assistance in the interpretation of the history of papyrus in ancient Egypt. Members also provided answers to questions on the conservation and preservation of rolls and fragments of ancient papyri in particular, Ted Bernhardt, Dr. Thomas Kraus, and Professor Cornelia Roemer. Thanks to Elaine Evans, curator of the McLung Museum at the University of Tennessee for her thoughts on replicas of famous papyri, and Dr. Neal Spencer, keeper of the Deptartment of Ancient Egypt and Sudan, British Museum, for his help, suggestions, and access to the Papyrus of Ani and British Museum Study Rooms.

Special thanks go out to the staff at the new Museum of the Bible in Washington, DC, for their advice and information on the artful display of facsimile pages of ancient papyrus paper. In particular, the help of Brian Hyland and Bethany Jensen, associate curators of Manuscripts, is appreciated. I also thank Alex van Oss of the Foreign Service Institute, Washington, D.C. for comments on early drafts.

The American Research Center in Egypt helped greatly in funding a speaking tour that allowed me to test out some of my ideas on their members, and they helped promote my work as it applied to ancient Egypt. For their help over the years, I thank Carol Boyer, president of the ARCE Washington, DC, chapter; executive director, Jane Zimmerman; and Robin Young.

Thanks also to Mr. Shady Nabil, tourism manager at the Pharaonic Village, Cairo, Egypt; Dr. Sayyed Hassan, director of the Papyrus Department at the Egyptian Museum, Cairo, Egypt; Dr. Magdy Mansour, director of conservation, Coptic Museum, Cairo, Egypt; Hossam El Deeb and Wael Mohamed, Restoration Laboratory at The Library in Alexandria, Egypt; Corrado Basile, Siracusa, Italy; and Dr. Abdel Salam Ragab, chairman and CEO of the Pharonic Village, Cairo, Egypt.

Much of the text was written at a small table in Greenberry's Coffee House, an extraordinary meeting place in McLean, Virginia, where I have been coddled and "refilled" over more years than I care to remember.

Supplementary Illustration Credits

Photo and figure credits: Map 1, Tura Caves, Mayfair, I., 1954. UK Military Series, HMSO, London. Map 3, Courtesy of Prof. Willy Clarysse and the University of Leuven (Leuven, Belgium) Fayum Project.

COLOR INSERT

PAGE 1: TOP left, Brooklyn Museum, Charles Edwin Wilbour Fund, 37.1699Ea-c; center, Wikipedia Commons-Fredduf/Orig. Louvre; bottom, composite after Wikipedia Commons-Walaa/Orig. Egyptian Museum.

PAGE 2: Top, after E. A. Wallis Budge, The gods of the Egyptians, 1904; center, left and right photos courtesy of S. Johnson (SAREP, Gabarone, Botswana) & G. Petersen (HYDROC, Langballig, Germany); bottom: after N. de Garis Davies, 1922.

PAGE 3: Top, Map A, after Larrasoaña, Roberts and Rohling, 2013 and N. Drake,et al., 2011; below left, after Alma-Tadema, 1888; below right, after Jean-Baptiste Wicar, Wikipedia Commons-Sailko/Orig. Art Institute of Chicago (Creative Commons Attribution 3.0 Unported license).

PAGE 4: Below, after Alma-Tadema, 1885.

PAGE 5: Top left,after Wikipedia Commons-Didia/Orig. British Museum (Creative Commons Attribution-Share Alike 3.0 Unported license);top center, Jon Bodsworth, Egypt Archive; top right Wikipedia Commons-Benh Lieu Song (Creative Commons Attribution-Share Alike 3.0 Unported license).

PAGE 6: Top, Map B based on James Rennell, 1830; below, Map C, after McCormick, 2001.

PAGE 7: Bottom, Canadian Govt. Asia/Canada (https://tinyurl.com/yawm5apb).

PAGE 8: Set of four trading cards from the author's collection.

Appendix

Table 2. Estimated production of Papyrus Paper in Ancient Egypt[*]

Period	Time	No. of years	Estimated Sheets/yr. (millions)	Rolls (millions)	Sheets (millions)	Tons
Early Egypt	3100–2800 B.C.	300	0	.03	.6	3
Old Kingdom	2700–2200 B.C.	500	.001	.5	10	43
Middle Kingdom	2100–1800 B.C.	300	.01	3	60	261
New Kingdom	1700–1100 B.C.	600	.05	30	600	2,609
Late Period	1000–300 B.C.	700	2	70	1,400	6,087
Ptolemaic	300–30 B.C.	270	20	270	5,400	23,478
Roman	30 BC–395 A.D.	425	50	1012	21,250	92,391
Arab	395–900 A.D.	505	15	379	7,575	32,935
Total		*3,600*		*1,764*	*36,296*	*157,807*

[*] Tonnage based on modern standard multipurpose paper, 500 sheets 8.5 x 11 = 4lb 14 oz. or 78 oz. = 6.4 sheets/oz. = 102.6sheets/lb. = 2,240 lb./ton = 230,000 sheets/ton.

Calculations Used for Table 2

1. Potential standing crop of papyrus paper under normal swamp conditions*

A. Size of stems: Assume stems of maximum growth 15–18 ft. tall and 6 in. diameter at base. In African swamps 2 unelongated stems, 4 juvenile elongated stems, 9 mature green stems, and 13 old, dead stems occur per square meter (Gaudet, 1976 and Terer, et al, 2012). For estimate, assume 12 useable green stems per 10 square feet = 1.2 useable green stems per square foot

B. Number of slices: One tall stem (15 ft.) trimmed (thin upper part and the umbel are discarded) into 18 in. long pieces yields 8 usable pieces. Each 18 in. long piece allows about 6 slices yielding 48 slices per stem or 57 slices per square foot

C. Number of slices needed per sheet of papyrus paper: Using modern papyrus sheets (8 in. by 12 in.) about 32 slices per sheet (or 1.5 sheets per stem)

D. Number of sheets possible from a square mile of swamp: One sheet will require 0.56 square feet of swamp production. Thus, 27,878,400 (no. of square feet in one square mile) ÷ 0.56 = 50 million sheets per square mile.

E. Area available and maximum harvest possible in ancient Egypt: Of the total area 2,500 square miles perhaps 20 percent available for papermaking = 500 square miles. Thus 500 × 50 million = 25,000 million sheets possible as a biological maximum one-time yield.*

(*Note: this calculation assumes clear cutting, a one-time event)

2. Annual Sustainable Yield, if contractor constraints are followed**

A. Number of stems harvested: In Roman times (13 B.C.) as noted by Lewis (1974), contractors in one particular papyrus swamp had to pay interest in kind of 200 armfuls per day. One armful load conservatively contained 25 stems, or 5,000 stems per day. If this interest represented, say, 20 percent of the production, then 25,000 stems per day could be expected.

B. Total area required to maintain this rate of production: Assume 200-day regeneration cycle (requires 200 days maximum to grow back, 6 months or 180 days minimum); then 25,000 stems per day requires: (20,833 square feet × 200 days) ÷ 27,878,400 = 0.15 square mile (where 27,878,400 = no. of square feet in one square mile). This is the minimum size papyrus swamp plot needed. Average plantation required space for fallow, waterways, etc., thus would probably be a much larger area, say two square miles in area.

C. Maximum total sheets produced: 5,000 stems over 200 days (assume flooding during rest of year) × 1.5 = 7.5 million sheets per year.

D. Using this rate of production under contractor constraints for all of ancient Egypt:

Total swamp available in Egypt = 2,500 square mile, of which perhaps 20 percent was available for paper production, or 500 square miles = 250 plantations (2 square miles each) × 7.5 million sheets per year = 1,875 million sheets maximum sustainable yield under contractor constraints.

(**Note: this calculation assumes sustainable growth, cutting on a rotational basis)

3. Annual sustainable reasonable yield (realizing the wishes of the cartel)

A. Number of sheets produced per year: The cartel limited the labor pool (Lewis, 1974) and the area farmed. Also considering that plantations (*drymoi*) varied from 20 square mile (Great Swamp[1]) to 0.5–1.8 square mile (Arsinoite Nome[2]) and that modern papyrus papermakers estimate only about 100 sheets could be produced by one worker per day; best estimates are thus much less than the maximum. They are listed in Table 1 as "Sheets/yr."

References

PROLOGUE

Darnton, Robert. *The Kiss of Lamourette: Reflections in Cultural History*. New York: W. W. Norton, 1991.

1: THE INSPECTOR PUTS PEN TO PAPER

Avrin, Leila. Scr*ibes, Script and Books: The Book Arts from Antiquity to the Renaissance*. Chicago: American Library Association, 1991.

Emery, Walter B. and Zaki Yusef Saad, *Excavations at Saqqara, The Tomb of Hemaka*. Cairo: Government Press, 1938.

Emery, Walter B., *Great Tombs of the First Dynasty II*. London: Egypt Exploration Society, 1954, 127.

Emery, Walter B. *Archaic Egypt*. Middlesex, UK: Penguin Books, 1961.

Shaw, Donald L., Chris Vargo, Richard Cole, and Milad Minooi, "The Emerging Papyrus Society: How We Are Using Media to Monitor Civic Life, Find Personal Community, and Create Private Identity." Paper presented at Digital Communication in the Time of Disclosure, Yarmouk University, Irbid, Jordan 2014. https://tinyurl.com/y959vmym.

Standage, Tom. *Writing on the Wall: Social Media—The First 2,000 Years*. New York: Bloomsbury, 2013.

Tallet, Pierre. "Ayn Sukhna and Wadi el-Jarf: Two Newly Discovered Pharaonic Harbours on the Suez Gulf." *British Museum Studies in Ancient Egypt and Sudan* 18 (2012), 147–68.

Tallet, Pierre. "Des papyrus du temps de Chéops au ouadi el-Jarf." *Bulletin de la Société française d'égyptologie* 188 (2014): 25–49.

Wilkinson, Toby A. H. *Early Dynastic Egypt*. New York: Routledge, 1999.

Wilkinson, Toby A. H. *The Rise and Fall of Ancient Egypt*. London: Random House, 2010.

2: PRISSE LIKE MOSES, CARRIES HOME STONE TABLETS AND PAPER SCROLLS

Avrin, Leila. *Scribes, Script and Books: The Book Arts from Antiquity to the Renaissance*. Chicago: American Library Association, 1991.

Deuel, Leo *Testaments of Time: The Search for Lost Manuscripts and Records*. New York: Knopf, 1965.

Norton, Mary. "Prisse, a Portrait." *Saudi Aramco World* 41, (1990), http://archive.aramcoworld.com/issue/199006/prisse-a.portrait.htm.

3: THE UNDERTAKER'S SPECIAL AND THE FIRST BEST SELLER

Adkins, Lesley, and Roy Adkins. *The Keys of Egypt: The Race to Crack the Hieroglyph Code*. New York: Harper Perennial, 2000.

Budge, E. A. Wallis. *The Book of the Dead; The Papyrus of Ani*. London: British Museum, 1895.

Budge, E. A. Wallis. *A Short History of the Egyptian People*. London: J. M. Dent, 1914.

Budge, E. A. Wallis. *By Nile and Tigris: A Narrative of Journeys in Egypt and Mesopotamia on Behalf of the British Museum between the Years 1886 and 1913*. London: John Murray, 1920.

Budge, E. A. Wallis. *Egypt*. London: Williams and Norgate, 1925.

Denon, Vivant. *Travels in Upper and Lower Egypt*, trans. Arthur Aikin. London: Longman and Rees, 1803.

Larson, Charles M. *By His Own Hand Upon Papyrus: A New Look at the Joseph Smith Papyri*. Cedar Springs, MI: Institute for Religious Research, 1992.

Taylor, John H. *Journey through the Afterlife: Ancient Egyptian Book of the Dead*. Cambridge, MA: Harvard University Press, 2010.

4: THE BOOK OF THE DEAD

Budge, E. A. Wallis. *The Mummy: A Handbook of Egyptian Funerary Archaeology*. Cambridge: Cambridge University Press, 1894.

Goelet, Dr. Ogden. "A Commentary on the Corpus of Literature and Tradition Which Constitutes the Book of Going Forth by Day," in *The Egyptian Book of the Dead: The Book of Going Forth by Day*, ed. James Wasserman. San Francisco: Chronicle Books, 1998.

5: PAPYRUS PAPER, YOUR TICKET TO PARADISE

Budge, E. A. Wallis. *By Nile and Tigris: A narrative of Journeys in Egypt and Mesopotamia on Behalf of the British Museum between the Years 1886 and 1913*. London: John Murray, 1920.

Budge, E. A. Wallis. *The Book of the Dead; The Papyrus of Ani*. London: British Museum, 1895.

Gaudet, John. *Papyrus, the Plant that Changed the World*. New York: Pegasus, 2014.

Immega, Guy. "Ancient Egypt's Lost Legacy? The Buduma Culture of Lake Chad." Friends of Niger. Last modified 2012. www.friendsofniger.org/pdf/Buduma_Master_V4.pdf.

Schneider, Thomas. "The West beyond the West: The Mysterious 'Wernes' of the Egyptian Underworld and the Chad Palaeolakes." *Journal of Ancient Egyptian Interconnections*, no. 2: 1–14.

Taylor, John H. *Journey through the Afterlife: Ancient Egyptian Book of the Dead*. Cambridge, MA: Harvard University Press, 2010.

Travelers in the Middle East Archive (TIMEA). "The Nile Cruise, 1847 and 1897." http://timea.rice.edu/NileCruise.html.

Yeakel, Justin D., Mathias M. Pires, Lars Rudolf, et. al. "Collapse of an Ecological Network in Ancient Egypt." *PNAS* 111, no. 40 (2014). https://doi.org/10.1073/pnas.1408471111.

6: THE SANDS OF THE NILE GIVE UP THEIR TREASURES

Černý, Jaroslav. "Paper and Books in Ancient Egypt." Inaugural lecture, March 1947, at University College, London. Published London: H. K. Lewis for the College, 1952.

Deissmann, Gustav Adolf, and Lionel R. Strachan. *New Light on the New Testament: From Records of the Graeco-Roman Period*. Edinburgh: T. and T. Clark, 1908, 14–15.

7: THE AFFAIR OF THE ORANGES

Budge, E. A. Wallis. *By Nile and Tigris: A narrative of Journeys in Egypt and Mesopotamia on Behalf of the British Museum between the Years 1886 and 1913*. London: John Murray, 1920.

8: THE FLOODGATES OPEN

Bagnall, Roger S., *Early Christian Books in Egypt*. Princeton, NJ: Princeton University Press, 2009.

Hodgkin, Thomas, ed. *The Letters of Cassiodorus*. London: Henry Frowde, 1886. Oxyrhynchus Online. 2007. http://www.papyrology.ox.ac.uk/POxy/oxyrhynchus/parsons4.html.

9: THE BIRTH OF MEMPHIS AND PAPER

Anon. 2012. Johannes Gutenberg. Univ. Texas, Harry Ransom Center web site http://www.hrc.utexas.edu/exhibitions/permanent/gutenbergbible/gutenberg/#top.

Anon. 2018. Online Encyclopedia: Based on the 11th Edition of the Encyclopedia Britannica, 1922. http://encyclopedia.jrank.org.

Avrin, Leila. *Scribes, Script and Books: The Book Arts from Antiquity to the Renaissance*. Chicago: American Library Association, 1991.

Basile, C., and A. Di Natale. "*Per la storia e le origini del papiro in Sicilia*," in *Papyri*. Siracusa: Museo del Papiro, 1991, 5–29.

Breasted, James, ed. *Ancient Records of Egypt: Historical Documents from the Earliest Times to the Persian Conquest*, Vol. IV. Chicago: University of Chicago, 1906.

Budge, E. A. Wallis. *The Book of the Dead: The Papyrus of Ani*. London: British Museum, London, 1895.

Emery, Walter B. *Archaic Egypt*. Middlesex, UK: Penguin Books, 1961.

Emery, Walter B., and Zaki Yusef Saad. *Excavations at Saqqara: The Tomb of Hemaka*. Cairo: Government Press, 1938.

Evans, Elaine A. "Papyrus a Blessing upon Pharaoh." Knoxville: McClung Museum, University of Tennessee, 1–12.

Fischer, Steven Roger. *A History of Writing*. London: Reaktion Books, 2001.

Horne, C. F. *The Sacred Books and Early Literature of the East, Volume II*. New York: Parke, Austin, and Lipscomb, 1917, 62–78.

Johnson, M. *The Nature and Making of Papy*rus. Barkston Ash, UK: Elmete Press, 1973, 71.

Kenyon, F. G. *The Paleography of Greek Papyri*. Oxford: Oxford University Press, 1899.

Kilgour, F. 1998. The Evolution of Books. Oxford: Oxford University Press.

Leach, B. and J. Tait. "Papyrus," in *Ancient Egyptian Materials and Technology*, edited by P. T. Nicholson and I. Shaw. Cambridge: Cambridge University Press, 2000, 227–253.

Lewis, Naphtali. *Papyrus in Classical Antiquity*. Oxford: Clarendon Press, 1974.

Lewis, Naphtali. *Papyrus in Classical Antiquity: Supplement. Papyrologica Bruxellensia*. Vol. 23. Brusells: Fondation égyptologique Reine Élisabeth, 1989.

Lewis, Naphtali. "Papyrus in Classical Antiquity: An Update." *Chronique d'Egypte* 57, no. 134 (1992), 308–318.

Owen, Antoinette, and Rachel Danzig. "The History and Treatment of the Papyrus Collection at the Brooklyn Museum." *The American Institute for Conservatio*n 12 (1993).

Parkinson, Richard, and Stephen Quirke. *Papyrus*. Austin: University of Texas Press, 1995.

Pliny the Elder. *The Natural History,* Vol. XIII. Translated by J. Bostock and H. Riley. London: Taylor and Francis, 1855, 74–81.

Ragab, Hassan. 1980. "Le Papyrus." PhD thesis, Université de Grenoble and Papyrus Institute, 1980.

Roberts, C. H. "The Greek Papyri." In *The Legacy of Egypt*, edited by S. R. K. Glanville, 249–282. Oxford: Clarendon Press, 1963.

Wilkinson, Toby A. H. *Early Dynastic Egypt*. New York: Routledge, 1999.

Wilkinson, Toby A. H. *The Rise and Fall of Ancient Egypt*. London: Random House, 2010.

10: A GIFT FROM THE GODS

Breasted, James, ed. *Ancient Records of Egypt: Historical Documents from the Earliest Times to the Persian Conquest,* Volume IV. Chicago: University of Chicago, 1906.

Deissmann, Gustav Adolf, and Lionel R. Strachan. *New Light on the New Testament: From Records of the Graeco-Roman Period*. Edinburgh: T. and T. Clark, 1908, 14–15.

Evans, Elaine A. "Papyrus a Blessing upon Pharaoh." Knoxville: McClung Museum, University of Tennessee, 1–12.

Howard-Williams, Clive, and John Gaudet. "The Structure and Function of African Swamps." In *The Ecology and Management of African Wetland Vegetation*. Edited by Patrick Denny, 153–175. Springer Netherlands, 1985.

Johnson, M. *The Nature and Making of Papyrus*. Barkston Ash, UK: Elmete Press, 1973, 71.

Kantor, H. "Plant Ornament: Its Origin and Development in the Ancient Near East." PhD Thesis, University of Chicago, 1945.

11: THE MONOPOLY

Lewis, Naphtali. *Papyrus in Classical Antiquity*. Oxford: Clarendon Press, 1974.

Lewis, Naphtali. *Papyrus in Classical Antiquity: Supplement. Papyrologica Bruxellensia*. Vol. 23. Brusells: Fondation égyptologique Reine Élisabeth, 1989.

Lewis, Naphtali. "Papyrus in Classical Antiquity: An Update." *Chronique d'Egypte* 57, no. 134 (1992): 308–318.

12: GROWING AND MANAGING PAPYRUS

Anon. 2018. Online Encyclopedia: Based on the 11th Edition of the Encyclopedia Britannica, 1922. http://encyclopedia.jrank.org.

Evans, Elaine A. "Papyrus a Blessing upon Pharaoh." Knoxville: McClung Museum, University of Tennessee, 1–12.

Gaudet, John. "Nutrient Relationships in the Detritus of a Tropical Swamp." *Archiv fur Hydrobiologie* 78 (1976), 213–239.

Lewis, Naphtali. *Papyrus in Classical Antiquity*. Oxford: Clarendon Press, 1974.

Muller, K. 2007. K.U. Leuven–Fayum Project (http://www.fayum.arts.kuleuven.ac.be).

13: THE EMPEROR AND THE LEWD PAPERMAKER

Basile, C., and A. Di Natale. "*Per la storia e le origini del papiro in Sicilia*," in *Papyri*. Siracusa: Museo del Papiro, 1991, 5–29.

Horne, C. F. *The Sacred Books and Early Literature of the East*, Volume II. New York: Parke, Austin, and Lipscomb, 1917, 62–78.

Kenyon, F. G. *The Paleography of Greek Papyri*. Oxford: Oxford University Press, 1899.

Owen, Antoinette, and Rachel Danzig. "The History and Treatment of the Papyrus Collection at the Brooklyn Museum." *The American Institute for Conservatio*n 12, 1993.

Parkinson, Richard, and Stephen Quirke. *Papyrus*. Austin: University of Texas Press, 1995.

Ragab, Hassan. 1980. "*Le Papyrus*." PhD thesis, Université de Grenoble and Papyrus Institute, 1980.

14: TAKING ON THE WORLD—AND LEAVING A LEGACY

Basbanes, N. *On Paper: The Everything of its Two-Thousand-Year History*. New York: Vintage, 2013.

Bloom, J. *Paper Before Print: The History and Impact of Paper in the Islamic World*. New Haven, CT: Yale University Press, 2001.

Harris, W. *Ancient Literacy*. Cambridge, MA: Harvard University Press, 1989.

Hazzard, S. Papryrology at Naples. Our Far-Flung Correspondents. N*ew Yorker*, August 29, 1983.

Lewis, Naphtali. *Papyrus in Classical Antiquity*. Oxford: Clarendon Press, 1974.

Roberts, C. H. "The Greek Papyri." In *The Legacy of Egypt*, edited by S. R. K. Glanville, 249–282. Oxford: Clarendon Press, 1963.

The Zenon Papyri. "Reading the Papyri." Last modified 2004. (http://www.lib.umich.edu/reading/Zenon)

15: EARLY LIBRARIES, PAPER AND THE WRITING BUSINESS

Anon, 2012. The Iron Gall Ink Website of the Cultural Heritage Agency, Netherlands (https://irongallink.org/)

Bülow-Jacobsen, Adam. "Chapter 1: Writing Materials in the Ancient World." In *The Oxford Handbook of Papyrology*. Oxford: Oxford University Press, 2009.

Carvalho, David N. *Forty Centuries of Ink, or A Chronological Narrative Concerning Ink and Its Backgrounds*. New York: Banks Law Publishing, 1904.

Elliott, R., and R. Waltz 2007.Ancient writing materials. In The Encyclopedia of New Testament Textual Criticism. (A work in progress: http://www.skypoint.com/members/waltzmn/WritingMaterials.html).

Huntington, Sharon J. "Think ink!" *Christian Science Monitor*, September 21. 2004. https://www.csmonitor.com/2004/0921/p18s02-hfks.html

Leach, B., and J. Tait. "Papyrus," in *Ancient Egyptian Materials and Technology*, edited by P. T. Nicholson and I. Shaw. Cambridge: Cambridge University Press, 2000, 227–253.

Parsons, P. *City of the Sharp-Nosed Fish: Greek lives in Roman Egypt*. London: Weidenfeld and Nicolson, 2007, 320.

Pollard, J. and H. Reid. *The Rise and Fall of Alexandria: Birthplace of the Modern Mind*. New York: Viking, 2006.

16: A LIBRARY TO END ALL LIBRARIES

Athenaeus of Naucratis. *The Deipnosophists*. Edited and translated by C. B. Gulick. Cambridge, MA: Harvard, 1961, 7 vols.

Hannam, J. "The Mysterious Fate of the Great Library of Alexandria." *Bede's Journal in Bede's Library*, 2007. www.bede.org.uk/library.htm.

Jacob, C. 2002.From Alexandria to Alexandria: Scholarly interfaces of a universal library. Arts and Social Sciences, Univ. Calif., Santa Barbara (http://dc-mrg.english.ucsb.edu/conference/2002/documents/christian_jacob.html).

Johnson, M. *The Nature and Making of Papy*rus. Barkston Ash, UK: Elmete Press, 1973, 71.

Kilgour, F. *The Evolution of Books*. Oxford: Oxford University Press, 1998.

Pollard, Justin and Howard Reid. *The Rise and Fall of Alexandria: Birthplace of the Modern Mind*. New York: Viking, 2006.

17: THE ROMANS AND THE BOOK TRADE

Alexander, L. "Ancient Book Production and the Circulation of the Gospels." In *The Gospels for All Christians: Rethinking the Gospel Audiences*, edited by R. Bauckham. Grand Rapids, MI: Eerdmans, 1997.

Anon. 2018. Online Encyclopedia: Based on the 11th Edition of the Encyclopedia Britannica, 1922. http://encyclopedia.jrank.org.

Bréhier, L. 1910. Manuscripts. (and Illustrated Manuscripts.) In *The Catholic Encyclopedia* Vol. IX. Transcribed by B. Johnson. New York: Robert Appleton 1910.

Fielden, Jerry. "Private Libraries in Ancient Rome." Last modified 2001. www.jerryfielden.com/essays.

Grenfell, B. "Oxyrhynchus and Its Papyri." *Egyptian Exploration Fund Archaeological Report (London 1896-97),* 1–12.

Lewis, Naphtali. *Papyrus in Classical Antiquity.* Oxford: Clarendon Press, 1974.

Lewis, Naphtali. *Life in Egypt Under Roman Rule.* Oxford: ClarendonPress, 1983.

Parsons, P. *City of the Sharp-Nosed Fish: Greek lives in Roman Egypt.* London: Weidenfeld and Nicolson, 2007.

Pollard, J. and H. Reid. *The Rise and Fall of Alexandria: Birthplace of the Modern Mind.* New York: Viking, 2006.

18: ROMAN LIBRARIES

Carlin, Martha. "Libraries and Archives of the Roman Empire." Prof. Martha Carlin's Home Page. Last modified 2013. http://tinyurl.com/kgu6hk7.

Casson, L. *Libraries in the Ancient World.* New Haven, CT: Yale University Press, 2001.

Clark, J. *The Care of Books.* Cambridge: Cambridge University Press, 1901.

Houston, G. *Inside Roman Libraries.* Chapel Hill, NC: University of North Carolina Press, 2014.

Kilgour, F. The Evolution of Books. Oxford: Oxford University Press, 1998.

Roberts, C., and T. Skeat. *The Birth of the Codex.* London: Oxford University Press, 1983.

Spoon, J. "Ancient Libraries of Greece and Rome, A Summary of Research Findings." Last modified 1999. www.ithaca.edu/hs/history/journal/papers/sp02ancientlibraries.html.

19: THOSE PRECIOUS, TENDER-HEARTED SCROLLS

Barker, E. *Buried Herculaneum.* London: A. and C. Black, 1908.

Economou, G. *Harmonies and Fits (Translated Poems of Philodemus).* Norman, OK: Point Riders Press, 1987.

Gabb, S. "Epicurus: Father of the Enlightenment." Lecture given to the 6/20 Club in London, 2007. www.seangabb.co.uk/pamphlet/epicurus.htm.

Porter, J. "The Herculaneum Papyri and Classical Scholarship." In *Antiquity Recovered: The Legacy of Pompeii and Herculaneum.* Edited by V. Coates and J. Seydl. Los Angeles: J. Paul Getty Museum, 2007.

Sider, D. *The Library of the Villa dei Papiri.* Los Angeles: Getty Publications, 2005.

Wordsworth, W. *The Complete Poetical Works.* London: Macmillan, 1888.

20: PAPYRUS PAPER SAVES THE DAY

Barnish, S., trans. *Cassiodorus: Variae.* Liverpool: Liverpool University Press, 1992.

De Maupassant, Guy. *Au Soleil, or African Wanderings.* New York: Review of Reviews, 1903.

Lewis, Naphtali. *Papyrus in Classical Antiquity.* Oxford: Clarendon Press, 1974.

21: MEDIA ONE MAKES ITS MARK IN THE WORLD

Bagnall, R. and R. Cribiore. *Women's Letters from Ancient Egypt, 300 B.C.–A.D. 800*. Ann Arbor, MI: University of Michigan Press, 2014.

Barnish, S., trans. *Cassiodorus: Variae*. Liverpool: Liverpool University Press, 1992.

Blechman, A. *Pigeons: The Fascinating Saga of the World's Most Revered and Reviled Bird*. New York: Grove Press, 2007.

Bloom, J. *Paper Before Print: The History and Impact of Paper in the Islamic World*. New Haven, CT: Yale University Press, 2007.

Mark Pack's blog http://thedabbler.co.uk/author/mark-pack.

Standage, Tom. *Writing on the Wall: Social Media—The First 2,000 Years*. New York: Bloomsbury, 2013.

Suetonius. *The Lives of the Twelve Caesars (Augustus 49.3)*. Cambridge. MA: Loeb Classical Library, Harvard University Press, 1913.

Thompson, M. "Holy Internet: Communication Between Churches in the First Christian Generation." In *The Gospels for All Christians: Rethinking the Gospel Audiences*. Edited by R. Bauckham. Grand Rapids, MI: Eerdmans, 1997.

Turner, E. "Greek Papyri, an Introduction." Oxford: Oxford University Press, 1968.

22: THE LAST BASTION, THE CHURCH OF ROME

Frost, G. "The American Institute for Conservation. Adoption of the Codex Book: Parable of a New Reading Mode." Discussion Group Session, AIC 26th Annual Meeting, June 1–7, 1998, Arlington, VA.

Thurston, H. *The Catholic Encyclopedia*, Volume III, transcribed by M. Donahue. New York: Robert Appleton, 1908.

Wordsworth, W. *The Complete Poetical Works*. London: Macmillan, 1888.

23: CONSTANTINOPLE AND THE LONG GOODBYE

Abbott, N. "The Kurrah Papyri from Aphrodito in the Oriental Institute." Chicago: University of Chicago Press, 1938.

Alston, George Cyprian. "Abbey of Saint-Denis." *The Catholic Encyclopedia*, Volume XIII. New York: R. Appleton Company, 1912. http://www.newadvent.org/cathen/13343b.htm.

Basbanes, Nicholas. *On Paper: The Everything of Its Two-Thousand-Year History*. New York: Vintage, 2013.

Bréhier, L. "Manuscripts. (and Illustrated Manuscripts.)" *The Catholic Encyclopedia* Vol. IX. Transcribed by B. Johnson. New York: R. Appleton Company, 1910.

Geary, P. *Phantoms of Remembrance: Memory and Oblivion at the End of the First Millennium*. Princeton, NJ: Princeton University Press, 1994.

Hutton, W. *A Short History of Constantinople*. San Diego: Didactic Press, 2013.

Jones, L. "The Influence of Cassiodorus on Medieval Culture." *Speculum*, no. 20 (1945): 433–442.

Kleve, Kurt. "In the Bellagio Report 2010." www.clir.org/pubs/reports/bellagio/bellag1.html.

Malczycki, M. "The Papyrus Industry in the Early Islamic Era." *Journal of the Economic and Social History of the Orient* 54 (2011): 185–202.

McCormick, M. *The Origins of the European Economy*. Cambridge: Cambridge University Press, 2001.

O'Donnell, James. *Cassiodorus*. Berkeley, CA: University of California Press, 1979. Postprint in 1995. www9.georgetown.edu/faculty/jod/texts/cassbook/toc.html.

Oikonomides, N. "Writing Materials, Documents, and Books." In *The Economic History of Byzantium: From the Seventh through the Fifteenth Century*. Edited by Angeliki E. Laiou. Washington, DC: Dumbarton Oaks Studies, 2002. www.doaks.org/etexts.html

Thurston, Herbert. "Bulls and Briefs." *The Catholic Encyclopedia*, Volume III. New York: R. Appleton Company, 1908. http://www.newadvent.org/cathen/03052b.htm.

Twede, D. "The origins of paper, based packaging." Conf. Historical Analysis & Research in Marketing Proceedings 12 (2005): 288–300.

24: END OF THE ROAD FOR PAPYRUS PAPER AND THE BATTLE OF THE TALAS RIVER

Basbanes, Nicholas. *On Paper: The Everything of Its Two-Thousand-Year History*. New York: Vintage, 2013.

Bloom, J. *Paper Before Print: The History and Impact of Paper in the Islamic World*. New Haven, CT: Yale University Press, 2007.

Kilgour, F. *The Evolution of Books*. Oxford: Oxford University Press, 1998.

Kurlansky, M. *Paper; Paging through History*. New York: W.W. Norton, 2016.

Pollard, Justin and Howard Reid. *The Rise and Fall of Alexandria: Birthplace of the Modern Mind*. New York: Viking, 2006.

Wiegard, W., and D. Davis. *Encyclopedia of Library History*. New York: Garland, 1994.

25: THE MYSTERY OF THE DISAPPEARING PLANT

Anon., 2000. An introduction to the history and culture of Pharonic Egypt. (http://www.reshafim.org.il/ad/egypt/).

Bagnall, Roger, and B. Frier. *The Demography of Roman Egypt*. Cambridge: Cambridge University Press, 1994.

Butzer, K. *Environment and Archaeology: An Ecological Approach to Prehistory*. Chicago: Aldine/Atherton, 1971.

Hurst, H. *The Nile, a General Account of the River and the Utilization of Its Water*. London: Constable, 1952.

Hoffman, A. *Egypt Before the Pharaohs: The Prehistoric Foundations of Egyptian Civilization*. Austin: University of Texas Press, 1991.

Kassas, M. "Impact of River Control Schemes on the Shoreline of the Nile Delta." In *The Careless Technology*. Edited by T. Farvar and J. Milton. Garden City, NY: The Natural History Press, 1972.

Lewis, N. 1989. *Papyrus in Classical Antiquity: Supplement. Papyrologica Bruxellensia*. Vol. 23. Brussels, 42.

26: THE PHARAOH'S OWN CONQUERS THE VATICAN

Avrin, Leila. *Scribes, Script and Books: The Book Arts from Antiquity to the Renaissance*. Chicago: American Library Association, 1991.

Kurlansky, M. *Paper: Paging through History*. New York: W. W. Norton, 2016.

Leach, B., and J. Tait. "Papyrus," in *Ancient Egyptian Materials and Technology*. Edited by P. T. Nicholson and I. Shaw. Cambridge: Cambridge University Press, 2000, 227–253.

Meyer, M. *The Gnostic Discoveries: The Impact of the Nag Hammadi Library*. New York: Harper One, 2006.

Robinson, J. *The Story of the Bodmer Papyri*. Eugene, OR: Cascade Books, 2011.

27: THE ROAD BACK

Colla, E. *Conflicted Antiquities: Egyptology, Egyptomania, Egyptian Modernity*. Durham: Duke University Press, 2007.

Cuno, E. *Who Owns Antiquity? Museums and the Battle over Our Ancient Heritage*. Princeton, NJ: Princeton University Press, 2008.

Gibbons, K. "The Elgin Marbles, A Summary." In *Who Owns The Past?* Edited by Kate Fitz Gibbons. New Brunswick, NJ: Rutgers University Press, 2005.

Hoffman, D. "The fictitious gospel of Judas and its sensational promotion." Christian Research Institute. 2008. http://www.equip.org/article/the-fictitious-gospel-of-judas-and-its-sensational-promotion.

Krosney, H. *The Lost Gospel, the Quest for the Gospel of Judas Iscariot*. Washington, DC: National Geographic Society, 2006.

Lau-Lamb, L. "APIS Guidelines For Conservation of Papyrus." Last modified 2008. www.lib.umich.edu/pap/conservation/guidelines.html.

Leach, B., and J. Tait. "Papyrus." In *Ancient Egyptian Materials and Technology*. Edited by P. T. Nicholson and I. Shaw. Cambridge: Cambridge University Press, 2000, 227–253.

Lewis, Naphtali. *Papyrus in Classical Antiquity*. Oxford: Clarendon Press, 1974.

Opoku, K. "Affirmations and Declarations: Review of James Cuno's *"Museums Matter"* Africavenir web site, 2014. https://tinyurl.com/y996as6f

EPILOGUE: THE ROAD AHEAD

Evans, Elaine A. "Papyrus a Blessing upon Pharaoh." Knoxville: McClung Museum, University of Tennessee, 1–12.

Heyerdahl, T. *The Ra Expeditions*. New York: Doubleday, 1971, 341.

Waxman, S. *Loot: The Battle over the Stolen Treasures of the Ancient Wor*ld. New York: Times Books, 2003.

Endnotes

AUTHOR'S NOTE

1 Sharpe S. *Egyptian Antiquities in the British Museum*. London: J. Russell Smith, 156.
2 The Dartford Town Archives. Last modified 2017. www.dartfordarchive.org.uk/technology/paper.shtml
3 Turner, E. *Greek Papyri, an Introduction*. Oxford: Clarendon Press, 1968.
4 Hunter, D. 1943. *Papermaking: The History and Technique of an Ancient Craft*. New York: A. Knopf.

PROLOGUE

1 The earliest known occurrence of the spells included in the *Book of the Dead* is from the coffin of Queen Mentuhotep, of the Thirteenth Dynasty (1700 B.C.), where the new spells were included amongst older texts known from the *Pyramid Texts* and *Coffin Texts*. By 1550 B.C. it had become a very common item among the funerary objects in tombs (Source: Taylor, 2010).
2 Gaudet, John. 2014. *Papyrus, the Plant that Changed the World*. New York: Pegasus.
3 The term media is used here as a mass noun: "The word media comes from the Latin plural of medium. The traditional view is that it should therefore be treated as a plural noun in all its senses in English and be used with a plural rather than a singular verb . . . In practice, in the sense 'television, radio, and the press collectively,' it behaves as a collective noun (like staff or clergy, for example), which means that it is now acceptable in standard English for it to take either a singular or a plural verb." (http://www.oxforddictionaries.com).

1: THE INSPECTOR PUTS PEN TO PAPER AND MAKES HISTORY

1 Jarus, Owen, 2013. “Giza Secret Revealed: How 10,000 Pyramid Builders Got Fed.” *Live Science.* www.livescience.com/28961-ancient-giza-pyramid-builders-camp-unearthed.html.

2 NOVA, PBS (http://www.pbs.org/wgbh/nova/ancient/who-built-the-pyramids.html).

3 Levy, J. 2005. *The Great Pyramid of Giza: Measuring Length, Area, Volume, and Angles.* New York: Rosen Publishing.

4 Tallet, P. “The Wadi el-Jarf site: a harbor of Khufu on the Red Sea”. *Jour. Anc. Egyptian Intercon.*5 (2013): 76–84.

5 Stille, A. 2015. “The World’s Oldest Papyrus and What It Can Tell Us About the Great Pyramids: Ancient Egyptians Leveraged a Massive Shipping, Mining and Farming Economy to Propel their Civilization Forward.” *Smithsonian Magazine,* October 2015. http://tinyurl.com/z9hu8jo.

6 Tallet, P. “*Des papyrus du temps de Chéops au ouadi el-Jarf.*” *Bulletin de la Société française d’égyptologie* 188 (2014): 25–49.

7 Lehner. M. 2015. “Feeding pyramid workers.” AERA website. www.aeraweb.org/lost-city-project/feeding-pyramid-workers.

8 Tallet, P. “Ayn Sukhna and Wadi el-Jarf: Two newly discovered pharaonic harbours on the Suez Gulf.” *British Museum Studies in Ancient Egypt and Sudan* 18 (2012): 147–68.

9 Wilkinson. T. 2001. *Early Dynastic Egypt: Strategies, Society and Security.* London: Routledge.

10 Tallet, P. 2014. “*Des papyrus du temps de Chéops au ouadi el-Jarf.*” loc. cit.

11 Grubbs, M. 2015. “Google Sheets 101: The Beginner’s Guide to Online Spreadsheets.” *Zapier,* 2015. https://zapier.com/blog/google-sheets-tutorial.

12 Lehner, M. “On the waterfront: canals and harbors in the time of Giza pyramid-building.” *AERAgram* Vol. 15 (2014). www.aeraweb.org/wp-content/uploads/2015/09/AG15_1_2.pdf.

13 The Graham Hancock Forum, 2013. A web log (http://tinyurl.com/gurxezk) that contains an extract from some notes taken from a public briefing in Paris by Pierre Tallet.

14 Stille, A. 2015. *The World’s Oldest Papyrus and What It Can Tell Us About the Great Pyramids.* loc. cit.

15 Tallet, P. 2014. “*Des papyrus du temps de Chéops au ouadi el-Jarf.*” loc. cit.

16 Parker, R., R. Braidwood, T. Jacobsen, and S. Weinberg. “Radiocarbon Dates and Their Implications in the Near and Middle Eastern Area.” *Memoirs Soc. Amer. Archaeology* 8 (1951): 52–53. and Dee, M.,et al., “An absolute chronology for early Egypt using radiocarbon dating and Bayesian statistical modelling.” *Proc. Roy. Soc. A: Mathematical, Physical and Engineering Sciences* 469 (2013).

17 Dr. Gunter Dreyer of the German Archaeological Institute, Cairo (personal communication) “. . . the earliest appearance of the sign representing a sealed papyrus scroll (Gardiner Y 2) is on a seal impression from a tomb at Saqqara (S 3504). The seal impression is well dated by the name of king Qa’, the last ruler

of Dyn. 1. It is published in: W. B. Emery, *Great Tombs of the First Dynasty II*, London 1954, p. 127 Fig. 200."

18 Wilkinson, T. 2010. *The Rise and fall of Ancient Egypt*. New York: Random House. and Dee, et al. 2013. loc. cit.

19 The Met, Heilbrunn Timeline of Art History (http://www.metmuseum.org/toah/hd/papy/hd_papy.htm) and Revolvy (http://www.revolvy.com/main/index.php?s=Papyrus%20stem%20(hieroglyph).

20 *Ancient History Encyclopedia* (http://www.ancient.eu/Egyptian_Papyrus).

21 Hodgkin, T., ed. 1886. *The Letters of Cassiodorus*. London: Henry Frowde.

22 McCrady, E. "Paper Permanence Debate Lends Drama to Paris Conference." Vol 1, no. 1 (1994). http://cool.conservation-us.org/byorg/abbey/ap/ap07/ap07-1/ap07-102.html

2: PRISSE, LIKE MOSES, CARRIES HOME STONE TABLETS AND PAPER SCROLLS

1 Norton, M. "Prisse, a Portrait." *Saudi Aramco World* 41 (1990). http://archive.aramcoworld.com/issue/199006/prisse-a.portrait.htm.

2 Norton, M. 1990. Ibid.

3 Marshall, I. 1996. *Passage East*. Charlotesville, VA: Howell Press.

4 El Shaarawi, S. 2016. "Egypt's Own: Repatriation of Antiquities Proves to be a Mammoth Task." http://newsweekme.com/egypts-repatriation-antiquities-proves-mammoth-task.

3: THE UNDERTAKER'S SPECIAL AND THE WORLD'S FIRST BESTSELLER

1 Deuel, L. 1965. *Testaments of Time: The Search for Lost Manuscripts and Records*. New York: A. Knopf.

2 Goelet, O. 1998. "A commentary on the corpus of literature and tradition which constitutes the Book of Going Forth by Day." In *The Egyptian Book of the Dead*, edited by J. Wasserman. San Francisco: Chronicle Books.

3 Deuel, L. 1965. Ibid.

4 Deuel, L. 1965. Ibid.

5 Allen, J. 2015. *The Ancient Egyptian Pyramid Texts*. Atlanta: SBL Press.

6 Spurlock Museum. "Mummification." 2016. www.spurlock.illinois.edu/exhibits/online/mummification/artifacts6.html.

7 Taylor, J. 2010. *Journey through the Afterlife: Ancient Egyptian Book of the Dead*. Cambridge, MA: Harvard University Press.

8 Taylor, J. 2010. Ibid.

9 British Museum Tumblr. https://tinyurl.com/y9u4ndd7

4: THE BOOK OF THE DEAD, GUARDIAN OF IMMORTALITY

1 Taylor, J. 2010. *Journey through the Afterlife*. loc. cit.

2 Scalf, F. 2017. "12. The Death of the Book of the Dead." In *Book of the Dead: Becoming God in Ancient Egypt* edited by F. Scalf, 139–147. Chicago: Oriental Institute University of Chicago.

3 Reeves, N. 1990. *The Complete Tutankhamun: The King, the Tomb, the Royal Treasure.* New York: Thames and Hudson.

4 Dorman, P. "2. The Origins and Early Development of the Book of the Dead," 29–40 and Kockelmann, H. "5. How a Book of the Dead Manuscript was Produced," 67–74. In *Book of the Dead: Becoming God in Ancient Egypt*, edited by F. Scalf. Chicago: Oriental Institute University of Chicago.

5 Black, J. "The Instruction of Amenemope: A Critical Edition and Commentary Prolegomenon and Prologue." PhD Thesis, University of Wisconsin–Madison, 2002.

6 Travelers in the Middle East Archive (TIMEA), http://timea.rice.edu/NileCruise.html.

7 Budge, E. A.Wallis. 1920. *By Nile and Tigris: A Narrative of Journeys in Egypt and Mesopotamia on Behalf of the British Museum between the Years 1886 and 1913.* London: John Murray.

8 Taylor, J. 2013. *Journey through the Afterlife.* loc. cit.

9 Budge, E. A. Wallis. *The Book of the Dead; The Papyrus of Ani.* London: British Museum, 1895.

5: PAPYRUS PAPER, YOUR TICKET TO PARADISE

1 Drake, N., R. Blench, S. Armitage, C. Bristow and K. White. "Ancient Watercourses and Biogeography of the Sahara Explain the Peopling of the Desert." *PNAS*, 2011. www.pnas.org/content/108/2/458.full.

2 Larrasoaña, J., A. Roberts, and E. Rohling. "Dynamics of Green Sahara Periods and Their Role in Hominin Evolution." *PLOS One*, 2013. https://doi.org/10.1371/journal.pone.0076514.

3 Van der Merwe, N., F. Masao, and M. Samford. "Isotopic evidence for contrasting diets of early hominids Homo habilis and Australopithecus boisei of Tanzania." 2008. loc. cit.

4 Förster, F., and H. Riemer, eds. 2013.*The Desert Road in Ancient Egypt and Beyond.* Cologne: H. Barth Institut.

5 Sikes, S. K. 1972. *Lake Chad.* London: Eyre Methuen.

6 Gaudet, J. 2014. *Papyrus, the Plant that Changed the World.* New York: Pegasus.

7 Bergmann, C., 2013 "Expedition of Winter 2012/13." *Advance Report*, 2013. www.carlo-bergmann.de.

8 Ward, C., and C. Zazzaro. "Evidence for Pharaonic Seagoing Ships at Wadi Gawasis, Egypt." *Internat. J. Nautical Archaeology* 39 (2009): 27–43.

9 Yeakel, J., et. al. 2014. "Collapse of an Ecological Network in Ancient Egypt." *Proc. Nat. Acad. Sci.* (Sept. 8).

10 Taylor, J. "The Amduat papyrus of Panebmontu." *British Museum Studies in Ancient Egypt and Sudan* 23 (2016): 135–151.

11 Schneider, T. "The West beyond the West: The Mysterious 'Wernes' of the Egyptian Underworld and the Chad Palaeolakes." *Journal of Ancient Egyptian Interconnections* 2 (2010): 1–14.

12 Aaru, the place where Osiris rules, Wikipedia.

13 Taylor, J. 2013. *Journey through the Afterlife.* loc. cit.

14 Immega, G. "Ancient Egypt's Lost Legacy? The Buduma Culture of Lake Chad." *Friends of Niger*, 2012. www.friendsofniger.org/pdf/Buduma_Master_V4.pdf.

15 As I discuss in my earlier book, *Papyrus, the Plant That Changed the World*. New York: Pegasus, 2014.

16 Fischer, S. 2001. *A History of Writing*. London: Reaktion Books.

17 Fischer, S. 2001. Ibid.

18 Wikipedia (https://en.wikipedia.org/wiki/History_of_the_alphabet).

19 Fischer, S. 2001. Ibid. Stephen Fischer is former Director of the Institute of Polynesian Languages and Literatures, Auckland, New Zealand, and is the first person ever to decipher two wholly different historical scripts.

20 Fischer, S. 2001. Ibid.

21 Scalf, F. 2017. Ibid.

22 Johnson, P. 1999. *The Civilization of Ancient Egypt*. New York : Harper Collins.

23 Pritchard, J. 2016. *Ancient Near Eastern Texts Relating to the Old Testament with Supplement*. Princeton: Princeton Univ. Press.

6: THE SANDS OF THE NILE GIVE UP THEIR TREASURES

1 Courcelle, P. "Nouvelles recherches sur le monastere de Cassiodore." *Actes des V Congres Internat. d'archiol. chretienne* (1954): 511–528.

2 Černý, J. 1952. "Paper and Books in Ancient Egypt." 1947. Inaugural Lecture, University College, London. Chicago: Ares Publishers. See also oldest papyrus and parchment fragments of the Koran dated to within thirty to seventy years of the Prophet's death (http://www.library.leiden.edu)

3 Deissmann, G. A. & L. Strachan, 1908. *New Light on the New Testament: From Records of the Graeco-Roman Period*. Edinburgh: T. and T. Clark, 14–15.

7: THE AFFAIR OF THE ORANGES

1 Budge, E. A. Wallis. 1920. *By Nile and Tigris: A Narrative of Journeys in Egypt and Mesopotamia on Behalf of the British Museum Between the Years 1886 and 1913*. London: John Murray.

2 Jebb, R. 1905. *Bacchylides: The Poems and Fragments by Bacchylides*. Cambridge: Cambridge University Press.

8: THE FLOODGATES OPEN

1 Cuvigny, H. 2009. "Chapter 2. The Finds of Papyri: The Archaeology of Papyrology." In *The Oxford Handbook of Papyrology*. New York: Oxford University Press.

2 Marouard, G. "Wadi al-Jarf—An early pharaonic harbour on the Red Sea coast." *Egyptian Archaeology* 40 (2012): 40–43.

3 Turner, E. *Greek Papyri, an Introduction*. Oxford: Clarendon Press, 1968.

9: THE BIRTH OF MEMPHIS AND PAPER

1 Saqquara.nl website maintained by the Friends of Saqquara Foundation (http://www.saqqara.nl/ichiga/location).

2 Rennell, J. 1830. *The Geographical System of Herodotus, Examined and Explained.* London: F. Rivington.

3 Redford, D. 2001. *The Oxford Encyclopedia of Ancient Egypt, Volume 3.* Oxford: Oxford University Press.

4 Lewis, N. 1974. *Papyrus in Classical Antiquity.* Oxford: Clarendon Press.

5 Lewis, N. 1934. *L'industrie du papyrus dans l'Egypte ichi-romaine.* Paris: Univ. of Paris, Sorbonne.

6 N. Garis Davies, 1922. *The Tomb of Puyemre at Thebes, Vol. I.* The Hall of Memories. Metropolitan Mus. Of Art, NY.

7 Dr. I. Hendriks, in a series of papers, proposed that the ancient papermakers used a peeling method by which they would rotate papyrus pulp against a razor edge or strip it with a needle to produce an endless sheet, similar to the process used to produce plywood veneers, a process that results in large thin sheets. Hendriks' method, summarized by Leach and Tait (2000), seems now to have little support, being slow, technically cumbersome and producing sheets of uneven surface.

8 Leach, Bridget. 2009. "Papyrus Manufacture." In *UCLA Encyclopedia of Egyptology*, edited by Willeke Wendrich. Los Angeles : UCLA. http://escholarship.org/uc/item/5n53q5fc.

9 Bülow-Jacobsen, A. 2009. "Chapter 1: Writing materials in the ancient world." In *The Oxford Handbook of Papyrology.* Oxford: Oxford University Press.

10 Lewis, N. 1992. *Papyrus in Classical Antiquity: An Update.* loc. cit., and Leach, B. and J. Tait. 2000. "Chapter 9 Papyrus." In *Ancient Egyptian Materials and Technology*, edited by P. T. Nicholson and I. Shaw, 227–253. Cambridge: Cambridge University Press

11 Skeat, T.C. "Was papyrus regarded as 'cheap' or 'expensive' in the ancient world?" *Aegyptus* 75 (1995): 75–93.

12 According to Smith and Gronovius the drachma was almost equal to the denarius. Even after drachmae had fallen off in weight, there was no doubt that they were at one time nearly enough equal to pass for equal. Smith, W. 1875. *A Dictionary of Greek and Roman Antiquities.* London: John Murray.

13 During the Roman Republic the sesterce was a small, silver coin issued only on rare occasions. During the Roman Empire it was a large brass coin. It would today be worth about $2.25 based on the value of wheat. (Since 6.67 kg of wheat in 79 A.D. Pompeii cost 7 sestertii according to Wikipedia.org, and the retail cost of organic hard red wheat, 25 lb. bag, would today be about $US 31.00). Olive oil (1 kg) cost 3 sestertii, vs. the modern cost of olive oil (1 kg) $5.00 (Sandra's guide to Roman money http://tinyurl.com/jz7znnr). If based on the price of silver it would be worth about $2.00 (http://tinyurl.com/z7koffo).

14 Blumell, L. "The Message and the Medium: Some Observations on Epistolary Communication in Late Antiquity." *J.Greco-Roman Christianity & Judaism* 10 (2014): 24–67.

15 Ammianus Marcellinus, History, Book XV. http://penelope.uchicago.edu/Thayer/E/Roman/Texts/Ammian/15*.html.

10: A GIFT FROM THE GODS

1 Terer, T., L. Triest, and M. Muasya. "Effects of harvesting Cyperus papyrus in undisturbed wetland, Lake Naivasha, Kenya." *Hydrobiologia* 680 (2012):135–148.

2 The same study showed that selective harvesting is best, versus clear cutting, which, if done twice a year, would diminish the whole population and results in a smaller crop each year (see also M. Jones, F. Kansiime, M. Saunders. 2016. "The potential use of papyrus [Cyperus papyrus L.] wetlands as a source of biomass energy for sub-Saharan Africa." *GCB Bioenergy*.)

3 McKenzie, J. 2007. *The Architecture of Alexandria and Egypt 300 B.C.–400 A.D.* New Haven, CN: Yale Univ. Press.

11: THE MONOPOLY

1 Lewis, N. 1974. *Papyrus in Classical Antiquity*. loc. cit.

2 Lewis, N. 1974. Ibid.

3 Strabo, 18 A.D. 1856. *The geography of Strabo*, translated by Hamilton and Falconer, 1801–1885. London: H. Bohn, London, 237.

4 Table 3.1 in Bagnall, R. 2009. *Early Christian Books in Egypt*. Princeton, NJ: Princeton University Press.

5 Sharpe S. 1862. *Egyptian Antiquities in the British Museum*. London: J. Russell Smith, 156.

6 Lewis, N. 1974. *Papyrus in Classical Antiquity*. loc. cit.

7 Bülow-Jacobsen, A. 2009. *Writing Materials in the Ancient World*. loc. cit.

12: GROWING AND MANAGING PAPYRUS FOR PAPER

1 Lewis, N. 1992. Papyrus in Classical Antiquity: An Update. loc. cit.,

2 Terer, T., L. Triest and M. Muasya, 2012. "Effects of harvesting Cyperus papyrus." Loc, cit.

3 Pollard J. & H. Reid. 2006. *The Rise and Fall of Alexandria*, 79. New York: Viking.

4 Baikie, J. 1925. *Egyptian Papyri and Papyrus-Hunting*. London: The Religious Tract Society.

5 Bernhardt, T. 2008. The Papyri Pages. (http://papyri.tripod.com/texts/cartonnage.html)

13: THE EMPEROR AND THE LEWD PAPERMAKER

1 Orias website (http://orias.berkeley.edu/spice/textobjects/imports-exports.htm).

2 Morley, N. 2005. "Feeding ancient Rome." BRLSI web site, Bath Royal Literary and Scientific Institution (https://tinyurl.com/ybahev6u).

3 An introduction to the history and culture of Pharaonic Egypt (http://www.reshafim.org.il/ad/ichi).

4 Lewis, N. 1999. "Life in Egypt under Roman Rule." Oakville, CT: *Amer. Soc. Papyrologists*. Professor Lewis (p. 139) cites the high cost of local 'chaparral' wood in Roman times, i.e., the wood of arid regions (acacia, tamarisk, and sycamore fig).

5 Lewis, N. 1974. *Papyrus in Classical Antiquity*. loc. cit. (p. 112).

6 Diringer, D. 2012. *The Book Before Printing: Ancient, Medieval and Oriental.* New York: Dover Publications.
7 Černý, J. 1952. *Paper and Books in Ancient Egypt.* loc. cit.
8 The Romans, like the Greeks, had separate words for plant and paper. The Latin word, *papyrus* means "the paper plant, or paper made from it," but also the word *charta* in Latin means "paper/papyrus (sheet)," according to the *Oxford Latin Dictionary*, 1982.
9 Libraries and Archives of the Roman Empire. Professor Martha Carlin Home Page (http://tinyurl.com/kgu6hk7)
10 Houston, G. 2014. *Inside Roman Libraries.* Chapel Hill, NC: Univ. N.C. Press.
11 In reference to standard sizes and the measurements given by Pliny, an argument has raged in the literature about whether or not Pliny meant height or width of the paper grades. William Johnson, professor of classical studies at Duke points out that Pliny never mentioned height. He defends Pliny's measurements. He feels that he was correct, the measurements he reported refer to widths. Since no one has ever found papyrus paper that matched these grades and "heights," Johnson's reading would seem to be as correct as any other. Johnson feels that width would be an indication of the writing surface available, an important quality in defining the value of different grades of paper. His argument proposes that Pliny never bothered to mention height because it was of no importance, the important measure was width and especially the space left after the sheets were joined into a roll. He backs up his argument with reference to extant rolls and sheets where height/width ratios vary in excess of what would be expected if Pliny meant height. See: Johnson, W. "Pliny the Elder and standardized roll heights in the manufacture of papyrus." *Classical Philology* 88 (1993): 46–50.
12 Diringer, D. 2012. *The Book Before Printing.* loc. cit.
13 Suetonius Tranquillus C. 1914. *The Lives of the Twelve Caesars, Volume 13: Grammarians and Rhetoricians.* Loeb Classical Library. https://tinyurl.com/y9zzzm2s".
14 Suetonius Tranquillus C. 1914. Ibid.
15 Sheppard, J. "Self-education and late-learners in The Attic Nights of Aulus Gellius." MA Thesis, Victoria University, Wellington, NZ, 2008.
16 Lewis, N. "Papyrus in Classical Antiquity: A Supplement." *Papyrologica Bruxellensia* 23 (1989), 42.
17 Budge, W. 1895. *The Book of the Dead, An English Translation of The Chapters, Hymns, Etc., Of The Theban Recension, With Introduction, Notes.* 3 Vols. Kegan Paul, Trench, Trübner & Co., London, and Budge, W., 1912. *The Greenfield Papyrus in the British Museum.* Harrison & Sons, London.

14: TAKING ON THE WORLD—AND LEAVING A LEGACY

1 The Zenon Papyri. Reading the Papyri. 2004. www.lib.umich.edu/reading/Zenon.
2 Harris, W. 1989. *Ancient Literacy.* Cambridge, MA: Harvard University Press.
3 2015. Select Papyri. Orig. Text PSI 333. Attalus (https://tinyurl.com/y8cxhsxz)
4 2015.Catalog Recordichigan.apis.1808-Bus.Letter (http://www.papyri.info/hgv/1924)

5 According to Shepherd 2008 this is: rel. hum. 45–55 percent, 18-22 degrees Celsius and light levels at less than 50 lux, with ultraviolet less than 75 microwatts per lume. See also an extensive discussion of deterioration, preservation and restoration in Leach, B. and J. Tait. 2000. "Chapter 9 Papyrus." In *Ancient Egyptian Materials and Technology*, edited by P. T. Nicholson and I. Shaw, 227–253. Cambrdige: Cambridge University Press.
6 Parkinson, R. and S. Quirke. 1995. *Papyrus*. Austin: Univ. Texas Press.
7 For a detailed account of the manufacture, history and preservation of papyrus paper see the comprehensive review by Bridget Leach, Conservator of Papyrus, British Museum and J. Tait, Univ. Coll., London ("Chapter 9 Papyrus" in *Ancient Egyptian Materials and Technology*. 2000. Camb. Univ. Press).
8 See my earlier book, Gaudet, J. 2014. *Papyrus, the Plant That Changed the World*. New York: Pegasus.
9 Terer, T., L. Triest and M. Muasya, 2012. Effects of harvesting Cyperus papyrus. Loc, cit.
10 British Association of Paper Historians—BAPH (http://baph.org.uk/ukpaperhistory.html)
11 British Association of Paper Historians. Ibid.
12 "Papyrus paper: a craft on the verge of collapse." *Egypt Independent*, November 23, 2014.
13 Statista. Production volume of paper and cardboard in major countries from 2009 to 2016. (https://tinyurl.com/yd8hvksu.
14 The story of paper from ancient times to present is retold in *On Paper* by Nicholas Basbanes (2013) and in *Paper Before Print: The History and Impact of Paper in the Islamic World* by Jonathan Bloom (2001).

15: EARLY LIBRARIES, PAPER, AND THE WRITING BUSINESS

1 Black, J. R. "The Instruction of Amenemope: A Critical Edition and Commentary Prolegomenon and Prologue." PhD Thesis, University Of Wisconsin–Madison, 2002.
2 Ryholt, K. 2013. "Libraries in ancient Egypt." In *Ancient Libraries*, edited by König, J., et al. Cambridge: Cambridge University Press.
3 Dollinger, A. 2016. An introduction to the history and culture of Pharaonic Egypt, website. Libraries (http://www.reshafim.org.il/ad/egypt/institutions/house_of_books.htm)
4 Reclus, E. 1886. *The Earth and its Inhabitants*, Vol. 1. New York: D. Appleton.
5 Casson, L. 2001. *Libraries in the Ancient World*. loc. cit.
6 Black, J. R. 2002. *The Instruction of Amenemope*. Ibid.
7 Parkinson, R. and S. Quirke, 1995. *Papyrus*. loc. cit. (esp. see page 38.)
8 Parkinson, R. and S. Quirke, 1995. *Papyrus*. loc. cit.
9 Wikipedia, https://en.wikipedia.org/wiki/Lawrence_Alma-Tadema
10 Danzing, R. 2010. "Pigments and Inks Typically Used on Papyrus." (http://www.brooklynmuseum.org)

11 Rasmussen, K. et al. 2011. "The constituents of the ink from a Qumran inkwell: new prospects for provenancing the ink on the Dead Sea Scrolls." *Jour. Archaeological Science* 39: 2956–2968

12 Carvalho, D. 1904. *Forty Centuries of Ink; A Chronological Narrative Concerning Ink and Its Backgrounds.* Huntington, S. "Think ink!" *Christian Science Monitor,* September. 21, 2014.

13 Avrin, L. 1991. *Scribes, Script, and Books.* loc. cit.

14 Krutzsch, pers. comm. and also see: Krutzsch, M. 2016. "Reading papyrus as writing material." *British Museum Studies in Ancient Egypt and Sudan* 23: 57–69.

15 Leach, B. and J. Tait. 2000. "Chapter 9 Papyrus." loc. cit.

16 A good comparison of all inks used in ancient times is given in Thomas Christiansen's recent paper, "Manufacture of black ink in the ancient Mederterranean," Bull. Amer. Soc. *Papyrologists* 54 (2017):167–195.

17 Gunther, M. 2016. "Ancient scrolls roll back first use of metallic inks by centuries. Chemistry World." (http://www.rsc.org/chemistryworld/2016/03/ancient-scrolls-herculaneum-papyrus-x-ray-fluorescence-ink) and Tack, P. 2016. "Tracking ink composition on Herculaneum papyrus scrolls." Scientific Reports 6 (http://www.nature.com/articles/srep20763).

18 Houston, G. 2014. *Inside Roman Libraries.* loc. cit.

19 An early recipe for iron gall ink can be found in the Encyclopedia of Seven Free Arts by Martianus Capella, who lived in Carthage in the 5th century A.D. In it, Capella describes "Gallarum gummeosque commixtio" as a writing ink.

20 Milbank, D. 2007. "Denying Genocide in Darfur—and Americans Their Coca-Cola." *Washington Post*, June 2007.

16: A LIBRARY TO END ALL LIBRARIES AND THE SWEET SMELL OF HISTORY

1 Cherf, W. 2008. "Earth Wind and Fire: The Alexandrian Firestorm of 48 B.C." In (ed. M. el-Abbadi & O.M. Fathallah) *What happened to the great library of Alexandria?* BRILL, Leiden, Netherlands.

2 Hannam, J, 2003. *The Mysterious Fate of the Great Library of Alexandria.* Bede's Library, Website (http://www.bede.org.uk/library.htm).

3 Bowie, E. 2013. *Libraries for the Caesars.* In König, J, et al. (Eds.) Cambridge: Cambridge University Press.

4 Pollard, J .& H. Reid. 2006. *The Rise and Fall of Alexandria.* loc. cit.

5 Casson, L. 2001. *Libraries in the Ancient World.* New Haven, CT: Yale University Press.

6 Blakey, H. 2014. Mouseion. House of the Muse Website. (http://www.dailywriting.net/Mouseion.htm)

7 Cherf, W. 2008. *Earth Wind and Fire.* loc. cit.

8 Pollard, J.&H. Reid. 2006. *The Rise and Fall of Alexandria.* loc. cit. (Page 79).

9 Casson, L. 2001. Libraries in the Ancient World. loc. cit.

10 Casson, L. 2001. Ibid.

11 McKenzie, J. 2007. *The Architecture of Alexandria and Egypt 300 B.C.–400 A.D.* loc. cit.

17: THE ROMANS AND THE BOOK TRADE

1 Affleck, M. 2013. *Libraries in Rome before 168 B.C.*. König et al. (Eds.) Ancient Libraries. loc. cit.

2 Winsbury, R. 2009. *The Roman Book: Books, Publishing and Performance in Classical Rome.* London: Duckworth Press.

3 Flood, A. 2014. Authors' incomes collapse to "abject" levels. *The Guardian* July 8, 2014.

4 Grafton, A., and M. Williams. 2008. *Christianity and the Transformation of the Book: Origen, Eusebius, and the Library of Caesarea.* Cambridge, MA: Harvard University Press.

5 Houston, G. 2014. *Inside Roman Libraries.* loc. cit.

6 Grafton, A., and M. Williams. 2008. *Christianity and the Transformation of the Book.* loc. cit.

7 *The Catholic Encyclopedia* Vol. IX (Transcribed by B. Johnson.) New York: Robert Appleton Company.

8 Casson, L. 2001. *Libraries in the Ancient World.* and Winsbury, R. 2009. *The Roman Book.* Locs. cit.

9 Winsbury, R. 2009. *The Roman Book.* loc. cit.

10 Anon, 1911, *Encyclopedia Britannica (*https://archive.org/details/EncyclopaediaBritannica1911HQDJVU)

11 Norman, J. 2014. *From Cave Paintings to the Internet* (http://tinyurl.com/m29xkov).

12 Houston, G. 2014. *Inside Roman Libraries.* loc. cit.

13 Parsons, P. 2007. *City of the Sharp-Nosed Fish: Greek lives in Roman Egypt.* Weidenfeld & Nicolson, London.

14 Dando-Collins, S. 2010. *The great Fire of Rome.* Cambridge, MA: Da Capo Press.

18: ROMAN LIBRARIES

1 Spoon, J. 1999. *Ancient Libraries of Greece and Rome* (http://www.ithaca.edu/history/journal/papers/sp02ancientlibraries.html)

2 Houston, G. 2014. *Inside Roman Libraries.* loc. cit.

3 Casson, L. 2001. *Libraries in the Ancient World.* loc. cit.

4 Houston, G. 2014. *Inside Roman Libraries.* loc. cit.

5 Schodde, C. 2013. Ancient scrolls: where are the wooden handles? Found in antiquity web page. July 17. (https://tinyurl.com/y93f2hav).

6 Anon, 1911, *Encyclopedia Britannica.* loc. cit.

7 Bowie, E. 2013. Libraries for the Caesars. In König, J, et al. (Eds.) *Ancient Libraries.* Cambridge: Cambridge University Press.

8 Nicholls, M. 2013. Roman libraries as public buildings in the cities of the Empire. In König, J., et al. (Eds.) *Ancient Libraries.* loc. cit.

9 Nicholls, M. 2013. Roman libraries as public buildings in the cities of the Empire. In König, J., et al. (Eds.) *Ancient Libraries.* loc. cit.

10 Rodriguez, J. 2015. *A Brief History of Roman Libraries.* Roman Empire Net (http://www.roman-empire.net/articles/article-005.html).

11 Boyd, C. 1915. *Public Libraries and Literary Culture in Ancient Rome.* Chicago: University of Chicago Press.

12 If one sesterce is valued in comparison to the current value of wheat and olive oil, as previously suggested, it would have been worth about $2.25. Thus he received the equivalent of $22,500.

13 Boyd, C. 1915. Ibid.

14 Casson, L. 2001. *Libraries in the Ancient World.* loc. cit.

15 Tucci, P. 2013. "Flavian libraries in the city of Rome." In *Ancient Libraries*, edited by J. König, et al. Cambridge University Press. loc. cit.

16 Grout, J. 2016. *Encyclopaedia Romana* (http://tinyurl.com/psxcmyd).

17 Affleck, M. "Roman Libraries during the Late Republic and Early Empire: With Special Reference to the Library of Pliny the Elder." PhD Thesis, Univ. Queensland, Australia, 2012.

18 Tutrone, F. 2013. "The case of the Aristotelian corpus." In *Ancient Libraries*, edited by J. König, et al. Cambridge University Press loc. cit.

19 Anon, 1911, *Encyclopedia Britannica*, and Casson, L. 2001. *Libraries in the Ancient World.* Locs. cit loc. cit.

20 Spoon, J. 1999. *Ancient Libraries of Greece and Rome.* loc. cit.

19: THOSE PRECIOUS, TENDER-HEARTED SCROLLS

1 Arensberg, S., and R. Molholt, 2008. *Pompeii and the Roman Villa.* Catalog, National Gallery of Art, Washington, DC.

2 Sider, D. 2005. *The Library of the Villa dei Papiri.* Los Angeles: Getty Publications.

3 Sider, D. 2005. Ibid.

4 Harris, J. 2007. *Pompeii Awakened, A Story of Rediscovery.* London: I. B.Tauris.

5 Sider, D. 2005. *The Library of the Villa dei Papiri.* loc. cit.

6 Banerji, R. 2016. "Unlocking the scrolls of Herculaneum." *BBC News Magazine.* (http://www.bbc.com/news/magazine-25106956).

7 *History of the Getty Villa.* 2013. Video www.getty.edu.

8 Porter, J. 2007. "The Herculaneum papyri and classical scholarship." In *Antiquity Recovered: The Legacy of Pompeii and Herculaneum*, edited by V. Coates and J. Seydl. Los Angeles: J. Paul Getty Museum.

20: SAVING THE DAY

1 O'Donnell, J. 1979. *Cassiodorus.* (www9.georgetown.edu/faculty/jod/texts/cassbook/toc.html).

2 Arvine, K. 1853. *Cyclopaedia of Anecdotes of Literature and the Fine Arts.* Boston: Gould and Lincoln, Boston. Google Books: http://tinyurl.com/ljjawwf.

3 Standage, T. 2013. *Writing on the Wall: Social Media, The First 2,000 Years.* New York: Bloomsbury.

4 König, J., K. Oikonomopoulou, and G. Woolf (Eds.). 2013. *Ancient Libraries.* loc. cit.

5 Lewis, N. 1974. *Papyrus in Classical Antiquity.* loc. cit.

21: **MEDIA ONE MAKES ITS MARK IN THE WORLD**

1 Bagnall, R., and R. Cribiore, 2014. *Women's Letters from Ancient Egypt, 300 B.C.–A.D. 800.* Ann Arbor, MI: University of Michigan Press.

2 Standage, T. 2013. *Writing on the Wall.* loc. cit.

3 Suetonius, 1913. *The Lives of the Twelve Caesars* (Augustus 49.3). Loeb Classical Library, Cambridge, MA: Harvard University Press.

4 Turner, E. 1968. Greek papyri, an Introduction. Oxford: Oxford University Press.

5 Head, P. 2009. Named Letter-Carriers among the Oxyrhynchus Papyri. *JSNT* 31: 279-300

6 Blumell, L. 2014. *The Message and the Medium: Some Observations on Epistolary Communication in Late Antiquity.* Jour. of Greco-Roman Christianity and Judaism Vol. 10.

7 Deuel, L. 1965. *Testaments of Time.* loc. cit.

8 Anon., 2015. *Greek and Roman History—Attalus. Cicero: Letters to and from Cassius.* (http://www.attalus.org/translate/cassius.html).

9 Barnish, S. 1992 (Transl.) *Cassiodorus: Variae.* Liverpool: Liverpool University Press.

10 Blechman, A. 2007 *Pigeons: The Fascinating Saga of the World's Most Revered and Reviled Bird.* New York: Grove Press.

11 Pliny. Nat. Hist. X.37 and Frontinus, Sextus Julius, Stratagems Book III 90 A.D. Loeb edition, (trans. 1925. C. Bennett. http://penelope.uchicago.edu).

12 Bloom, J. 2001. *Paper Before Print: The History and Impact of Paper in the Islamic World.* New Haven, CT: Yale University Press.

13 Especially see Simblet, S. 2010. *Botany for the Artist.* New York: DK. and Marganne, M-H. 1981. *"Inventaire analytique des papyrus grecs de medecine."* Geneva: Droz.

14 Anon. 2004. *Encarta Encyclopedia Standard; Illustrated Manuscripts* (section III).

22: **THE LAST BASTION, THE CHURCH OF ROME**

1 Lewis, N. 1974. *Papyrus in Classical Antiquity.* loc. cit.

2 Lewis, N. 1974. *Papyrus in Classical Antiquity.* loc. cit.

3 Lewis, N. 1999. *Life in Egypt under Roman Rule.* Oakville, CT: Amer. Soc. Papyrologists.

4 Morgan, R. 2016. *History of the Coptic Orthodox People and the Church of Egypt.* Victoria BC, Canada: Fiesen Press.

5 Kilgour, F. 1998. *The Evolution of Books.* loc. cit.

6 Clement, R 2014. Europe and the Invention of Modern Bookmaking, Manuscript Books. New Age World webpage (http://www.nawpublishing.com/expansionpages /ephemera/european_publishing.htm).

7 Skeat, T. C. "Was papyrus regarded as 'cheap' or 'expensive' in the ancient world?" *Aegyptus* 75 (1995): 75–93.

8 Johnson, W. 2013. "Bookrolls and scribes in Oxyrhynchus." In *Studies in Book and Print Culture.* Toronto: Univ. of Toronto Press.

9 Oikonomides, N. 2002. "Writing Materials, Documents, and Books." In (Angeliki E. Laiou, Ed.) *The Economic History of Byzantium: From the Seventh through the Fifteenth Century.* Washington, DC: Dumbarton Oaks Studies. www.doaks.org/etexts.html.

23: **CONSTANTINOPLE AND THE LONG GOODBYE**

1 O'Donnell, James. 1979. *Cassiodorus*. Berkeley, CA: University of California Press. Postprint in 1995 (www9.georgetown.edu/faculty/jod/texts/cassbook/toc.html).

2 Cassiodorus—see Barnish, S., trans. 1992. *Cassiodorus: Variae*. Liverpool: Liverpool University Press.

3 Hutton, W. 2013. *A Short History of Constantinople*. San Diego: Didactic Press.

4 Oikonomides, N. 2002. *Writing Materials, Documents, and Books*. loc. cit.

5 McCormick, M. 2001. *The Origins of the European Economy*. Cambridge: Cambridge University Press.

6 Malczycki, M. "The Papyrus Industry in the Early Islamic Era." *Jour. Economic and Social History of the Orient* 54 (2011): 185–202.

7 Abbott, N. 1938. *The Kurrah Papyri from Aphrodito in the Oriental Institute*. Chicago: University of Chicago Press.

8 Oikonomides, N. 2002. *Writing Materials, Documents, and Books*. loc. cit.

9 Bowman, A. and D. Thomas. 1994. *The Vindolanda Writing Tablets (Tabulae Vindolandenses II)*. London: British Museum Press.

10 Bowman, A. and D. Thomas. 1994. Ibid.

11 Wikipedia and Lowe. E., 1972. *A Key to Bede's Scriptorium, from: Palaeographical Papers 1907–1965*. edited by L. Bieler. Oxford: Clarendon. https://tinyurl.com/ychuzdwt.

12 Bréhier, L. "Manuscripts. (and Illustrated Manuscripts.)" *The Catholic Encyclopedia* Vol. IX, transcribed by B. Johnson. New York: R. Appleton Company, 1910.

13 Oikonomides, N. 2002. *Writing Materials, Documents, and Books*. loc. cit.

14 Abbott, N. 1938. *The Kurrah Papyri*. loc. cit.

15 Kleve, Kurt. In the Bellagio Report 2010, (http://www.clir.org/pubs/reports/bellagio/bellag1.html).

16 From an extensive list in Wikipedia based on 72 references.

17 Thurston, H. 1908. "Bulls and Briefs." In *The Catholic Encyclopedia*. New Advent website. www.newadvent.org/cathen/03052b.htm. and Jones, L. 1945. "The Influence of Cassiodorus on Medieval Culture." *Speculum*, 20 (1945): 433–442.

18 Avrin, L. 1991. *Scribes, Script, and Books*. loc. cit.

19 Thurston, H. 1908. "Bulls and Briefs." In *The Catholic Encyclopedia*. New Advent website. www.newadvent.org/cathen/03052b.htm.

20 1911. "Abbey of Saint-Denis." In *The Catholic Encyclopedia*. New Advent website. www.newadvent.org/cathen/13343b.htm.

21 Geary, P. 1994. *Phantoms of Remembrance: Memory and Oblivion at the End of the First Millennium*. Princeton, NJ: Princeton Univ. Press.

22 Kaleem, J. 2014. "'Gospel of Jesus' Wife' Papyrus Is Ancient, Not Fake, Scientists And Scholars Say." *Huffington Post*, April 10, 2014. www.huffingtonpost.com/2014/04/10/jesus-wife_n_5124712.html.

23 "The 'Jesus's wife' papyrus reveals another version of the Christian story." *The Guardian* (http://tinyurl.com/ltlkbca).

24: END OF THE ROAD AND THE BATTLE OF THE TALAS RIVER

1 Bloom, J. 2001. *Paper Before Print: The History and Impact of Paper in the Islamic World.* New Haven, CT: Yale University Press, 2001.

2 Pollard, J., and H. Reid, 2006. *The Rise and Fall of Alexandria: Birthplace of the Modern Mind.* New York: Viking.

3 Malczycki, M. "The Papyrus Industry in the Early Islamic Era." *Jour. Economic and Social History of the Orient* 54 (2011): 185–202.

4 Ghazanfar, S, 2004. *The Dialogue of Civilizations.* Found. Sci. Technol. and Civilization (http://www.bbi.catholic.edu.au)

5 Johannes Pedersen, 1984. *The Arabic Book.* transl. G. French, Princeton: Princeton University Press, 2007 (http://www.islamicmanuscripts.info/reference/books/Pedersen-1984-Arabic-Book.pdf).

6 Lewis 1974 (p. 11) and Pedersen, 1984 loc. cit.

7 Bloom, J. 2001. *Paper Before Print: The History and Impact of Paper in the Islamic World.* loc. cit.

8 Although throughout early history silk was expensive, Kurlansky in a recent book (Kurlansky, M. 2016. *Paper: Paging through History.* New York: W. W. Norton.) offers proof that by the 14th century in China some considered silk cheap.

9 "Paper wasp." Wikipedia, 2016. https://en.wikipedia.org/wiki/Paper_wasp.

10 Yangtze Yan, 2006. *Guangming Daily* (http://www.chinaview.cn)

11 Tsien, Tsuen-Hsuin. 1985. "Paper and Printing," *Joseph Needham, Science and Civ. in China, Chem. and Chemical Technology.* Vol. 5, part 1, Cambridge: Cambridge University Press.

12 The horizontal-axle watermill is said to have appeared around 240 B.C., with Byzantium and Alexandria as the assigned places of invention (Wikipedia).

13 Basbanes, N. (2013) *On Paper: The Everything of Its Two-Thousand-Year History.* New York: Vintage.

14 International Starch Institute, Aarhus, Denmark (www.starch.dk/isi/applic/paper.htm).

15 Basbanes, N. 2013. *On Paper.* loc. cit.

16 Carter, T. 1925. *The Invention of Printing in China and Its Spread Westward.* New York: Columbia University Press.

17 Kilgour, F. 1998. *The Evolution of Books.* loc. cit.

18 An early specific allusion to the quill pen occurs in the writings of Saint Isidore of Seville in the early part of the seventh century, but there is no reason to assume that it was not in use at a still more remote date (according to Anon., 1911. *Encyclopedia Britannica* (under the heading "Pen", www.studylight.org).

19 See page 116, Bloom, J. 2001. *Paper Before Print: The History and Impact of Paper in the Islamic World.* loc. cit.

20 Wiegard, W. and D. Davis. 1994. *Encyclopedia of Library History.* Garland, NY.

21 Wani, Z. and Maqbol, T. 2012. The Islamic Era and Its Importance to Knowledge and the Development of Libraries. Libr. Philos. and Practice. (http://digitalcommons.unl.edu).

25: THE MYSTERY OF THE DISAPPEARING PLANT

1 Lewis, N. 1989. *Papyrus in Classical Antiquity: A Supplement.* loc. cit. (p. 18).

2 Budge, W., 1895. *The Book of the Dead, An English Translation.* loc. cit.

3 Leach, B. and J. Tait. 2000. "Chapter 9 Papyrus." loc. cit. and Budge, E. A. Wallis. 1912. *The Greenfield Papyrus in the British Museum.* London: Harrison and Sons.

4 Lewis, N. 1974. *Papyrus in Classical Antiquity.* loc. cit.

5 Evans, E.A. 2002. "Papyrus a blessing upon Pharaoh." pp. 1-12. Occasional Paper, 2002. McClung Museum, Univ. of Tenn., Knoxville.

6 Kantor, H. "Plant Ornament: Its Origin and Development in the Ancient Near East." PhD Thesis, University of Chicago, 1945.

7 Gaudet, J. 2014. *Papyrus, the Plant that Changed the World.* loc. cit.

8 Strabo, 7–18 A.D. Geography. Vol. VIII. Loeb Classical Library edition. Cambridge, MA: Harvard University Press.

9 Gaudet, J. 2014. *Papyrus, the Plant that Changed the World.* loc. cit.

10 Butzer, K. 1971. *Environment and Archaeology: An ecological approach to prehistory.* Chicago: Aldine/Atherton.

11 Sloan, J. 2000. "The Crusades in the Levant (1097–1291)." Xenophon Group Military History Database. (http://www.xenophongroup.com/montjoie/crusade2.htm)

12 Serag, M. "Ecology and biomass production of Cyperus papyrus L. on the Nile bank at Damietta, Egypt." J. Medit. *Ecology* 4 (2003):15–24.

26: THE PHARAOH'S OWN CONQUERS THE VATICAN

1 Hanna, F. 2010. "Defending the faith with physical evidence." Chistendom College. (http://tinyurl.com/h6wxlw7).

2 Viegas, J. 2007. "Earliest Gospels Acquired by Vatican," *Discovery News.* (http://www.freerepublic.com/focus/f-religion/1823123/posts)

3 See the summary in Wikipedia (https://en.wikipedia.org/wiki/Bodmer_Papyri)

4 Voicu, S. 2007. *Bodmer Papyrus: History Becomes Reality. L'Osservatore Romano,* Weekly Edition in English page 8.

5 Tov, E. 2003. *The Corpus of the Qumran Papyri.* In (ed.L. Schiffman) *Semitic Papyrology in Context.* Boston: Brill.

6 Tov, E. 2003. *The Corpus of the Qumran Papyri.* loc. cit.

7 Crawford, S. 2016. "The Qumran Collection as a Scribal Library." *In The Dead Sea Scrolls at Qumran and the Concept of a Library*, edited by Crawford, S., and C. Wassen, 109–131. (Brill, Leiden and Boston; and Werrett, I. 2016. "Is Qumran a Library?" In Crawford, S. and C. Wassen, eds, 78–108. Ibid.

8 Somers, B. 2006. "Scientists Decode Dead Sea Scrolls with DNA and Infrared Digital Photography." *AAAS News Archives* (http://tinyurl.com/ht9k79o).

9 Gaudet, J. 2014. *Papyrus, the Plant that Changed the World.* loc. cit.

10 Avrin, L. 1991. *Scribes, Script and Books: The Book Arts from Antiquity to the Renaissance.* loc. cit.

11 Kurlansky, M. 2016. *Paper, Paging through History.* New York: W. W. Norton.

12 Robinson, J. 2011. *The Story of the Bodmer Papyri.* Eugene, Oregon: Cascade Books.

27: THE ROAD BACK

1 Krosney, H. 2006. *The Lost Gospel, the Quest for the Gospel of Judas Iscariot.* Washington, DC: National Geographic Society.
2 Krosney, H. 2006. Ibid.
3 Lewis, N. 1974. *Papyrus in Classical Antiquity.* loc. cit.

EPILOGUE: THE ROAD AHEAD

1 Heyerdahl, T. 1971. *The Ra Expeditions.* loc. cit.
2 Hawass, Z. 2000. *Valley of the Golden Mummies.* Cairo: American Univ. in Cairo Press.
3 Waxman, S. 2003. *Loot: The Battle over the Stolen Treasures of the Ancient World.* New York: Times Books, NY.
4 Zalewski, D. 2016. The Factory of Fakes, How a workshop uses digital technology to craft perfect copies of imperilled art. *New Yorker,* A Reporter at Large, November 28.
5 Sherief, A. 2012. The Papyrus village. *Daily News,* Egypt (http://www.dailynewsegypt.com/2012/11/15/the-papyrus-village/).
6 Summers, C. 2017. *The Bible: the Story behind the Museum of the Bible.* Franklin, TN: Worthy Books.
7 Kennicott, P. 2017. "The new Bible museum tells a clear, powerful story. And it could change the museum business." *Washington Post* (https://tinyurl.com/y8vah858)
8 Pietersma, A. 1980. *The Edited Text of P. Bodmer XXIV. Bull. Amer. Soc. Papyrologists* 17.1–2 (1980) 67–79.

ACKNOWLEDGMENTS

1 Prof. Lewis's original text appeared in 1974 and was further amended in 1989 in a "Supplement" and again in 1992 in an "Update."
2 In Nicholson, P., and I. Shaw. 2000. *Ancient Egyptian Materials and Technology.* Cambridge: Cambridge University Press.

APPENDIX

1 Lewis, N. 1989. *Papyrus in Classical Antiquity.* loc. cit.
2 Rowlandson, J. 2005. "The organization of public land in Roman Egypt." *CRIPEL* 25:173–196.

Index

A

Abusir Papyri, 30
Abydos King List, 29
Accounts/records, xviii, 7–11, 15, 19–22, 30
Acta Diurna, 19, 184, 185, 219–220, 243
Acta Senatus, 185
Aeneid, 193
Aeschylus, 174, 215
Aesop, 178
Affleck, Michael, 105, 195
Agrippina the Younger, 122, 185
Ahmes, 89
Aida, 186
Akhenaten, 139
Alcubierre, Roque de, 201–202
Alexander, Loveday, 178, 180
Alexander the Great, 84, 104, 112, 140, 155, 163, 169, 170, 173, 180–181, 196, 272
Alfred the Great, 212
Alma-Tadema, Lawrence, *157*, 160–161, 179
Alphabet, 13–14, 18, 61–65, *62*, 131, 142, 144
Alpinus, Prosper, 266
Al-Samman, Muhammed Ali, 276
Amalia, Maria, 202
Amduat, 58–60
Amenhotep III, 139
Amenhotep IV, 139
Amr Ibn al-Asi, 175, 255–256
Anabasis, 178
Ancient Shore, The, 207
Andrews, Carol, 79–80
Andronicus, Livius, 178
Ani Papyrus, 49–52, 73–78, 80–82, 134–135, 266, 300–303
Ankar, Peter, 293–294
Antiope, 125
Antony, Mark, 191–192, 221, 227
Apollonides, 180
Apollonius, 171
Appianus, Aurelius, 104
Archimedes, 117–118, 171
Aristarchus, 158–159, 171

Aristotle, 71, 73, 75, 80, 82, 155, 169, 196
Arius, 171
Asabil, Hanna, 284–288
Athalaric, 240
Athenaeus, 174
Athenian Constitution, 73, 80
Atrectus, 182–183
Atticus, Pomponius, 183, 196, 198
Augusta, Julia, 121, 122
Augustine of Hippo, 222, 237, 239, 244
Augustus, Emperor, 121–122, 128–135, 185, 190–193, 201, 218
Auletus, 155
Avrin, Leila, 31, 45, 144–145, 249, 283

B

Bacchylides, 73–75, 80–82
Bacon, Francis, 229
Bagnall, Roger, 217, 219
Baikie, James, 125
Baker, Florence, 108
Baker, Samuel, 108
Banerji, Robin, 208
Bankes, William, 29
Basile, Antonio, 300
Basile, Corrado, 119, 290, 300
Basiliscus, Emperor, 246
Battle of the Talas River, 254–256
Bawd, The, 73
Belon, Pierre, 266
Belzoni, Giovanni, 299
Ben Hur, 160
Benedict VII, Pope, 245, 276
Bergmann, Carlo, 57
Bible, 21, 35–36, 40, 45–46, 71, 77, 144, 176, 212, 229, 232–235, 264–265, 280, 283, 291, 305–306
Birmingham Library, 247
Black, James, 153
Bloom, Jonathan, 254–255, 262
Blumell, Lincoln, 105
Bodmer, Martin, 278–279
Bodmer Library, 274, 306
Bodmer Psalter, 306
Boethius, 222
Bonaparte, Napoleon, 41, 46–48, 77, 247, 265, 270
Book of Abraham, 40
Book of Breathing, 39–40, 64
Book of Caverns, 58
Book of Coming Forth by Day, 31
Book of Gates, 58
Book of Magic, 125
Book of the Dead, 15, 31–39, *33*, *34*, *36*, 41–54, 58–61, 64, 66–67, 72–73, 77–81, 89, 139, 162, 228–229, 266, 300
Book of the Dead Man, 49
Book of the Earth, 58
Book of the Heavenly Cow, 58
Book of the Netherworld, 58
Book of Traversing Eternity, 58
Books. *See also* Libraries
  book scrolls, xix, 14–15, 105, 110, 174, 180–183, *188*, 188–198
  book trade, 177–185, *182*, 236–237, 246–248
  illustrated books, 227–229
  paper and, xi, xix, 12, 124–125
  schoolbooks, 248–249
  textbooks, 89
Books of the Sky, 58
Borgia, Stefano, 72
Bowie, Ewen, 170
British Library, 104, 156, 195
Brown, Dan, 251
Bruce, James, 266
Brutus, Decimus, 227
Brutus, Marcus, 191, 221
Budge, E. A. Wallis, 35, 48–52, 70, 73–82, 111, 135, 266, 289, 303
Bülow-Jacobsen, Adam, 103
Byzantine Empire, 140, 256

C

Caepio, Fannius, 189–190
Caesar, Claudius, 135
Caesar, Germanicus, 121–122

Caesar, Julius, 155, 159, 167–175, 188, 191, 193, 201–202, 215, 219–221, 226–227, 246, 299
Cai Lun, 258
Caligula, 122, 133, 201
Cambyses, King, 140, 272
Camplani, Alberto, 252
Caracalla, 193, 196
Care of Books, The, 198
Cartel, 114–116, 129, 145, 175, 181, 271–272
Carter, Howard, 12, 15, 261
Carvalho, David, 162
Caskets, 38. *See also* Coffins
Cassiodorus, xi, 19, 69–71, 82, 107, 136–137, 143, 167, 198, 210–215, *211*, 222–223, 238–240, *239*, 244–248, 279
Cassius, Dio, 172, 221–222
Casson, Lionel, 170, 174, 189
Catholic Encyclopedia, 250
Celsus, 189
Census rolls, 88, 126, 184–185, 215, 227
Černý, Jaroslav, 129
Champollion, Jean-François, 41, 48
Charlemagne, 212, 250
Charles III, King, 201–202
Charta Borgiana, 72
Chester Beatty Library, 278
Chronicles of Narnia, The, 160
Church of Rome, 230–237
Cicero, 73, 178, 183–185, 196–198, 201–202, 221–223, 227
City of the Sharp-Nosed Fish, 85
Clark, John Willis, 198
Claudius, Emperor, 122, 131–135, 201
Clement, Richard, 234
Clement of Alexandria, 171
Cleopatra, 155, 159, 169, 191–192
Cleopatra (movie), 160
Cleopatra VII, 159
Cloth parchment, xiv. *See also* Parchment
Code of Law, 44
Codex
  burned codices, 206
  description of, xv, xx, 12, 46, 49
  disappearance of, 156
  evolution of, 227–229
  examples of, *233*, *239*
  facsimile codex, 306
  gospels, 287–289
  making, 232–233, *233*
  Nag Hammadi codices, xv, 144, 276–280
  parchment codices, 175–176, 181, 232–242, 260
  spread of, 237, 248–249
  worth of, 285
Coffin Texts, 42–43, 53
Coffins, 11–15, 31–33, *33*, 34–47, *42*, 53–54, 58–61
Commodus, Emperor, 194, 244
Confessio Genechiseli, 251
Constantine, Emperor, 175, 228, 231
Constantinople, 175, 180, 184, 210–212, 234, 238–253, *240*
Constantius II, 106, 175, 231, 246
Cook's Tourists' Handbook for Egypt, the Nile, and the Desert, 50
Coptic script, 61–63, *62*
Corpses, 32–35, *33*, 40–43, 170, 201, 220. *See also* Mummies
Corpus Hermeticum, 277–278
Crawford, Sidnie, 280–281
Cribiore, Raffaella, 217, 219
Cursive script, 6, 15–16, 30, 61–65, 157, 163
Cuvigny, Hélène, 86
Cyril, 232

D

Da Vinci Code, The, xv, 251
Dabbler, The, 220
Daedalus, xix
Dagobert, King, 250–251
Dando-Collins, Stephen, 185
Darnton, Robert, xi, xix–xx

Dead Sea Scrolls, 162, 280–284
Decius, 231
Deissmann, Gustav Adolf, 86–88
Delchevalerie, Gustave, 267
Demetrius, 180, 218
DeMille, Cecil B., 160
Demotic script, 61–63, *62*
Den, Pharaoh, 13
Denon, Vivant, 40–41, 46–49, 72, 303
Depp, Johnny, 78
Depuydt, Leo, 252
Deuel, Leo, 73
Diaries, 6–10, 30, 88
Dio, Cassius, 172, 221–222
Diocletian, Emperor, 175, 231
Diodorus, 180
Discovery News, 6
Dishna Papyri, 276–280, 284
Dispute Between a Man and his Ba, The, 31
Dius, 183
Djoser, Pharaoh, 28, 137–138
Domitian, 193, 195
Drovetti, 29
Drymoi, 110–111, 120–121
Dublin Papyrus, 51
Duchess Amalia Library, 247
Dumas, Alexandre, 207

E

Ebers Papyrus, 89
Edh-Dhib, Muhammed, 280
Edwin Smith Papyrus, 89
Egypt Exploration Society, 72, 83–84
Egyptian Book of the Dead, The, 77–79
Egyptian Empire, 139–140
Egyptian Scientific Institute, 247
Electronic mail, xxi
Elements, 85
Eloquent Peasant, The, 31
Elysian Fields, 53
Emery, Walter, 12–16
Epicurus, 197, 206
Epigrams, 183
Eragon, 69
Eratosthenes, 171
Euclid, 85, 171
Euergetes, 171–172
Euripides, 85, 125, 174, 215
Eustathius, 245
Evans, Craig, 252, 300

F

Facsimiles, 299–306
Faenerator, 208
Fagan, Brian, 303
Fam, Riyad, 284
Fannius, 132–135
Faulkner, Raymond, 39
Favorite Poet, 161
Felucca boat, *25*, 25–28
Ferdinand IV, King, 207
Field of Offerings, 53
Field of Reeds, 53–55, 59–60, 273
Fields of the Greeks, 53
Fires, 194, 247–248, 299
Fischer, Stephen, 63–64
Flood, Alison, 179
Forgery, 249–250
Fowler, Robert, 208
Frost, Gary, 236–237
Funeral bouquet, 40

G

Gabriel, Father, 285–286
Galen, 103, 171, 183
Galerius, 231
Garcia, Terry, 288
Garis Davies, Nina de, 304–305
Garis Davies, Norman de, 101, 304–305
Garrett, Stephen, 209
Gates, Bill, xx
Geary, Patrick, 251
Getty, J. Paul, 208–209, 301
Giza King List, 28
Gladiator, 160
Gnostic documents, 21, 71, 144, 278
Goelet, Ogden, 39
Gordian, 196

Gospel of Jesus's Wife, 252
Gospel of Judas, 287–289
Gospels, 71, 85, 223–224, 232–235, 276–280. *See also* Bible
Grave robbers, 32, 70, 78
Great Fire of Rome, 185, 194
Great Library, 140, 156, *169*, 174–175, 191, 246, 256
Great Pyramid, 3–5, *4*, 7–8
Grebaut, Monsieur, 50
Green, Frederick, 268
Green Sahara, 55–61
Greenfield, Edith, 81
Greenfield Papyrus, 51, 80–81, *81*, 134–135, 266
Gregory the Great, 119, 213, 234, 249
Grenfell, Bernard Pyne, 84–85, 88, 106, 126
Griffith, D. W., 160
Gross, John, 216
Grubbs, Michael, 8
Guardian, 179, 253
Guidano, F., 28
Gulgul, Ibn, 266
Gum arabic, 162, *164*, 164–166
Gutenberg, Johannes, xvii–xviii, 163–164, 263
Gutenberg press, xv, 163–164

H

Hadrian, 195
Hall of Judgment, 37–39, *38*
Hamilton, Lord, 207
Hammurabi, 44
Hanna, Frank, 276
Hanna Papyrus, 276, 279
Harpocration, 180
Harris, Judith, 203–204
Harris, Robert, 207–209
Harris Papyrus, 51
Harrison, Tony, 85
Harthotes, 120–121
Hasselquist, Fredrik, 266
Hatshepsut, Queen, 139
Haukal, Ibn, 213
Hawass, Zahi, 78–79, 288, 294
Hawqal, Ibn, 119, 266
Hayter, John, 206
Hazzard, Shirley, 142, 207–208
Hemaka, 13–15, 93, 172
Herodas, 73
Herodotus, 61, 65, 82, 165, 225
Heroninos, 104–105
Hesiod, 178
Heyerdahl, Thor, 57–58, 293–295, 302
Hieratic script, 6, 15–16, 30, 61–65, *62*, 157
Hiero II, King, 117–118
Hieroglyphs
  on coffins, 41–42, *42*
  deciphering, 41, 47–48
  development of, 15–17, 137
  examples of, *15*, *18*
  in Karnak, 26–27, *27*
  on paper, 6
  script styles, 61–64, *62*, 157
Hirtius, Aulus, 227
History of the Bible, 306
Holland, Tom, 253
Holstein, Duke of, 262
Homer, 125, 161, 178–179
Horace, 131, 177
Horemheb, *65*, 66
House of Books, *154*, 154–155. *See also* Libraries
Houston, George, 189
Hunt, Arthur Surridge, 84–85, 88, 106, 126
Hunter, Dard, xiv
Hyperides, 73
Hypsicrates, 180
Hypsipyle, 85

I

Ibrahim, Mohammed, 294
Ichneutae, 85
Ikram, Salima, 29–30
Iliad, 125

Illustrated London News, 229
Imberdis, Father, xiv
Immega, Guy, 60
Immortality, achieving, 54–68
Immortality, guardian of, xix, 1, 45–53
Imperial Library, 72, 175–176, 191–193, 247
Ink
  colored inks, 47, 61, 97, 227–228
  inkwells, *65*, 282
  making, 162–164
  pens and, xv, 65, *65*, 162–164, 261–263
  for printing presses, 144, 163–164
  quill pens and, xv, 163, 261–263
  removal of, 61, 124–125, 204, 244–245
  vaporizing, 204
  washable inks, 106, 125, 162–163
Institutiones Divinarum et Saecularium Litterarum, 248–249
Instruction of Amenemope, The, 153
Intolerance, 160
Isesi, Djedkare, 30
Islam, world of, 254–258, *255*, 263

J

Jarring, Gunnar, 293–294
Jason and the Argonauts, 171
Jealous Mistress, The, 73
Jefferson, Thomas, 222, 247
Jéquier, Gustave, 29
Joan of Arc, 251
John V, Pope, 250
John XV, Pope, 250
Johnson, J. de M., 228
Johnson, Paul, 63, 66–67
Jovian, Emperor, 246
Judas Gospel, 287–289
Julian, Emperor, 246

K

Kagemni, Vizier, 30–31
Kantor, Helene, 268
Karnak King List, 27–28
Kha Papyrus, 300
Khayyam, Omar, 158
Khufu, Pharaoh, 3–11, 27, 30–31, 56–57, 88, 93–95, 294
Kilgour, Frederick, 12, 260
King, Karen, 20, 251
King lists, 27–29
Kiss of Lamourette, The, xix
Kleve, Knut, 248
Koran, 71, 257, 260
Krosney, Herbert, 287
Kurlansky, Mark, 284

L

Leach, Bridget, 102
Learning centers, 70, 73, 113–114, 167–171, 210–213, 279
Legal documents, 87, 89–90, 126, 257
Lepsius, Richard, 28
Letter carriers, 218–219, 224, 226–227
Letters, writing, 85–87, 105–106, 125–126, 141–142, 150, 216–226, 257
Lewis, Naphtali, 100, 102–103, 110, 114–117, 119–124, 134, 145–146, 236–237
Leyden Papyrus of Qenna, 51
Libraries
  Birmingham Library, 247
  Bodmer Library, 274, 306
  British Library, 104, 156, 195
  Chester Beatty Library, 278
  church libraries, 242–243, 250
  Duchess Amalia Library, 247
  early libraries, 153–156, *154*, 186–199, *187*, *188*, *189*, *194*, 208–212, 231–236, 262–263
  fires at, *168*, 168–169, 175, 194, 246–248, 299
  Great Library, 140, 156, *169*, 174–175, 191, 246, 256
  Imperial Library, 72, 175–176, 191–193, 247
  Library of Alexandria, 155, 167–171, *168*, 175, 247, 281, 290, 297–301, *298*

Library of Antioch, 247
Library of Congress, 156, 158, 195, 247, 281
Library of Marcellus, 192–193
Library of Nalanda, 247
Palatine Library, 194–195
private libraries, 170–171, 181, 190–197
Royal Library, 124, 155, 159, 168–170, 172–174, 297
Ulpian Library, 189, *194*, 194–195
Vatican Library, 251, 275–276, 279
Libraries for the Caesars, 170
Linnaeus, Carolus, 203
Livia, 122, 131
Living history, 296–299
Livy, 203, 206
Loot, 298
Lord's Prayer, 276
Louis VII, King, 250–251
Louis XVI, King, 46
Lowe, Adam, 299, 301–302
Lucullus, 196
Luijendijk, AnneMarie, 252

M
Magazines, 227–229
Malczycki, Matt, 241
Malerba, Luigi, 118
Marcellus, 192–193
Marouard, Gregory, 6
Martial, 105, 182–183, 233
Mathematical papyri, 31, 89
Maupassant, Guy de, 214
Maximian, 231
Mayet, Princess, *42*
McCormick, Michael, 241, 244
McLuhan, Marshall, 21–22, 251, 302
Media One, xx–xxi, 216–229
Medical papyri, 31, 89, 154
Medical texts, 89
Mehrez, Gamal, 294
Memphis, 93–106, *94*, *98*
Menander, 85
Mentuhotep II, King, 42
Merer, Inspector, 5–11, 30
Meyer, Marvin, 144, 277, 279
Milbank, Dana, 165
Mimes, 73
Minutoli, Heinrich de, 267
Money, making, 115, 122–123, 145–146, 172, 179, 225–226, 270
Morse, Samuel, 24
Moses, 21, 24, 237, 280, 283
Mosher, Malcolm, 78
Mostafa, Anas, 100–101, 273, 299
Mount Vesuvius, 132, 163, 200–201, 208
Mummies, 10, 31–35, *33*, 40–43, 61, 70, 83, 125, 138, 261. *See also* Corpses
Mummification, 32–35, 44, 52
Mummy cases, 43, 61, 125. *See also* Coffins

N
Nag Hammadi codices, xv, 144, 276–280
Natural History, 99
Naville, Édouard, 83
Neapolitan Lovers, The, 207
Necho, Pharaoh, 57
Nefertiti, 139
Nero, 122, 133, 185, 201, 225
Nesitanebtashru, Princess, *38*, *81*
New Testament, 11–12, 223–224, 252. *See also* Bible
New York Times, 207, 216
New Yorker, 142, 207, 299
Newsletters, 155
Newspapers, 19, 184, 185, 219–220, 227–228, 243
Nicholls, Matthew, 191
Nile Basin, 55, 273
Norton, Mary, 27
Nussberger, Frieda Tchacos, 287–288

O
Octavia, 192–194
Odes, 73, 80
Odoacer, King, 103
O'Donnell, James, 238

Oikonomides, Nicolas, 241–242
Old Testament, 264–265, 283. *See also* Bible
Olearius, Adam, 262
On Nature, 197
On the Sizes and Distances of the Sun and Moon, 158
Origins of the European Economy, The, 241
Ovid, 178, 190
Oxyrhynchus Papyri Project, 84–90, 161, 180, 217

P

Pachomius, Abba, 277–278
Pack, Mark, 220
Paderni, Camillo, 203, 205–206
Pagina, 160
Pakourianos, Gregory, 245
Palaemon, Quintus Remmius, 132–135
Palatine Library, 194–195
Palermo Stone, 28
Paolini, Christopher, 69
Papal bull, 244–245, 250–251
Paper. *See also* Papyrus; Parchment
  Arab paper, 241, 258, 260–262
  birth of, 93–106
  books and, xi, xix, 12, 124–125
  cartel, 114–116, 129, 145, 175, 181, 271–272
  Chinese paper, 242, 254–255, 257–259, 262
  cost of, 104–105, 122–124
  discovery of, xi, 12–13
  Egyptian paper, 103, 129, 134, 235
  finish on, 261–262
  legacy of, 136–150, 289–291
  monopoly of, 112–119
  origins of, xiii–xix
  paper mills, 147–148, 241, 258–262
  production of, xiv, 91–100, *98*, *101*, 102–135, 145–148, *147*, 209, 235, 258–265, 296–302
  pulp paper, xiv–xv, xix, 102, 117, 140–144, 257–263, 291, 295
  replica roll, *18*
  as scratch pad, 244–245
  types of, 124–132, 142–147
  usage amounts, *148*, 148–149
  wood paper, 243–244
Paper Before Print: the History and Impact of Paper in the Islamic World, 255
Pappus, Tiberius Iulius, 131
Papyrus. *See also* Paper
  ancient papyrus paper, 5–7, *6*, 14–16, *18*
  boats for, *56*, 56–60, 96–97, 123–124, 294–296, *296*, 302
  cost of, 104–105
  disappearance of, 264–273
  durability of, xv
  facsimiles of, 299–306
  flooding, 94, 138, 226, 267–271
  importance of, 19–20
  meaning of, xiii–xiv
  modern sheet of, *6*
  origin of, xiii–xiv
  plantations, 100–101, 109–115, *110*, 122–123, 129, 140–141, 148, 172–174, *173*, 225, 230, 267, 271, 294–296, 299–300
  plants, xiii, 11–12, *16*, 16–19, 33–35, 40, 46, 52–60, 72, 93–110, *96*, *108*, *110*, 111–119, *115*, 120–126, 140–149, 172–173, 213–215, 225–228, 242, 258–259, 264–273, 282–283, 294–296, 299–300
  production of, 93–106, *98*, *101*, 112–114, 120–126
  swamps, 12, *16*, 16–19, 35, 52–55, 60, 93–113, *110*, 120–124, *121*, 140–142, 146, 172–173, 213–215, *214*, 264–273, 278, 299–300
  versatility of, 16–19
Papyrus in Classical Antiquity, 100
Papyrus Institute, 100, 295–297, *296*, 300
Papyrus of Ani, 49–52, 73–78, 80–82, 134–135, 266, 300–303
Papyrus of Hunefer, 51

Papyrus of Kha, 300
Papyrus of Nebseni, 51
Papyrus of Qenna, 51
Papyrus Society, 22–23
Paradise, reaching, 54–68
Parchment. *See also* Paper; Vellum
  advantage of, 124–125
  cloth parchment, xiv
  parchment codices, 175–176, 181, 232–242, 260
  preference for, 241–247, 260–263
  price of, 114–115, 212, 225–226
  replacing, 142–144
  as scratch pad, 198
  sleeves, 190
  transcribing to, 71, 82, 279–284
  use of, xvii–xviii, 11, 71, 82, 124–125, 163–164
  for wrapping dead, 35
Parsons, Peter, 85, 88, 161, 185, 217
Pasha, Ibrahim, 25–26
Pasha, Mohammed Ali, 25–26, 28
Paul the Apostle, 224–226
Paullus, General, 196
Pearl of Great Price, A, 40
Pedersen, Johannes, 257
Pens, xv, *65*, 65, 162–164, 261–263
Per-em-hru, 49
Perseus, King, 196
Peter the Apostle, 225
Petitions, 87, 89–90, 126, 217
Petrie, Flinders, 13, 83, 125
Phaedo, 125
Philadelphus, 109, 171
Philippics, The, 221
Phillip the Good, 250
Philo, 171
Philodemus, 201, 206–208
Philosophical Transactions, 203
Piaggio, Antonio, 205–206
Pietersma, Albert, 306
Pigeon post, xxi, 226–227
Pimp, The, 73
Pindar, 73, 82, 85
Piso, Lucius Calpurnius, 202, 208
Placidus, Julius, 183
Plato, 71, 125, 278
Pliny the Elder, xiii–xiv, 33, 99–103, 113, 130–135, 143, 145, 168, 191, 227
Plotinus, 171
Polion, 180
Pollard, Justin, 156, 170–171
Pollio, Gaius Asinius, 191–193
Pompeii, 208
Pompeii Awakened, 204
Porter, James, 206, 209, 227
Printing presses, xv, 144, 163–164
Prisse d'Avennes, Émile, 21, 24–30, *26*, 48
Prisse Papyrus, 27, 30
Ptahhotep, Vizier, 30–31
Ptolemy, Claudius, 171
Ptolemy I, 169–171
Ptolemy II, 109, 113, 117, 124, 140–141, 156, 171, 196–197, 212
Ptolemy III, 171–172, 174
Ptolemy IV, 172
Ptolemy Soter, 170–171, 173
Ptolemy V, 159
Pulp paper, xiv–xv, xix, 102, 117, 140–144, 257–259, 291, 295. *See also* Paper
Pyramid Texts, 42–43, 52

Q

Qa'a, King, 15–16
Quibell, James, 268
Quill pens, xv, 163, 261–263
Qumran collection, 280–283

R

Ragab, Hassan, 100, 102, 116–117, 273, 294–299, 301
Rainier, Archduke, 72
Ramesses I, 139
Ramesses II, 29, 47, 139
Ramesses III, 51, 139
Ramesses XI, 140

Rape of the Nile, The, 303
Reading from Homer, A, 161, 179
Ready-made documents, 34, 43, 89, 182
Records, xviii, 7–11, 15, 19–22, 88, 126, 184–185
Reid, Howard, 156, 170–171
Reign of Martyrs, 231
Reign of Terror, 206
Reis, Piri, 173
Reisner, George, 28
Rennell, James, 95
Republic, 277–278
Rise and Fall Alexandria, The, 170
Rites of baptism, 52
Rites of dead, 83
Rites of passage, 35
Rituals, 35–39, 52, 83, 154. *See also* Spells
Roberts, C. H., 104
Roberts, Colin, 225, 237
Robinson, James, 278, 284
Roman Empire, 19, 113–114, 127–135, *128*, 139–143, 181–185, 227–242, 256, 302
Romanianus, 237
Royal Library, 124, 155, 159, 168–170, 172–174, 297
Rubaiyat, The, 158
Ryholt, Kim, 154

S

Saint Anthony, 277
Saint Augustine, 222, 237, 239, 244
Saint Benedictine, 249
Saint Denis, 242, 250–251
Saint Mark, 35, 176, 231
Sammonicus, 196
Sansevero, Duke of, 203–204
Sappho, 71, 85
Saqqara King List, 29
Sarcophagus, 5, 12, 49, 69–70. *See also* Coffins
Satire on the Trades, The, 67
Scalf, Foy, 47
Schodde, Carla, 190
Schoolbooks, 248–249
Scientific texts, 89
Scorpion II, King, 268
Scratch pads, 198, 244–245
Scribes, 6–8, 12, 31, *36*, 43–47, 63–68, *65*, *66*
Scribes, Script, and Books, 31, 45
Script styles, 61–65, *62*, 157. *See also* Cursive script
Scrolls
  book scrolls, xix, 14–15, 105, 110, 174, 180–183, *188*, 188–198
  charred scrolls, 203–208, *204*, *205*
  discovery of, xviii, 7, *14*, 14–15, 27, 32–34, 201–203, *202*
  examples of, *14*, *18*
  explanation of, 14–15, 45
  funerary scrolls, xviii, 33–34, 37–39, 41, 47, 58, 64–65, 77
  length of, 30, 34, 49, 51–52, 75–76, 84–86, 103, 129–132, 300
  reading, 156–161, *157*, *159*
  sealed scroll, 15, *18*, 18–19, 34
  writing style, 156–161, *157*, *159*
Secundus, 182–183
Sekhet A'aru, 53, 59. *See also* Field of Reeds
Seleucus, 180
Serageldin, Ismail, 297
Sergius I, Pope, 250
Seti I, 28, 29, 139, 298–299
Severus, Septimius, 193, 195, 231
Sharpe, Samuel, 117
Shaw, Donald, 22–23, 139
Silvanus, 106
Skeat, T. C., 104–106, 181, 225, 235, 237
Smith, Edwin, 89
Smith, John, 40
Smith Papyrus, 89
Sneferu, Pharaoh, 31
Sobekmose scroll, 52
Socrates, 71, 182

Sophocles, 85, 174, 215
Soter, 170–171, 173
South Saqqara Stone, 29
Spells, 31, 37–39, 43, 47, 138, 155. *See also* Rituals
Spencer, H., 80
Spoon, Jacalyn, 188, 198
Spreadsheets, 8, 10–11, 15, 30. *See also* Records
Standage, Tom, 22, 149, 220, 223–224, 234
Statius, Caecilius, 208
Stephen II, Pope, 251
Stille, Alexander, 10, 11
Story of Sinuhe, The, 31
Story of Wenamun, The, 144
Strabo, 114, 172–173, 196, 271–272
Strudwick, Nigel, 304
Stylus, 163, 261
Suetonius, 132–133, 135, 185, 218–219
Sulla, 196

T

Tablet, clay, 11–12
Tablet, cuneiform, 11–12
Tablet, stone, 21, 24–31
Tablet, wood, 243–244
Tacitus, 207
Tale of the Shipwrecked Sailor, The, 31
Tallet, Pierre, 5–12, 88
Tauran, Jean-Louis, 275–276
Taylor, John, 43, 46, 52–53, 58, 60
Teaching of King Merikare, 31
Telegraph, xx–xxi, 24
Temple of Amun, 24, *27*, 27–28
Temple of Horus, *154*, 268
Ten Commandments (movie), 160
Ten Commandments (text), 21
Testaments of Time, 73
Textbooks, 89
Themistios, 246, 248
Theodoric, 69, 212, 239–240
Theodosius I, Emperor, 246
Theophilus, 174, 231, 242
Theophrastus, 99
Thersagoras, 180
Thievery, 74–80
Thompson, Edward Maunde, 111
Thompson, Michael, 224–225
Thurston, Herbert, 250, 252
Thutmose III, 139
Tiberius, 113, 121–122, 133, 193, 194, 201
Torah, 21, 283
Trackers of Oxyrhynchus, 85
Trump, Donald, 133
Tura Caves, *5*, 5–6, 8–9
Turin King List, 29
Tut, King, 12, 15, 38, 47, 294, 299, 301
Typikon, 245

U

Ulpian Library, 189, *194*, 194–195
Umar, 175, 255–256
"Undertaker's specials," 32, 42–43
Unwin, Francis, 304
Usurer, The, 208

V

Valens, Emperor, 181, 246
Valentinians I, Emperor, 246
Valentinians II, Emperor, 246
Valerian, 231
Varro, 196
Vatican Library, 251, 275–276, 279
Vedder, Elihu, *157*, 158
Vellum, xvii–xviii, 212, 237, 242–244, 279, 282–283. *See also* Parchment
Verdi, 186
Vespasian, 183, 194
Vesuvius eruption, 132, 163, 200–201, 208
Virgil, 131, 193, 203, 206
Voicu, Sever, 279

W

Waltz, Robert, 11–12
Washington Post, 165, 305
Wassen, Cecilia, 280–281
Wasserman, James, 79

Watson, Francis, 252
Waxman, Sharon, 298–299
Weber, Karl, 202, 208
Westcar Papyri, 30
Wicar, Jean-Baptiste, 193
Wilkinson, Charles, 304
Wilkinson, Toby, 16
Williams, Hank, 39
Winsbury, Rex, 179, 181–182, 192
Wireless technology, xxi, 22
Women Worshippers, The, 73
Women's Letters from Ancient Egypt, 218–219
Wordsworth, William, 206
Writing business, 156–161, *157*

X
Xenia, 105
Xenophon, 178

Y
Yan Zhitui, 259

Z
Zalewski, Daniel, 299
Zenon, 141–142, 217